P9-BZH-679

Jonathan R. Eller

Ray Bradbury
Unbound

UNIVERSITY OF ILLINOIS PRESS Urbana, Chicago, and Springfield

Lewes Public Library
111 Adams Ave.
Lewes, DE 19958
302-645-4633

© 2014 by Jonathan R. Eller
All rights reserved
Manufactured in the United States of America
C 5 4 3 2 1
∞ This book is printed on acid-free paper.

Library of Congress Cataloging-in-Publication Data
Eller, Jonathan R., 1952–
Ray Bradbury unbound / Jonathan R. Eller.
pages   cm
Includes bibliographical references and index.
ISBN 978-0-252-03869-3 (cloth : alk. paper)
ISBN 978-0-252-09663-1 (ebook)
1. Bradbury, Ray, 1920–2012. 2. Authors, American—20th century—Biography.
I. Title.
PS3503.R167Z67   2014
813'.54—dc23 [B]   2014010893

Frontispiece:
Ray Bradbury with UCLA student art illustrating his recent science fiction stage plays, July 20, 1964. Photograph by Mary Frampton. Copyright © 1964. *Los Angeles Times.* Reprinted with permission.

For Ray Bradbury

    Who lived the storyteller's life

and Maggie Bradbury

    Who believed in the storyteller's dreams

I went to Hollywood every day for *years* . . .
from the time I was thirteen 'til I was eighteen,
in front of the studios. . . . But this *thing* in me
wanted to go over the wall. I knew that some
day I would. . . . When I finally got in there,
I looked at the block across the street and
I could see my ghost standing there. That boy
of thirteen who wanted to go over the wall.

—Ray Bradbury, October 4, 2004

Contents

Acknowledgments

In October 1965, on the eve of his first venture onto the New York stage as a playwright, Ray Bradbury maintained that "the theater is no place for Realism. . . . Theater should be as magical as Blackstone." Magic also provides the foundation beneath the consuming realities of biographical writing, and I have been blessed with a great deal of miraculous support and guidance as I researched and wrote *Ray Bradbury Unbound*.

Crucial aspects of my research were supported in part by Indiana University's New Frontiers in the Arts & Humanities Program, funded by the Office of the President and administered by the Office of the Vice Provost for Research. A 2010 travel grant under this program supported three weeklong working visits in Mr. Bradbury's Los Angeles home during the most intensive phase of research for this book. Earlier travel grants under this Indiana University program, funded by the Lilly Endowment, supported a number of working visits from 2004 to 2009 for research that, in various ways, provided foundational research for both *Ray Bradbury Unbound* and its prequel, *Becoming Ray Bradbury* (2011).

The remarkable six-decade correspondence between Ray Bradbury and his literary agent, Don Congdon, was essential to the preparation of both of these biographical volumes, providing the essential insights needed to present the early and middle years of Ray Bradbury's multifaceted career in American literature and culture. Bradbury's side of the correspondence is preserved in his agent's archives at Columbia University's Butler Library; I'm grateful to Ben Camardi for access to earlier years of the Bradbury-Congdon correspondence in Columbia's Harold Matson Agency deposit, and to Michael Congdon, now head of Don Congdon Associates, for access to subsequent years of author-agent correspondence in Columbia's Congdon Agency deposit.

I owe Michael Congdon an even greater debt for permitting me to quote from his father's letters to Bradbury, and for reading *Ray Bradbury Unbound* as it approached completion. Cristina Conception also read the entire manuscript and provided encouragement as she coordinated permissions for Don Congdon Associates. Access to the Congdon half of Bradbury's author-agent correspondence was provided by Professor Donn Albright of the Pratt Institute, Bradbury's longtime bibliographer, who has preserved the earlier decades of these letters in his private collection.

Mr. Bradbury provided access to all of his correspondence during his lifetime, and I'm grateful to his daughter Alexandra for allowing access since his June 2012 passing. In this way I was able to consult the later decades of Bradbury's author-agent correspondence, as well as many letters bearing on the midcareer transitions and achievements of his professional and personal life documented in *Ray Bradbury Unbound*. Permission to quote from Bradbury letters and his published and unpublished work, and to publish selected photographs, was provided by Marsha Rothman LuMetta, Executor and President, the Ray Bradbury Living Trust.

My gratitude for access to materials radiates out to a number of research institutions and libraries as well. Librarian Carolyn Davis of Syracuse University's Bird Library contributed proxy research into Bradbury's Mercury Press correspondence with *The Magazine of Fantasy & Science Fiction* editor Anthony Boucher as well as his correspondence with author Frederik Pohl during his years as editor of *Galaxy Science Fiction* magazine. Archivist Keith Call of Wheaton College led me to commentary on Bradbury in the letters of C. S. Lewis. I'm grateful as well for his friendship and encouragement and to the equally important and enthusiastic friendship and support of Bradbury biographer Sam Weller, who was the first researcher to discover Bradbury's FBI file through the Freedom of Information Act.

My discovery of Bradbury's letters to Bernard Berenson led to Berenson's Villa I Tatti estate in Tuscany, where his remarkable library is now part of the Harvard University's Center for Italian Renaissance Studies. I am grateful to Dr. Michael Rocke, the Nicky Mariano Librarian of the Biblioteca Berenson, for his pivotal role in this discovery. Closer to home, Faye Thompson of the Margaret Herrick Library guided me into the impressive resources of the Academy of Motion Picture Arts and Sciences in Burbank, California. I'm especially grateful to Kristina Krueger of the National Film Information Service for providing invaluable proxy research through the Herrick's photograph archive. The *Los Angeles Times* proved to be another excellent source of photographic research on Bradbury, and I greatly appreciate the help and genuine interest of Ralph Drew in securing permissions for the Mary Frampton portrait of Bradbury.

Both Faye Thompson and Ralph Drew proved to be Bradbury enthusiasts, as did nearly everyone I encountered during my speaking and research association with the California Institute of Technology. Bradbury's years of engagement with Caltech students and scientists were central to the narrative of *Ray Bradbury Unbound*, and I'm indebted to archives assistant Loma Karklins and to Shelley Erwin, Head of Archives and Special Collections, for allowing me to explore the rich audiovisual record of Bradbury's Caltech legacy and to secure illustration permissions.

As in the past, my research on this second biographical volume was enriched by the encouragement of writers William F. Nolan and Sid Stebel, whose friendships with Bradbury spanned more than six decades, and Doug Menville, who worked with the Famous Artists Agency, Bradbury's first media representatives during the 1950s. Writers Greg Miller, Steven Paul Leyva, and Jason Marchi; family friends Nik Grant, Patrick Kachurka, and John King Tarpinian; and Ruth Alben Davis, Bradbury's longtime speaking agent, all contributed background information and much encouragement.

Media scholar Phil Nichols of the University of Wolverhampton, U.K., was both auditor and advisor throughout the writing of *Ray Bradbury Unbound*, offering important insights into Bradbury's media adaptations and reading through all three major stages of revision. Professor Emeritus William F. Touponce, cofounder and first director of Indiana University's Center for Ray Bradbury Studies, as well as independent scholar Michael Quilligan, offered key insights into Bradbury's aesthetics and his uneasy relationship with Modernism and the postmodernist world.

Donn Albright, Bradbury's longtime bibliographer and his close personal friend, provided unconditional access to his comprehensive collection of Bradbury-related books, papers, and unpublished works. He spent more hours reading drafts and discussing aspects of *Ray Bradbury Unbound* than anyone else, and I'll always be thankful for his encouragement and optimism. His daughter, Elizabeth Nahum Albright, provided photographic documentation for many of my research trips to the Bradbury home and has come to share her father's abiding archival instincts.

I appreciate the very creative support of many people at the University of Illinois Press, including Joan Catapano, now retired but sponsoring editor of the prequel *Becoming Ray Bradbury*, and UI Press Director Willis G. Regier, whose great enthusiasm for scholarship and for a well-told tale motivated me to take up the story once again and write *Ray Bradbury Unbound*. Bill Blomquist, Dean of the Indiana University School of Liberal Arts, has gone the extra mile to support the Center for Ray Bradbury Studies and to encourage my research. My wife Debi invested long hours in reading successive drafts and helped me to find the essential story of Ray Bradbury's middle years.

Alexandra Bradbury, who worked closely with her father in all of his writing and speaking endeavors, reinforced and refined my understanding of his creative mind; her sisters Susan, Ramona, and Bettina have, with their families, extended my great appreciation of Bradbury values and traditions; their encouragement, and that of Brad Bradbury, cousin and keeper of much family history, and Marsha Rothman LuMetta, Ray Bradbury's longtime counselor and now executor, contributed greatly to my understanding of a remarkable writer's life.

Between 1998 and 2002, Maggie Bradbury's reflections on the nature of her husband's creativity and success provided important foundational insights as I began to form the dim outlines of this book and its prequel in my mind. In 2004, a year after her passing, Ray Bradbury and I worked over a single-book outline that evolved into both *Becoming Ray Bradbury* and *Ray Bradbury Unbound*. His simple blessing—"O.K. R.B."—remains on that sheet today, a starting point for all the years of discussion that followed.

A working relationship that began in the late 1980s culminated in these two volumes; I had the great good fortune to see *Becoming Ray Bradbury* in his hands, to finish the final phase of research for *Ray Bradbury Unbound* with him, and to read draft passages to him during the final months of his life. He was encouraging to the end, and the hardest exercise in the whole process was changing all of my present- and progressive-tense references to him into the past tense. This book is dedicated to both Ray and Maggie Bradbury, who together shared the storyteller's life.

Introduction

In late October 1946, one of Ray Bradbury's first story submissions for the popular CBS prime-time radio show *Suspense* arrived at the network's New York office with this note, typed on a red-bordered sticker affixed to the address label: "In the Event of My Death—The Contents of This ENVELOPE Are To Be Destroyed Without Being Opened Or Read. Ray B." Taken together, the package and its somber instruction represent a revealing transitional marker in Bradbury's early career. Here, at age 26, was perhaps the last manifestation of his teenage fear that he would die before he could mature into the master storyteller he knew he could be. From this point on, such fears would surface only in the edgy twists and turns of his best dark fiction.

If the package label offered the last vestige of his very tangible teenage fear, its contents represented one of the first artifacts of the media prominence that would extend his active writing career well into the twenty-first century. Eventually seven Bradbury tales would be adapted for *Suspense* on radio, and by the mid-1950s he was firmly established in Hollywood's vast and overlapping film and television empires as well. These opportunities would have an irreversible impact on his ability to write masterful short stories, however, and would alter the creative trajectory of his long career. The 1950s and 1960s changed everything for one of the most recognized names in midcentury American fiction, and these years define the focus of *Ray Bradbury Unbound*.

Becoming Ray Bradbury, the prequel to the present volume, narrates the story of his development and achievements through the summer of 1953, just as he completed his final *Fahrenheit 451* revisions. *Ray Bradbury Unbound* continues on through the middle decades of Bradbury's richly productive literary career; during these years he discovered—through a combination of unexpected opportunity and willful determination—that he was no longer bound to the short story form that had established him as a master storyteller. In his early thirties Bradbury began to write, with ever-increasing frequency, performance adaptations not intended (at least initially) for publication at all. These double tensions—his exploration of new fields of writing and his determination to translate his published stories into various dramatic forms—would play out across the next forty years of his career, slowly diminishing his ability to produce the kind of original short fiction that had come so easily to him during the first dozen years of his professional career.

He briefly entered the Hollywood studio world in 1952, earning original story credits for Universal's *It Came from Outer Space* and (on the strength of a single scene) the Warner Brothers release of *The Beast from 20,000 Fathoms.* Two very short stints at Twentieth Century–Fox were unsuccessful, but these missteps were followed by a nine-month adventure that greatly accelerated his drift away from the world of bound books. Bradbury spent the fall of 1953 and the winter of 1954 in Ireland, writing the screenplay for the Warner Brothers production of Melville's American classic, *Moby Dick.* Before returning to America, he encountered the full force of Renaissance Italy under the tutelage of Bernard Berenson, the most prominent Italian art historian of his day. By virtue of these two life-changing experiences, a very different writer returned to America in late May 1954.

He soon found himself writing with great success for television and, after a few years' hiatus, writing once again for the silver screen. These media passions were eventually matched by his growing mastery of stage adaptation, a process that began in 1955 under the tutelage of Charles Laughton and culminated, in the early 1960s, with the establishment of Bradbury's own acting company and production record—achievements that continued for nearly five decades. By 1962 Bradbury had also become a respected writer on writing, a coveted catch for major market magazine interviews, and an increasingly popular public speaker; he began to write and publish verse and completed his first full-length novel. In full command of his multigenre creative possibilities, he was no longer bound to the short story form at all.

In fact, his reputation (and his growth as a writer) no longer depended on the publication of each new book. After the release of *Something Wicked This Way Comes* in 1962, his subsequent stories and books became literary milestones by which to frame and contextualize the constant refashioning of his early work for other media forms of creativity. There were, however, unforeseeable consequences for this gamble; Bradbury's often Herculean efforts to finance and produce his own stage dramas played out against an equally time-consuming cavalcade of cinematic projects involving *The Martian Chronicles, The Illustrated Man, Fahrenheit 451, Something Wicked This Way Comes,* and a half dozen of his best short stories. In many cases, these achievements were obscured or altered by the competing talents of directors and producers, and by the all-too-frequent refusal of studio executives to produce his work at all. Most of these projects became dreams deferred, or worse—productions hijacked by Hollywood and produced with only a thin shell of Bradbury's creative magic within.

But what of the short stories first published during these midcareer decades? A fair number of new compositions had the old Bradbury magic, but many of the best were brought forward from the files of the 1940s and early 1950s. Some still carried the delicate whimsy and poetic fantasy of his earlier work, especially through the late 1950s and early 1960s. Too often, though, the sentimental and nostalgia-driven impulses in his creativity would become dominant. Bradbury always had to guard against descriptions verging on purple prose, but now the distinct Bradburyesque edginess, the quirky, dark, and off-trail ideas springing out of ordinary situations, was largely absent. More often, his characteristic brilliance of effect and emotional impact was reprised in other forms, rechanneled as he refashioned his classic work for stage and screen.

The real-life drama of these years may very well represent the best Bradbury tale of all—a story centered on his willing entrapment in media work and the compensating freedom provided by his emerging role as a free-wheeling cultural commentator and a visionary spokesman for the Space Age. The extrapolative impulse inherited from his beloved H. G. Wells soon spilled over into the award-winning 1960s nonfiction he penned for *Life* magazine to inspire and validate our first steps into the Cosmos. He railed against those who, like Wells's Time Traveler, "saw in the growing pile of civilization only a foolish heaping that must inevitably fall back upon and destroy its makers in the end." In spite of his ingrained romanticism, Bradbury's response to such judgments was firmly grounded in reality, often echoing the Wellsian narrator who tells the Time Traveler's story: "If that is so, it remains for us to live as though it were not so."

Bradbury would never speak with the measured rhythms of Wells, however; he preferred to witness and celebrate rather than narrate and analyze, and he never felt quite at ease when *Life*'s editors would prompt him to narrate the factual milestones of the American space program. He was far more interested in emotional truth than scientific fact; the 1950s wonderment phase of his space fiction, often told from the perspective of adolescence or young adulthood, was rechanneled during the 1960s into his *Life* magazine articles, unproduced screenplays, media interviews, and an increasing number of college campus lectures. Some of his most cogent observations on humanity and the state of our arts and sciences were no longer clothed in story form, and often did not reach print at all. Many key comments on the space program and politics, equal parts inspirational and controversial, survive only at Cal Tech and a few other college archives; equally insightful and, at times, harsh commentaries on the history and aesthetics of motion pictures also survive only in a few Hollywood and academic institutions.

Ray Bradbury Unbound pursues a young writer at the top of his form as he moves into new creative territory, writing and speaking beyond the boundaries he had observed, more or less, during his earlier rise to prominence as a unique and masterful storyteller. With fame came the confidence to speak out more and more openly as an independent-minded visionary determined to go his own way; as a consequence, his stories sometimes became polemic, and this tendency would often spill over into his articles and lectures. Yet his style remained engaging regardless of genre, and there are literary treasures hidden in dozens of his stage and screen adaptations of this period.

That they remain hidden to this day suggests that there was a price to pay for working beyond the boundaries of genre convention. His instinctive emphasis on description and dialogue often obscured the dramatic and structural progression of his stories when he adapted them for stage and screen; in his mind, spectacle and stage magic always took priority over the development of conflict between characters, and all too often studio executives felt that Bradbury's approach could not hold an audience in the way that his books held readers. He had fair success writing teleplays for *Alfred Hitchcock Presents*, but many of Bradbury's radio, television, and screen credits of the 1950s and 1960s were adaptations by other writers.

Bradbury's midcareer universe sparkled in many ways, but the star-points were fewer than they had been during the first dozen years of his career. Dark matter filled the interstices, in the form of unproduced screenplays, teleplays, and screen treatments that swallowed up great portions of his time and creative energy. The void also masked the many significant lectures that never reached the broader reading or viewing public—lectures that go a long way toward illuminating the ways that Bradbury captured the American imagination during the greatest period of space exploration.

The published milestones in fiction after his return from Europe—*The October Country, Dandelion Wine, Something Wicked This Way Comes*, and the various story collections that presented the best of his midcareer fantasies through the 1960s—cannot be effectively evaluated unless they are considered within the context of other writings, his successful media ventures, and the far broader but largely hidden record of his unproduced adaptations and unpublished lectures. In the end, the record bears up not as a tragic story of dreams deferred, but as a remarkable testament to the boundless creative energy of a writer who could touch the heart and reveal the fundamental emotions and aspirations that define our humanity.

Part I

A Place in the Sun

The Cinerama had opened [in 1952], and I sat there with Maggie and looked at the scenes of Paris and Egypt and London and Rome, and tears streamed down my face. And Maggie looked at me and said, "Why are you crying?" I said, "When are we going to have some money so we can travel?" I wanted to go to those places. So by God, the next year John Huston offers me *Moby Dick*, and we're off and running to Paris and to London and to Dublin.

—RB, 2004

1 Loomings

On the surface, everything seemed fine.

By the late summer of 1953, 33-year-old Ray Bradbury had become one of the most recognized names broadly associated with fantasy and science fiction. His initial pulp fiction successes had quickly opened out into an ever-widening range of major market magazines since the end of World War II, and his first three Doubleday titles—*The Martian Chronicles*, *The Illustrated Man*, and *The Golden Apples of the Sun*—were already on their way to becoming perennial classics. His newest title, Ballantine's *Fahrenheit 451*, was nearing release amid a barrage of prepublication publicity. During the previous six years, individual Bradbury tales had been featured in three of the annual *Best American Short Stories* anthologies and two volumes of *O. Henry Prize Stories*. In little more than a decade, he had published nearly 200 professional stories.

But privately, he was increasingly tormented by doubts that were making it more and more difficult for him to let go of his newest creative efforts. Fewer and fewer stories made their way east from his Los Angeles home to the New York office of his agent, Don Congdon. Bradbury had finally transformed the core of his novella "The Fireman" into *Fahrenheit 451* during June of 1953, but only after months of worry and broken deadlines. This breakthrough achieved much, but it changed nothing about his creative worries; the closer *Fahrenheit* came to completion, the more Bradbury anguished over the final product, sending increasingly smaller installments to Congdon as the summer dragged on.

Finally, with Ian Ballantine in danger of losing the printing window for his most heavily advertised book, Bradbury sent the final pages in for galley composition; in early August, Ballantine's trusted colleague Stanley Kauffmann closeted himself with Bradbury in Los Angeles for a final revising pass through the galleys, leaving at the last possible minute to drop off the galley sheets with the Chicago printer before returning home to New York. It was a close call, but the reading public knew nothing of the drama going on behind the scenes.

Don Congdon was deeply concerned, for he had seen this obsession with perfection building throughout his seven-year association with Bradbury. To some degree, it was a natural consequence of Bradbury's abiding hatred of slanting or writing to please a market. The meager penny-a-word pay of the pulp houses where he began had tempted him, but he rarely succumbed after learning to avoid the influence and subjects of his mentors and turn to his own experiences and emotions for inspiration. Nevertheless, his rapid rise to prominence was paralleled, beneath the surface, by a growing unease with work that was, in reality, ready for submission to his agent. Scores of fascinating stories were in his files, and many of these should have been in circulation. This wasn't just about stories, however; the Illinois novel he had contracted with Doubleday was now nearly two years overdue, and nowhere near ready for submission.

These private dramas were symptoms of a deeper tension in Bradbury's creative psyche. In late July 1953, just before Kauffmann arrived to work through the galleys, Bradbury wrote Congdon to confess a persistent uneasiness with the way the core ideas of *Fahrenheit 451* had played out: did he even know enough about literary traditions and purposes to provide believable motivation for Fireman Montag? Could he express the core intellectual implications of the novel well enough to avoid charges of naïveté or excessive sentimentality? Bradbury felt that his command of emotional situations had outrun his understanding of the intellectual purposes of art and literature.

Congdon waited until the final stage of galley revision had passed and then reminded Bradbury that his ability to bring vitality and focused intensity to many of his stories had already brought him widespread popularity. He also applauded Bradbury's desire to develop his intellect, to study the world of ideas in ways that would deepen and broaden his writing. But Congdon was dead set against Bradbury's mounting desire to hold back a story until it seemed perfect: "You should have more faith in yourself and in your achievements from day to day and not be afraid to publish and communicate while you are struggling; as I say, you will always be struggling with this, and in many instances, it is not for you to say what is your best, or worst work. The public and the writer seldom agree."

Then, unexpectedly, a new challenge suddenly suspended all thoughts of this creative dilemma, and ended any chance of taking up the long-deferred Illinois novel. The expatriate motion picture director John Huston had returned from Europe for a brief Hollywood visit to finalize financial backing and studio distribution with Warner Brothers for his next project, an ambitious attempt to film Herman Melville's classic novel *Moby Dick*. But Huston also had a more private and unpublicized objective in mind—he wanted Bradbury to come back to Europe with him and write the screenplay. Huston was notorious for his unpredictable personnel decisions, but there was a history behind this unexpected choice.

Bradbury had, in fact, sought out Huston more than two years earlier. His own media agent, Ray Starke, knew Huston well, and at Bradbury's request he arranged a dinner with Huston at Michael Romanov's restaurant on Saint Valentine's night, 1951. Bradbury brought all three of his books that evening—*Dark Carnival*, *The Martian Chronicles*, and *The Illustrated Man*—and would always recall making this declaration: "Mr. Huston, it's very simple. I love your films, I love you, and if you love these books half as much as my affection for you, I want you to hire me some day." The evening went well, perhaps because Starke could vouch for the growing Hollywood interest in Bradbury's work.

The next night Huston invited Bradbury to a preview showing of *The Red Badge of Courage* at the Pickwood Theater, and during the course of the evening he saw firsthand how Huston's passion for adapting novels to film played out with a classic title as subject. Bradbury (and the critics) thought the film was too long in its first release form, but his desire to work with Huston remained unabated.[1] Huston was in the midst of a very productive period in his career, yet nevertheless found time to read some of the young writer's offerings. He wrote within two weeks with comments on stories from both *Dark Carnival* and *The Illustrated Man* and declared *The Martian Chronicles* "most beautiful & wise & moving."[2]

For the next two years Huston worked out of London and various locations on *The African Queen* and *Moulin Rouge* and eventually settled his family on a leased estate twenty miles outside of Dublin. Meanwhile, the English edition of *The Martian Chronicles*, re-titled *The Silver Locusts*, came out in September 1951 and Bradbury immediately sent several copies on to Huston. Between films, in late December 1951, Huston wrote Bradbury thanking him for the new edition and noting that the *Chronicles* "would make a great picture." He didn't think his London production company could handle the technical challenges, but he sent a copy of *The Silver Locusts* on to Sir Alexander Korda, the only English filmmaker that Huston thought capable of mounting such a large-scale production.[3]

Huston nevertheless held out the possibility of directing an American studio production of the *Chronicles* some day. He was in no hurry to return to the Hollywood witch hunts of the McCarthy era (in fact, he would not make another film in America until *The Misfits* in 1960). He spent much of 1952 on the production of *Moulin Rouge*, which quickly achieved great critical and box office success. In early 1953 Bradbury sent Huston an insightful note about the pioneering Technicolor effects of *Moulin Rouge*, along with another offer to work on a Huston film. Huston considered the feasibility of integrating several Bradbury tales into a single film, but in the end asked for longer fictions: "I would infinitely prefer to do one long one with you."[4]

The catalyst for that one long film was actually one of Bradbury's shortest story masterpieces, "The Fog Horn," originally published in a June 1951 issue of the *Saturday Evening Post* as "The Beast from 20,000 Fathoms." On January 14,

1953, Bradbury sent Huston an advance copy of *The Golden Apples of the Sun*, the first Bradbury collection to privilege fantasy over the hallmark science fiction and weird tales of his earlier years. The collection opened with "The Fog Horn," and Huston read it in England as he began work on his next film, *Beat the Devil*. At this point, Bradbury did not know that Huston had read the story. The only hint was a rare straightforward compliment in Huston's February 1953 letter: "yours is just about the most striking and original talent in America today."

Eventually, after he began to work with Huston on *Moby Dick*, Bradbury discovered that this story above all others had sold Huston on his work. In 2006, he could still recall Huston's October 1953 revelation: "I read the story 'The Fog Horn,' and I smelled the ghost of Melville." In particular, Huston found Bradbury's self-contained paragraph about the creation of the foghorn to be "pure Melville." The paragraph presents the old light-keeper's theories about the origins of the foghorn in a passage that Bradbury would always regard as one of his best pensées, or prose-poems:

> One day many years ago a man walked along and stood in the sound of the ocean on a cold sunless shore and said, "We need a voice to call across the water, to warn ships; I'll make one. I'll make a voice like all of time and all of the fog that ever was; I'll make a voice that is like an empty bed beside you all night long, and like an empty house when you open the door, and like trees in autumn with no leaves. A sound like the birds flying south, crying, and a sound like November wind and the sea on the hard, cold shore. I'll make a sound that's so alone that no one can miss it, that whoever hears it will weep in their souls, and hearths will seem warmer, and being inside will seem better to all who hear it in the distant towns. I'll make me a sound and an apparatus and they'll call it a Fog Horn and whoever hears it will know the sadness of eternity and the briefness of life."

This paragraph, like Bradbury's well-known description of his Tyrannosaurus Rex in "A Sound of Thunder," has the self-contained qualities of a prose poem. Both of these pensées appeared in the *Golden Apples* collection, and no doubt both made an impact on Huston. He had only a very distant familiarity with *Moby Dick* as a work of literature, but he knew enough from his own experiences with the cinematic adaptation of literary works to know that here, in Bradbury, he had found his screenwriter. All he had to do was convince Bradbury that he was right for the job.[5]

Huston already had a production plan in mind before he arrived in Los Angeles. Harold and Walter Mirisch had produced Huston's successful *Moulin Rouge*, and they agreed to use some of the profits from that film to back *Moby Dick*. Warner Brothers put up the rest of the financing in return for worldwide distribution rights.[6] Bradbury knew none of this, but he was aware that his favorite director was in Los Angeles. Huston's looming presence remained in the back of his mind as he set off on a daylong expedition in search of books on dinosaurs at Acres of Books in Long Beach. That evening he was astounded to find out from Maggie that John Huston had called and wanted to meet with him the very next evening—Huston's last evening in town. It seemed a purely social visit for the first five minutes, until Huston asked him point-blank if he would come to Europe in September to begin work on the screenplay for *Moby Dick.* Bradbury had not yet read *Moby Dick*, but Huston needed an answer by the next day.[7]

Bradbury had less than twenty-four hours to get a sense of the task at hand and make his decision. He read selectively through a Modern Library edition that he purchased on the way home from Huston's hotel, and at every point of entry he seemed to hit a poetic high: the seas of mysterious microscopic "brit" that float with the currents and feed the whales; the "'Spirit Spout,' seen in the spectral whiteness at night"; the remarkable catalog chapter on the whiteness of the whale, and finally Ahab's mystically persuasive speech to Starbuck aloft before the final three-day chase. Bradbury had great reverence for Melville's reputation, and immediately sensed a kinship with Melville's style and poetic vision. He already had some idea of what *wouldn't* work; three weeks earlier, he had seen the 1930 John Barrymore version, with Joan Bennett as Ahab's wife—a role created out of thin air by the screenwriter—and no Ishmael at all.[8] The next day he told Huston that he was ready to take on the challenge.

Against all odds, Huston's long-shot hunch that Bradbury was up to this challenge would soon prove true to the mark. Bradbury could not overcome his abiding fear of flying, however, and his slow journey by land and water began to take on overtones of "Loomings," the opening chapter of the book he would live with for many months to come; like Melville's Ishmael, he slowly began to make his way down to the sea, and beyond.

2 Strangers in a Strange Land

Bradbury's wife, two young daughters, and a governess were able to travel on a screenwriter's budget, which was far more money than he had yet earned from story and book sales. On September 2, 1953, Bradbury signed a seventeen-week contract for $650 a week plus travel and living expenses and enough money up front to cover the logistics of an immediate departure for Europe. They were scheduled to meet Huston in Paris on September 26, but little else was certain. The original plan had been to write with Huston in Biarritz, but with fall rapidly approaching Huston decided to begin work at his home in Ireland to take advantage of the fox-hunting season.[1] Passports were the most immediate problem, and Warner Brothers provided a letter to expedite the process. The Bradburys quickly engaged Regina Ferguson, Susan's preschool teacher, as a governess-nanny for both Susan (almost 4) and Ramona (aged 2), and departed Los Angeles on the evening of the 12th.

He wrote the first page of his screenplay on September 13, 1953, en route to New York by train, little knowing that it would be seven months to the day before he would run the last draft of the final page through his portable typewriter. In New York, during his September 15th–16th layover before boarding his liner for Europe, Bradbury had brief meetings with his Bantam paperback editors and received informal prepublication praise for *Fahrenheit 451* from Theodore Sturgeon and science fiction anthologist Groff Conklin. On the 16th, he had a working lunch with his Doubleday editor Walt Bradbury and his agent Don Congdon to discuss his latest draft and outlines for the long-awaited Illinois novel.[2] He would leave these still incomplete materials with Walt Bradbury for review, but all three men knew that the challenge of the great white whale would keep Bradbury occupied for months to come. He nearly finished the first of nine full readings of *Moby Dick* on the afterdeck of the SS *United States*, during one of the worst storms that the grand liner ever encountered.[3]

The *United States* docked at Le Havre on September 22nd, and Bradbury, with family in tow, traveled to Paris for several days at the Hotel St. James where he finished his first reading and began to discuss specifics with Huston. Both men wanted a script that would "reflect the philosophical, religious, and literary overtones of the original." But they also shared a respectful boldness toward the book, and Huston had made it clear from the start that Bradbury would have a free hand in developing the script.[4] This freedom was quickly put to the test; by the time he arrived in Paris, Bradbury was convinced that Fedallah, the sinister and mysterious chief of Ahab's personal longboat crew of Lascars, represented the principal yet perhaps most expendable obstacle to production. He asked permission then and there to "throw him overboard" and allow Ahab to absorb his function. Huston readily agreed, and this support would provide a key catalyst for Bradbury as he prepared to move beyond the opening scenes of the script.[5]

Paris also initiated Bradbury into Huston's high-profile world of celebrities and fast living. During his two or three days out with Huston he was introduced to the racing scene at Havre de Grace and actually came out ahead with his timid wagers at the Longchamps track. Here was a strange land indeed; as a child and teenager Bradbury had experienced the migrations and poverty of the Great Depression, but his adult life had been relatively uneventful. Now, in Paris, Huston introduced him to the noted combat photographer Robert Capa, who would be killed by a land mine in French Indochina less than a year later. Bradbury also met novelist Irwin Shaw and actress Suzanne Flon, whose role in *Moulin Rouge* had led to an ongoing affair with Huston.

On the evening of September 28th, Bradbury had dinner with screen idols Lana Turner and Lex Barker. He immediately wrote notes and openings for four short stories based on these people, but he was still too naïve to absorb the subtleties of the situation and these pages came to nothing.[6] Before leaving Paris Bradbury offered a lighthearted assessment of his director in a letter home to his bibliographer, the budding genre author William F. Nolan: "Huston says he is out to corrupt me; he looks forward to putting me on a horse, riding me to foxes, jetting me in a speed-plane, and generally introducing me to dope, drink, and dames." These playful words, clever and detached, also reveal just how little he realized, in these early days, that Huston meant exactly what he said.

The Bradburys arrived in London on October 2nd and settled into Brown's Hotel for what turned out to be a brief stay. There was not much work to do at Huston's Moulin Productions office in London, for Huston had decided that most of the preproduction work would center on Courtown, his rented Irish estate. Instead, Huston made final preparations for the release of *Beat the Devil* and hosted a screening of the film.[7] The screening, and a dinner at Huston's private club, allowed Bradbury to get acquainted with legendary director William Wyler; Jeanie Sims, secretary at Huston's London office; and screenwriter Peter Viertel, who would be continuing on to Ireland with Huston. Sims was delightfully "English," and a wonderful production assistant, but Huston had already found another secretary for the advance work in Ireland. On the way to the screening Huston taunted her in ways that surprised Bradbury even though Sims took it all in stride, leaving Bradbury with the uneasy feeling that this kind of verbal abuse might be the price one paid for being part of Huston's world. "At the time I thought it was terribly mean, but I couldn't say anything, because these were my first days in London with John."[8]

Bradbury had time in London to meet his British publisher, Rupert Hart-Davis, who invited him to dine with New Zealander Sir Edmund Hillary, recently knighted for his conquest of Mount Everest.[9] On Sunday September 27th, the *London Observer* published the title story to Bradbury's *The Golden Apples of the Sun* collection as a prelude to the Hart-Davis release of the book in its British edition the following day. This was a coup on two counts; as John Montgomery of the Peters Agency in London pointed out in a note to Don Congdon a week earlier, "*The Observer* carries immense literary prestige, and seldom publishes fiction."

There were other surprises waiting in London; Bradbury found to his great embarrassment that Hal Chester's science fiction B-film, *The Beast from 20,000 Fathoms*, was premiering at a theater in London's Piccadilly Circus, with Bradbury's name prominently displayed as the writer. Its only merit rested with friend Ray Harryhausen's stop-action special effects, but the title (and a minor scene depicting the beast's destruction of a lighthouse) were based on the story that Huston knew as "The Fog Horn." Bradbury had in fact had little to do with the film, and Huston knew quite well that the film itself had little to do with the original story that had sold him on Bradbury's talent. Nevertheless, Huston loved the incongruity of having Bradbury associated with this sensationalized sea monster film while working for Huston on perhaps the greatest novel of the sea in modern literature. As Bradbury recalled many years later, "John was very philosophical about this and very amused. In fact, he liked to use it to twit his friends."[10]

In early October the Bradburys traveled by rail and ferry to Ireland for the principal preproduction work. There was some delay at Dun Laoghaire, their port of entry for Dublin, while customs officials examined Bradbury's copy of *Moby Dick* to see if it was on the Catholic Church listing of banned books; it wasn't, but many early- and mid-twentieth-century classics were. The irony was not lost on Bradbury, whose *Fahrenheit 451* was about to endure a far broader and more public cultural scrutiny under the "climate of fear" that still affected American writers and readers. Bradbury and his family, along with Regina Ferguson, settled into the Royal Hibernian Hotel in Dublin on the 6th, and he immediately entered the frenetic world of Huston's unpredictable schedules and moods.

The young writer loved Hollywood, but he was naïve in its ways; he was constantly trailing behind the horse racing, drinking, and cardplaying life at

Huston's Courtown estate and the adjacent town of Kilcock on the northern edge of County Kildare, west of Dublin. Huston's inner circle included veteran screenwriter Peter Viertel, who had recently published his enduring study of Huston, White Hunter, Black Heart; it was typical of this topsy-turvy world that Viertel had allowed Huston himself to read galleys of his searing portrait in the months prior to publication. Newly arrived Lorrie Sherwood provided secretarial support at the stately Georgian mansion, and Huston's fourth wife Ricki was also in residence with their two young children, Tony and Anjelica.[11] John Godley, a decorated naval aviator and postwar journalist who had recently inherited his father's title as Lord Kilbracken, joined the circus on October 16th to dine with the Hustons, the Bradburys, and Peter Viertel at the Russell Hotel in Dublin.[12]

While Huston spent his days attending to business matters and various social adventures, Bradbury would write in his rooms at the Royal Hibernian. Sometimes business or pleasure would bring Huston into Dublin, but he would rarely work with Bradbury there. He clearly wanted work to center on Courtown and was annoyed when Bradbury chose to keep his family in the more predictable environs of the city. Several days a week a hired car (always driven by "Mike") would take him out to Courtown House, where Huston would review progress before retiring to a lively dinner table, gambling cards, and drinking. Bradbury found it difficult to spread his energy so thin and drank only as much as he felt he had to before calling down to the local pub for "Nick," a Kilcock cab driver who provided his return ride to Dublin.

Most of Huston's insiders regarded Bradbury as somewhat odd—he steered clear of the card table most nights and always required his drivers to respect his fear of high-speed automobile travel. But some respected Bradbury's desire to keep his family life centered in Dublin, where he loved to frequent the small shops and take in the rich tones and unfamiliar speech patterns of the merchants. John Godley found Bradbury sincere, loyal, and full of a fascination with Huston's strange new world of expatriate filmmakers. He loved Bradbury's unbounded enthusiasm and dedication to the project at hand, but found it curious that Ray was still somewhat surprised, even dazed, at his own success as a writer and the new world that this success had brought him to.

Writing nearly forty years after the fact, Peter Viertel recalled that both Ray and Maggie spent some time at Courtown together, and that Ray occasionally came to working lunches as well. During Huston's August trip to Los Angeles, he had finalized a two-picture deal with producers Harold and Walter Mirisch for Moby Dick and Kipling's The Man Who Would Be King. Huston settled Viertel in on the Kipling script but began to spend more and more time with Bradbury discussing *Moby Dick*.[13] This attention did not, however, bring Bradbury any closer to Huston's inner circle, and Viertel was soon able to detect how distant the Bradburys remained from it:

> Neither had ever been to Europe . . . so that their new surroundings were a culture shock to say the least. They appeared to be a devoted young couple, protective of each other, and doubtful at the prospect of joining a house party made up of strangers. . . . Conversation at the luncheon and dinner table would on occasion veer off into the subject of writing, which was a relief from the constant talk of horses and hunting, which initially, Ray confessed to me once we had become friends, had made him and Maggie feel that they had been interned in a madhouse.[14]

It may not have helped that Bradbury had read Viertel's *White Hunter, Black Heart*, which revealed all the personal and professional challenges of working with Huston. Before he ever left Los Angeles, Viertel's estranged wife offered a more personal warning about Huston's dark side. Nevertheless, the Bradburys were well-liked by many members of Huston's circle. Jeanie Sims began an enduring friendship with the Bradburys, but in these early days she worked with publicist Ernie Anderson and assistant director Jack Clayton in the London office. At the Courtown end, Ray soon became attached to a wider audience of characters from one of Kilcock's local pubs, far removed from the "fillum-making gentleman" at the manor house. Nick, the cab driver who regularly ferried him between Kilcock and Dublin, and other villagers would soon infuse Bradbury with characters and story lines that would surface in his fiction and stage plays for decades to come.

3

Indecisions, Visions, and Revisions

Bradbury's work was enjoyable at first. His initial focus on structure was reinforced by Peter Viertel's advice to compose the first draft as if he were scripting a silent movie, then add in the dialogue.[1] Bradbury wrote 20 pages on the screenplay by mid-October and reached 55 before the month was out. None of these pages had passed before Huston's critical eye, however, and to this point there was very little directorial pressure. Bradbury was fascinated by the stories that Huston and Viertel would tell over dinner out at Courtown House, and the natural surroundings soon added to the magic. For the first time in nearly twenty years, Bradbury was experiencing autumn in all its glory. He had not known such a season since his Midwest childhood, and his October 30, 1953, letter to Bill Nolan conveys how the sight of his first fox hunt accentuated the sensations: "All the leaves on the trees ablaze with autumn. Clear, cool, wonderful weather, horns blowing, hounds baying, by God, a fine day!"

In early November, Huston read the evolving screenplay for the first time, and Bradbury began to see just how challenging the rewriting would be. He was entering uncharted waters, and the dangers increased as the *Moby Dick* shooting schedule was moved ahead; location filming was set to begin in April 1954, and Huston now focused on critiquing Bradbury's script. By November 26, 1953, Bradbury had worked through three drafts of the first 43 pages—only a third of the way to the shooting script goal of 120 to 140 pages.[2]

In the space of a month, the pleasure he expressed to Bill Nolan on October 30th ("I'm enjoying *Moby Dick* very much") had completely evaporated; on November 28th, he turned down a story request from Arkham House publisher August Derleth by noting "my time is completely taken up with the project, since it is the toughest damn book to adapt." He also had to tell Charles Beaumont that he would not be able to write an introduction for his first book.[3] This was not an easy decision, for he was a great fan of the young writer and had helped him revise a number of stories over the previous two years.

During November, Bradbury had an odd encounter that seemed to foretell the challenging winter to come. On the 10th, an extensive bookstore search was rewarded when he found the latest title by his beloved Dylan Thomas—*The Doctor and the Devils*, based on the chilling story of the notorious nineteenth-century

Edinburgh anatomy lecturer Thomas Rock and the two murderers who maintained his supply of cadavers. Bradbury had always been attracted to the lyric power with which Thomas navigated the boundaries between life and death in his poetry, and this new experimental work, written in the form of a screenplay, greatly fascinated him as well.

He also purchased a daily paper with the book, and was horrified to find himself in front of the clerk with Thomas's latest book in one hand, and the front-page news of Thomas's sudden death in the other.[4] The sensational details of the 39-year-old Thomas's fatal collapse during a New York reading tour, triggered by bouts of heavy drinking, served as a shocking reminder of the price of fame; this tragedy also reminded Bradbury that he was closer to the world of fame than he had ever been before.

His elaborate commute to and from Courtown House in Mike's car and Nick's taxi was a constant reminder of the distance that was growing between *Moby Dick*'s director and his screenwriter. Huston was an effective motivator and shared Bradbury's passion for Melville, but Bradbury never knew just what Huston was looking for. For his part, Huston simply wanted Ray Bradbury's sense of the story, fresh and new and unencumbered by critical subtleties, and he often encouraged his writer to work things out for himself.[5] Fortunately, Bradbury had already developed distinct strengths as a screenwriter; his earlier contract work at Universal exhibited deep directorial detail, and he brought a director's sense of camera shots and event timing to *Moby Dick* as well. Bradbury was able to write for the camera, and this innate talent was crucial to compressing the action without destroying the magnitude of the original fiction.

One sees this in the brief opening montage, which captures the essence of Melville's entire opening section: how gentle brooks and streams lead men away from the land, delivering them, at last, to the sea. This was, in fact, the very text that he had drafted on the train to New York in September, and it remained with little change in the final shooting script. One sees this quality as well in Bradbury's compression of the final three-day hunt into a single lowering of boats, and his risky elimination of Fedallah. This last gamble was eventually covered by Bradbury's skillful transfer of Fedallah's prophecies to Elijah, and, during his final push to finish the script in April 1954, by his transfer of Fedallah's fatal entanglement with the white whale to Ahab himself.

But Bradbury did more than think in terms of scenes and shots; he also realigned events, and with *Moby Dick* he would need the confidence of a diamond cutter reshaping a crown jewel. In his 1955 credit arbitration summary, and again in his unpublished 1961 UCLA interviews, Bradbury provided a detailed look at the way he recharted events for the screenplay. He had the first third of the screenplay in stable form by late November 1953, carrying through the departure of the *Pequod* from New Bedford. Many late-night conferences with Huston out at Courtown led to seemingly endless rewrites of the final two-thirds, although Bradbury had a clean first draft done by January 10, 1954. By this time he had established what he called three major movements for the final two-thirds of the script: the calm, the typhoon, and the lowering of the boats for Moby Dick. The becalming of the *Pequod* has no true corollary in the novel; Bradbury took a brief passage about a calm, along with the Doubloon chapter, a minor man overboard episode, and parts of the funeral chapter—all from widely separated sections of the novel—and created a major new scene. In Bradbury's version, the loss of the sailor highlights the curse on Ahab's obsession, and brings on the punishing calm.[6]

For *Green Shadows, White Whale*, his 1991 novelization of the six months spent in Ireland, Bradbury portrayed the central significance of the doubloon and its radiating metaphors as the key to his reorganization of the action in the middle and final third of the script: "What nailed it fast was hammering the Spanish gold ounce to the mast. If I hadn't fastened on that for starters, the other metaphors, like pilot fish and minnows and shark followers and sharks, might not have surfaced to swim in the bleached shadow of the Whale. Capture the big metaphor first, the rest will rise to follow. Don't bother with the sardines when Leviathan looms. He will suction them in by the billions once he is yours."

Bradbury established his doubloon sequence by early February 1954, revising from that point on with a stable structural platform already in place.[7] His carefully preserved and dated drafts and discard pages confirm this time line, and his unpublished 1961 UCLA interview offers a screenwriter's perspective on the process:

> So, [Ahab] dedicates the men not only with his insanity but with his gold. After nailing it to the mast, this first man who goes up to look for Moby Dick, falls in. The calm begins; and, in the calm, the image of the sun is seen, again and again, blazing down on this solid sheet of metal which is the sea. The men are suffering above and below decks. There isn't a wisp of wind, and the sun blazes in the sky and the doubloon blazes on the mast. The men then circle around the doubloon and talk about all this. . . .
>
> All of this scene which is one of the best scenes in the film (I'm very proud of it) takes place at its own rate and its own time, and dares to take a longer time because we have scenes of action before it and after it. The ship is becalmed: there's the doubloon: there's the sun in the sky looking like the doubloon: there's the doubloon looking like the sun, and the glare of the gold and the glare of the heat of the sun burns all [the] men golden, makes them sweat and gets them thinking. (254–255)

Even with this structural breakthrough the first full draft would take nearly four months of work, and during that time Bradbury had only periodic contact with events in America. News from Don Congdon came in weekly letters throughout the fall and early winter. *Fahrenheit 451* had been released in America on October 19th, and with few exceptions received excellent reviews. Orville Prescott, writing in the October 21, 1953 issue of the *New York Times*, felt that the alarming parallels to tendencies in our own world offered compelling evidence that "the degraded ideal of mindless happiness and slavish social conformity" was "the most sinister threat to modern man." This was the first Bradbury book that Prescott had read, but he already considered him "the uncrowned king of the science-fiction writers" and acknowledged his international reputation.

Three weeks later, the *Times* followed up with a more critical review by Mick McComas, who took Bradbury to task for being too polemic and too spare on character development. Congdon was furious that McComas and Tony Boucher, who penned a similar review (as "H. H. Holmes") in the October 18th *New York Herald Tribune*, had apparently lost their sensitivity for an author who had consistently supplied them with significant stories for their joint editorial venture, the *Magazine of Fantasy & Science Fiction*. But strong reviews by August Derleth (*Chicago Tribune*), Don Guzman (*L.A. Times*), and a balanced political analysis by Carter Jones in the *Washington Star* were soon followed by excellent magazine reviews in the *Nation* and *Harper's*. Ballantine's unprecedented distribution of 6,000 paperback review copies resulted in nearly fifty reviews in American periodicals, and this kind of grassroots exposure helped counteract the McCarthy period bias against nonconformist fiction back home.

As the holidays approached, Huston's unpredictable working schedule began to complicate Bradbury's plans to finish and revise the screenplay. A hoped-for Christmas vacation in London and the south of France never materialized; winter entertainments were scarce, and Bradbury, along with most of the crew, had fallen into the habit of working on Sundays. On New Year's day, Bradbury had breakfast with Gregory Peck, who by now was locked into the lead role. He liked the quiet actor from the start, but still had misgivings about his suitability for the role; a week later he summed up his feelings in his New Year's letter home: "It is a little hard for me to imagine him as Captain Ahab in this film, for it is hard to find the right kind of maniacal fury and drive in him that would be necessary for this bitter, plunging, wild character. If it is in Peck at all, Huston will bring it out."[8]

Bradbury's most immediate concern was the screenplay itself, and it looked like he would complete it on schedule. He had 140 pages completed by January

7th, and three days later finished his first complete 159-page draft.[9] Cutting seemed inevitable until he had an unexpected opportunity to see MGM's *Julius Caesar*, which had just opened in Dublin. He had seen it back home but quickly decided to see it again; this opportunity would provide a chance to revisit the central challenge of translating literary classics into film—in other words, to see whether he had moved too far away from intellectual content in his *own* efforts to maintain the attention of a motion picture audience. He attended not one but two showings of *Julius Caesar*—the second time sitting up front in the second row to make sure he could hear every word. This odd litmus test revealed a great deal. After the Dublin viewings, it was apparent to Bradbury that this adaptation carried a greater density of dialogue than nonliterary cinema, but it was also apparent that writer-director Joseph Mankiewicz was able to carry it off without losing the mainstream audiences that paid to see it.[10]

Bradbury immediately began to add back dialogue and then cut carefully to find the kind of textual balance achieved in *Julius Caesar*. He restored as much of the rich texture of Melville's dialogue as he dared, now somewhat more confident that an audience could follow great literature on screen without necessarily absorbing every line of dialogue. Beginning on the 16th, Bradbury (with secretarial support) retyped his layered first draft into a fairly clean working copy of 162 pages.[11] But he knew he would eventually have to make cuts that would get the script closer to the ideal shooting length. On January 17, he described this dilemma in a letter to Hart-Davis: "I'm now trying to cut it down to 140 pages, which is a hellish job. I think it can be done. But, God, how heartless it seems, at times, to throw out some of the beauty in Melville to make way for more significant beauties."[12]

By now, Bradbury had other concerns as well—Maggie was exhausted from supervising family life in a strange city and was deeply concerned about the toll that working with Huston was taking on her husband. So far, Bradbury had persuaded her to help him maintain an illusion and not bring her powerful analytical mind to bear on Huston's darker nature.[13] But now, in late January of a seemingly endless winter, he knew that Maggie could not handle much more strain. On the evening of January 27, 1954, he sent his family and Regina to Taormina in Sicily with a promise that he would follow in a few weeks when revisions were done.

4 | Fatal Attraction

Bradbury soon proved he was up to the challenges of revision, even when they included further shifts of plot elements. As he began to revise, he extended the becalming of the *Pequod*—an event that he had originally expanded from a minor Melvillean episode into the first ill omen for the crew; the calm now extended through the sighting of the Spirit Spout, the miragelike spouting of the whale that entices the crew to lower boats and try to row the *Pequod* toward both spout and wind. The next shift of plot sequence resulted from Huston's desire to have a second "ill omen" event lead into the typhoon. Bradbury built to this next stage of fury by bringing the *Rachel* episode forward in the story; as he refashioned it, Ahab does not stop to aid the *Rachel*'s search for the captain's young son, and the storm gathers as a consequence.

Not being a man of the sea, Bradbury needed directorial descriptions that could capture the anatomy of Melville's storm. He found the language he needed in Joseph Conrad's *Typhoon* and *The Nigger of the Narcissus*. Bradbury borrowed no plot elements, but his use of Conrad's vocabulary in his shot directions provided the production crew with a clearer sense of the shooting challenge for this scene. He had little choice but to reposition certain plot elements in this way, for he had to create the drive and dramatic unity that is essential to a film of this kind: "I got a sequence of events, each of a larger texture, each of a more dramatic size and impact so that the hunt gets increasingly more turgid, more fervent, more dedicated, more heated, and so small events build to large ones."[1]

His ability to work comfortably with Melville's language was crucial, and his own metaphors are often hard to distinguish from Melville's. One scene in particular reveals just how well Bradbury could work outside the novel, yet in concert with it, to advance the action of the film. Bradbury recalled his invention of this scene more than fifty years after the fact:

> [H]ow come Queequeg came out of his death spell? It's never explained in the novel. He simply comes out of it without any help. So I wrote a scene in which Queequeg rolls the bones and sees his death, calls for the coffin-maker to make him a coffin, and goes into a trance from which Ishmael cannot bring him out. During the time when the ship is becalmed, late at night, a sailor

approaches Queequeg and begins to cut a new tattoo on his chest with a knife. Ishmael, seeing this, grabs the sailor and fights with him and finds himself pinned to the deck, with the sailor brandishing the knife to kill him. This act, of course, is the thing which brings Queequeg out of his trance. . . . His love for his shipmate causes him to come out of his death trance, grab the sailor, and try to crack his spine over his knee. At which moment we have the entrance of Moby Dick; we've prepared a proper time for the entrance of the whale.[2]

His stylistic inspiration was further enriched in February, when he purchased a secondhand copy of Conrad's *The Mirror of the Sea*. Here he found both a language model and creative reinforcement, another bridge between Melville and his own writing in the form of Conrad's brief mood piece on the power of the sea:

If you would know the age of the earth, look upon the sea in a storm. The greyness of the whole immense surface, the wind furrows upon the faces of the waves, the great masses of foam, tossed about and waving, like matted white locks, give to the sea in a gale an appearance of hoary age, lusterless, dull, without gleams, as though it had been created before light itself.[3]

Conrad's description is a precursor to the self-contained prose-poem at the heart of Bradbury's "The Fog Horn"—just the kind of writing that had sold Huston on Bradbury in the first place. Finding himself heir to both Melville and Conrad was a blessing—in Conrad's books he now had a new voice to break the solitude of the long winter evenings in Dublin.

Other language models came from one of Melville's own inspirations—the Bible. Bradbury equipped himself with Volume I of the Old Testament Revised version, part of a four-volume set of the Oxford World Classics. The first volume contained Genesis through Deuteronomy, and was almost certainly a local purchase—Bradbury signed this copy of the Pentateuch with a further annotation that it was "used working on screenplay of *Moby Dick*, January—February 1954 Dublin." It remains one of many documentation markers of his time writing for Huston and shows how carefully Bradbury wished to preserve every instrument and artifact used in bringing the White Whale to life.

The only instrument he couldn't influence was the musical score; he wanted Huston to engage Bernard Herrmann and had a phonograph recording of Herrmann's *Moby Dick* cantata sent over from the States. Bradbury even played the recording on Huston's phonograph, but he could not win over his director (Anglo-French composer Philip Sainton was eventually contracted to score the film).[4] Herrmann's compositions had fascinated Bradbury ever since he first saw *Wuthering Heights* more than a decade earlier; another decade would pass before he was rewarded with Herrmann scores for two Bradbury episodes of the *Alfred Hitchcock Hour* and the Truffaut film adaptation of *Fahrenheit 451*.

February and March, without Maggie's support, proved to be the toughest months of his stay in Ireland. He was largely cut off from American periodicals and relied on Congdon and others to tell him what was in print and worth reading. Over the winter Congdon sold *Fahrenheit 451* reprint rights to a new American magazine, but the situation didn't fully register with Bradbury until Forry Ackerman wrote to say he was surprised to find *Fahrenheit*, already a Stateside success in book form, serialized in a controversial new Chicago-based magazine called *Playboy*. Bradbury was, at first, stunned: "Wha' hoppen? I never even heard of the magazine before. I'm writing my agent to see if this was a legal transaction."[5] But Congdon was quite pleased with the sale, for no other magazine owners had yet followed Ian Ballantine's lead in publishing this powerful and controversial new book. *Fahrenheit 451* helped sustain *Playboy* through its second, third, and fourth issues, and Hefner always credited Bradbury as a key factor in the early survival of the venture.

His Dublin friendship with UPI bureau chief Len Probst and his wife Beth was a lifesaver during these months away from his family. They were sympathetic to his situation; one of Len Probst's assignments the year before had been to interview Huston, and he was very much aware of the pressure that the director could bring to bear on his writers. Probst also brought him news from the wider world; in late January, he called Bradbury down to the UPI offices for a special news bulletin. Together, they followed the teletype line by line as it revealed Ernest Hemingway's air crash in Uganda, his presumed death, his rescue, and the second, nearly fatal air crash a day later. Bradbury kept the teletype tearsheets for decades, convinced that this was, in effect, the end of the great writer's career. The experience of watching the news pour forth from the teletype was both exciting and unsettling, for it made him feel as if he had been present as one of his literary heroes was crippled for life.

The new series of deep revisions stretched on through the rest of the winter, and Bradbury once again found himself trying to prove his worth to the director he had dreamed of working with ever since he had seen *The Maltese Falcon* more than a decade earlier. Bradbury's desire to win Huston's respect was intensified by the very nature of his perceived relationship with his director. Eight years later, during his extensive but unpublished UCLA interviews, Bradbury reflected on what he had brought into the relationship: "I don't think he's ever had anyone around him that came as blindly as I did. I look back now, and realize I was much too blind. I put him on too high a pedestal. No one can live in rarified country

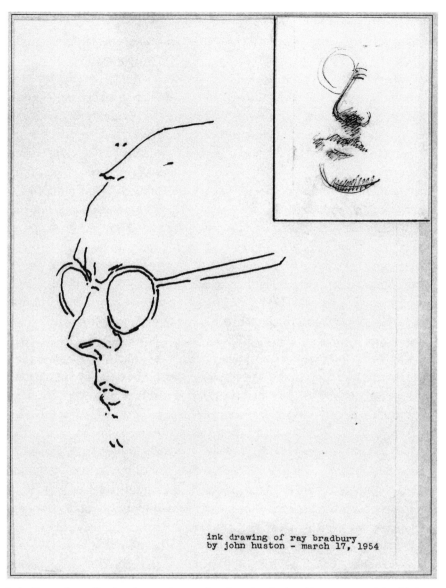

ink drawing of ray bradbury
by john huston - march 17, 1954

John Huston's profile sketch was given to Bradbury just before Huston moved the *Moby Dick* preproduction crew from Ireland to London. The incomplete full-face sketch (inset above) appears on a fragment of Bradbury's script copied out in Huston's hand. From the Albright collection; courtesy Donn Albright and the estate of Ray Bradbury.

like that, and I suppose you can say my adulation was stupid; but there it was. I had to live by it and for it, and I was, of course, so thrilled to be doing my first big film with my hero."[6] He was thrilled when Huston penned a simple profile of his face, and kept it among his working papers for many years.

Through most of the time in Ireland, Huston did not needle Ray any more than he needled everyone else who fed at his large table. But he could not resist toying with people who idolized him or who showed weakness. Bradbury was vulnerable on both counts, and Huston very casually hit his weak points from time to time. Furthermore, Bradbury's avoidance of Huston's sometimes suicidal adventures was beginning to irritate the director, and he eventually convinced himself that Bradbury had his own black heart of secrets. Late in life, Huston confided this observation to biographer Lawrence Grobel: "There's a monster there, too. I remember Ray talking about his love for his children and what he'd do to anyone who kidnapped them, how he would tear them to pieces. And he began to enjoy it, defending his children. He's that kind of a monster."[7] This incident was, of course, simply a variation on Bradbury's lifelong process of working out primal fears through sometimes shocking but purely imaginative storytelling. This was not Huston's way of dealing with the world, and he never understood it.

His way of making Bradbury pay for not fitting into his own world was sometimes amusing. In early March 1954, Huston had Lorrie Sherwood prepare a fake telegram from producer Walter Mirisch: "ASTOUNDED THERE IS NO WOMAN'S PART OF CONSEQUENCE IN FIRST SEVENTY-ONE PAGES OF SCRIPT. WARNER BROTHERS FLATLY REFUSE TO PROCEED UNLESS RICH WOMAN'S ROLE WRITTEN IN."[8] The hoax had Bradbury in tears for some time before Huston let him off the hook. But other pranks, preying on his fear of being trapped in a speeding automobile and his abiding fear of air travel, began to sap his confidence as a writer. Nothing was safe from the game; when Bradbury received word of an unexpected but prestigious thousand dollar grant from the National Institute of Arts and Letters, Huston relentlessly prodded him to bet the money at the racetrack. Bradbury was not able to do this any more than he was able to ride to the hounds, and once again he felt isolated from the man he idolized more than any other Hollywood figure of his time. When Huston joked in front of Tim Durant, who had once worked as an assistant to Charlie Chaplin, that his screenwriter didn't seem to be up to the challenge of *Moby Dick*, Bradbury was no longer able to distinguish harsh humor from chilling reality; until Huston revealed the joke many hours later, Bradbury was certain that he was about to be fired.[9]

Sometimes Bradbury's own words would come back to haunt him. Three years earlier, at his first dinner with Huston, he had professed his love for

Huston's work and sworn that if Huston loved his stories half as much, they would be sure to make a film together someday. Now, in the midst of the *Moby Dick* script revisions, Huston threw these words back with an enigmatic revision of his own: "No Ray, our problem is, you don't love me half as much as I love you." The great unspoken agony may have centered on Huston's inability to translate his great genius as a filmmaker into a genius for writing. For the rest of his life, Bradbury believed that his own hard-earned success in fashioning a script from Melville's classic novel, more than any other factor, ended any possibility that Huston would ever work with him again. Earlier, in Paris, Huston and his agent had seriously revisited the possibility of a *Martian Chronicles* project. "Seven months later, John had to put up with me, and he discovered a terrible thing: I could write. And he tried to teach me to write screen plays, and gave me an example of how bad his writing was. I didn't say anything about it. I was embarrassed. But along the way my script turned out so well that *The Martian Chronicles* was impossible."[10]

Peter Viertel, in interviews for Weller's biography of Bradbury, looked back on the relationship in similar ways: "Huston was really a somewhat frustrated writer. He had always had his input to whatever script was being prepared, but writing didn't come easily to him. . . . John was very satisfied with Ray's adaptation for most of the time they were together." Viertel, like Huston, knew that quality of work was not an issue, but he could see that Bradbury was losing his Muse as the winter rolled on. Huston himself was not sure what he wanted in the script revisions, and that didn't help matters at all. Viertel felt that the two were simply together too often, too long, and the strain began to tell.[11]

5 | A Whale of a Tale

Finally, sometime in early March, Bradbury made a fatal mistake at the dinner table. He had always been guarded at meals, conscious that he was in a strange world and mindful as well of one of his first dinners in Ireland with Huston; there, at Courtown back in October, Huston had suddenly slipped into a dark mood and quickly brought his wife Ricki to tears in front of everyone. No one really knew when he would turn on his large captive audience at meals, so Bradbury kept his normally outgoing table talk in check—until one night in March, when the conversation turned to hypnotism.[1]

This was a favorite subject for Huston; he had successfully hypnotized many of his guests, including both Ray and Maggie. But now Ray saw a chance to turn the tables on Huston by spoofing hypnosis with the other guests and proposing to hypnotize Huston himself. He comically reasoned that, since Huston constantly ridiculed Ray for riding the ferry between England and Ireland instead of flying, Huston himself must be afraid of the ferryboat in the same way that Bradbury was afraid of air travel. He offered to "cure" Huston through hypnosis. He extended the sketch nicely, and drew the kind of attention and laughter normally reserved for the head of the table. It all came together in one of those delightful social moments, but it turned out to be all wrong. It was not just a matter of upstaging the host. Bradbury didn't see it at the time, or even for some days to come, but in the UCLA interviews he looked back on this evening as the pivotal moment in his relationship with Huston:

> I think that caused the break in our wonderful relationship because, up until that time, I was the student: he was the teacher. I was the idolator, and he was the idol. Everything was going toward him; and now, suddenly, I pulled back if only for an hour and criticized him with humor which I gather maybe he couldn't take after having me worship at the shrine so long. I think that our whole attitude toward one another and the whole shape of our relationship changed as of that evening. I was too dense to see it at the time. I didn't realize I'd done anything. We all seemed to have had a fine evening and come away laughing, and quite suddenly, I was a mad ape out of the jungle. The next day

Peter Viertel saw me coming through the lobby of the hotel and cried, "Go get some chains! Here he comes!"[2]

Viertel and a few others in Huston's circle knew immediately that it was a dangerous development. Huston began to needle Bradbury more than ever before, first over the National Institute grant money and then over the unfavorable *London Times* review of *Fahrenheit 451*, which had just been released in England. Bradbury was now being put to a test that was normally reserved for the inner circle. Years later, for Grobel's Huston family biography, Jeanie Sims observed that Huston "tested his love for people and theirs for him to such an extent that it could break. He had to be cruel to see whether you were going to come through that and still be fond of him. And he was continually doing that to people."[3] For his part, Bradbury could work only for someone he liked and respected; for months he had told Maggie that he had to overlook Huston's behavior or he would never be able to finish the screenplay. But now his family was half a continent away, and Huston was about to put Bradbury to the ultimate test.

The test came in mid-March, just as the preproduction staff was preparing for a move to London. It was understood that this relocation would also serve as a minivacation for Bradbury, who had been working on the screenplay since October 6th and had negotiated the last two months of the Irish winter without his family. By this time he rarely saw anyone outside of Huston's circle and had even begun to write journal-like notes in the books he purchased. Still saddened by the premature death of Dylan Thomas four months earlier, Bradbury bought a copy of *Under Milkwood* for companionship and remembrance. His inscription is most revealing: "Mar. 20–25 1954. Last week in Dublin. London next, to finish *Moby Dick*. RB." He added "Ray and Marguerite Bradbury," a signing habit that reinforced the double wish for closure and reunion that was buried between the lines of his inscription.

The day before departure, however, Huston came to Ray and told him that he must fly to London or remain in Dublin until the script was done. Bradbury refused and went out to buy his ticket for the Dun Laoghaire to Holy Head ferry and train connection to London, scheduled to depart at ten o'clock the following night. He didn't take Huston's calls all the next day and was having a farewell dinner at the Royal Hibernian with Len and Beth Probst when Huston caught up with him. Over premeal cocktails, Huston turned the conversation to racing and became insulting when Len Probst confessed to knowing very little about racehorses. Probst had interviewed Huston some months earlier, but now the director curtly turned the tables and demanded to know how a news bureau chief in Ireland could know nothing of horses. Huston quickly left without offering an apology or even a final swipe at Bradbury for taking the forbidden form of transport.

When everyone regrouped in London, tensions were still high between the two men. Casting was finalized during this period, but not before a large dinner at Huston's private club with some of the production staff and other friends of Huston's, including the silent film stars Bebe Daniels and her husband Ben Lyon, who had become television entertainers in the U.K. since leaving Hollywood. This group included Jeanie Sims; Lorrie Sherwood; Peter Viertel; Richard Brooks, who had been Huston's cowriter on *Key Largo* in 1948; and Jack Clayton, who would go on to direct *Room at the Top*, *The Innocents*, and, eventually, Bradbury's *Something Wicked This Way Comes*.

But this evening was heavy with ghosts from seasons past. The events that followed became one of Bradbury's most celebrated anecdotes, and the magnitude of this tale was apparent in the way that each participant brought slight variations to each telling down through time.[4] Huston was in a dark mood, for the flight had aggravated a recent back injury. During dinner he started in on everyone in turn. He began to disparage Bradbury's friends the Probsts, in absentia, and his fear of flying. When Bradbury thanked the waiter with his habitual "God bless you," Huston demanded that he stop blaspheming and shouted, "What do you mean, 'God bless you'? Are you the Pope?" He started in again on the Probsts, and at this point Bradbury cut him off with a profanity. Peter Viertel helped calm Bradbury, but more words after dinner led to a scuffle outside. Huston threatened to throw a punch and Bradbury offered to take it; Viertel remembered later that an elderly lady standing nearby, unaware of the cause of the fight, assured them all that there was no need to fight over a cab at that hour. Jack Clayton managed to get Huston into a cab; Viertel pulled Bradbury away and helped negotiate a meeting with Huston in the morning.

Both Viertel and Lorrie Sherwood, among others, felt that Huston had pushed Bradbury too far. Huston probably knew this, but he also knew that he needed Bradbury for the final revisions and agreed to make amends in the morning. In fact, he appeared to be rather proud that Bradbury had stood up to him outside the restaurant. In these last London weeks, out from under Huston's tyranny and the endless rain and cold of Dublin, Bradbury was able to rewrite the final third of the script. This new focus, along with the sea chanteys he had been composing at intervals throughout the winter months, helped him feel a new closeness with Melville during the final weeks of work in London. Bradbury worked from his room in the Mount Royal Hotel, commuting only when necessary to consult with Huston at the Moulin Productions offices. On Sunday, April 2nd, Bradbury had his best writing day of all and rewrote the final 36 pages (the typhoon and the final lowering of the boats) in a single eight-hour stint: "That last Sunday, I felt more like Melville than any other time in my whole experience. . . . [I]t came right, it came absolutely right."[5] On this day he also took his earlier deletion of Fedallah's role to its logical final step and transferred his fate to Ahab: "My inspiration was to have Moby Dick take Ahab down and wind him in the coiled ropes and bring him up among the harpoons on this great white bier, this great cortege, this funeral at sea. Then we see, 'My God, these two should be together forever through eternity, shouldn't they—Ahab and the white whale?' It's not in the book, but I do believe that Melville would have approved."[6]

Here was a final Bradbury touch that soon worked its way into film culture as if it were authentic Melville: "The tidal motion causes [Ahab] to gesture and the men look, and one of them says, 'Look, he beckons, he beckons.' That's not in the book. . . . Even though he's dead, he's able to destroy them with his madness. I'm so proud of that."[7] Years later, in his 1968 novelization of 2001: A Space Odyssey, Bradbury's friend Arthur C. Clarke even developed an allusion to this scene as Dave Bowman sees Frank Poole's arm "wave" while he oscillates lifelessly at the end of his tether: "Poole's gesture was an echo of Captain Ahab's when, lashed to the flanks of the white whale, his corpse had beckoned the crew of the Pequod on to their doom."[8]

In a most creative way, then, Bradbury had convinced himself that he *was* Melville, at least for the eight hours it took to type those last 36 pages of script. He drew on the same form of willpower, verging on self-hypnosis, which had allowed him to silence the warnings of his wife and even his own rational mind as his working relationship with Huston became more and more untenable. And in the end, he was able to turn this illusion to great comic effect in Huston's very presence: "When I ran across London I threw the script in John Huston's lap and said, 'There! I think it's finished! All in one day!' He read it and said, 'My God, yes! What happened?' I said, 'Behold! Herman Melville stands before you!' And then I added, 'But look quickly, because he'll be gone in five minutes!'"[9]

Bradbury completed a few final revisions by April 14th with a sense that he had paved the way for a quality production. Peter Viertel, who was sad to see Bradbury leave the crew, agreed. In all, Bradbury had prepared more than thirty outlines and 1,500 pages of text, and left a final script that was still 150 pages long. He had ribbon or carbon copy for his drafts and discards, and Lorrie Sherwood kept copies of his principal drafts for reference in preparing the initial shooting script. He parted on good terms with Huston, who was now assembling his cast and finalizing plans for the location filming. Bradbury knew that revisions and script cuts during the shooting stage were inevitable, and he assumed that he would be able to send revisions even though he was no longer on contract. But in the afterglow of a job well done, Bradbury was anxious to rejoin his family in Italy and made no formal arrangements for further work on the script. He did, however, make one final gesture of reconciliation that would come back to haunt him. The last time he saw Huston, they exchanged gifts (a silver bowl from a shop in the Regent High Street for Huston, and a silver fish charm for Bradbury), and then Bradbury offered to share the screen credit in return for everything he had learned from Huston about shaping and focusing a script. Huston thanked him but declined, and that was all Bradbury ever expected to hear on the subject.[10]

In the two weeks between his April 2nd epiphany and his departure for Sicily on April 15th, he made time to check in with his British publisher, Rupert Hart-Davis, who had recently published *Fahrenheit 451*. He had asked Hart-Davis to send a copy to Nobel laureate Bertrand Russell, who found it to be a powerful cautionary tale: "The sort of future society that he portrays is only too possible."[11] Russell asked to meet the author, and Bradbury made the trip to Lord Russell's estate in Richmond, Surrey on April 7.

His journey began in high anxiety. A decade earlier he had read around in Lord Russell's *History of Western Philosophy*, but those dim memories failed to reassure; his lack of higher education was bolstered only by his reading of Russell's recent and somewhat whimsical science fantasy tales. That, at least, would get him past the handshake. Fortunately, Russell wanted to discuss *Fahrenheit 451* and, most particularly, how Bradbury could transform *Moby Dick* into a screen presentation. Bradbury was still too close to this work to have a practiced answer, but did manage to focus on his determination to preserve the power of Melville's language and characters even as he modified Melville's dramatic development of events.

The evening went well enough, but his hosts were clearly more entertained than enlightened. Shortly after returning to America, he wrote Hart-Davis about his visit: "I may have hit Russell on an off evening. I may have had little to give him, being constrained myself. In any event, while it was a nice evening, it didn't have that sort of feeling where your own champagne-bubbles foam up behind the eyes while you're talking to people you're really at ease with." But before he ever met Lord Russell, Bradbury had already gained something that he would always value; his letter of invitation contained a picture of Russell in his armchair, pipe in hand and his copy of *Fahrenheit 451* in the chair beside him.

6

"Floreat!"

As Bradbury prepared to leave the British Isles and rejoin his family in Taormina, his mind turned to the long-deferred European vacation. The original plan had been to spend perhaps two months on the screenplay and tour Europe for eight or nine months.[1] In actuality, the time line was nearly reversed—Bradbury spent seven months to the day working on *Moby Dick*. As Easter 1954 approached, they would have to decide exactly where they could afford to go in terms of both money and time. With Maggie and the girls already in Sicily, it became clear that the final month should be spent touring Italy. They would indeed spend most of the next month in Rome and northern Italy, with a primary focus on visiting the distinguished Renaissance art historian and attribution expert, Bernard Berenson.

Their quest to reach Berenson was almost a year in the making. In late May 1953, shortly after Bradbury's "Day after Tomorrow" essay appeared in the *Nation*, Berenson wrote what he called the first "fan letter" of his life to congratulate Bradbury on his refreshingly simple and sincere approach to the art of writing science fiction. Berenson was not a fan of the genre, but the two substantive sentences of his short letter indicate how much Bradbury's view resonated with his own general views on creativity in the arts: "It is the first time I have encountered the statement by an artist in any field, that to work creatively he must put flesh into it, & enjoy it as a lark, or fun, or a fascinating adventure. How different from the worker in the heavy industry that professional writing has become!"

Their subsequent conversations reveal that Berenson was also impressed by Bradbury's characteristic homage to the influence of tradition. In defining science fiction for his essay, Bradbury maintained that "It *can* be poetry. It *has* resulted in some of the greatest writing in our past, from Plato and Lucian to Sir Thomas More and Francois Rabelais and on down through Jonathan Swift and Johannes Kepler to Poe and Edward Bellamy and George Orwell." This observation was impressive in its simple directness, and offered yet again another indicator that Bradbury's library-based reading had exceeded the limits of his unevenly absorbed high-school education.

Berenson's remarkable letter ended with an invitation to visit him in Florence. This seemed impossible until the unexpected opportunity to work with

John Huston on a Hollywood pay scale suddenly provided the means. In mid-January 1954, Bradbury sent Berenson a copy of *Fahrenheit 451*, but it would actually be mid-April before he was able to join his family in Sicily and begin the long-awaited tour of Italy with a two-week stay in Rome. With almost no warning, it suddenly became apparent to Bradbury and his wife that Rome marked the beginning of the greatest cultural awakening of their lives.

To be sure, Maggie was well versed in the broader aspects of European history and literature; nevertheless, the magnificent art and architectural grandeur of Rome opened entirely new cultural vistas for both of them. The first milestone was the Vatican Museum; during their second week in Rome both Bradburys spent days exploring the exhibits and galleries, and this adventure provided a deep exposure to both ancient and medieval art. The days spent in the Vatican Museum provided the perfect prelude to the world of the Renaissance that Bernard Berenson would reveal to them in the northern cities of Florence and Venice.

On May 7, 1954, the Bradbury party left Rome for Tuscany, arriving in Florence and settling into the Grand Hotel Baglioni Palace for what would be a six-night stay. Bradbury had written ahead to Villa I Tatti, the hillside estate just below the village of Settignano where Berenson spent all but the hottest months of the year. That afternoon Bradbury called and had his first conversation with Nicky Mariano, who together with Berenson managed all aspects of life at the Villa and its world-famous library. She informed him that the aged Berenson was slightly ill but felt confident that this was a passing indisposition and invited the couple to I Tatti for lunch the next day.

: : :

In many ways Bradbury felt more prepared to meet Berenson than he had felt earlier in April when he met Bertrand Russell. He knew much more about Berenson, but he also knew that Berenson was ready to question Bradbury's reliance on the framework of science fiction when his work clearly had more universal relevance. In mid-March, Berenson had offered his first comments after reading *Fahrenheit*: "I cannot & do not mean to try to persuade you that your framework seems to me superfluous. Perhaps you can write only with that trellis to climb on. But your sense of people, their reactions as well as spontaneous actions is so fine, so delicate that I could wish you were creating novels & stories of character, & characters not engaged in fantastic events."

Berenson's background seemed quite exotic to Bradbury: a European Jewish heritage, early childhood in Lithuania, youth and schooling in New York, college and graduate school at Harvard, all before 1890. Although he retained his United States citizenship for the rest of his long life, the 89-year-old Berenson had spent nearly seven decades in Europe pursuing a dual career—his voca-tion was art history, but his reputation as an art historian was largely built on his avocation as an attributor of Renaissance Italian paintings. In many ways, Berenson was already an institution through his living connection with the history of modern thought.

At Harvard, William James had been both a mentoring professor and a friend, and he had made a lasting impression on Henri Bergson. Lord Bertrand Russell was for many years his brother-in-law through Russell's marriage to his wife's sister Alys Smith, and thus Berenson interacted with the only two philosophers to win Nobel prizes in the twentieth century. He was now at the other end of life's cycle and remembered how intellectuals of the past like Bergson and Walter Pater had, inexplicably, enjoyed meeting the young Berenson. They had shown a surprising interest in him and now, unexpectedly but in much the same way, Berenson wanted the young to continue to visit him.[2]

Upon arriving at I Tatti, the Bradburys were immediately put at ease by Nicky Mariano, who provided a full tour of the house before settling her guests into the study. Berenson arrived about a half-hour later; he presented a delicate and well-groomed figure, diminutive but clearly a commanding intellectual presence in spite of his calm manner. By the end of the day Berenson had established the kind of rapport he hoped to spark in all of the new young writers and artists who visited him in these later years. A parting gift, however, would overshadow all other aspects of their growing friendship—an unusual itinerary of Florentine sites and museum exhibits, veering off from the usual tourist attractions to reveal the deep history of the Renaissance world.

The following day, May 9, Berenson took up his diary and reminded himself of Bradbury's refreshingly unaffected manner and his unsophisticated passion for art. The unspoken question behind Berenson's diary note is not difficult to di-vine—would the young writer's unproven potential lead to meaningful discover-ies? The wife was well grounded in history and languages, but he wasn't yet sure about Bradbury himself. A luncheon invitation for Monday May 10 was extended by Nicky at the last minute, allowing Berenson to continue his gentle probing of Bradbury's largely self-taught aesthetic.[3] Was this largely self-educated American writer ready to encounter the full force of the Renaissance? There was no way to be sure until Bradbury confessed to an accidental discovery of the Church of the Carmine and the frescoes of Masaccio. As Bradbury would privately recall a half-century later, he had sensed that Masaccio represented "a change in the way of painting, turning the figures and giving a round to them, giving shadows.... I felt like I was looking at a change in the way painting existed in the world."[4] From this point, Berenson knew that Bradbury's eyes were open to a new world.

In three days—Sunday May 9th through Tuesday the 11th—they managed to visit and study most of the principal sites on Berenson's very unusual list. His instructions for the Duomo, the landmark cathedral church of Florence known officially as Basillica di Santa Maria del Fiore, were typical. Berenson did not want them to focus on the church as it is today, or even on Brunelleschi's magnificent red-brick dome. Instead, he directed the Bradburys to the Opera Del Duomo, the Museum of Cathedral Works hidden away behind the grand edifice of the Duomo, where Bradbury was able to walk through five centuries of reconstruction and see as well the statuary "retired" to the museum after each successive wave of rebuilding. Either by chance or design, Berenson had sent Bradbury to the one part of the Duomo complex that would mean the most to the young writer—a magnificent stone time machine, perhaps the greatest cathedral museum outside of Rome.

At the church and convent of San Marco, Berenson wanted them to focus only on the convent cells of the fifteenth-century Dominican friars. The humble friars' cells link the entire Dominican history together through the art of the great Fra Angelico, and this was what Berenson wanted Bradbury to see. There was a pictorial language conveyed in the gestures of the figures—gestures of adoration, grief, pain, and supplication that invited deeper meditations on faith, and these paintings represented a visual analogue to the challenge that Bradbury faced every day of his writing life: how to release the creative unconscious from the restrictions and distractions of external reality.

All of the principal sculptures and paintings he encountered persisted as vivid images in Bradbury's mind, stimulating new and broader brushstrokes in his own writings. Even the Renaissance foes of art interested him (he would eventually attempt a stage play based on Savonarola's life and discourses). To this point in his life he had admired certain modern artists, but he knew them largely in *vacuo*, with little understanding of what came before. Now the larger picture was starting to take shape, and he had new artistic loves to go with his reading loves. And by the end of the week, there would be more discoveries in Venice—the late Renaissance innovations in light and dark contrasts pioneered by Titian and Tintoretto, representative works by Bellini and Veronese, and Da Vinci's drawing of Vitruvian Man.

A scheduled research visit brought Berenson to Venice as well, and the Bradburys caught up with him for at least one lunch and a dinner during their three-day stay. In both Florence and Venice, Berenson often turned the conversation to Bradbury's work. He even suggested a sequel to *Fahrenheit 451* designed to lure his young friend away from science fiction: a further future when the book people might finally have the freedom to reveal their memorized classics, but they unknowingly reestablish them in forms distorted by fading memories and the passage of time.[5] A surviving developmental note from that week shows just how far he had fallen under Berenson's spell:

What of the old men with the memories of great books in their minds? How did they remember the books?
    distorted, of course.
    rewritten.
    added to, detracted from, misshapen, etc.
    you could do an entire book of twelve chapters on twelve men with 12 books in their minds and the changes the characters of these men wraught on the books.
    an incredible idea.

What Berenson had suggested would have turned Bradbury toward a highly experimental form of postmodernist or postapocalyptic fiction that ran counter to his temperament; in spite of his initial fascination, he never attempted it. But Berenson was more interested in a project that Bradbury already had under contract—stories of his Illinois childhood that would eventually reach print, in part, as Dandelion Wine. Berenson sensed that this autobiographical project would help Bradbury move beyond the science fiction of Fahrenheit 451 and the science fictional framework built into (and around) many of his best-known early stories. In Venice, Berenson approached the subject once again,

Bradbury still felt most comfortable nesting his creations within a loose framework of science fiction, projecting the present out into the future. Hadn't he proclaimed this to the readers of the Nation, only a year earlier? Now Berenson was suggesting that Bradbury could write about enduring themes and the issues of the day without such an armature around the emerging text. He had already proven that he could write stories of great emotional impact in the nostalgic small-town context of his youth, but could he sustain this level of creativity through longer works of interpretive fiction? It was worth thinking about, especially now as he prepared to return to his own writing for the first time in nearly a year.

He would not see Berenson again before departing Venice. On Saturday, May 15, 1954, the Bradburys prepared to board the Orient Express for Paris, leaving a gift of flowers delivered in person to Berenson's hotel. Bradbury had considered taking his family through Milan and on to Genoa for the ocean voyage home, but rapidly rising expenses and the swiftly falling sands of time made it much more expedient to retrace their steps to Paris for three days before proceeding on to the port of Le Havre. They boarded the SS United States, the same ocean liner that had brought them from America in September 1953, and departed Europe on May 21, 1954.

In his quiet way, Berenson greatly appreciated the vitality and enthusiasm that the Bradburys had brought into his life, and the promise of a new correspondence through his declining days. He had already formed his settled opinion of Bradbury's innate strengths; on the day following their first meeting, Berenson made this entry in his diary:

May 9th, I Tatti

Ray Bradbury, the writer of "science fiction," and his wife. He is only thirty-three, simple, easygoing, no inferiority complex, not shy nor on the defensive. No "education" after fourteen. Began to write at fifteen. Seems to have escaped being stuffed with pseudoproblems that worry young writers, and make them howl to the moon. Tried to persuade him to drop the framework of science and to write without that cast-iron skeleton, assuring him he had enough psychological creative power and gift of words to become a novelist of the Classical tradition. Extraordinary in many ways. . . . Nothing "self-made" or culturally *nouveau-riche* about him. Floreat![6]

"Floreat!"—'May he flourish.' A command, a blessing, and a prophecy, expressed through the tense and mood of a single Latin verb. Berenson would live five more years—long enough to see the prophecy fulfilled.

7

A Place in the Sun

Bradbury's readjustment to America actually began just as his grand adventure with Bernard Berenson came to a close. On May 15, 1954, his final day in Venice, he wrote to his parents, slipping effortlessly back into the "gee whiz" mask he usually adopted in writing to them. But the letter was meant to be informative rather than deceptive; the life-changing nature of the European experience came through in a tone that simply reflected the most basic aspect of Bradbury's genuine wonderment at the discoveries: "This trip has been an opening up of our lives for us; we have seen so much and learned so many new things about the world and about ourselves and about living. We'll look back on this time as our own private Renaissance, I'm certain. We've learned to come to personal terms with the paintings we've seen, and all through meeting Mr. Berenson and reading his books." A few weeks later, the more intimate letter he sent to Rupert Hart-Davis revealed the full impact of the encounter: "Italy, Berenson, Tintoretto, Rubens, Fra Angelico fell on us in an avalanche of color. To see the really great artists for the first time in your life is a shattering and exhilarating experience. You get the terrific and powerful sense of discovery—as if the Renaissance had never existed until you created it yourself with your eyes."[1]

The impact of these discoveries would change everything, but these changes would emerge slowly; for now, Bradbury returned from his nine months in England, Ireland, and continental Europe eager to take up the exciting literary projects that he had unexpectedly suspended nine months earlier to work with John Huston. He had a backlog of story drafts and concepts filed away from the seven incredibly productive years preceding his September 1953 departure for Europe, and he had the Illinois book to take up again—a project that Bradbury, Don Congdon, and Doubleday editor Walt Bradbury all earnestly hoped would soon mature into a fully novelized cycle of stories. On May 27, 1954, the day after debarking from the SS United States in Manhattan, he met with both men to plan a strategy for completion of the book, still titled Summer Morning, Summer Night. Walt Bradbury was certain that the Illinois book would take Ray Bradbury to another level of recognition in the broader markets beyond the science fiction and fantasy field, and in the process firmly establish him at home and abroad as a master of both the short story and the novel. All three men felt that the time was right, and perhaps already overdue, for Bradbury to move out of the SF genre niche where Doubleday executives had tried to center his marketing image. In spite of his wide international prominence in major market magazines and his growing reputation in school classrooms and libraries, his Doubleday titles still reflected the limited sales objectives symbolized by the company's science fiction logo.

But before leading his family home by rail to Los Angeles, he would also receive an indisputable literary honor that proved to be a harbinger of things to come. By sheer good fortune, the National Institute of Arts and Letters annual awards ceremony fell on May 26th, the day of his arrival in New York, and he was able to appear on the dais with five other grant recipients in literature, including C. Vann Woodward (a great fan of Bradbury's fiction) and Hannah Arendt, author of the very timely *Origins of Totalitarianism*. Bradbury had received news of the $1,000 grant during his troubled time in Ireland; now, however, free of these pressures and seated among authors, editors, and critics of the first order in American literature, he felt himself yet another step closer to the literary canon as he received his award citation from Pulitzer Prize–winning novelist John Hersey.

The American Academy of Arts and Letters cohosted the Institute ceremonies, and Bradbury was seated on stage with the attending members. This experience brought to life all of his youthful hopes of earning a place among his literary loves on library bookshelves. He always associated a book with its author and spent much of his early life in close communion with the creative spirits he imagined to be all around him in the many public libraries he frequented. This form of worship did not fade as he matured and in fact supplied a large part of his unflagging will to write. Suddenly, he found himself seated within a living library; here were playwrights Maxwell Anderson, Lillian Hellman, and Robert Sherwood; historian Jacques Barzun; poets Robert Lowell, Archibald MacLeish, Carl Sandburg, and William Carlos Williams; novelists Pearl Buck, John Dos Passos, John Hersey, and Thornton Wilder; and some of the best-known literary scholars and critics in America.

Surprisingly, the recent critical success of *Fahrenheit 451* was not mentioned at all; the program citation described him as the author of *The Martian Chronicles* and *The Golden Apples of the Sun* and went on to offer the first solid evidence that he had carried aspects of genre fiction into the world of high literature: "Ray Bradbury . . . has brought to the genre of popular weird tales, especially that new sort known as space fiction, a complexity and intensity and strange beauty that lift much of his work to a level very close to that of poetry."

Describing science fiction as "that new sort" of weird tale reveals just how hard it was for academe to accommodate his achievement. To this point, his acceptance within literary circles had largely been limited to West Coast British expatriates such as Christopher Isherwood, Aldous Huxley, and their broader circle of friends on both sides of the Atlantic. Individual American and British writers usually discovered Bradbury's work from his many magazine and anthology appearances, which often then led them to his books. But he would always remain an outsider, a writer with a unique and at times masterful poetic style who violated nearly every genre-based rule of plot and characterization in order to focus on the deeper emotions of the human soul. His selection of an aphorism by Juan Ramon Jimenéz as the epigraph for *Fahrenheit 451* aptly characterized the way that many literary figures would always see him: "If they give you ruled paper, write the other way."[2]

Bradbury's highly emotional approach to literature was certainly at odds with the high modernist technique of minimizing authorial presence within the work. Don Congdon had pinpointed the main intellectual objection to Bradbury's dramatic presentation of ideas just before Bradbury's departure for Europe: "to them, such ideas would presume to be more commonly known, and they demand, consequently, a more restrained, almost ironic approach to the idea, so that no one could ever accuse them of having joy at such discovery. . . . The great thing, which is pure, distilled Bradbury, is the skill with which you dramatize an idea and entertain the reader while he is absorbing it." The National Institute of Arts and Letters prize was a crucial step toward broader recognition, and Bradbury's European excursion had done much to fulfill Congdon's predeparture prediction of further creative growth: "The more you deepen your own understanding and experience with ideas, the more effective you will become."[3]

Similar private encouragements had also arrived by mail during his time in Europe. One of the most treasured had been forwarded to him during his first weeks in Ireland from Nelson Algren, then at the peak of his powers as a mainstream realist. Bradbury would always draw back from Algren's naturalistic studies of urban life, but he was greatly encouraged by the letter that Algren sent to Ballantine's Stanley Kauffmann after reading *Fahrenheit 451* and its companion stories: "Mr. Bradbury can bring the future closer to the reader than most writers can bring the present. This is because, no matter how prophetic, he is always topical: like Orwell, his fantasies are never so remote but that we see their beginnings all about us. His understanding of our own times affords a special force to his portraits of man's future, and a humor not possessed by any other science-fiction writer."[4]

The televised Army-McCarthy hearings had begun in April 1954, just weeks before Bradbury's return to America, and he was concerned that the continuing climate of fear back home might affect sales of *Fahrenheit 451*. Ian Ballantine quickly assured him that he was not disappointed that the steady sales of

Fahrenheit had not come close to best-selling status, and he summarized the essential political challenge facing the book: "It is an irony of our time that some of the most important things that are happening to us are not talked about because people have been made afraid, and I think that *Fahrenheit* and every other nonconformist book faces the obstacle of this fear."

It would, in fact, take seven years for Ballantine's first paperback printing of 250,000 to sell out. In England, however, where Senator McCarthy and America's climate of fear was largely irrelevant to the literary critics, *Fahrenheit* was well-received. The British edition was released in the spring of 1954, and the major reviews followed him home to Los Angeles. Although Angus Wilson was not as enthusiastic as he had been for *The Martian Chronicles*, there was an enthusiastic radio broadcast from Idris Parry, the BBC's foremost literary reviewer, as well as strong reviews from the future Poet Laureate John Betjeman and a very young Adrian Mitchell, just embarking on his long career as Britain's most prominent antiwar literary voice.

Ballantine's April 7 letter had reached him at Taormina, and after his return to America in late May there were strong indicators that *Fahrenheit 451* would overcome the obstacle of fear and advance Bradbury's reputation within the mainstream literary establishment. The National Academy honors were soon followed by news that the novel would receive the 1953 gold medal as the best fiction book written by a California author. On September 15, 1954, Bradbury accepted this honor from the Commonwealth Club of San Francisco, where he found himself in good company; silver medals were awarded to Leon Uris for *Battle Cry* and to the best-selling aviation writer Ernest K. Gann for *The High and the Mighty*. Bradbury was not comfortable speaking in such a venue—he had not been required to speak at the National Academy ceremonies—and decided to focus his Commonwealth Club address on the bitterly divisive polarization of politics and media reporting that had, in part, fueled his vision of a future world where an examined life is no longer possible.

His remarks, preserved in a partially handwritten draft, indicate his unease, but they also carry the kind of emotional impact that would characterize many of his subsequent public addresses. His words also reflected the impact of recent travels: "I wrote *Fahrenheit 451* to let us remind ourselves that the world is out there. The world outside our borderlands is there, it is a fact, it cannot be turned from, it cannot be hidden away, it cannot be covered up, it refuses to be ignored. I wrote *Fahrenheit 451* to remind us that we must be careful how we funnel that world into our minds." Not unexpectedly, the content was more visionary than practical, offering an impossible solution that nevertheless struck at the heart of the nation's traumatizing ideological divisions: "I would like to see a page, an entire page appear in every newspaper in America, where the facts on any given situation would be presented by a Board of Reporters, Democratic, Republican, Socialist, who would present the actions of a given day or hour and say this is what happened today. On the other pages you will find what this newspaper thinks of what has happened."

Other recognitions were just as encouraging as the awards and demonstrated the wide range of Fahrenheit's impact. The Nation, which had previously published Bradbury's widely read essay on science fiction as well as a short story, now promoted Fahrenheit 451 as a featured book club selection. The AFL-CIO published a major summary of the novel and offered copies of Fahrenheit to new union members. Best of all, the book had also attracted a new friend who would provide a crucial boost to Bradbury's acceptance within the intellectual literary community—the Columbia University scholar and critic Gilbert Highet. Bradbury, who had developed the habit of reaching out to mainstream authors and critics with copies of his books, had written to Highet from Dublin in early November 1953. But Ian Ballantine's wide circulation of review copies may have reached him first, for Highet had already penned an endorsement of Fahrenheit 451 for the December issue of Harper's magazine.

Highet's personal response to Bradbury's letter was even more encouraging: "Goodness, you have a sensitive style; such things are rare, and have to be born in people, like color-sense; and then kept constantly alive. I wish we could meet, for I am rapidly becoming a fan of yours." Over the next year, this appreciation of Bradbury would motivate a major shift in Highet's long-held opinion of science fiction as "merely childish fairy tales without moral or intellectual content." This negative stance represented his view as late as the 1953 publication of World to World: People, Places and Books. But in November 1954, Bradbury received Highet's gift of his new book, A Clerk of Oxenford: More Conversation about People, Places and Books. It contained Highet's extensive discussion of Bradbury's early weird tale "The Crowd," offered "partly because it is a splendid story, partly because Ray Bradbury is an exceptionally good author who deserves to be better known, and partly because I want to take back something I wrote in an earlier book."

In this way, Highet used Bradbury's work as preamble to his concession that there is much good work in the field of science fiction. His confessional had major implications for the way that the broader literary world might view genre fiction, but this was only the beginning of Highet's impact on Bradbury's recognition as a major writer. He would soon become an arbiter of popular and intellectual literary taste in his role as a board member of the Book-of-the-Month Club, and in 1965 he would write the Random House introduction to The Vintage Bradbury—the first truly retrospective collection of Bradbury's short fiction.

Highet would eventually designate Bradbury a neoclassical fabulist, a myth-maker of great relevance to the modern literary scene, but his revised view of genre fiction was still conflicted in ways that reflected the broader views of the intellectual community: "I have read a large number of genuine 'science fiction' romances and short stories. Thinking them over, I must say that most of them are trash, on the same level as cowboy tales, cheap ghost stories, and 'lost world' exploration fantasies, poorly imagined and vulgarly written. But a surprising number of them are good, far better conceived, and more interestingly written than many of the dull realistic novels and machine-made historical romances that pour off the printing presses."

Highet and his wife, the writer Helen MacInnes, would soon become close friends of the Bradburys and would join an increasing number of literary authors and critics who found Bradbury, at his best, a writer who transcended genre boundaries of all kinds. But Highet's qualified and frank assessment of science fiction was also an indicator of the resistance that Bradbury would continue to encounter throughout his career. All too often, he was portrayed as a writer who rose through the support of genre fans and fellow genre writers and then denied them; conversely, other critics portrayed him as a writer of popular fiction who had dared to pull himself into the world of serious literature.

Ray Bradbury—always the two names, read or spoken as a single password of recognition—was becoming one of the best-known figures in contemporary American literature; he had finally found a place in the sun, a bright prominence where an increasing number of readers, authors, and critics acknowledged his transcendent gifts as a master storyteller, prose stylist, and mythmaker for the emerging Space Age. But he was also seen as a writer trying to navigate the unsettled margins between popular success and high literary standing—a very dangerous proposition indeed. Would *Fahrenheit 451* find traction as an enduring work of literary relevance and philosophical value? Not while the Climate of Fear influenced political and sociological thinking. But as E. B. White and others were beginning to observe, Senator McCarthy's public rallies were no longer drawing capacity crowds. Only the passing years would tell if Bradbury's best work could stand the test of time.

Part II

The End of the Beginning

I was in Plandome, Long Island, to visit an aunt of mine when I was twenty-six. I stayed overnight in her house. She was a wonderful lady. She took me down to the train station the next morning, and I stood there on the platform and tears came to my eyes. I said, "Oh God, I hate to go; everything's ending." She said, "Oh no, my dear, everything's beginning. You go home and begin." A great lady. She was right. She really nailed it. So that's the attitude you have. Every day is a beginning.

—RB, 2005

8 Post-Scripts

After settling back into the familiar routines of Clarkson Road in June 1954, Bradbury unexpectedly found himself unable to write for several weeks—the inevitable aftereffect of his intense but successful struggle to produce the *Moby Dick* script under Huston's brilliant but tormenting tutelage. He soon found his Muse again, but before he resumed any of his suspended works-in-progress, he was drawn back to the screenplay he had so recently left behind in London. The sensation was unsettling, much like an amputee feeling phantom pains and movement in a lost limb, for he had left the preproduction crew long before the inevitable rewriting required for the final shooting script.

Throughout the summer of 1954, distanced from the long months with Huston, he began to exorcise his own demons by revising a copy of his script back in Los Angeles. He assumed that Huston would welcome these revisions, but the director and his inner circle blocked further discussion of the screenplay. The first hint of this isolation came when Lorrie Sherwood failed to forward a copy of the screenplay to Rupert Hart-Davis. Bradbury had made this request before he left England; he wanted Hart-Davis's opinion, but he also wanted to see if there was any interest in publication of the screenplay as a book.[1] Bradbury would eventually send copies off to several publishers, but Warner Brothers actually owned the final form of Bradbury's work and nothing ever came of these efforts.

He now took time to learn more about Melville, not only to inspire revision but also, and perhaps more importantly, to verify in his own mind that he had captured the heart and soul of the novel in his script. When he arrived in Dublin the year before, Bradbury had purchased copies of *Redburn* and *White-Jacket*, the novels that Melville had written just before turning to *Moby Dick*, as well as an edition of Melville's collected stories. Now he had time to read these works, but his attention quickly turned to Melville's critical legacy.[2] He purchased and read a number of volumes, and the most important of these, from Bradbury's perspective, turned out to be the most creative and the most unconventional of them all—*Call Me Ishmael*, the controversial 1947 study of *Moby Dick* written by the American poet and literary critic Charles Olson.

Bradbury found Olson's highly subjective, direct, and emotional style very accessible, and found his theories absolutely fascinating. He would eventually write a poem on this discovery, "That Son of Richard III," quoting from Olson's central premise in his introduction to a private-press printing of the poem: "Moby Dick was two books written between February 1850 and August 1851. The first book did not contain Ahab. It may not, except incidentally, have contained Moby Dick." The evidence of this break in composition centered on Melville's first reading of Shakespeare during the summer of 1850. There is little textual evidence to support the "two-texts" theory, but Olson's reading of *Moby Dick* in a Shakespearean context remains a pioneering critical achievement today. Bradbury had felt the impact of the Bible and Shakespeare in all of his many readings of *Moby Dick* over the previous year, but he had had no critical context at all. Now, seeing (through Olson's eyes) exactly *how* Shakespeare's drama informed Melville's masterwork, Bradbury felt that his own approach in writing the script, his decision to focus on the development of character and the measured rise and fall of dramatic action, had been the right approach all along.

Indeed, his fascination with Ahab's character threatened to eclipse any rational aspects of his revising hand. As he continued to write and read in isolation during the summer of 1954 he confided, in a letter to reviewer and critic Clifton Fadiman, his growing conviction that *Moby Dick* "is a far wickeder book than first imagined."[3] He had by now grown suspicious of Melville's Father Mapple sermon and its conventional Christian insights: "But the small unblinking eye of us that sees a Truth beyond our religious rituals, puts in with Ahab when he cries out that he will accept neither blind obedience nor any philosophical obfuscation."

He had also developed a deep psychological kinship with Ahab, and in one sense (the sense of a family man who loved his wife and children) he found that a bit troubling; nevertheless, his admiration for Ahab became an important milestone in his maturing notion of tragedy, and his summer reading came into full focus as he wrote to Fadiman: "If *Moby Dick* were but an object lesson to be tied, line by line, to Christian doctrine, it would not be so great a book, do you agree? It is in its very blasphemous and outrageous qualities, personified in Ahab, that the book becomes a purer and nobler substance."

Bradbury was finally beginning to come to terms with his screenplay, if not yet with his director, and he soon offered Berenson a first self-assessment: "I feel now that my first intuitive and selfish act, last year, in approaching the book blind and fumbling, was, for all its errors, correct. After all, when the chips were placed, the thing that mattered most was what *Moby Dick* meant to me. It all comes back to that, finally. And if I was wrong and a fool, then I would have to take the responsibility. But one thing is certain, it is better to be wrong your own way than someone else's way."

There were, however, more treacherous waters yet to navigate. In the spring of 1955, Warner Brothers and the Writer's Guild of America (West) notified him that the screenplay credit would carry Huston's name as coauthor. Bradbury filed an appeal, and since Huston also received credit as director, the Writer's Guild was required by policy to initiate an arbitration.[4] The Guild's Credit Arbitration Committee determined that Huston's role was that of a mentor and teacher throughout the screenwriting process, and on June 1st found in favor of Bradbury's claim to sole credit.[5] But Huston returned to America briefly later that year and had the case reopened. On November 16, 1955, Bradbury submitted a more detailed account of the way he successfully restructured the events of the novel as he wrote the screenplay. Nevertheless, the original ruling in Bradbury's favor was reversed in January 1956, on the grounds that Huston had offered daily input and had rewritten scenes during production.[6]

John Godley, who worked on the shooting script with Huston during July and August 1954, privately sided with Bradbury. As Godley himself noted in his letters to his friend, much of the work he did with Huston simply restored Bradbury's text or alternate readings, and anything else they added was usually derived directly from Melville's underlying text. For his part, Bradbury never denied Huston's influence on the original screenplay drafts. He offered an early description of their working dynamic in an April 28, 1954, letter to Bill Nolan from Rome, just two weeks after finishing the revised screenplay in London:

> John did little actual writing on it, but much in the way of straightening out my thinking and making me rework page after page, over and over again. Sometimes Huston wrote three or four pages to give me an idea of what he wanted; and then I took over to do a final draft. It is "essence of Melville" which means Melville boiled down, I hope, to his essentials. We have had to rearrange some of his scenes and ideas to give us a step-progression for films, in other words a series of quiet scenes, dramatically loud scenes (you might say) and a series of small climaxes building to a grand finale. It is, in a way, a symphony.

These comments are not colored by the conflict that followed, and probably offer an accurate view of the way that Huston, always working from Bradbury's initial draft, would sometimes write out an idea of how a brief scene might play out in revision. Huston's influence was clearly pervasive, but the screenplay itself showed little or no evidence of his composing hand. Six years later, after working with Carol Reed and a number of other directors and producers in Hollywood,

Bradbury reiterated the distinction he saw between authorship and influence in his UCLA interviews:

> Well, the function of the producer is to do what John did, to keep driving me until I'd brought out the quality of the book, and he gave me a lot of advice on construction. Without John there, I'm sure I would never have gone on with all those outlines. I did ten, twenty, thirty outlines, I've forgotten how many I did of the book, until, finally, everything fell into place. But this is not work John did at the typewriter. The function of the producer is to give advice, to buck up one's spirits, to be a teacher, actually. If any man should know this, John should, because he was taught by other people, and he's passing on the knowledge of film making. Most directors have enough sense to realize this and don't go out for credit.[7]

In spite of the unexpected loss of sole credit, Bradbury moved into the ranks of experienced and respected screenwriters with the 1956 release of *Moby Dick*. Huston won the New York Critics Award, and the film made the list of top ten moneymakers. Bradbury's early decision to focus on the dramatic aspects of the story was crucial to this success; as he told Berenson shortly after the premiere, "when I realized that here and there, anyway, we had captured Melville on film, I was so happy and excited that a chemical change came over me. . . . Suddenly my little prides and vanities, my irritations and angers, vanished." Nevertheless, Bradbury's evolving opinion of Huston was not such a simple process; he went on to offer Berenson his first attempt to fit Huston's personal failings into the larger view:

> Huston the man is one thing, I can still know him as a man and know him, unhappily for what he lacks there, but over that picture I must constantly super-impose the image of his creativity. He has electricity in his fingertips and an eye that sees more than the normal eye can ever hope to see. . . . So often, it seems, the artist is cut off from the very benefits he offers mankind, he strews riches on the earth and dies of hungers in so doing. Huston feeds the world and yet cannot feed himself, an unhappy, tormented, and in some ways, Ahab-type of man.[8]

Yet Bradbury never forgot that his ultimate success with Huston had opened many doors in Hollywood. In the late 1980s, while dining at the Bistro Gardens restaurant in Beverly Hills, Bradbury saw Huston dining with Jack Nicholson and Ray Starke, the man who had introduced Huston to Bradbury so many years ago. Bradbury went over to Huston's table and thanked him for what he had

Lewes Public Library
111 Adams Ave.
Lewes, DE 19958
302 6

taught and for the opportunity he had provided.[9] The timing was providential, for John Huston passed away a few weeks later.

: : :

Throughout the summer and fall of 1954, Bradbury had no idea that Huston's distant production work would have enduring consequences for his authorship; he was far more focused on the wondrous thread of correspondence he was slowly weaving with his new friend and mentor Bernard Berenson. He had been unable to share his final morning in Venice with Berenson, but now he had enough of a command of his senses to paint a picture through words. In his letter of June 29th, Bradbury focused on just one famous hall of one venue:

> I had gone walking to the Academy and had found my way, alone, to the room where Tintoretto had opened windows into vast wonderfully lit spaces. From window after window I fell into the voids he had created. I was Christ brought down from the cross, St. Mark being carried into the square, Cain struggling with Abel, and, at last, God rushing through the universe creating his animals. I came forth into sunlight so happy to be alive and so truly grateful for Italy and Venice and Tintoretto and you that it was impossible to decide who to thank first.

This passage was in many ways an annunciation of his rebirth, made all the more intense by his clear realization that the experience would preserve the fire of his creativity even as it sent him off in a new direction with his writing: "How grand it is to be discovering new thresholds every year, when so many people I have known in the past have stopped and frozen on the first step. . . . You gave me the last small nudge which sent me headlong over the rim into wonder and beauty."

He could (and did) discuss the inner workings of his creativity with Maggie and with Don Congdon, but now he had as mentor an Ancient of Days who had spent a lifetime studying the responsibilities of creative genius. The magic returned slowly, however, after a summer where his Muse remained, for the most part, uncharacteristically silent. Finally, on December 12, 1954, Bradbury could tell Berenson of his own regenerated creativity: "Last weekend, in a great burst of enthusiasm, and energy, completely at ease with my techniques and thus unaware of them, I wrote six short stories in a period of 40 hours."

He was still following his time-tested method for bringing up his subconscious inspirations: "All of the stories that leapt from my typewriter were the result of my experimenting with word-associations." But these stories bore little, if any, of the trappings of science fiction. Three of the six clearly sprang from his newly extended horizons as an artist. One—"Mr. Smith and the Tintorettos"—was about Berenson himself, and it was by Bradbury's own admission a wish-fulfillment at the most basic levels of wonderment: "I can at least try to produce an aura of Berenson, conjured up from your books and ideas and your enthusiasms." This proved to be too much of a mood piece, and was never published.

Another of these six new stories was "The Day It Rained Forever," perhaps his best-known tale and metaphor of creative renewal. It remains one of the best stories he wrote after his return from Europe, and his early summary of it for Berenson reveals a high level of development from the very first draft:

> I have written a story about some old men lost in a desert town for many many years, waiting for the one day each year when the rain comes over the town. And when the one day comes, this year, the rain holds off, and the old men are held in the ruinous heat of the sun until an old woman, a traveling musician, comes by in the hot twilight with a great golden harp closeted in the back-seat of her antique car. When she plays her harp, in the sun-blazed lobby of the deserted hotel, the old men quicken. For here, at last, with a touch of the hands on the strings, quickly, softly, is the sound of the rain. The cool sound of the harp moves through the rooms of the hotel and the old men know that the long season of drought is over and that the good years of the gentle rains have begun.

Bradbury felt that this summary was all too brief, but it came out letter-perfect from his typewriter, a nested version of the larger tale presented to his mentor across the continents and oceans that separated them. All of the interactive metaphors of the finely crafted story are present in miniature, a clear sign that Bradbury had regained his form after two of the most stressful years of his career. Bradbury took the time to describe a third story from this same creative burst of energy, a marvelous fantasy about the creative process itself. His summary for Berenson indicates how closely he now identified the eloquent intricacies of the written word with the beauty of visual art:

> I have written one about a man in a small town who discovers that the local maker of tapestries, which are incredible displays of forest coloring, grass-greens, flower whites and blues, touches of water and white pebble and brown stone, like the floor of a woods in spring and summer—that the maker of these tapestries, I say, employs jeweled spiders which he takes from the meadowlands and forests and trains and brings into his shop where the

spiders re-create the natural life they experience in the town. The tapestries these spiders spin and weave are, of course, beyond belief.

The description leads to a typescript in the Albright Collection titled "The Tapestry," a 5-page undated opening episode set in the evening hours of a typically Bradburyan Midwest town, narrated by a young man who secretly observes the spiders at work through the window of the tapestry shop of "J. Solidarian." It was natural for Bradbury to merge the art of man and the art of nature in this way; in fact, the central images of this story are reminiscent of the spider "histories" woven on the far-distant planet described in Bradbury's 1952 story "A Matter of Taste," which itself remained unsold and neglected for more than fifty years.

But in "The Tapestry" the fantasy is sustained without the science fiction superstructure of the earlier story, and represents yet another celebration of the creative renewal that had quickly returned to Bradbury after the sudden career transitions of the early 1950s. Less than two years after penning his highly regarded defense of science fiction in the pages of the *Nation*, and barely a year after transforming his most sustained science fiction novella into *Fahrenheit 451*, Bradbury was close to completing his journey into the broad mainstream of American literature and American culture.

This journey sometimes opened out in unexpected ways, including an essay commissioned by the *New York Times Magazine* on the fiftieth anniversary of the death of Jules Verne. He accepted the commission even though he was still very uncomfortable with the essay form, and decided to structure "Marvels and Miracles: Pass It On!" as a time-traveling interview with Verne himself. In this essay, Bradbury has Verne (who knows as much about the twentieth century as his interviewer knows about Verne's nineteenth) describe the powers that will help Mankind survive the Atomic Age: "Curiosity and our obsession for pattern and meaning, and our wanting to bring order out of chaos."

Here Bradbury's vision wells up from the same fundamental but imperfect power of visualization that Berenson found to be essential to the creation and appreciation of art. In March 1955, Bradbury sent a copy of "Marvels and Miracles" to Berenson, who shared many of Bradbury's assumptions about the powers of the mind even if he could not share Bradbury's hope that Mankind would use these powers to reach other worlds. Berenson's response was penned on Easter Sunday 1955: "It is full of ideas that I rejoice to share with you, altho' I am not so sure about MAN'S future. He has never lost his MONKEY curiosity & will experiment, no matter what the consequence. Even if self-destruction & earth's destruction. If MAN has a distant future it will be on this puny Earth, & in turning himself into a god, that is to say a complete work of art . . ." (ellipses Berenson's).

Berenson clearly had doubts about Mankind's staying power, but he had no doubts about his young friend. Bradbury was immensely grateful for the double blessing of Berenson's friendship and encouragement. Now more than ever he had the confidence to navigate the treacherous waters between popular and serious literature. Meanwhile, he and Maggie continued to study the art and life of the Renaissance through a series of UCLA lectures, an activity that played to her intellectual strengths and, from time to time, brought her out of the shadow of Bradbury's own career.[10] And they looked for any opportunity that might take them back to Italy and to Berenson, while he still lived.

9 Invitations to the Dance

The letters he wrote to Berenson during the last six months of 1954 emerged during the few retrospective moments he had away from pressing new creative activities. But these were neither new stories, nor the older stories gathered for his long-deferred Illinois novel; in fact, the stories that reached print during 1954 had all been written prior to his departure for Europe, and most of the weird tales in his forthcoming Ballantine story collection, *The October Country*, were refashioned from stories he had previously published in his 1947 *Dark Carnival* collection. Clearly, much of his creative energy was now moving away from the short story form.

The temptation had been there for months. Barely five weeks after his return from Europe, Bradbury had received (by his count) four Hollywood offers to film *Fahrenheit 451*. Ben Benjamin, his principal representative at the Famous Artists agency, had negotiated his first film deals during 1952 and had kept Bradbury properties in active negotiation throughout his long absence. Benjamin and Congdon were still working out control of Bradbury's television negotiations, but the major film studios were already responding to word that Bradbury had produced a viable screenplay for the demanding John Huston. With the exception of *Forbidden Planet*, which MGM asked him to script from the Irving Block and Allen Adler screen story "Fatal Planet," the offers he refused were all mainstream productions.[1]

By midsummer 1954, Famous Artists had generated interest in Bradbury from William Wyler (*The Friendly Persuasion*), Britain's Alexander Korda, and Henri-Georges Clouzot, who approached Bradbury directly to write his second film, *Diabolique*. A tentative offer to adapt Nelson Algren's *The Man with the Golden Arm* for Otto Preminger came from Preminger's agent-brother Ingo. David O. Selznick tried to engage Bradbury for *War and Peace*, one of the few film ventures that could have rivaled the complexities of adapting *Moby Dick* (Selznick's funding failed to materialize, and this project went to Paramount). Twentieth Century–Fox offered him *Good Morning, Miss Dove*, starring Selznick's wife, Academy Award–winner Jennifer Jones. But Bradbury was still working out the psychological consequences of the Huston experience; these emotions, and the additional pressures of the seemingly stillborn Illinois novel, persuaded him to defer all such offers for the next year.

The contents for *The October Country* were set by October 1954, but in early December Bradbury was unexpectedly drawn into an adaptation offer that he simply could not resist. It involved "The Black Ferris," a story that he had held out of the original 1947 *Dark Carnival* because he saw greater possibilities for it. This tale of a mysterious carnival that enslaved rather than entertained had grown into a concept for a novel-in-pictures by 1952, but it had not gone beyond the preliminary concept art prepared in close consultation with California artist and illustrator Joe Mugnaini. His work on *Fahrenheit 451* and the *Moby Dick* screenplay soon intervened, but when he returned from Europe he found that Sam Goldwyn Jr. had picked up the television rights to "The Black Ferris" and produced a short show with a Mel Dinelli script that aired locally in Los Angeles on *Starlight Summer Theater*. In November, Goldwyn showed the production to Bradbury and encouraged him to work up a feature-length script for television or cinematic release.

Bradbury spent much of December 1954 generating a 50-page treatment for such a film, but he was drawn back to other projects before anything more final could develop with Goldwyn. There was, in his mind, an urgent need to revise, and in some cases, rewrite the stories he had pulled forward from *Dark Carnival* for *The October Country*. And there was a new impulse rising from his recent European experiences; in late January 1955 Bradbury confessed to Doubleday's Walt Bradbury that "all of the months of walking the Dublin rains is now beginning to simmer up in me." Over the next two years a number of Irish stories would emerge as a new experiment in storytelling and dialogue; eventually one of these Irish tales, "The Anthem Sprinters," became the prototype for a number of the one-act plays he would adapt from his own stories.

But much still depended on the Illinois novel, and during the winter of 1954–55 Bradbury eased his conscience by using every spare hour to work through a somewhat haphazard regimen of background reading. It was yet another way around facing up to the fact that this work, so long in the making, was far too densely packed with incident and digressive reverie to stand as outlined. Many of the individual stories were drafted, and a number had reached print as stand-alone tales of children, young adults, and the elderly residents of a small town in Illinois during the 1920s.

On January 27th, he sent a long letter to Walt Bradbury that provided a catalog of these readings, which included works ranging from André Maurois' *The Art of Living* to Mark Twain's *Huckleberry Finn*; volumes of poetry by Robert Frost, Robert Hillyer, Robert P. Tristram Coffin, and Walter de la Mare; *An Almanac for Moderns*, by Donald Culross Peattie; books on clocks and children's toys; books on the sense of smell, the human face, and country children; *The Boys of Bobb's Hill* series, by Charles Pierce Burton; and many volumes of poetry for and about children.

Bradbury assured his editor that he worked at his typewriter from three to eight hours a day, adding "What I *do* at the typewriter of course, is as predictable as the Irish mind." But not everything in the letter was meant to excuse; there was a defendable purpose to the wide range of outside readings that Walt Bradbury could certainly appreciate—a search for just the right symbols to enrich the sense of time and memory that had inspired all of the Illinois tales: "Cellars, closets, attics, pantries, anything I can lay hands on that help me to handle the thoughts and situations and pin them down so they can be turned over in the hand and in the mind. These are things I look for in my own past, and I find them turning up all the time when reading such things as books of children's verses." He felt that new symbols, like new metaphors, would help him say more by saying less.

Bradbury agreed to Walt Bradbury's request for one chapter a week from the Illinois novel, as long as Doubleday could wait until he sold enough stories to cover the spring income tax deadline. Walt Bradbury would have to wait a lot longer, however, for Bradbury's focus was once again diverted from the Illinois novel as his various agents continued to cultivate attractive film offers. During March 1955, the A. D. Peters Agency in London—representing all of the Matson Agency's authors in Great Britain, including Congdon's—generated producer Peter Rathvon's interest in Bradbury as a possible screenwriter for Orwell's *1984*. Bradbury declined to pursue this possibility, but he took note of the way that the *Studio One* CBS television production of *1984* (along with the BBC's more recent one) had quickly led to a feature film deal.[2]

Back in Los Angeles, Ben Benjamin reported William Wyler's continuing interest in Bradbury for *The Friendly Persuasion*. Bradbury's love of Jessamyn West's midwestern fiction finally broke down his resistance to further screenwriting, but Wyler could not agree to Bradbury's request to wait until the fall of 1955. He confided his disappointment to Congdon: "I can hardly imagine a screenplay that would be more heartwarming for me to do. I have always felt that this book would be around on the American scene long after many Hemingway books were lost in the past. A drastic observation, perhaps, but it's a natural feeling I have for West's ability, especially in that one volume."[3]

But a third project soon became irresistible, and it emerged directly from his ever-broadening Hollywood connections. Bradbury had known MGM star Gene Kelly for several years and had followed Kelly's efforts to release *Invitation to the Dance*, a 1952 experimental four-part anthology musical without dialogue. Kelly finally won a screening from MGM for a shortened three-part feature version in the spring of 1955 and invited the Bradburys. This encounter proved pivotal, for the opening segment's circus setting, presented in combined dance and mime, reminded him of the recent history of his own *Dark Carnival* concept. Bradbury's wordless novel-in-pictures of 1952–53 had already evolved into the 50-page screen treatment he had prepared for Sam Goldwyn Jr. just a few weeks earlier.

In its original short story form, a strange carnival raises the curiosity of two small-town boys who sneak in after hours and find one of the owners riding the Black Ferris in reverse to transform himself into a small child. The evil child-in-man preys on the town until the boys catch him in the transformation and jam the Ferris machinery forward in time until the owner dies of old age. Dinelli's teleplay had changed the Ferris into a carousel, just as Bradbury had done several years earlier for his textless novel-in-pictures concept of the tale.

Bradbury now extended the story from one night's terror into a week of revelations as the boys, encouraged by the town library's custodian, discover how the carnival returns like a plague every few generations to enthrall the weak and the solitary, enslaving their souls within the ever-expanding tattoos of the co-owner. Evil is finally defeated, but only just. Kelly was immediately won over, and promised to seek funding in Europe during the summer of 1955. In early August, as he exchanged telegrams with Kelly and simultaneously courted studio interest in Hollywood, Bradbury described the thematic essence of his *Dark Carnival* in a letter to Bernard Berenson, indicating that it was still partially in a prose narrative form:

> I hope to make another motion picture of a small book I recently finished in manuscript form about a Gothic carnival that arrives one October midnight in a small Illinois town; the carnival having traveled all about the earth, with its alchemists and sorcerers, for hundreds of years, posing the problem of good and evil, and tilting the scales in its own favor—that is, of course, toward evil. I was in a fever, doing the story, for many days, earlier this year, not unlike some I have run with a fine head and chest cold, but without any of the discomforts. After a number of days of absolutely glowing in the dark, and feeling somewhat drunk, the carnival let down its black velvet tents and stole away, leaving me exhausted but happy, at my typewriter . . . [4] [ellipses Bradbury's]

The extended metaphor presented yet another variation on the quotidian fever that seized him whenever his Muse was stimulated. Unfortunately, Kelly was unable to find backing for *Dark Carnival*, and the eventual box office failure of *Invitation to the Dance* discouraged any further attempts with MGM. For the rest of 1955, he continued to develop and market his *Dark Carnival* screenplay through the Famous Artists agency but found little interest. Hollywood wanted him to work on proven Bradbury properties or to adapt the work of other writers, as he had done so successfully for John Huston.

Bradbury's creative challenges with the Illinois novel, already complicated by his *Dark Carnival* screenplay, were further complicated by the constant but all too often ephemeral television offers for various other works. Bradbury (working through Famous Artists) had extended his screen outline of "The Fox and the Forest," one of the most popular Bradbury stories gathered into *The Illustrated Man*. There was now interest from CBS for a possible hour-long episode of this story for *Climax*; this possibility, along with an option for "The Screaming Woman," was never finalized ("The Screaming Woman" foundered over a producer's obsession with how long a woman could survive in a buried coffin). There was also interest from Ford Theatre for "The Whole Town's Sleeping," one of the darkest stories in the Illinois novel materials. Congdon advised against any television film options on published stories, which, unlike the short-term live broadcast options, could tie up a property for seven years. He especially wanted to hold back any of the projected chapters for the Illinois novel from such entanglements, which would jeopardize the big screen film possibilities of the novel for a year after publication.

Congdon was increasingly frustrated that Bradbury allowed Ben Benjamin at Famous Artists to negotiate live or film television options for published stories. Bradbury, who felt a great deal of guilt in turning down the steady stream of motion picture offers that Famous Artists developed for him, wanted his Hollywood agency to maintain some share of the television work in compensation. During the spring of 1955, Congdon agreed that Benjamin could continue to negotiate television options on original (unpublished) stories, as well as the Bradbury Showcase television series concept that still attracted occasional attention in Hollywood. CBS had almost finalized a Showcase deal a year earlier, but settled for occasional stand-alone shows instead, eventually producing Bradbury's "Great Wide World" for a July 1955 episode of *Windows*. It seemed that these occasional options, along with new CBS and NBC radio productions of their various 1950–51 era adaptations, would represent the extent of his media presence for 1955.

CBS had also made an earlier try for a television adaptation of *Fahrenheit 451*, and Congdon was pleased to see renewed interest from NBC's *Television Playhouse*. Series writer Bob Aurthur had been angling for Bradbury story properties for some time, and in late April 1955 he led new NBC negotiations for a Bradbury script of *Fahrenheit 451*. Congdon had seen a similar hour-long production of *1984* for *Studio One* generate great public interest earlier in the year; now that *1984* was entering motion picture production in Britain, Congdon and Bradbury both felt that a high-quality summer production of *Fahrenheit 451* could result in a film contract by the fall.

The initial NBC offer came to Congdon on May 6. Bradbury would receive $1,250 in return for a live television option terminating on October 1, 1955. He would not write the adaptation, but would retain ownership of it. NBC was planning for a September broadcast and tentatively designated *Fahrenheit 451* as the season premiere for *Television Playhouse*. Aurthur told Congdon that network plans also called for significant publicity. Bradbury was ecstatic, but in mid-May the deal bogged down as designers and other technical staff debated over the various production challenges that the novel presented. The deal unraveled quickly from that point; this turn of events was, at first, incredibly disappointing for Bradbury, but he would soon find that when one door closes in show business, another may open. Freelance producer Paul Gregory, who had been eyeing several Bradbury projects for some time, immediately began negotiations for a stage version of *Fahrenheit*.

CBS and NBC had now failed twice to secure a major live television adaptation of Bradbury's most controversial work—first, producer John Haggott's 1952 attempt to secure the earlier "Fireman" version, and now, writer Bob Aurthur's attempt to option the *Fahrenheit 451* version. Congdon and Bradbury would soon successfully negotiate the stage option with Paul Gregory, and Ben Benjamin had already received several tentative (but unsatisfactory) film offers for the novel. All three men knew that better film offers were just a matter of time. What none of them knew, however, was that CBS would eventually find another way to present the substance of *Fahrenheit 451* without Ray Bradbury. This crisis was still several years off in the future, but the resulting courtroom drama would involve the highest courts in the land.

10

Pictures within Pictures:
The October Country

Ballantine Books released the hardbound edition of *The October Country* right on schedule in October 1955, but the projected simultaneous release of the mass-market paperback issue was delayed until March 1956. In spite of this delay, the mass-market paperback would achieve legendary longevity, ensuring that Bradbury's final refashioning of his earliest weird tale success would never go out of print. The initial release of the hardbound edition, however, printed in relatively small numbers for reviewers and traditional booksellers, included only a brief dust jacket note indicating that most of the contents were revised from his earliest published stories, leading some key reviewers to misunderstand the entire concept of the new collection.

On one level, his *October Country* interlude represented yet another way to defer Doubleday's *Summer Morning, Summer Night* Illinois novel until he could find a way through his writer's block with novel-length concepts. Throughout the winter of 1954–55, Bradbury made a final selection of fifteen stories from the twenty-seven tales of *Dark Carnival*, and brought a revising hand to all of them. These included "The Man Upstairs," relating a young boy's discovery that a vampirelike alien is living in his grandmother's boarding house, and "Homecoming," a tale of a normal boy raised by a family of fantastic vampires and shape-changers.

He now also rewrote "The Emissary" (a dog who brings his bedridden young master all the sensations of the outside world) and "Jack-in-the-Box" (a housebound boy who doesn't even suspect that there is an outside world). Among the eleven *Dark Carnival* tales he eliminated were the most gruesome ("The Maiden," "The Smiling People," "Interim," "The Handler"). These and other omissions continued the process (begun with the *Dark Carnival* collection itself) of elevating and showcasing the best of his early weird tales by eliminating the vulgar lowlife aspects of carnival.

In the end, *The October Country* transcended the earlier collection completely. Bradbury added four uncollected stories that had appeared during 1954 in newer digest-size genre pulps ("The Dwarf" and "The Watchful Poker Chip") and in established major-market slicks ("Shopping for Death" and "The Wonderful Death of Dudley Stone"). These had all been written before Bradbury's September 1953 departure for Europe, but all were conceived after Bradbury had moved away from dark horror in the late 1940s. These were fantasies or light horror tales that, for the most part, reflected newer interests while retaining the characteristic oddness and cultural inversions that had established him as a unique observer of life.

"The Watchful Poker Chip" extended his emerging views on art into an engaging parody of the avant-garde. In "Shopping for Death" (re-titled "Touched with Fire") Bradbury's "what if" premise (What if science can identify the victim before the crime?) leads readers to a victim who cannot be stopped from provoking her own murder. He used the final two new stories to add a commentary on authorship—by opening the refashioned collection with "The Dwarf" and closing it with "The Wonderful Death of Dudley Stone," Bradbury was signaling that, on one level, he would no longer be bound by critical opinion.

But if Dudley Stone's successful departure from the anxieties of authorship provided a closing sense of achievement, critical responses to The October Country quickly reawakened Bradbury's own anxieties as a writer. A number of reviews were positive, and to some degree the small-press origins of the Dark Carnival stories made that possible. The 1947 Arkham House edition had been limited to 3,000 copies, and by the early 1950s sales had diminished to the point that Bradbury was able to purchase the remaining stock himself. Consequently many of these tales had not been seen in years, and the new collection reawakened an appreciation in some critics for a metaphor-rich style that had always seemed to transcend genre boundaries anyway. Ballantine's hardbound vanguard for the projected six-figure paperback issue promised to bring a broader readership to these nineteen tales, key exemplars of Bradbury's creative origins.

The somewhat obscure publishing history of these stories was also an invitation to confusion, and this history was further confounded by the lack of a prominent prefatory note to indicate that most of these titles were the product of an early stage of his professional career, representing a kind of writing that he had largely left behind. The following spring Bradbury added a preface to the paperback issue, but this was far too late for the October 1955 release of the hardbound edition;[1] as a result, Bradbury's intent in revising and rewriting the best of these older stories, and carefully nesting them within four newer stories that reflected more refined themes, was lost on the reviewers who assumed that the entire collection represented new work. Carlos Baker's review in the New York Times, framed by that assumption, proved to be the most damaging: "For some time now, there has been a feeling among critics that this author was really on the verge of something significant. The verge he skirts in these stories, one regrets to report, is the crumbling cliff-edge of the banal."[2]

Baker's story-by-story dismissal of the collection as emotionally overcharged ended with an ominous judgment: "This is too bad for a man of such talent, for the only direction this kind of writing can follow is down." Tony Boucher, a well-known critic and reviewer in his own right, sent the *Times* an editorial rebuttal for publication.[3] Boucher's corrective never reached print, but an anonymous *Time* magazine review was even more problematic—it closed by invoking a new label that was perhaps more damaging than Baker's: "This book shows skill and ingenuity in the business of saying 'boo' to grownups, but sometimes the 'boo' does not ring true. Bradbury would do very well if he came out from under that fright wig."[4]

Worse still, the *Time* magazine review reversed everything that Bradbury had been trying to achieve in the years since most of these stories had been written, relegating Bradbury once again to the genre tradition of Mary Shelley, Bram Stoker, and John Collier, writers who "appeal to the middle or relatively uncorrugated brow, rather than the highbrow, who finds more than enough to bite his nails over in the Age of Anxiety without faking up a little more." Two years earlier, a very favorable *Time* review of *The Golden Apples of the Sun* had earned him at least a probationary status among highbrows as the "Poet of the Pulps"; now, however, the "fright wig" crowned him with the consequences of his growing tendency to live in the past.

For middlebrow readers, however, Bradbury's backward glance was not taken as a negative development. *The October Country* brought renewed interest from television executives for the better stories such as "The Next in Line," and within a year two of these stories would enter production for the first season of *Alfred Hitchcock Presents*. The new collection also consolidated his status as an innovative stylist who brought the horror tale out of its traditional settings and into the suburbs and cities of the contemporary world. Future horror writers (including Stephen King, Peter Straub, and Clive Barker) admired his nerve in bringing these marginalized forms into the mainstream at a time when the Cold War's "climate of fear" still controlled what was acceptable reading in the broader American culture.

In fact, *The October Country* had evolved across a three-year span that witnessed the height of book burning, censorship, and the anticomic crusade. Local book and comic burnings by concerned parents, clergy, and even military veterans (tacitly and even openly supported by school board officials) frequently made the news, and both of Bradbury's paperback publishers (Bantam and Ballantine) were assailed with threats of censorship. Against this backdrop, six of the *Dark Carnival* stories (including three that carried forward into *The October Country*) had been adapted to graphic form by the EC Comics syndicate, and this represented a greater vulnerability to authority than *Fahrenheit 451* had ever faced.

Furthermore, the very original and eye-catching American Gothic illustrations prepared for *The October Country* by Bradbury's good friend Joseph Mugnaini also hinted at the blurred line between narrative and graphic storytelling in fiction of this kind. His growing association with EC's illustrators represented a far greater danger, however; Bradbury had found that early "lifts" of his plots by EC were carefully adapted from his texts and well-illustrated by some of the best rising artists in the industry, and from 1953 through 1954 he had given his blessing to a total of sixteen story adaptations for various EC comic titles. But he soon came under pressure for this indulgence, especially from his Hollywood connections; by 1954, he asked EC publisher William M. Gaines to take his name off the covers of future issues containing his stories, and to minimize the author's biographical note as well.

That same year saw the publication of Fredric Wertham's Seduction of the Innocent, a controversial indictment of the comics industry that quickly led to United States Senate hearings, industrywide adoption of a strict publishing code, and, indirectly, the end of the EC Comics line. Bradbury was concerned about this new threat, for earlier Wertham works were deeply woven into his fifteen years of background reading on psychotic types and the psychology of violence. Bradbury's reading of criminology and personality studies dated to the early 1940s, but his 1949 discovery of two Wertham titles had signaled a new plateau in his reading focus. These books brought home to him the complex relationship between literature and the fundamental patterns of behavior that it often reflects.

It's not clear which came first, but sometime in 1949 Bradbury purchased two significant Wertham titles that spanned the decade. Show of Violence had just come out that year, and it provided a view of the world of clinical psychiatry and courtroom drama that Wertham had worked in since coming to New York from Germany in the 1920s. It revealed a wide spectrum of violent behavior through case studies drawn from his years as senior psychiatrist for New York City's Department of Hospitals—a job that often took him to the criminal wards of various hospitals, competency hearings, and high-profile criminal trials.

But his purchase that same year of Wertham's disturbing 1941 case study, Dark Legend, would have had far more impact on his imagination. This book illustrated how difficult it is to find the causes behind violent crimes committed by those who live in "the shadow of madness." In exploring the deeply hidden motives of a likeable young man who suddenly and brutally murders his mother, Wertham focused on fundamental questions at the center of some of Bradbury's best horror stories: "When and how are thoughts translated into action? When does a desire, an impulse, leave the world of fantasy and enter the world of reality?"

In an even broader sense, Dark Legend and Show of Violence joined a long list of background readings that had extended Bradbury's ability to pose rich variations on the numberless mechanisms of death. "Touched by Fire," prompted on one level by another criminologist's assertion that more murders are committed at ninety-two degrees Fahrenheit than at any other temperature, has its deeper roots in Wertham's assertion that analysis cannot predict the transformation of thought into action. Despite his distancing preface in subsequent paperback editions of *The October Country*, Bradbury would never fully abandon his off-trail genius for the weird tale form; "Touched by Fire" was only one of a number of edgy murder tales written during the early 1950s that Bradbury would eventually revise and publish, including "At Midnight, in the Month of June," "Some Live Like Lazarus," "Mr. Pale," "A Touch of Petulance," "Pilgrimage," and "Memento Mori."

In this way, Bradbury's reading history added a very private dimension to the public debates over Wertham's *Seduction of the Innocent*. Undoubtedly, Bradbury's association with EC Comics added indirectly to his concern as well. He knew that the art was well-executed, and Al Feldstein's narratives were accurate condensations of his own story texts; but the overt violence and sexual overtones found across the comics industry had now been analyzed by an acknowledged expert in human behavior, and his findings seemed to pinpoint specific causes for juvenile delinquency and other social maladies at a time when any kind of deviation from the norm was viewed with suspicion or even open hostility. The Senate Judiciary Committee wasted no time in appointing a Subcommittee on Juvenile Delinquency.

The closely watched subcommittee sessions (April 21, 22, and June 4, 1954) were highlighted by the back-to-back testimony of Dr. Wertham and EC's William M. Gaines. Certain points of Gaines's straightforward but vulnerable testimony ended up in newspaper headlines, but in reality the various EC publications were fairly tame when compared to the crime comics of other publishers. Wertham's approach was heavy-handed and did not distinguish between the violent and often sadistic overtones of the crime and horror comics and the somewhat milder superhero and weird fiction comics. His approach was aggressively polemic, matching the more broad-based public demonstrations and schoolyard burnings of the day. Ironically, some of the burning comics contained stories that had originated with the author of *Fahrenheit 451*. Bradbury was probably saved from direct scrutiny by Gaines's quick decision to terminate his various horror, weird tale, and science fiction comic lines and instead elevate his *Mad* comic to a magazine format that soon became an offbeat cultural mainstay.

The October Country was published in the fall of 1955, a year after all of these events culminated in an industrywide Comics Code and the disappearance (along with the more literate EC) of the hard-core crime and gangster publications. Bradbury's story collection was not drawn directly into this fray, but one controversial illustration in *Seduction of the Innocent* implicitly made a chilling connection between graphic art and literature. Wertham's close-up illustration from a rather tame action comic focuses attention on a man's shoulder muscles, contending that the lines and shading can also be seen as a woman's naked thighs. This interpretation is not credible and can be easily dismissed as playing into the hysteria of the times, but his caption had far-reaching implications: "In ordinary comic books, there are pictures within pictures for children who know how to look."

This simple statement reached beyond Wertham's seven-year campaign against the comics culture, which began in an influential 1947 *Saturday Review* article. Wertham's implication went all the way back to *Dark Legend* and a more rational insight that Bradbury had read years earlier: "[L]iterature does not exist in a vacuum. . . . Literature is a link between science and society." Even the best of Bradbury's older weird fiction could be twisted to form narrative "pictures within pictures," and he was clearly taking a great chance bringing this work back into the public eye at such a time. Echoes of the comic book crusade represented the great unspoken bias against the stories of *The October Country*, and the negative reviews reflected this cultural overtone at least as much as they reflected disappointment with what was misunderstood as regression in a well-respected author.

An entire aesthetic was under attack, and Bradbury was only a graphic pen away from condemnation. At the time he could not know that *The October Country* (as well as the Mugnaini illustrations and cover art) would become perennial favorites for generations of readers. All he knew was that 1955, his first full year back in America from his European enlightenment, had become increasingly challenging—his *October Country* worries and the constant lure of the television and film studios were aggravating the ever-present writing block that now threatened to force the Illinois novel into a devastating dead end.

11 Laughton and Hitchcock

The dramatic qualities of Bradbury's published work had attracted every major performance dream of his youth except the New York stage. But throughout the fall of 1955, he was further distracted from the Illinois novel by just such an opportunity. The failure of the NBC offer for a *Fahrenheit 451* television production opened the door for Paul Gregory and his business partner, the legendary British stage and screen actor Charles Laughton. Gregory and Laughton envisioned a New York production, and in spite of the time commitment Bradbury agreed to adapt *Fahrenheit* himself.

Gregory's promotional abilities and his power to persuade had forged a five-year partnership with Laughton that showcased the actor's natural talents in dramatic reading; notable successes had followed with critically acclaimed ensemble reading tours of Shaw's *Don Juan in Hell* and Steven Vincent Benet's book-length poem, *John Brown's Body*. Gregory had also introduced Laughton to stage and film direction and was always on the lookout for potential new properties that he could produce around Laughton's acting or directorial skills.

The link to Gregory came through Don Congdon and went back to the fall of 1953 while Bradbury was still in Ireland. Congdon also represented the novelist Davis Grubb and was actively marketing Grubb's *The Night of the Hunter* for film adaptation. In November 1953, Congdon sent a copy to Bradbury, who found this dark novel fascinating; Grubb's itinerant serial killer, preying on women in the guise of a lay preacher, was not unlike the proprietors of his own evolving *Dark Carnival* screenplay. Congdon asked Bradbury to recommend *The Night of the Hunter* to John Huston, but by mid-December Congdon was close to a deal with either Paramount or Paul Gregory and released Bradbury from the obligation. In the spring of 1954 Gregory formally acquired the rights and arranged for Laughton to direct. *The Night of the Hunter*, a unique film in terms of texture and its progression of dreamlike scenes, occupied them through the rest of 1954, but before the year was out Congdon had interested Gregory in a range of Bradbury properties. *Fahrenheit 451* was still in play with NBC, so Congdon pitched an alternative concept for a loosely connected film anthology of Bradbury stories.

This concept was near and dear to Bradbury, who had wanted to film an anthology of his weird tales ever since seeing the British Ealing Studios production of *Dead of Night* in 1945. But Congdon wanted to steer Gregory toward Bradbury's science fiction and fantasy work from the newer collections, suggesting a mix of stories connected by the now famous *Illustrated Man* Prologue-Epilogue frame. Congdon's undated outline, apparently prepared in close consultation with Bradbury, recommended that Laughton take on the role of the Illustrated Man to frame up a film sequence that would include the stories "Marionettes, Inc.," "A Sound of Thunder," "The Playground," "The Veldt," "The Fog Horn," and the "Illustrated Man" story itself (unrelated to the framing device).

But by the spring of 1955, Gregory and Laughton found themselves disappointed with the initial reviews of *The Night of the Hunter*, and their latest film venture—an adaptation of Norman Mailer's *The Naked and the Dead*—was beginning to prove problematic. They decided to defer another film deal and began to discuss stage adaptations with Congdon instead. Gregory had read a great deal of Bradbury's work, and was initially enthusiastic about securing a stage adaptation by Bradbury for "Way in the Middle of the Air," the *Martian Chronicles* tale of African Americans that was, given the previous year's U.S. Supreme Court decision in Brown vs. Topeka Board of Education, very timely: "As you know I have always been wild about Bradbury and I am delighted that you have sent me these things." But by May, Gregory had decided to negotiate for a stage version of *Fahrenheit 451* instead, and with television negotiations over this much-sought-after prize at an impasse, Congdon encouraged Bradbury to meet directly with Gregory to consider adapting the work himself.

Bradbury was in the perfect state of mind to strike a deal. By a stroke of good fortune, Laughton's Broadway directorial success with *The Caine Mutiny Court Martial* had returned to Los Angeles, and in early May 1955, Bradbury was able to see how Herman Wouk (working under Laughton's guidance) had managed to adapt the dramatic core of his best-selling novel to the stage. Eventually, Bradbury would discover just how stressful this process had been for Laughton, who had to cut Wouk's script twice during the pre-Broadway run before a stageable version of the court martial fully emerged. At the time, however, all Bradbury knew was that the critical success of Wouk and Laughton's collaboration had given him the confidence he needed to respond to Gregory's offer. He later told Walt Bradbury just how quickly the project evolved the night he saw the play: "I stayed up until four in the morning writing an outline and the openings of all the scenes for F.451. I then sat down and did a series of watercolor sketches of all the sets. Within a few weeks, I presented all the material to Paul Gregory and now, quite unbelievably, the project is in the works."[1]

By the end of August 1955, Bradbury had completed a draft of the first act, and Gregory felt confident enough to announce the project as both a stage and film deal. In early September, the *New York Times* revealed Gregory's intention to make *Fahrenheit 451* his next joint-venture film project with Laughton, to be preceded by a stage version tentatively scheduled to open in New York in late February 1956. Gregory had produced Laughton's *Caine Mutiny* run, and he quickly began negotiations with two veterans of that cast, Hollywood stars Lloyd Nolan and John Hodiak, for the principal roles of Fire Chief Beatty and Montag. But Laughton's work on *The Naked and the Dead* was not progressing well, and there were other potential properties in the wings; much depended on how fast Bradbury could complete and revise a playable script.

Bradbury soon found himself caught between the need to compress his novel for the stage and an ever-increasing impulse to develop his central characters. In 1953 he had discovered, as he completed the final proof revisions of the novel, that he was only just beginning to discover the inner realities of Montag's personality. Now, during the late summer of 1955, he described the new fire that drove his evolving stage adaptation to his Doubleday editor and friend, Walt Bradbury: "It is an exciting project and in writing it I have seen my characters grow six feet taller than ever before. . . . It is good to have this chance to make changes in the book, by indirection; I know so much more about the characters and their processes now." This newfound ability to interrogate his characters was clearly a sign of maturity, but it was also the result of his intense and repeated soundings of Melville's complex characters during his months with John Huston.

In a larger sense, though, Bradbury also felt that he was approaching another plateau in his development as a writer. In late August, he worked through this sensation in his letter to Walt Bradbury:

> I have always had to judge the various times and timings of material in my mind—for instance I've waited for 15 years to do a play. The last play I did was in the spring of 1940 and it was so miserable that I took a vow never to write another play until I was past thirty and had gathered a little sense to myself. During the last three years I have felt the gatherings of an ability to do a play. There's no way, really, to describe it, but in its simplest form it is just the disappearance of a sense of inferiority, replaced by a sense of adventure and a slight fever.

Here was the potential for another major surge in self-confidence, one that might have been as significant as the confidence that emerged from the encouraging words of Aldous Huxley, Christopher Isherwood, and Gerald Heard a few years earlier. It all depended on how well he could bring off the first major adaptation of his own work; as the summer of 1955 progressed into fall, he found that Gregory's successive critiques would lead through five drafts by mid-October.

Throughout these months, Laughton himself was locked in a similar struggle with an equally challenging adaptation. During the summer he had taken over sole responsibility for scripting Norman Mailer's *The Naked and the Dead*, and he worked intensely on the screenplay until November. His style and sensibilities were, in crucial ways, similar to Bradbury's; in the end he had fashioned a lyric and compassionate screenplay from this brutal war novel, but it was far too long to be filmable. Bradbury and Laughton worked at their separate solitary tasks among many distractions; for Bradbury, this included the release of *The October Country*, the beginning of his television work for *Alfred Hitchcock Presents*, and constant requests from Don Congdon for new stories.

During this time Gregory had perhaps more time to work with Bradbury than Laughton did, but by December 1955 it became apparent to both men that Bradbury's *Fahrenheit 451* adaptation would have to be rejected in its present form. Like Wouk's initial stages of adaptation for *The Caine Mutiny Court Martial*, *Fahrenheit 451* was still far too long to be staged effectively. They gave him the verdict with compassion, taking the time to get the inexperienced drinker thoroughly drunk on cocktails before breaking the news as gently as possible.

Bradbury's account of this evening is well known, but his telling always stops here. Various draft stages of the play survive, however, and these materials reveal the structural flaws that a more experienced playwright might have been able to avoid. The problem centered on his intention to give Montag and Beatty more depth of characterization. These new passages would have intrigued readers, but would leave a dramatic audience cold. Bradbury expanded the two Montag-Beatty debates into unplayable scenes that show Fire Captain Beatty's full descent into "the intellectual turned destroyer" and Fireman Montag's self-transformation into a "vital man of humane action." But in the process, the characters of Clarisse and Mildred are greatly diminished, and the pace of events is grindingly slow.

Bradbury had indeed achieved depth of character, but he had failed to let these characters build any compelling sense of tragedy. This much Laughton and Gregory no doubt told him, but they would not have gone into the larger factors at play in the decision to reject the play. Gregory had brought Laughton five years of great success, but there was an element of control and dominance that the veteran actor had grown to resent. Laughton suddenly terminated the partnership in early 1956, and the rising tension may have played into the December 1955 decision to terminate the *Fahrenheit 451* stage and film project. Fortunately, this would not bring an end to Bradbury's personal friendship with Laughton, which grew significantly in the months and years to come.

: : :

In May 1955, just as Bradbury began the ill-fated stage project with Paul Gregory, another door unexpectedly opened in Hollywood. His work for *Alfred Hitchcock Presents* would divert him even further from writing new stories, but it also provided an essential restorative to the *Fahrenheit* disappointment that played out that year. Hitchcock had read "And So Died Riabouchinska" in the June–July 1953 issue of *The Saint Detective Magazine*, and began negotiations to acquire the rights for the inaugural 1955–56 season of his new television venture. The high level of interest was apparent to Congdon, who characterized the initial inquiry for Bradbury in a May 10th letter: "[I]t is one that Hitchcock read and liked and they obviously are serious or we wouldn't have got to the price discussion."

Hitchcock may have known some of the ten-year history behind Riabouchinska, which Bradbury had initially submitted, unpublished, to Bill Spier at CBS radio a decade earlier. It was soon adapted to good effect by Mel Dinelli for a summer 1946 episode of *Suspense*, but radio could not fully capture the impact that Bradbury imagined for the ventriloquist's beautiful dummy—one who is far more complicated than she initially seems to be. Bradbury's fascination with the living connection between ventriloquist and dummy dated back to his early childhood, and included Lon Chaney's Mr. Echo in *The Unholy Three* (1925, 1930) and Erich von Stroheim's *The Great Gabbo* (1929). But at the time he wrote the story, the most immediate inspiration would have been Ealing Studios's 1945 British release, *Dead of Night*, a story anthology film that had an effect on his writing for more than a decade. For Bradbury, the most memorable story within the *Dead of Night* cycle was John Baines's "The Ventriloquist's Dummy." It featured Michael Redgrave as an entertainer driven to attempted murder and eventually to insanity by his dummy, which exhibits a controlling consciousness of its own.

Bradbury was enthralled by the Redgrave performance, which was carefully rehearsed and self-coached prior to filming. This remarkable process, recalled by Redgrave in his memoirs, reveals the underlying psychology of the performance: "I was to play a schizophrenic ventriloquist. It was not an easy part. For one thing, the ventriloquist has to remember to keep his mouth open. I managed that all right, but still I wanted an entirely different voice, though my own, for the dummy. I asked a friend, Diana Graves, to help. I would speak the dummy's lines; she would copy me, following as closely as possible my inflections and timing; then I would copy her copying me."[2] Bradbury could not have known the rehearsal strategy behind Redgrave's performance, but he undoubtedly responded to the eeriness of the two intertwined identities. He would strive to perfect his own cross-gendered psychosis in his many drafts for the 1953 published version of "Riabouchinska," whose distinct voice and tone, as well as her haunting silences, provides a rich subtext to the story.

In late May 1955, Hitchcock's production company purchased the rights to "Riabouchinska" for $1,000 on a seven-year nonexclusive lease and an option to purchase exhibition rights for another $1,500 if the Hitchcock series ever went into theater release. Hitchcock's writers included some of the old CBS *Suspense* radio and television veterans, and "Riabouchinska" went to Mel Dinelli once again for the teleplay. The three-year restriction on other media productions was reasonable in Congdon's eyes, and Dinelli's script aired on February 12, 1956, starring Claude Raines and Charles Bronson. But it would not be the first Bradbury episode of *Alfred Hitchcock Presents*; Congdon soon sold "Shopping for Death," a 1954 story that had been reprinted in the February 1955 issue of *The Saint Detective Magazine*, and Bradbury wrote the teleplay himself. "Shopping for Death," which aired on January 29, 1956, benefited from the final touches that Bradbury gave the original short story as he moved it into *The October Country* collection under the better-known title "Touched With Fire." Longtime Hitchcock associate Joan Harrison produced the initial Bradbury episodes, and her talents combined with excellent direction to ensure a new level of quality for genre-based television drama.

For Bradbury, the Hitchcock credits culminated a ten-year effort to bring his best dark fantasies to Hollywood. In early 1947, he had sent tear sheets from four of his off-trail weirds to Val Lewton, whom he idolized for his fine touch with terror films such as *The Cat People*, *The Leopard Man*, and *Isle of the Dead*.[3] Over the next year he sent copies of *Dark Carnival* to a number of Hollywood directors and radio producers, and to British writer-director Ivan Foxwell, in the hope that Foxwell could find a way to link some of the *Dark Carnival* stories into a reprise of Ealing Studios's success with the bridged stories in *Dead of Night*. Now, nearly a decade later, he had two episodes featured in the first season of Hitchcock's highly regarded television series.

The only sticking point in the contract negotiations involved the intricacies of what Congdon referred to as the "adroit morals clause." This public behavior clause was more often applied in acting contracts, where production companies and studios had a far greater investment in personnel. Congdon explained the concept to Bradbury in his letter of June 24, 1955: "As perhaps you know, this is the clause that says you have to be decent, law-abiding, non-Communist, etc. Otherwise, they have the absolute right to withdraw from the contract, or in this case, take your name off the film."[4] The New York representatives of Shamley Productions, Hitchcock's overarching enterprise company, had explicitly written the clause into Bradbury's initial contract for "Riabouchinska"; it did not appear in the subsequent "Shopping for Death" contract, and Congdon's Shamley and MCA contacts indicated that they didn't believe it would be needed at all.

But Shamley would not fully guarantee Bradbury's title credit, and Congdon recommended that Bradbury strike the clause from the contract. They had not been lumbered with the clause in other television deals, and Congdon felt that Shamley would back down if both author and agent presented a united front. Bradbury at first agreed to accept the clause if the political activity restriction were to be stricken from it, but in the end he and Congdon were apparently able to have it removed. It was a wise move; Bradbury's forceful "Letter to the Republican Party" in 1952, and his publication of *Fahrenheit 451* a year later, had revealed his nonconformist spirit, and he did not want his characteristic tendency to speak his mind restricted as he became more involved with Screen Writer's Guild activities. He was no Communist, and hated the totalitarian agendas of both the far Left and the far Right—foreign and domestic. This viewpoint was not always popular, and it would not keep the FBI from opening a file on him before the end of the 1950s.

12

"The First to Catch a Circus in a Lie Is a Boy"

Bradbury's breakthrough with the first season of *Alfred Hitchcock Presents* coincided with his final significant work as an anthologist of fantasy. *The Circus of Dr. Lao and Other Improbable Stories* proved to be another mass-market paperback success for Bantam Books, but behind the scenes the evolution of this project had proven stressful for all concerned. Bradbury's 1952 Bantam anthology, *Timeless Stories for Today and Tomorrow*, had successfully extended fantasy beyond genre boundaries by including work from mainstream writers, and Bantam's Saul David immediately declared his intention to publish a companion anthology under Bradbury's editorship in the near future.[1] During the winter of 1952–53, David urged Bradbury to feature Dr. Lao as the title story. But it would take nearly four years to publish, and the problem centered on the strange and rather mystifying title novel itself.

Bradbury's wariness of Charles Finney's slim 1935 fantasy *The Circus of Dr. Lao* dated back to 1948, when veteran genre writer Robert Bloch persuaded him to read it. At the time Bloch was trying to break down his friend's instinctive dislike of slanting to a market, but as far as Bradbury was concerned, Dr. Lao was just another example of this practice. Years later, Bradbury would observe privately that he found it "to be very sparse, only fitfully imaginative, somewhat vulgar, and not at all the set of fireworks my friends had led me to expect."[2] Before his 1948 reading of Dr. Lao, Bradbury had already developed the basic elements of his own dark carnival from "The Black Ferris" and an even earlier 30-page gathering of prose sketches and chapter openings for a predatory carnival. He had no intention of rereading Finney's novel until he had the actual plot progression of his own expanded tale fully established.

Unexpected delays bought Bradbury time; the copyright trail that ran through an obscure 1945 small-press second edition of Dr. Lao was unclear for a time, and it took even longer to track down Charles G. Finney himself—his low-profile career as a Tucson journalist had gradually come to overshadow his prewar prominence as a writer of dark fantasy. Bantam subsequently deferred the project during Bradbury's unexpected nine-month sojourn abroad in 1953–54, but by September 1954 Saul David was becoming more and more direct in his appeals for an introduction. Up to this point, Bradbury had limited his involvement to planning the mix of stories that would follow the title novel. In this he was aided by William F. Nolan, who was about to launch his own professional career as a writer. Nolan had been his bibliographer and close associate since 1950, and during the selection process he served as a second set of eyes as Bradbury attempted to survey the entire range of genre and mainstream magazines.

Selection of the stories would prove to be the one bright spot in the entire editorial experience. From Bradbury's perspective, this process formed the creative heart of his role as an editor; these authors were his "characters," and his selections reveal a great deal about how his own reading passions intersected with the stories he chose. Where he could, he advanced his claim that fantasy was alive and flourishing in the major market magazines, and the ten stories he was able to squeeze in behind the 92-page *Dr. Lao* included three from the *New Yorker*, two from *Charm*, one from *Harper's*, and two from earlier Knopf hardbound anthologies. Only two stories emerged from the golden age pulp heyday of John Campbell's *Astounding* and its fantasy companion *Unknown*, and in the context of the new anthology these stories complemented the sense of strangeness and wonder that Bradbury was trying to achieve.

The *Astounding* story was "Threshold," by Henry Kuttner, an important writer across several midcentury genre fields whose heavy use of pseudonyms (on his own and with his accomplished wife, C. L. Moore) obscured his importance as a master of plot development. He had been Bradbury's most demanding early mentor, and in some ways he exceeded the impact of Leigh Brackett as an influence on his development; Kuttner had written the final twist in "The Candle," Bradbury's first sale to *Weird Tales* in 1942, and the twist that concludes Kuttner's dark fantasy "Threshold" is reminiscent of that effect. His selection of this tale offered homage to Kuttner as both a professional and personal influence in his life.

Bradbury's decision to close the volume with "The Man Who Vanished," by Robert Coates, represents still another revealing choice. Genre editor and critic Anthony Boucher, a close Bradbury friend, considered Coates to be a master "of the unaccountable and disturbing moment," a subtle form of terror that had fascinated Bradbury since his discovery of Cornell Woolrich's fiction in the early 1940s. Bradbury had selected a chilling Coates story in this tradition for *Timeless Stories*, but this time the Coates selection was more nostalgic than terrifying. The title character gradually realizes that he can control his vanishing episodes, but he also realizes that the affliction represents his deeply repressed desire to return to the past and make different choices in life. His ability to see, smell, and touch deep memories allows him to jump through time for a second chance at love. This tale struck a deep chord with Bradbury, whose latest work on the Illinois novel was beginning to concentrate more and more on similar bridges to the past.

At least two of Bradbury's choices would probably not have been selected by any other author. During the late 1940s, Bradbury had discovered anthropologist Loren Eiseley's ability to convey sensation through rhythmic and metaphor-rich prose in the pages of *Harper's*, and he chose "Buzby's Petrified Woman," a rare Eiseley venture into fiction, for the new anthology. This choice was based more on personal admiration than editorial judgment, but Eiseley's insights into human nature compensate for the almost total lack of fantasy. "Earth's Holocaust," Nathaniel Hawthorne's most improbable vision of a global bonfire of the vanities, also held special attractions for Bradbury. The story's long passage on book burning indicts not only rulers, but also authors who take themselves too seriously (the latter category would always be a favorite Bradbury target). Furthermore, Hawthorne's closing commentary on the importance of the heart over intellect echoed Bradbury's core conviction that the writer must be, first and foremost, an emotionalist; in this way Bradbury used Hawthorne's words to convey, in the new anthology, what Bradbury himself had said in his earlier introduction for *Timeless Stories*: "while the scientific man can tell you the exact size, location, pulse, musculature and color of the heart, we emotionalists can find and touch it quicker."

Saul David had projected as many as fourteen supporting stories for the *Dr. Lao* anthology, but a few fell by the wayside during the unusually long period of volume development. Bradbury traded out Oliver La Farge's "Mr. Skidmore's Gift" for "The Resting Place," a new La Farge story of Native American anthropology that extended the eerie and forlorn mood of Eiseley's anthropological tale into a higher level of mystery and wonderment. Other factors eliminated four tales during the winter of 1955–56. All along, Bantam had been on the lookout for possible conflicts of contents with the new anthology; at one point David told Bradbury that his staff members were "twitching like rabbits, fearing that every time they crack a competitive anthology that our stories will be in it." Jack Finney's "Missing Persons" had to be dropped at the last minute when Dell brought it out in a new anthology, and another Bantam paperback forced the elimination of Saki's "Tobermory." Marcel Aymé, one of Bradbury's favorite European contemporaries, never answered Bantam's request to use "The Man Who Could Walk through Walls," and James Thurber refused permission for "The Unicorn in the Garden."

Four of the ten stories in the final table of contents had not even reached magazine publication when Bradbury signed his spring 1953 contract for the anthology—yet another indicator of Bradbury's long and uneasy relationship with the title novella that preceded all of these stories on the contents page. But he kept this personal history to himself, and managed to put off the introduction for a year and a half after his June 1954 return from Europe. Saul David was baffled, but he remained hopeful that Bradbury would come through. But by December 1955, Finney's agent was threatening to cancel the *Dr. Lao* permissions for this long-overdue volume unless publication could be assured for 1956.[3] Finally, assured in his own mind that his *Dark Carnival* screenplay had nothing of Finney's circus in it, he returned to *Dr. Lao* to see if the passing years might soften his view of it. They did not, and his introduction showed the strain of trying to find a middle way between hollow praise and outright criticism.

The overshadowing presence of *Dr. Lao*, as well as the small number of stories in the anthology, prevented Bradbury from striking a blow for mainstream relevance as he had in his introduction for *Timeless Stories for Today and Tomorrow*. In that earlier anthology, Bradbury had described his concept of "the hidden theatre of the mind" and the way that good fantasy could convey both the terror and the wonderment of the fantastic tale through the minimum of suggestion. Finney's *Dr. Lao* seemed antithetical to Bradbury's "theatre of the mind" and its admonition to suggest, but do not show. The metaphorical mirror that *Dr. Lao* holds up to the people of Abalone, Arizona, fairly explodes with harsh Juvenalian satire and explicit examples of the brutal and coarsely sensual urges that hide within the darker side of human nature. Finney's cynical tone adds force to his underlying conviction that human nature cannot accept the fantastic in any life-affirming way.

Such a viewpoint ran counter to Bradbury's abiding faith in the redemptive possibilities of the fantastic. In his introduction, Bradbury conceded the relevance of Finney's message, but did so with the implication that Finney didn't really write fantasy at all: "Certainly Mr. Finney has given us a long stare at Reality, and done so by dressing it up in fantastic guises. He catches us off guard by pretending to show us something not real, which, at a crucial moment, unshells itself to reveal the raw center of existence. Too late, we turn away. Eyes shut, book closed, we examine his images in private." Bradbury noted how Finney seemed to have reversed the old saying that "the first to catch a circus in a lie is a boy" by having Dr. Lao catch life "in many of its lies." But the overall tone of Bradbury's discussion is ambiguous, suggesting that the boy—perhaps now a writer of introductions, but still a boy at heart—may yet have his eye on the circus.

There is the faint hint of disapproval in all this, but Bradbury abandoned subtlety entirely in discussing the apparently intentional loose ends and unexplained mysteries of this oddly structured novel:

The reader, like the inhabitants of the small desert town, is left with a strewn jigsaw which he must fit together in his own time, according to his own temper, believing or disbelieving the entire menagerie, depending on his real or romantic needs.

There is a fifty-fifty chance you may emerge from the good Doctor's tent vaguely dissatisfied with questions posed and left unanswered. But we must examine not what Mr. Finney might have done (and I, for one, am curious to know the circus's effects on the futures of the people of Abalone, Arizona) but what he really accomplished with his materials.

This is not the kind of introductory commentary one might expect from an editor who supposedly chose the contents of his anthology. But he had not freely chosen The Circus of Dr. Lao, and ultimately he could not bring himself to commend it to his readers. One often sees Bradbury listed as perhaps the most significant author influenced by Finney's early sojourn into dark fantasy, but the correspondence trail combines with the volume introduction itself to suggest that quite the opposite is true. The hidden pressures of the situation diminished the quality of the introduction, which is not nearly as visionary or influential as that of Timeless Stories had been just four years earlier. This time his approach was more didactic, and even in discussing the other stories in the collection he invoked a fairly restrictive definition of fantasy based on how it is not like science fiction.

But his didactic stance and the negatively charged passages concerning the title novel represent an even deeper regression in editorial style and intent. The judgmental tone and rhetorical strategy is eerily similar to the first draft of the first introduction that Bradbury ever attempted—a failed draft for Theodore Sturgeon's 1948 story collection, Without Sorcery. Bradbury's abiding suspicion of financially motivated formula fiction, fueled in those early years by his own repressed fear of succumbing to such pressure himself, initially prevented him from showcasing the truly innovative and creative aspects of Sturgeon's work. His first draft was neutral and qualified, and said very little about the stories themselves; Sturgeon showed it to William Tenn, who also felt it was completely off-trail—a "study in aesthetics, devoted to the problem of why American science-fiction had not to date produced a single definite and unquestioned work of art."[4] Sturgeon gently challenged Bradbury by return mail, suggesting that the problem centered on Bradbury's preoccupation "with artistic form at the expense of substance." Bradbury took the point, and within a week he refashioned a fully celebratory and publishable introduction that reflected his actual belief in Sturgeon's talent.

To some degree, the impulses that had initially blocked his ability to write a balanced introduction for Sturgeon came out again as he wrote the Dr. Lao introduction, which he sent to Saul David (by way of Don Congdon) in early January 1956. His unease with Dr. Lao and the limited number of companion stories in the volume led him to focus on aesthetic questions of morality and symbolism above all else. Only fifteen of the 150 typographical lines in the introduction addressed the short stories (and only five of the ten stories were even mentioned at all). Bradbury spent much of his introduction asserting that responsible fantasy is not facile escape fiction, and he seemed to sacrifice some of his own favorites in the process: "In spite of world conditions today, we can certainly indulge in even those fantasies, say, of Edgar Rice Burroughs and A. Merritt, whose sole purpose is enchantment and high adventure. In practical terms, they make life worth living, survival important, for millions of boys each year."

Saul David was greatly surprised, but masked his concern in a carefully crafted critique. On January 17, 1956, he began with gentle hints that the Dr. Lao passages might be in need of revision before going on to suggest that the introduction seemed too intent, in an unfocused way, on forcing fantasy literature into a rigid obligation to moral responsibility: "All this seems so polemic. Where do we leave a whole body of fantasy which is more closely related to Coleridge's Kublai Khan than to Butler's Erewhon? Do you feel that the times make such work indulgence? Or would you extract a moral purpose from SHE and the Merritt things? . . . Since the question is raised not only by the introduction but also by much more of your recent work, I wonder if you might not speak more directly to it here?"[5]

Don Congdon was concerned in a more general way, implying that in introducing these tales Bradbury had drifted too far from his more spontaneous heartfelt joy in the fantastic: "you may be trying too hard to be intellectual and philosophic in your approach. It doesn't have quite the feeling of ease that the introduction to the other anthology had, at least for me."[6] Bradbury apparently made minimal adjustments during the late winter of 1956, but his introduction remained essentially the same when The Circus of Dr. Lao and Other Improbable Stories was released in October of that year. Bantam's mass-market wrapper design didn't help matters at all; the cover art placed Bradbury's name, as volume editor, directly above the large-font title of Finney's novel; Finney's name appeared in much smaller type, grouped in the lower half of the cover with some of the other authors collected in the volume.

Bradbury had nothing to do with the cover layout, but the situation only added to the private tensions behind the making of this anthology. It would sell well enough, but it never achieved the level of market and critical success that Timeless

Stories for Today and Tomorrow had achieved under his editorship. Bradbury probably never thought of his troubled introduction for *Dr. Lao* as a regression, but Congdon's warning about being too intellectual and philosophical harkened back to his *Fahrenheit* crisis of 1953 and his fear that he had not yet mastered the ability to write with confidence about the ideas behind his fiction—or, for that matter, about the fiction of others. The few introductions he would subsequently write for other authors would tell more about himself and his beliefs than the works at hand. Ironically, this was just what many of his subject authors wanted; Bradbury would always be the focus of much critical debate, but he was also becoming one of the most recognized names among American fiction writers.

In February 1956, Bradbury privately expressed his frustration with the *Dr. Lao* anthology to Tony Boucher: "Finally finished, and had accepted, my editorial introduction. . . . God, what hard work. My brain feels cracked down the middle. . . . To hell with being an editor."[7] In years to come, however, he would continue to present concepts for anthologies aimed at broadening mainstream acceptance of fantasy and science fiction; this had been a passion since the late 1940s, and Congdon dutifully promoted these plans even though he knew there was little money in it. But none of these projects ever reached print, or even got beyond a preliminary stage of development. So far, his best nonfiction writing had emerged much earlier, during a relatively short period in 1952—his Brandeis Library presentation ("No Man Is an Island"), his *Nation* article ("The Day after Tomorrow"), and his *Timeless Stories* introduction. In these works, he had not attempted to be intellectual or philosophical, but had instead turned to two of his most fundamental passions: why readers read and why writers write.

13 | Various Wines

It was only natural, then, that Bradbury would direct his nonfiction prose into a more familiar channel of creativity—writing about writing. Even before the *Dr. Lao* anthology was released, he wrote his first essay for *Writer* magazine. He had deferred an earlier request from the editors of *Writer* in 1951, but his accumulating lecture notes had finally ripened enough to produce "The Joy of Writing" for the October 1956 issue. Earlier plantings demanded his attention first, however, and these matters absorbed much of his time during the early months of 1956.

The most threatened harvest was the Illinois novel, *Summer Morning, Summer Night*. Both the author and Doubleday's Walt Bradbury often referred to it as "the Illinois novel"—perhaps because of its brevity, but possibly because the very title had come to signify something that might never come to fruition. The failure of the *Fahrenheit 451* stage adaptation had opened Bradbury's eyes to the possibility that his aspirations for a work might not always play out as he intended. In December 1955, these feelings coincided with a fateful letter from Walt Bradbury, who had finally decided to force an end to the five-year creative crisis over the Illinois novel by salvaging as much of the original work as possible. Bradbury was now ready to face the task of extracting some of the lighter story-chapters and bridging them into a far more wide-ranging summer's tale than the darker and more narrowly focused whole that had been accumulating for the better part of a decade.

Initially, the strange and sometimes dark exploration of child psychology at the heart of the original 1945 Illinois novel concept had been inspired by the odd pirate-children of Richard Hughes's *Innocent Voyage* and the great, almost racial divide between children and adults found in Christopher Morley's *Thunder on the Left*. Almost from the beginning, however, this psychological structure was slowly but relentlessly compromised by Bradbury's insertion of more and more stories that filtered the ambiguities of life and death through his own nostalgic memories of life in the midwestern town where he was born and raised for most of his first fourteen years. For these more wistful and romantic Green Town stories, the influence came to him through the airwaves rather than through books.

This underlying source of inspiration was the remarkable *Vic and Sade*, perhaps the most popular radio show in America during its twelve-year run. The 15-minute shows were broadcast daily out of Chicago on most networks from 1934 to 1946—perhaps 3,000 shows, all written by the remarkable Paul Rhymer. Through the characters of Vic Gook, his wife Sade, their adopted son Rush, and Uncle Fletcher, Rhymer was able to capture quintessential aspects of small-town life during the great Depression and the war years that followed. Bradbury was deeply affected by this fictional family and the host of nonspeaking characters (introduced through telephone sketches) that revealed the wider life of the town. By virtue of his own postwar contacts at NBC, Bradbury was able to express his feelings directly to Rhymer in 1949: "I was born up in Waukegan, Illinois in 1920, and Waukegan is pretty much Vic and Sade's town. There are thousands like it all over the country. I've been out West for sixteen years, but not a day passed when your show did not recall the small green town I had left behind."[1]

Vic and Sade, and to a lesser degree Jean Hersholt's portrayal of a rural physician in the *Dr. Christian* radio series, inspired the Green Town stories that slowly worked their way into the novel's structure between 1946 and 1955. Bradbury rehearsed his own vision of small-town American life in his 1949 letter to Rhymer, written just after *Vic and Sade*'s final reprise as a short series of television shows: "I cannot think of another program that so well represented what the real America is like. . . . *Vic and Sade* was the best argument ever advanced for a way of life in which we all grew up with our courthouse squares and Bijou theatres and Thimble Clubs and Sacred Knights of the Milky Way." Bradbury had moved away from Waukegan for the last time just as the first *Vic and Sade* episodes aired in 1934; for the next fifteen years the show represented a daily link with that past, prompting him to thank Rhymer "for having given back to all of us some certain portion of our lives, our childhoods, our adolescences, our fathers, our mothers, in a shape where we could recognize and be gently amused by them."

Bradbury's Green Town could not stand on humor alone, for he had been torn away from that world by the great dislocations of the Depression years. But his 1949 reflections on *Vic and Sade* reinforced his sense that the Green Town novels, already in outline and even manuscript form, would also serve as an enduring marker of a bygone age. In 1961, with *Dandelion Wine* already a perennial seller and *Something Wicked This Way Comes* nearing the final stages of revision, Bradbury answered a fan's inquiry with dead certainty:

> You ask me about *Vic and Sade*. I think it was the finest single 15-minute program ever to go on the air in the history of radio. I think it showed middle-class America to itself and showed it wonderfully and warmly, with just the nicest

hint of satire, but with no real hurt. . . . I'm sure the program had much to do with influencing my own thought and career as a writer, later on. Whatever its influence, I will remember it for a lifetime.[2]

The exact influence of *Vic and Sade* was indeed hard to pin down, since the broadcast vignettes were not nearly of the magnitude or emotional force that Bradbury would develop in his nostalgic Green Town novels. But his love would never fade, and in 1972 he wrote the introduction to a volume of Rhymer's scripts—a treasure in its own right, since the network had destroyed all the archived recordings of the show decades earlier.

By the mid-1950s, such gentle reflections on time and memory had already eroded the original outline of the Illinois novel. The core story-chapters—those centered on the plot episodes of tension between the young and the old—had never emerged as stand-alone stories, but many of the more nostalgic time pieces had already been published, or were circulating. And time was now of the essence; in November 1955, Doubleday's Walt Bradbury made a West Coast trip and offered a creative way out of the writer's block—could the sidebar mood and local color episodes be pulled out of the novel's fabric to form a preliminary story collection? By mid-December Ray Bradbury accepted this new alternative, and spent much of 1956 developing more integral bridges for these tales than he had attempted for *The Martian Chronicles*. But the process was slow and at times proved to be as disappointing as deferring the novel itself.

∶ ∶ ∶

Nevertheless, the first months of 1956 brought an unexpected and delightful new creative opportunity, and the agent was none other than Charles Laughton himself. Their time-constrained working relationship of late 1955 was about to blossom into an abiding personal relationship that would last until Laughton's death in 1962 and continue through his widow Elsa Lanchester for the rest of her long life. Here was an unexpected second chance, an opportunity to work with an Academy Award–winning actor whose broad understanding of literature was a treasure known only to those who knew him personally. Laughton's friend and fellow actor Walter Slezak summed up the imaginative characteristics that Bradbury would find most intriguing about Laughton: "[H]ere was one of those rare people in whom truth and fiction, reality and imagination had completely fused. Like water colors they had run together with the line of demarcation no longer visible."

Laughton had first captivated the teenage Bradbury through his title role in Alexander Korda's 1936 feature film biography *Rembrandt*, produced three years after Laughton's Academy Award–winning performance in Korda's *The Private Life of Henry VIII*.[3] Laughton's wife, Elsa Lanchester, had costarred in both films, and of the two celebrities it was Lanchester whom Bradbury would first see perform in person. In 1941 or early 1942, while still working his corner newspaper stand, Bradbury scraped together enough pocket change to attend a new kind of theater custom-built into a large house at the north end of La Cienega Boulevard. The Turnabout Theatre was the brainchild of the Yale Puppeteers, who had occasionally presented their combined marionette and live-actor shows in the carnivalesque environment of Olvera Street during the 1930s. Bradbury was very familiar with all the various Olvera Street entertainments, and when the core group of Yale Puppeteers created a permanent home in Los Angeles, Bradbury attended some of the first season's performances.

Audiences sat in turnabout chairs fashioned from discarded Red Car trolley seats, and turned to face either the live-actor stage at one end of the theater, or the marionette stage at the other end. This intimate musical venue was perfect for the cabaret kind of second career that Elsa Lanchester was already fashioning for herself, and she immediately became a regular star at Turnabout. Laughton himself often attended, and on one occasion he actually performed. In spite of its niche-market appeal and the rise of televised competition, Turnabout Theatre managed to stay in business from 1941 through 1956; for the first dozen years Bradbury attended perhaps thirty or forty performances, often bringing friends and family members.[4] During the 1940s, as Elsa's dedication to the Turnabout experiment became the focus of her professional life, Laughton had followed a parallel course into another medium by reading dramatic radio narratives for Norman Corwin, including *American Trilogy* and *Thomas Wolfe's America*. But the performances that fully fired Bradbury's love of Laughton's world were the stage readings that Laughton took on tour during the early 1950s, most notably Dylan Thomas's *Under Milkwood* and the *Don Juan in Hell* interlude from George Bernard Shaw's *Man and Superman*.[5]

Paul Gregory had been the moving force behind these dramatic endeavors, and had brought Laughton into the world of stage and film direction. Although the abrupt termination of their partnership at the end of 1955 had ended any chance to salvage Bradbury's *Fahrenheit 451* script, Laughton now had time to reassess his personal and professional life. He had taught young actors in his house periodically since 1948, and in a less intense way Bradbury fit naturally into the pockets of free time he now had. He admired Bradbury's poetic prose style and the emotional intensity he brought to his work, but there was a more personal dimension as well. Laughton's recent unsuccessful experience adapting *The Naked and the Dead* generated great empathy for the ordeal that Bradbury, working *for* Laughton, had just gone through.

Other shared experiences included a mutual love of fairy tales and a deep appreciation of the dramatic potential of Biblical texts; Bradbury's success in bringing the Biblical overtones of *Moby Dick* into his screenplay was very similar to the effect that Laughton achieved in directing *The Night of the Hunter*. Bradbury idolized him, but there was little chance that their growing friendship would follow the course of his disastrous relationship with Huston. Both Elsa and Charles genuinely liked the Bradburys and their growing family of daughters (Elsa would always call them "the graces"), and occasionally visited their modest Clarkson Road home during the winter and spring of 1956. Charles guided Bradbury through his first visit to Disneyland that year and cut a fine figure playing Captain Bligh on the jungle-ride boat excursion.

It was this shared passion for performance that gave strength to the new friendship, and Bradbury (often accompanied by his two older daughters) began to spend time swimming at the Laughton's Curson Avenue home in Hollywood. Lloyd Wright, a son of Frank Lloyd Wright, had designed the heated pool for Laughton, who greatly enjoyed reciting literature and working out his approach to new acting projects with his friends in and around the water. For the next three years, between the various film commitments, stage productions and dramatic reading tours that took Laughton away from Los Angeles for months at a time, Bradbury found himself a willing auditor at the Curson Avenue house, encouraged to offer occasional reactions to Laughton's performance strategies. At these moments he performed a role often filled by Elsa, Christopher Isherwood, and other family intimates, but in Bradbury's case there was a learning component as well—Laughton was providing insights into the works of Shaw and Shakespeare that soon led to new levels of understanding. Bradbury had returned from Europe with a new passion for these masters, and Laughton provided inspiration (if not direction) for further study. Shaw in particular was now much on Laughton's mind. During the spring of 1956, he agreed, after much soul-searching, to direct and star in a New York revival of Shaw's *Major Barbara*, and much of his poolside conversation involved this upcoming project and the insights he had gained from his earlier reading adaptation of Shaw's *Don Juan in Hell*.

During these months Bradbury learned crucial lessons that would bear fruit in the 1960s as he began to adapt and produce his own stories on small-stage venues around Los Angeles. Perhaps the most significant insight that Laughton imparted involved language; Bradbury did not yet know how to compress his fiction for the stage, but he was beginning to learn from Laughton that he must continue to value his own voice in the transformation of story into drama. In earlier years, British expatriates like Huxley and Isherwood and Heard had given him great confidence by telling him he was a prose poet; now another British expatriate gave him confidence on a new level: "Remember you're a poet. Let your imagination free on your tongue."[6] Laughton also showed him how "the free spirit of language," combined with good acting and directing, minimized the need for sets, a lesson Bradbury took to heart when he began to produce his own plays. His observations of Laughton in performance, going back to 1950, also showed him how important it was to have an observer on the set. Laughton had worked, on occasion, with Burgess Meredith, who could gently critique Laughton's direction without disrupting a production. For many years, Bradbury would perform the same function for his longtime director Charles Rome Smith.

These interactions also had an immediate impact on his creativity; when the *Fahrenheit 451* project was terminated, the Laughtons encouraged Bradbury to try his hand at composing a verse operetta for Elsa in the tradition of the Restoration stage. He rapidly became comfortable with the form, and the result was entertaining if not elegant: he would later describe *Happy Anniversary 2116* as "a one act science fiction farce about an elderly couple who buy robot duplicates of themselves as gifts for their fiftieth wedding anniversary." He never fooled himself about the quality of this work, but his March 23, 1956, reflections to Bernard Berenson show just how much this activity healed the trauma of the failed *Fahrenheit 451* stage venture:

> Here again was a delightful experience, where I was released from my inferiority complex by Mr. Laughton coming to me and telling me I had the ability to try and succeed at this form which I had never thought of in my life. To write a lyric! Impossible! And yet I have done it. I have much to learn here, too, but at least a friendship has broken my doubts for me and I am on my way. Here, too, it seems to be a creative truth, that so often a single person believing in us and telling us we *can* succeed, helps us over barriers. We go on, with the strength of ten. The power of friendship, the power of love, how rarely we consider it, how rarely we realize the interior mountains it can blast apart and shake to nothing.

The sentiment that emerges in such observations is revealing. This is a newer Bradbury voice, a product of the crucial months in Europe and the new urge, imparted by Bernard Berenson, to explore the nature of art. Here too is the voice of George Bernard Shaw; Bradbury's discovery of *Saint Joan* on a Dublin stage and his subsequent conversations with Laughton paralleled his accumulation of a large library of Shaw's works, and his growing love of Shaw's prefaces is evident in the very next lines of his letter to Berenson: "The one thing I try to do when I lecture classes in the short story, once or twice a year, is knock down the inferiority I find in student after student, the devil imps that tell them they cannot do what in their hearts they most wish to do." An element of Shaw's often didactic and philosophical superrealism would continue to creep into Bradbury's fiction as well, and this would not always be for the better; eventually, the edginess and freshness of his fiction would become diluted in a Shavian form of dialogue and anecdote.

During March and April, Congdon worked with Laughton on a contract to produce *Happy Anniversary 2116* in New York during the fall of 1956, and Laughton went so far as to have model sets prepared by his friend James Whale, who had directed Laughton in *Old Dark House* (and Elsa in *Bride of Frankenstein*) during the 1930s and was now retired from film direction. This proved to be a pleasant experience for Whale, who hadn't sketched and modeled sets since his early days as a director and designer for 1920s London stage productions. Bradbury met him at Laughton's house during planning meetings and subsequently visited Whale's Pacific Palisades home with Laughton to see and discuss the sets, little knowing that Whale's mysterious death would occur here exactly a year later.[7] But none of these plans were firmed up before Laughton's summer 1957 departure for New York to cast, direct, and star in Robert Joseph's production of *Major Barbara*. Bradbury had nevertheless benefited greatly from listening to Laughton work through his anxieties about the Shaw project, and during these months an enduring friendship was cemented.

It was a time of great transition for the Laughtons, and Bradbury could not help but notice all that went on in the background. Laughton's break with Gregory had also coincided with the end of his relationships with his male companions of this period; the end was also in sight for Turnabout Theatre, and Elsa wound down her long years of involvement with the Yale Puppeteers and decided to spend the fall and winter of 1956–57 in New York with Charles. There was an oddness in the loving complexity of their long marriage that fascinated Bradbury, who had seen a wide range of homosexual lifestyles since coming to Hollywood as a teenager in 1934. Many of the Lonelies who joined him in the 1930s to seek autographs at the studio gates also had secret lives, and by the mid-1950s his various Hollywood assignments had brought him in contact with the parallel lives that often went on within the studio walls as well.

James Whale also maintained a homosexual lifestyle that had become more and more reclusive over the years, and Bradbury saw firsthand the withdrawn and mysterious nature of his final year. It was not surprising that Bradbury was beginning to write about these aspects in much the same way he had been drawn, in the mid- and late-1940s, to begin to write fiction that explored the complex and often ambiguous relationships between husbands and wives. He thought of these people compassionately and with friendship, and the occasional stories were always quite distinct from the lives of the people he had known. The McCarthy era was winding down, but it was still a liability to be different in Hollywood; Bradbury thought of Laughton as part of a "twilight world," and in the 1960s he considered bringing together an anthology of themed stories that he called *The Fire Walkers*. This project was never developed, but a half-dozen stories dealing with this side of the human equation were published, solitary and unsequenced, over the next fifty years.

14 The End of the Beginning

The 1956 release of *Moby Dick* coincided with Bradbury's growing awareness of recent advances in astronomy and planetary science. He eagerly awaited the boost that the upcoming International Geophysical Year would have on the space program, but his eagerness was counterweighted by anxieties that he loosely gathered under a vague articulation of "the uneasy time." An unpublished note from the summer of 1956 captures the root question at the core of his unease far more candidly than anything he was yet prepared to publish:

> There is special significance in the fact that even as Mars will be closer to Earth on September 1st, 1956 than she has been since 1874, so Mankind on Earth is closer to Mars than he has ever been since he leapt down from the tree, or shuffled out of the cave. With the geophysical year looming, with Mars swinging close, we find ourselves on the outer edge of a Renaissance of thought and exploration. That Renaissance which surged northward from Italy in the 14th to 17th centuries swerved us from thinking of man and heaven toward consideration of man on [E]arth. Now we are fast approaching the time when we will reverse the process with a vengeance. Man in heaven again, via rocket, by 1975, is our goal.
>
> It follows that in the uneasy time before the dawn of space-travel, we groundlings consider just what the rocket will mean to us. The question to be asked and answered is why the space-ship, why travel at all to the moon, to Mars, from Mars to Jupiter or Saturn and thus on out to all the planets.

Bradbury framed this statement in terms he would not have thought to use before his discovery of the Renaissance with Berenson, or before his engagement with the California Institute of Technology, where the faculty and staff scientists were beginning to reach out to him for poetic inspiration. The vast military-industrial complex that formed both a Cold War deterrent and a formidable instrument of global diplomatic leverage could not overshadow the closely guarded research treasures represented by Cal Tech's Mount Wilson and Mount Palomar observatories. Bradbury had grown up with the great advances in cosmology made possible by Mount Wilson's pioneering 100-inch reflector, where Edwin Hubble was able to determine that many of the nebulae seen from smaller telescopes were, in reality, massive galactic islands far beyond our own Milky Way.

This new conception of island universes in a rapidly expanding and perhaps infinite Cosmos comprised the fourth teaching unit in Bradbury's fall 1937 high-school astronomy course; in the years immediately following World War II, as Bradbury reached his peak as a writer of darkly haunting science fiction tales, he witnessed the quantum leap in magnitude represented by the June 1948 dedication of the 200-inch Hale telescope on Mount Palomar. Suddenly Mankind could see twice as far as ever before by means of a fourfold increase in light-gathering power, opening up eight times the volume of deep space that the Mount Wilson observatory had been able to scan. To a large degree Palomar's revelations were open to the broader scientific community, but the facility itself was guarded with nearly the same security as an atomic test site.

Bradbury's senior-year astronomy class may have actually been given passes to observe a November 1937 lunar eclipse at Mount Wilson, but touring the Palomar complex proved to be an entirely different challenge. In late August 1954, Bradbury tried unsuccessfully to see the Hale telescope at Palomar, but even an inscribed copy of *Fahrenheit 451* couldn't win admission. Cal Tech's Robert Richardson apologized, noting how "the observatory has a strict policy about admitting visitors, and the front office very seldom makes an exception." But Bradbury soon became a popular visitor at the more accessible Cal Tech campus in Pasadena; Ballantine Books had sent four of their science fiction titles to the faculty six months earlier, and Richardson reported to Bradbury that these had been widely circulated among the scientists and their wives, who favored *Fahrenheit* by a wide margin over the other titles.

In early April 1955, Bradbury was invited to Pasadena to lecture at Cal Tech. He had not yet overcome his fear that his lack of a college education—and perhaps the lack of hard science in his stories—would make it difficult for him to connect with his audience. What he found, however, was an audience that had adopted his own dreams of Mars and other worlds as their own, and his relief was close to the surface of the account he sent to Don Congdon: "Had a wonderful time last week one night, out at Cal-Tech, lecturing to about a hundred young and enthusiastic scientists and scientific engineers on science-fiction, philosophy (ha!) and their own work. They kept me stepping to a fast pace, but I got through with my skin pretty much in one piece."

He was given a parchment-printed bound copy of the 1948 dedication ceremony for Palomar, documenting the essential funding provided by the Rockefeller Foundation. The dedication address by foundation chairman Dr. Raymond Fosdick had expressed the same fundamental questions that the marvels of modern astronomy (and the perils of the Atomic Age) were leading Bradbury to address in his more recent science fiction: "Are there other planets that have burst into consciousness like our own? Is there an answering intelligence anywhere in space? Is there purpose behind the apparent meaninglessness and incomprehensibility of the universe? What is this divine spark of awareness which we call consciousness? And finally, in the words and spirit of the Psalmist, what is man?"

Bradbury had never been comfortable with beginnings and endings, and as he turned away from the edgy and emotionally charged dark science fiction he had written through the late 1940s, he also turned away from the mounting evidence for the Big Bang theory implicit in Palomar's great advances in observational cosmology and stellar evolution. He remained far more comfortable with the Steady State theory that emerged in the late 1940s as an alternative concept of continuous creation. This was much more like Bradbury's universe, which accommodated the master metaphor of his 1948 O. Henry prize story "Powerhouse"—"for every light that was put out, another could come on."[1]

Relieved of the psychological burden of accepting a universe that must someday dissipate in entropy, Bradbury allowed his growing sense that Mankind is its own salvation to inform his final phase of development as a writer of science fiction. The more intriguing dark tales of the mid- and late-1940s, and the somber but occasionally hopeful stories that he would bridge into *The Martian Chronicles*, slowly gave way to a style of science fiction based on wonderment and reverie. Such stories had only rarely surfaced in his earlier fiction, but the first of these—published as "King of the Gray Spaces" in the December 1943 issue of *Famous Fantastic Mysteries*—was the precursor for what was to come. The submitted title, "R Is for Rocket," captured the initial child's-eye view of the Cosmos that frames the opening of the tale; for Bradbury, this story proved to be a breakthrough in terms of focused storytelling that is true to the human heart.

Whenever this approach surfaced in Bradbury's maturing work, it was usually muted, as in "The Rocket Man," where the young boy's last sight of his father is the shooting star formed in the night sky by his father's exploding rocket. But a more positive vision of space exploration, stripped for the moment of the sense of isolation and overwhelming loneliness that marked much of Bradbury's best science fiction of the 1940s, surfaced in "The Million Year Picnic," a 1943 composition that would become the famous second-chance conclusion of *The Martian Chronicles*. By the 1950s, these stories were appearing with more frequency, beginning with "The Rocket" (originally published as "Outcast of the

Stars" in 1950), where a father uses the power of imagination to transform the relics of a junkyard into a backyard rocket for his son. "The Gift" (1952) soon followed, capturing the moment when a homesick boy, embarking with his family for a Martian colony, discovers the wonders of the Cosmos as seen from interplanetary space.

The better-known Bradbury tales that passed as science fiction, stories such as "To the Future" ("The Fox and the Forest"), "The Veldt," and "A Sound of Thunder," were Earthbound tales that had appeared in major market magazines, and to some degree they overshadowed the final evolution of his space-based fictions. Broadly speaking, Bradbury never developed the kind of technological sublime that his peers (and their successors) had hoped to see in his science fiction; even the gothic effect that stretches into the sublime in his fantasies is absent from his 1950s science fiction subjects. Instead, the emerging effect is picturesque, a contained sublimity that he keeps in the safe and familiar zone of childlike wonderment. This impulse reached its peak in 1956, as Bradbury published two more inspirational tales of space exploration. "Next Stop, the Stars" and "Icarus Montgolfier Wright" presented variations on the first attempt to reach another celestial body, providing a more focused and elemental answer to the question of man's purpose in the universe than he had so far attempted.

In terms of creativity, "Icarus Montgolfier Wright" became the high ground for Bradbury's brand of short story science fiction. The story moves through a montage of dreams that come to an astronaut the night before his departure on the first rocket to the moon. Bradbury continued to transform "Icarus Montgolfier Wright" into new forms, first as a wordless picture book built around art by Joe Mugnaini, then, with advice from his mentor Charles Laughton, as a verse narrative, and finally, in the early 1960s, as an Academy Award–nominated short-subject film.

R Is for Rocket (1962) and the companion volume S Is for Space (1966) represented a successful harvesting of a wide range of Bradbury stories that would reinforce his presence in school and public libraries for decades. "King of the Gray Spaces," under its original prepublication title "R Is for Rocket," opened as the first volume's title story, followed by "Next Stop, the Stars," prophetically re-titled by Bradbury as "The End of the Beginning." All of the other wonderment phase stories were included in the two volumes, as Bradbury, perhaps unconsciously, celebrated his last full engagement with this subject.

After 1956, the science fiction that Bradbury published or presented was derivative, or, at best, represented creative digressions from other work. The short novel *Leviathan '99*, weaving in and out of radio- and stage-play form, was an extension of his *Moby Dick* motion picture triumph; "The Lost City of Mars" emerged from his *Martian Chronicles* screenplays. Most of the science fiction stories that occasionally surfaced in later story collections were unpublished or uncollected stories from the richly creative period of the 1940s and early 1950s; the rest were latter-day compositions, infused with an almost anecdotal dialogue-heavy structure that masked minimal plot development and almost nonexistent characterization. The many stage plays adapted (by Bradbury and others) from his science fiction stories combine with this later work to obscure the crucial change of the mid-1950s. In all these ways, 1956 marked "the end of the beginning"; his science fiction materials would continue to attract generations of readers, but his truly creative advances in this form were at an end. As a fiction writer, his turn to fantasy, and to a gently reflective form of realism, was final.

From this point on, the critical mass of his growing popularity would propel him into the role of occasional spokesperson for the genre he was no longer practicing, and this complicated the way other science fiction writers regarded him. Damon Knight, who had known Bradbury since his late teens, was convinced that Bradbury never really wrote science fiction at all, but Knight appreciated his images and range of ideas: "As his talent expands, some of his stories become pointed social commentary; some are surprisingly effective religious tracts, disguised as science fiction; others still are nostalgic vignettes; but under it all is still Bradbury the poet of 20th-century neurosis. Bradbury the isolated spark of consciousness, awake and alone at midnight; Bradbury the grown-up child who still remembers, still believes."

Bradbury's friend Ken Crossen, who had successfully merged the worlds of pulp fiction and superhero comics in his own writing, was representative of those who saw Bradbury as "the voice of the poet raised against the mechanization of mankind. . . . To him there has been only a difference of degree between the atom bomb and man tossing beer-cans into Martian canals. One destroys the whole man; the other indicates the inner man is already destroyed."[2] Ironically, the specter of nuclear war, which loomed or became manifest in so many of Bradbury's earlier stories, disappeared entirely from the science fiction he wrote after his return from Europe.

Across the Atlantic, Brian Aldiss, like Crossen, grouped Bradbury with those writers, such as Ted Sturgeon and Clifford Simak, who were "clearly in revolt against the trends of science." Aldiss found Bradbury's reconfigured weird tales of *The October Country* to be more literary and less folksy than his earlier fantasies, but he preferred Bradbury's earlier, darker science fiction to the wonderment tales of the mid-1950s.[3] This was also true of J. G. Ballard, whose evolving "we're all doomed from the start" premise of science fiction was in tune with the range of Bradbury's darker explorations of the genre in the late 1940s: for most postwar science fiction writers, the terror and unease of such extraterrestrial stories as "Purpose" ("The City"), "No Particular Night or Morning," "The Lonely Ones," and "Death Wish"; the *Martian Chronicles* stories "Ylla," "—And the Moon Be Still as Bright," and "The Long Years"; and his dark marionette tale "Changeling" were far more interesting than what was to come.

Bradbury's role in the field would always be debated, but his achievement as a stylist was rarely disputed. In his annual review of science fiction in Britain, Michael Edwards closed out 1956 by acknowledging that Bradbury, "the master of the American school, is the direct heir of Poe and Hawthorne, and seems to have modeled his style on Joyce, Faulkner, and the French surrealists." Even Ballard, looking back across half a century, would rank Bradbury as a first-tier stylist: "At its best, in Borges, Bradbury and Edgar Allan Poe, the short story is coined from precious metal, a glint of gold that will glow for ever in the deep purse of your imagination."[4]

Bradbury's final phase of SF was a natural outgrowth of the myths he had been evolving since the mid-1940s. His was a form of mythopoeia not far distant from that of C. S. Lewis; both men exhibited the same richness of metaphor common to many of the best mythmakers and storytellers. Arthur Quiller-Couch traced Lewis's achievement back to Aristotle's sense of metaphor as innate genius that cannot be taught. Bradbury, working without such a studied academic view of metaphor, was already certain that this ability could not be explained in any other way. By the mid-1960s, Russell Kirk noted the mythopoetic similarities between Bradbury and Lewis. For his part, Bradbury was quite fond of *The Screwtape Letters*, but he was only remotely aware of Lewis's richly mythological science fiction trilogy.

Lewis, however, had already encountered Bradbury's science fiction, commenting as early as April 1951 that "Bradbury is a writer of great distinction." Lewis went on to suggest subtle differences between his own work and Bradbury's fiction: "Is his style almost too delicate, too elusive, to nuancé for S.F. matter? In that respect I take him and me to be at opposite poles; he is a humble disciple of Corot and Debussy, I an even humbler disciple of Titian and Beethoven." These brief but intriguing comments offer insights that anticipate the direction Bradbury's science fiction took after his return from Europe, stripped, as it was, of the scientific and technological and even psychological conventions of the genre. He would instead explore the psychological *response* to space travel—less often as the voyager, more often focusing on the responses of those who observe the voyage. Lewis's invocation of Corot, who both anticipated and celebrated the French Impressionists, is apt—Bradbury was beginning to cast himself as a witness, a patron who provides a central point of view for interpreting the work of others. It was natural that his responses to the Space Age would turn more and more to nonfiction and, eventually, to poetry.

The general reading public accepted his most recent science fiction stories along with what little they had seen of the darker tales in parts of The Martian Chronicles and The Illustrated Man. Within a few years, the scientists, technicians, and administrators of America's rapidly expanding space programs also accepted (and celebrated) these more visionary stories as inspirational glimpses of an exciting future. Bradbury's settled form of the science fiction story was not unique, but the newer stories were full of vivid images for readers of all ages, told with an understated elegance that attracted an entirely new generation of young readers. His vision of how Mankind could fulfill destiny would eventually radiate out into his Space-Age essays of the 1960s, heightened to a more emotional pitch by his reading of Nikos Kazantzakis. These rich variations would appeal to the broader culture in lasting ways, even as they generally failed to appeal to his fellow writers.

Don Congdon wasn't particularly concerned with the reactions of other writers in the field; he was more attuned to Bradbury's readership and considered the style of "Icarus Montgolfier Wright" to be "absolutely masterful."[5] He had other concerns, however, about troubling tendencies he was finding in Bradbury's story submissions, and he began to address these trends in the summer of 1956: "It's a fact that you have been much less interested in story-telling in the last few years, and much more interested in ideas and in perceptions of human behavior." This shift was most obvious in the new brand of science fiction stories, but it also spread out into his broader fiction; there was, at times, a tendency to support a story with dialogue rather than narrative. He was continuing to read (in translation) most of the short stories of Luigi Pirandello, whose narratives were almost as dialogue-dependent as his stage plays. This influence, along with the increasing distractions of the dialogue-rich world of his various television projects, may have diminished his ability to concentrate on new short fiction.

Congdon could only guess at the specific causes, but he sensed that Bradbury's writing was more and more strained "by the urgency you feel to say something truthfully and with accompanying beauty." He urged him to pull back somewhat and "move closer to plotting, closer to old-fashioned story-telling with some of these situations you attack." Privately, Congdon had more concrete reasons to offer this advice—Bradbury was submitting and publishing far fewer stories than he ever had before. The author of more than 220 professional tales had published only five new stories in 1955 and would stall at the same figure in 1956 (his lowest annual totals since 1942, his first full year as a professional writer). Other than the stories projected for *Dandelion Wine*, only two new stories would reach print in 1957. Hollywood beckoned, and Bradbury found himself looking down a path from which he might not return.

Ray Bradbury, early winter, 1952–53. Bradbury used another shot from this sequence for the dust jacket of *The Golden Apples of the Sun*—the collection that convinced John Huston to hire Bradbury as screenwriter for his motion picture adaptation of *Moby Dick*. The photographer was Bradbury's good friend Morris Dollens, well known for his science fiction artwork. From the Albright Collection; courtesy Donn Albright and the estate of Ray Bradbury.

Ray Bradbury (left), Maggie Bradbury, and John Huston at the reception following the wedding of Huston assistant Tim Durant and Mary Bacon, held at Huston's Courtown House, Kilcock, Ireland, January 9, 1954. Already in coat and breeches, Huston would ride to the hounds later that day; these events eventually became the subject of Bradbury's story-memoir, "The Hunt Wedding." Copyright © by the Irish News Agency. Bradbury's presentation copy from the Albright Collection; courtesy Donn Albright and the estate of Ray Bradbury.

Director John Huston (left) and Bradbury reviewing progress on Bradbury's *Moby Dick* screenplay adaptation in Courtown House, Kilcock, Ireland, February 1954. Huston allowed Bradbury time to work through a nearly complete first draft before entering into deep consultations and revisions. Lorrie Sherwood, Huston's secretary, is in the background. Photograph by MacNally of Dublin. From the Albright Collection; courtesy Donn Albright and the estate of Ray Bradbury.

                    THE VOICES (faintly)
          Homeward bound, boys! We're homeward bound!
          Grog! Grog for all! A full ship and homeward
          bound. Solong, lads, solong. Luck, boys,
          luck. . .luck. . .

The men in the two boats sit listening to the music and laughter
fade. Then the BACHELOR is gone. The sea is quiet all around.

The men look at the water.

Suddenly the waters nearby slowly swell in broad circles; then are
quickly upheaved, as if sideways sliding from a submerged berg of
ice, swiftly rising to the surface. A low rumbling sound is heard;
a subterranean hum.

The men in the boats hold their breath.

STUBB turns.

STARBUCK turns to stare.

Bedraggled with trailing ropes and harpoons and lances, a vast form
rises shrouded in a thin drooping veil of mist into the air. The
water flashes like heaps of fountains and sinks in a shower of flakes.
MOBY DICK lies nearby on a surface creamed from his purging tail.

The men in the boats stiffen.

As does STUBB.

As does STARBUCK.

As does ISHMAEL.

Lashed round and round to the fish's back, pinioned in the turns upon
turns of line reeled around and around, the sodden body of AHAB
is seen, like a corpse bourne upon a great white marble bier floating
through the sea.

We see the body, the face in nightmare, the eyes distended.

STUBB sees the body and takes it like a blow that slowly burns him
to anger.

STARBUCK looks upon the whale and its terrible gift from the sea.

As does FLASK.

As does ISHMAEL.

As do all the crew, hardening, stiffening, angering and filling out
with iron purpose.

Very early in the process of drafting his screenplay, Bradbury decided to eliminate the character of Fedallah, whose body ends up caught in the fouled lines and harpoons on Moby Dick's flank. He initially substituted the harpooner Tashtego, but in this subsequent draft of the final scenes Bradbury had the sudden insight to cross through Tashtego's name and insert Ahab as the entangled corpse; while the whale rocks in the waves, Ahab's lifeless arm seems to beckon his crew to their doom. Bradbury's alteration remains one of the most easily recalled images of the entire film, and it is often mistaken as Melville's invention. From the Albright Collection; courtesy Donn Albright and the estate of Ray Bradbury.

"The sort of future society that he portrays is only too possible." Lord Bertrand Russell at home in Richmond, United Kingdom, about the time of Bradbury's spring 1954 visit, with a British edition of *Fahrenheit 451* on the arm of his reading chair. Photo by Harold White; original in the Bertrand Russell Papers, McMaster University, Ontario, Canada. Bradbury's presentation copy from the Albright Collection; courtesy Donn Albright and the estate of Ray Bradbury.

Bradbury's mentors of the 1950s. Renaissance art expert Bernard Berenson (left) in his Villa I Tatti outside Florence, Italy, 1955. Bradbury's spring 1954 visits with Berenson in Florence and Venice opened his eyes to the Italian Renaissance and its consequences for the Western world, prompting a significant correspondence and a second visit during the summer of 1957. The Academy Award–winning actor Charles Laughton (late 1940s) greatly expanded Bradbury's appreciation of Shakespeare and George Bernard Shaw through many hours of discussion as Laughton prepared for various performances during the mid- and late-1950s. Berenson photograph by David Seymour, 1955 (courtesy Magnum Photos); Laughton photograph by Clarence Bull, 1943 (licensed by Warner Bros. Entertainment Inc. All rights reserved; image provided courtesy of the Margaret Herrick Library).

Literary Hollywood, November 1958. Bradbury was one of the sponsoring celebrities for poet Carl Sandburg's eightieth-birthday commemoration in Los Angeles. Those pictured at the pre-gala banquet include (standing, left to right) playwright Clifford Odets, novelist Robert Nathan, Ray Bradbury, presidential science advisor Dr. Joseph Kaplan, Bell Laboratory television host Dr. Frank Baxter, and (seated, left to right) Groucho Marx, television journalist Georgianna Hardy, and Carl Sandburg, whose actual birthday had been celebrated with far less fanfare back in January. Bradbury's friendship with Sandburg continued through the rest of the poet's life; he was brought into the planning group by radio legend Norman Corwin and film director George Stevens Sr., who together organized the event on behalf of expatriate German writer and Sandburg enthusiast Lion Feuchtwanger. Photograph by Neil Cleman. Courtesy of the Feuchtwanger Memorial Library, Special Collections, University of Southern California. Bradbury's presentation copy from the Albright Collection; courtesy Donn Albright and the estate of Ray Bradbury.

Part III

Dark Carnivals

The art of writing is that the author takes time to step aside from the plot. *Dandelion Wine* works because it's not a straight-line plot—it's full of asides: about the weather, about being alive, about making wine, about dying—the Grandma's death is an aside. It has nothing to do with the plot. It's beautiful, beautiful.

—RB, 2005

15 Strange Interlude: *Dandelion Wine*

Bradbury's marked decline in short story production was offset (and masked) by new media adaptations. Antony Ellis wrote radio adaptations of "Zero Hour," "Kaleidoscope," and the ever-popular murder tale "The Whole Town's Sleeping" for 1955–56 broadcasts of the long-running CBS radio show *Suspense*. In February 1956, the more literary *CBS Radio Workshop* followed up its highly regarded radio adaptation of Aldous Huxley's *Brave New World* with two more Ellis adaptations of Bradbury fantasies, "Hail and Farewell" and "Season of Disbelief."[1] The *CBS Radio Workshop* broadcasts opened with introductions read by Bradbury himself. Unfortunately, these years represented network radio's last hurrah in programming, and the CBS episodes would be the last two Bradbury radio adaptations produced by any network for more than a decade.

Television, the great slayer of radio shows, provided more prominence for Bradbury than he had yet experienced in either medium. "Cora and the Great Wide World," an emotionally powerful tale that reveals how letters in a mailbox give an illiterate hill-country woman her first contact with the outside world, was adapted for two different networks. The CBS *Windows* episode "The World out There," featuring Anthony Perkins (in one of his first roles) as the nephew who writes letters for his illiterate aunt, had aired in 1955. The Dumont network *Studio 57* version, "The Great Wide World," seemed destined for oblivion when Dumont ceased dramatic broadcasts in 1955; fortunately this episode, starring longtime film actress Spring Byington as Cora, made its way into syndication and was aired nationally in May 1956.

"Merry-Go-Round," Mel Dinelli's adaptation of "The Black Ferris," had languished for almost two years after its local Los Angeles debut on *Starlight Summer Theatre*, but in July 1956 it aired nationally as the pilot for NBC's *Sneak Preview* series. Bradbury's next television credit—a November 1956 episode of *Jane Wyman Presents*—was produced from an original Bradbury teleplay titled "The Marked Bullet." The show's producers approached him for an original romantic story appropriate for Jane Wyman, and Bradbury decided to combine two carnival story lines to create a highly emotional tale of estrangement and reconciliation.

His 1945 story "The Electrocution," one of his first dark studies of husbands and wives, provided the basic plot: a routine carnival act (the wife as electric chair "victim," the husband as executioner) turns deadly when the husband learns that she loves another man. For Jane Wyman Presents, Bradbury transferred these basic tensions to a real-life circus act that had fascinated him since childhood—the fantastic performances of Ching Ling Soo, the man who could catch a speeding bullet in his teeth. The illusion was based on firing an exploding wax bullet to distract the audience as the victim "catches" a real bullet he has secretly palmed earlier in the act. Bradbury hated to slant his work for any market, but his chance to steer an Academy Award–winning actress into his favorite world of carnival and illusion was too tempting to pass up. In the end, Bradbury had the shooter-husband reconcile with his wife, who finds the chance to revitalize their marriage more appealing than the handsome young man in the crowd.

With the help of Ben Benjamin and other agents at Famous Artists, Bradbury was still shopping the Dark Carnival screenplay around Hollywood. His wider circle of advisors included such Hollywood friends as Fritz Lang and the Hungarian director Lazlo Benedek. Charles Laughton's New York production of Major Barbara left Bradbury without his trusted advice during the fall of 1956, but he was nevertheless able to generate interest from Columbia and Disney studios. No offers resulted, however, and throughout 1956 the creative energy he had invested in this screenplay and other media projects continued to overshadow most of the literary work he had in hand.

The opening acts of the international space race tempted him to revive his 1952 plans for a Martian Chronicles television series, but another Chronicles-related project claimed priority through much of 1956—the daring conception of a Martian Chronicles musical. The lyrical potential of Bradbury's Chronicles narratives had attracted Lerner and Loewe as early as 1952, and NBC radio writer-producer Van Woodward (assisted by Earl Hamner) spent the better part of two years developing an unproduced adaptation of his own. By March of 1956 Bradbury had worked up his own musical concept in collaboration with Leonard Rosenman, who had just scored East of Eden and Rebel Without a Cause for Warner Brothers, and the successful pop songwriter Wayne Shanklin.

Bradbury owed the rebirth of this idea to Charles Laughton, who had convinced him to extend his writing into other creative forms. Initially, Bradbury hoped that Laughton's producer Paul Gregory could be involved, but the breakup of that partnership was already in progress. Laughton agreed to remain, behind the scenes, a creative advisor for the Chronicles musical, which Bradbury initially called Rocket Summer. Bradbury intended to write the book adaptation, sharing royalties and subsidiary rights with Rosenman and Shanklin.[2] With Gregory out of the picture, Congdon began a long series of negotiations with David Susskind, who showed great interest in the project. Susskind had not yet begun the pioneering television talk show that would make him a celebrity, but he was already a proven producer of stage and screen adaptations.

While the *Chronicles* stage musical and the Bradbury television series remained viable projects, other ventures slowly unraveled through the spring and summer of 1956. One was particularly disappointing—the Space-Age operetta that Bradbury had so enjoyed creating for the Laughtons was now unlikely to reach Broadway. Laughton had planned to take Bradbury's blend of Restoration domestic comedy and futuristic marionette fantasy to New York; while he directed and starred in a fall-winter production of George Bernard Shaw's *Major Barbara*, his wife Elsa Lanchester, a great enthusiast of cabaret and dance hall, could star in a revue that would combine Bradbury's operetta with Sam Rosen's adaptation of Max Beerbohm's story "The Duke and the Dairymaid." Ray Henderson put both works to music.[3]

Without Paul Gregory, it soon became evident to Congdon that the Oscar-winning actor had little experience with preproduction negotiations. Negotiations were further slowed when retired Hollywood director James Whale, who had sketched and built miniature sets for the operetta back in Los Angeles, suffered a debilitating stroke. Sporadic negotiations continued without any real progress until May 1957, when *Major Barbara* closed and Laughton returned with his wife to Los Angeles. But Congdon had long since relegated this negotiation to the background; throughout the spring and summer of 1956, he was far more concerned with Bradbury's lack of story production.

He had received only three new stories since January, and these were proving problematic to place in major market magazines. Such sales were beginning to bring in upward of $1,500 apiece, but Bradbury had not sold an original story at that level since March of 1955, when the *Saturday Evening Post* took his Green Town story, "The Sound of Summer Running." Publicly, Bradbury remained prominent through the various radio and television adaptations, reprints of his older stories, and steady paperback sales of his earlier books; but privately, he was enduring a strange interlude in his writing career and producing virtually nothing new for Congdon to circulate.

Early in 1956, Congdon almost sold one of the new space stories, "The End of the Beginning," to *Life* magazine, but settled for the lower-paying Canadian slick *Macleans*. On May 14, he noticed that Bradbury was still claiming, in his latest published interview, that he was writing a story a week, and immediately sent Bradbury this half-serious rejoinder: "I'm beginning to get a strong feeling that this is the year I should come out and have a look at that mythical file of stories." For a brief time, such proddings brought impressive results. Bradbury had just sent Congdon "In a Season of Calm Weather," a beautiful story that he had been holding back for nearly two years: what if an American tourist in Biarritz comes across Picasso, drawing a masterwork on the sands of the Mediterranean shoreline? Is there time to take it all in before the tide turns? It took almost a year to sell, but in the end Congdon was able to leverage a significant new price plateau from *Playboy* magazine.

For a brief moment, he managed to overcome his obsession with perfection and sent two more stories to Congdon: "The Beautiful Sleep," a preschool Green Town memory of his great-grandmother that had found its way into the Illinois novel structure, and "The Day It Rained Forever," a striking story of beauty and creativity in a desert town of the American Southwest. These two tales were fully formed and transcended the anecdotal tales, mood pieces, and polemic stories that were becoming more and more difficult for Congdon to place.

Two major television projects soon added to Bradbury's growing list of near misses. During the summer of 1956, NBC's Mort Abrahams approached Congdon with the possibility of securing *Fahrenheit 451* for *Producer's Showcase*, a pioneering dramatic television series that produced live color episodes in a 90-minute format ideal for literary and stage adaptations.[4] On the West Coast, Bradbury's Famous Artists agents almost brokered a deal with CBS to produce Bradbury's script of "The Fox and the Forest" as an hour-long episode of the network's *Climax* dramatic series. This popular time-travel story was fast-paced and rich in character development, but in the end neither "The Fox and the Forest" nor *Fahrenheit 451* were optioned that summer. With no stories—new or old—ready to circulate, and the Illinois materials buried in a never-ending writer's block, Congdon reluctantly advised Bradbury to consider a return to the virtual anonymity of screenwriting.

∴ ∴ ∴

All of Bradbury's complicated and time-consuming media negotiations were playing out against the far more urgent drama of the Illinois novel, which had been under contract since 1952 with Doubleday. Bradbury's fateful December 1955 decision to extract the nonessential stories to form a new collection of Green Town tales should have lifted the writing block—the newer stories represented a more nostalgic and wistful late-blooming fruit that should have been easy to harvest from the deep genealogical stems of the original work, but this was not the case at all. The only milestone that Bradbury reached during the winter and early spring of 1956 was to settle on "Dandelion Wine," a memory of his grandfather's cellar winepress venture, as the title story for the extracted collection.

This unexpected twist to his writing block was agonizing; the generational conflict concept of the Illinois novel (young boys against the town's authority figures) was fully developed during the mid-1940s, and by the time he signed his 1952 contract with Doubleday, many of the story-chapters were drafted. But Bradbury's innate comfort with the short story form never really extended to sustained fictions—even *Fahrenheit 451* had been built around the armature of a short novella. He had never been able to weave the ever-changing skein of story-chapters into a novel form, and now he found himself unable to provide any unifying structure to the extracted stories. He continued to distract himself with media ventures; when he did turn to the Green Town materials, he became obsessed with puzzling out the residual episodes of the deferred core novel and ignored the extracted stories. Neither Congdon nor Doubleday's Walt Bradbury were aware that their author was approaching the end of his tether until April 1956, when the usual belt-tightening of the tax season led Ray Bradbury to bargain for a $1,000 advance from his publisher.

The bargain he proposed quickly revealed how desperate he was to avoid work on *Dandelion Wine*. During the winter he had taken one of his newest space exploration stories, "Icarus Montgolfier Wright," and adapted it to verse for a children's picture book. This was not an unnatural impulse in and of itself, for Bradbury was always ready to bring the fantastic genius of Joe Mugnaini's artwork into any of his own creative ventures. But he asked Walt Bradbury to advance the needed funds on the strength of the picture-book proposal and the promise of another story collection based on the pieces he had published or worked on during the two years since his return from Europe. Such a collection would not require bridging, but the very suggestion of this project seemed a clear signal to both Congdon and Walt Bradbury that the bridging required for the Illinois stories was going nowhere.

Ray Bradbury had published no new work for Doubleday in more than three years, and the two books he had subsequently refashioned for Ballantine—*Fahrenheit 451* and *The October Country*—were derived from even older works. Walt Bradbury was deeply concerned and tried one more time to highlight the vital importance of *Dandelion Wine*: "[A]s you remember, this was to be not only an interim book before the novel but a curtain-raiser, by its nature, to the novel and thus it is a logical planned publication in your career—rather than 'just another Ray Bradbury collection.' We have got to give your readers and critics a valid book which indicates development and progress; otherwise some of the carpers will begin to sound the note of question as to whether you have reached an indefinite plateau."

The prospect of the indefinite plateau jolted Bradbury, but he would still need a devil's bargain to force himself back to work on *Dandelion Wine*. By the end of April he offered Walt Bradbury the promise that he would send a new table of contents and the first 100 pages in return for $250 and would receive another $250 for each 100 pages of typescript. Both Walt Bradbury and Don Congdon assured Ray that they didn't distrust him, but both men knew all too well how easily he could be distracted by new projects and ideas.

Much to Congdon's annoyance, Bradbury had tipped his hand that *Dandelion Wine* was far from complete in terms of story sequence and bridging narrative; Congdon felt that the installment payments, which were expected to top out at $1,250 for five 100-page installments, was far less than a formal advance for a complete submission. But he knew that Walt Bradbury had a strong personal attachment to *Dandelion Wine* and would do what he could when it came time to finalize the advance. As it was, Ray Bradbury's promise to submit timely installments proved unrealistic—it would take almost four months to work up a stable outline for the story sequence. On August 14, 1956, Bradbury finally sent off a working outline for *Dandelion Wine*, and it did not disappoint.

The outline shows evidence of a crucial shift in Bradbury's state of mind. He was no longer trying to bring the old Illinois novel's youth rebellion plot structure to life; since April, he had managed to turn his imagination to the task of weaving continuities into the extracted stories that had become *Dandelion Wine*. They had been pulled from all sections of the novel, and for the most part represented the episodes that had the least direct relevance to the narrow plot of the original work.

He tied these episodes together by linking the common elements—the wonderful machines, both human and technological, that the boys of Green Town encounter during the summer of 1928: Mr. Tridden's antiquated town trolley; the eccentric electric car of Miss Fern and Miss Roberta; the memories of the Civil War and the great western buffalo herds that make old Colonel Freleigh a living time machine; Leo Auffmann's plans for a Happiness Machine; and the mechanical tarot witch of the carnival arcade. One by one, these marvelous machines fail, or die, and the despondent Douglas Spaulding falls into a life-threatening fever.

Bradbury would later reflect on this crisis in very personal ways, for the great unseen character that emerges from *Dandelion Wine* isn't the murderous Lonely One, waiting for Lavinia Nebbs to come up out of the ravine and meet her fate; it is, in reality, the writer himself:

> It was a rummage through a fabled attic or basement storehouse. . . . I believe the past is both bad and good, it can both wound and heal. If one goes to it to suffer, to self-lacerate, of course the junk must go out of the attic into the incinerator. But if it can be used to instruct, then a man extends himself in

time, and becomes whole. . . . A man cannot possibly speak futures, unless he has a strong sense of the past. . . .

So in writing *Dandelion Wine*, I was doing more than time-traveling fueled by nostalgia. I was picking up and putting down objects which represented Noon and Midnight, good and evil, the vast cry of terror or the easeful sigh of relaxation on a summer evening early.[5]

By the end of 1956, the story progression and the emerging narrative bridges formed more than a sentimental exercise in nostalgia—here instead was an insightful glimpse of the passing age of innocence common to all. Time and memory, reflected in Grandfather Spaulding's dandelion wine and the junkman's dreaming wine, will preserve the past and give Douglas the strength to bear the passage into unknown futures. After a year of exhaustive experimentation, *Dandelion Wine* was finally complete. The remaining structures of the original Illinois novel (eventually re-titled *Farewell Summer*) would pick up the story line from there as Douglas enters the inevitable age of rebellion, but it would take Bradbury another fifty years to make the story whole.

16 | Return to Hollywood

Given the way that stage and television work was beginning to consume Ray Bradbury's time and creativity, it seemed odd—at least to Don Congdon and Walt Bradbury—that he remained hesitant to jump back into screenwriting. Part of his aversion centered on his reluctance to work for another dominating director like John Huston, but he was also wary of the midwife nature of the craft—adapting the work of another writer, a writer who would always have primacy over the adaptation as well as the original work. Screenwriters were, for the most part, anonymous in Hollywood, unless they had earned a reputation as original writers.

Since his return he had turned down (or failed to pursue) opportunities to work on *The Man with the Golden Arm*, *Diabolique*, *War and Peace*, *Good Morning Miss Dove*, 1984, *The Friendly Persuasion*, the unproduced *Lorenzo the Magnificent*, and various lowball offers for *Fahrenheit 451*. He maintained and extended his circle of Hollywood friendships, and the Famous Artists agency, hoping Bradbury would come around, kept his name in front of film and television producers. Finally, in early 1957, with *Dandelion Wine* at press, his resolve weakened.

Bradbury was drawn back into the business side of Hollywood by the rapid rise of the independent production team of Harold Hecht and Burt Lancaster, who together sustained the rebirth of United Artists throughout the mid-1950s. Hecht-Lancaster films produced with UA financial backing and distribution included *Vera Cruz*, the unexpectedly successful *Marty*, and *Trapeze*; in late 1956, Lancaster brought James Hill into the partnership to oversee the writers hired to develop the various properties. Ironically, it was Bradbury's personal experience with John Huston, rather than his screenplay for Huston's production of *Moby Dick*, that triggered his first Hecht-Hill-Lancaster (H-H-L) writing assignment. In early 1957 he was teamed with veteran writer John Gay to adapt Peter Viertel's vivid study of Huston, *White Hunter, Black Heart*.

Success seemed so very easy at Hecht-Hill-Lancaster, but the interpersonal relationships were complex and sometimes difficult. Bradbury initially discovered shared passions that helped him fit in—he and Lancaster had both been publicly critical of the McCarthy era, and they also shared a strong enthusiasm for opera. Lancaster had also lived in the world of the circus performer—both on-screen and in his early life—and Bradbury was privately thrilled to work so closely with the tradition that had informed his imagination since childhood. But Burt Lancaster was a man of many moods, and the constant pressures of success were manifest in the tensions that often broke through the surface illusions of open expense accounts and the new luxury offices on Canon Drive.

Bradbury greatly enjoyed his work with John Gay on the *White Hunter, Black Heart* adaptation. Viertel's novel described the 1952 location filming of *The African Queen*, focusing on Huston's instinctive brilliance as well as his chilling fixation on dominating and toying with those around him. Bradbury knew this world only too well, and John Gay found his insights useful as they outlined a treatment for *White Hunter, Black Heart*. Bradbury's familiarity with the material soon became a significant distraction, however, and his contributions to the script inevitably slipped away into anecdotal storytelling and psychological speculation. Together they completed only 30 pages of script outline; the project soon became a creative dead end, and the property would not be filmed for more than thirty years.

The Sweet Smell of Success, H-H-L's current film, was becoming problematic, and for a time Bradbury advised on the editorial process. Clifford Odets had been hired to step up the dialogue for this searing tale of a powerful New York gossip columnist who is intent on controlling the lives of all who surround him. It came close to the edge in terms of its rough language and potential for legal action; J. J. Hunsecker, played by Lancaster, was clearly inspired by the career of Walter Winchell. Tony Curtis's brilliant characterization of toadying publicist Sidney Falco was even more repellant. Falco's violently predatory actions toward his own secretary establish his dark character early in the film; Bradbury felt that the scene was gratuitously predatory, and he urged that it be cut down. The released version of this scene was in fact toned down, and to some extent Bradbury's viewpoint would have played into this decision.

Bradbury also argued against the ending that eventually took shape during postproduction. Throughout the film Lancaster's Hunsecker had been intent on controlling his younger sister and destroying her engagement to a jazz musician. Hunsecker almost succeeds, but he's psychically destroyed when his sister runs off and escapes his dominating will forever. The film ends in the gray light of a winter dawn viewed through long shots in street-level Manhattan, where Falco receives a vicious beating for failing Hunsecker. This sequence was settled only after great debate; during these often heated arguments, Bradbury offered a solution that bypassed the sequencing issue entirely. Given his position as a peripheral contract writer in the studio hierarchy, and the fact that his solution required additional shooting, it apparently received little serious consideration.

Despite its impracticality, however, Bradbury's recommendation reveals a great deal about his emerging views on cinematic action.

In contrast to his moderating view of the film's opening, Bradbury felt that the closing scenes should take a full measure of revenge on Lancaster's masterful portrayal of Hunsecker. In 2002 he would look back, in private conversation, on the failure of the film to take this course of action: "It's a fascinating film, but the ending's wrong, to me. . . . There's only one way to end this . . . you've got to kill him. It's not enough to have his sister walk away into the wilderness, you know, out of the city, with her boyfriend, because they're both wimps anyway. They never really stood up to the Lancaster character. They walk away at the end, and there's an incestuous overtone here, that because she's left, he's destroyed. I don't believe that for a minute. He's too strong a character. . . . Give me an unhappy ending that's justified."[1] For Bradbury, *The Sweet Smell of Success* required the satisfaction of vendetta, and in later years he would often cite the vengeful killings of John Borman's *Point Blank* as the perfect example of this formula.

Although he spent a great deal of time writing at his Hecht-Hill-Lancaster office, Bradbury was never regarded as a full-time screenwriter. He was too well established as a freelance fiction writer, and during the spring of 1957 many of his ongoing projects occasionally took priority over his work at H-H-L. During May 1957, Mort Abrahams made a second proposal on behalf of NBC for *Fahrenheit 451*. The previous year's proposal for *Producer's Showcase* was now replaced with an offer to option *Fahrenheit 451* for Alfred Hitchcock's new NBC venture, the hour-long dramatic series *Suspicion*. Bradbury had maneuvered himself into a position where he had to write or revise treatments for NBC; perhaps it was best that, just like the previous summer, the new *Fahrenheit* venture failed to materialize. Even so, such adaptation projects took him further away from the kind of original story writing that formed the very foundation of his reputation.

These conversations were soon overshadowed by the revived prospects for the science fiction television series that Bradbury had offered to the networks as early as 1952. His friend John Fulton, who had interested Kirk Douglas in the series early on, returned to the scene and convinced Bradbury, a cautious Ben Benjamin, and a very reluctant Don Congdon to sign an exclusive contract that allowed Fulton to represent the project, now known as *Report from Space*. Bradbury's plan was to project the first decade or two of space exploration in a docudrama format, with continuity provided by the interrelated *Chronicles* structure and, presumably, by modifying some of his freestanding science fiction stories. But he remained worried about the quality of television drama slotted into 30-minute programming, and confided to Tony Boucher that he held little hope for science fiction when other genres were set to dominate the 1957 prime-time schedule:

"The elephants follow each other's tails, and this autumn promises to be crime-western season, with horses rushing 'thataway' through Baker Street."[2]

As enjoyable as it sometimes was, his assignments at Hecht-Hill-Lancaster might have gone the way of his brief stints at MGM in 1952 and 1953, where the shifting financial fortunes and executive indifference to his materials led to a swift parting of ways. Then, unexpectedly, a most improbable stroke of luck intervened. Most of the major H-H-L negotiations began and ended at Harold Hecht's desk, and Bradbury was not surprised when an April 1957 visit to Hecht's office was interrupted by a trans-Atlantic telephone call from Sir Carol Reed in London inquiring about contact information for a Los Angeles–based author. He was, however, stunned to see Hecht look up at him and tell Reed that the author in question was standing in front of his desk.

Reed's quarter-century career as a director had evolved from the London stage through an impressive record of film successes, including his acclaimed 1949 adaptation of Graham Greene's early Cold War novel The Third Man. Greene had, in fact, set Reed off on his search for Bradbury; he had read Bradbury's "And the Rock Cried Out," either in an American edition of Fahrenheit 451 (the British edition deleted the companion tales), or, as "The Millionth Murder," in the May 1954 British edition of Manhunt magazine. He was impressed by Bradbury's speculations on Westerners stranded in Central America in a near future where the Cold War has suddenly escalated into a nuclear holocaust. Greene, already the expatriate author writing about politically charged places in the sun, had explored similar postcolonial themes in his most recent novel, The Quiet American; sometime in early 1957, he suggested to Reed that he might want to consider filming Bradbury's 7,000-word story.

By this point in his career Reed operated outside of the British studio system and had become an international director who negotiated his own productions from properties that he personally found creatively compelling. He preferred to work directly with authors, and once he decided that "And the Rock Cried Out" had a literary complexity that could be extended through film, he tried unsuccessfully to negotiate rights through a British producer. He had recently directed Trapeze in Paris for Hecht-Lancaster, and when the British negotiations failed to make contact, Reed decided to make the fateful call to Hecht. Within a few moments he was talking with the astonished Bradbury, who immediately expressed his willingness to adapt the story himself. Bradbury's agents at Famous Artists quickly negotiated an option through Hecht-Hill-Lancaster, where everyone was more than willing to renew their association with Reed.

17

"And the Rock Cried Out"

Hecht arranged for Sir Carol Reed to fly out to Los Angeles over the weekend of May 11–12, 1957, for three weeks of conferences centering on Bradbury's story and another property, the Robert Krepps novel *Tell It on the Drums*, which did not carry the foreboding sense of the near future that Bradbury's story promised.[1] Reed worked primarily with Bradbury on a detailed outline to determine if "And the Rock Cried Out" could be extended effectively for feature film production. The experience was marvelous for Bradbury, who found in Reed a director who valued authors and privileged storytelling above spectacle. In the end, Bradbury's 35-page outline extended well beyond the original story, which remained largely unchanged as the opening sequence of the film.

In early June 1957, Reed flew back to England and resumed work on his current film, *Stella* (his working title for *The Key*), but before leaving Los Angeles he convinced H-H-L to send Bradbury to London for the summer so that he could transform his outline into a feature-length screenplay in close consultation with Reed. Bradbury, still unwilling to attempt air travel, followed by rail to New York and embarked on June 7th aboard the SS *America*; four days later, Maggie and their three daughters followed from New York on board the French liner *Liberté*. The short-notice trip was reminiscent of their similar whirlwind departure in pursuit of John Huston almost four years earlier.

Bradbury began to transform his outline into a screenplay on June 13th, while still at sea. By June 20th, the family had settled into the Kensington Palace Hotel, not far from Reed's Chelsea home. Reed had arranged for Bradbury to work in seclusion where virtually no one could find him—a sparsely furnished office at the back of the top floor of 144 Piccadilly. It was both functional and odd in a way that appealed to Bradbury, if not to his few visitors. Near the end of his seven-week stay he was finally located by cinema reporter Peter Evans, who failed at first to convince two of the building's staff that Bradbury was there at all (they kept trying to send him to see a Mr. Cadbury instead). Evans noted the building's tomblike entrance and coffin-shaped elevator, which transported him to Bradbury's hideaway: "Finally, I discovered Bradbury seated behind a giant desk which was absolutely clear except for a portable typewriter and a sheaf of typing paper. This apart, the room was so bare it made Mother Hubbard's cupboard look overstocked. The window was open and there was an undisturbed view of a fire escape and a brick wall."

Bradbury's Muse was constantly inspired by this setting, which seemed to transfer the claustrophobic shadows of Melville's "Bartleby the Scrivner" from old New York to postwar London. The closeness of the room was free of the multitude of distractions he had experienced three years earlier in Ireland as he negotiated John Huston's mad world of manor houses and fox hunts. To be sure, he was thrilled to be working with another legend of film; *The Third Man* had made a vivid impression on Bradbury, who had taken Maggie to see it twice in the early 1950s and even bought the soundtrack phonograph recording at a time when the household budget could hardly afford such an indulgence.[2]

But the similarities between Huston and Reed ended with the element of fame that attracted him to both men. In early July, 1957, Bradbury described the crucial difference in a letter home to Bill Nolan: "[M]y relationship with Reed is delightful, I must say . . . far different from the Huston relationship, where I stood in too much awe of a god I had created out of whole cloth . . ." (ellipses Bradbury's). Bradbury himself was greatly relieved at the way that Reed encouraged him from the start. He had little trouble creating scenes to establish and extend his original story, which centered on the way that his characters John and Leonora Webb, traveling through Central America, respond to a sudden and total inversion of the world they had always known.

The original story of "And the Rock Cried Out," written during 1951, was relatively straightforward, but it had grown in interesting ways during the many months that it circulated. Congdon cycled it through twenty-three refusals before the genre pulp *Manhunt* took it for the September 1953 issue, changing the title to "The Millionth Murder." The editors saw both versions, but purchased the original shorter form; Congdon noted at the time that *Manhunt*'s editors "felt the new material which was pure philosophizing seemed to stick out in the story too much like a sore thumb."[3] A series of surviving longer drafts implicitly reflect Bradbury's growing frustration with the reluctance of mainstream magazines to take a story about race and postcolonial cultural divides. *Mademoiselle*, after a tentative acceptance, had paid Bradbury *not* to force them to publish it. He was able to publish a longer form of the story under its original title within the three-story *Fahrenheit 451* volume; now, nearly four years later, he returned to the basic story form to construct the new screenplay for Carol Reed.

A sudden atomic war across the entire northern hemisphere has left the Webbs to face life alone in a small jungle village along the Caribbean coast of Central America. Overnight, their status has changed; their passports mean nothing now, and they must work menial jobs in harsh servitude or die at the hands of people who hate what they stand for—centuries of exploitation by white colonial masters who have now endangered the entire planet with their genocidal war. The Webbs will not be scapegoats, however; they choose to walk out into the square, unafraid, and face the final vengeance of the mob. The title allusion to an old spiritual rings true: "I went to the Rock to hide my face | And the Rock Cried out, 'No Hiding Place, | There's no Hiding Place down here.'"

On June 28, barely a week into his working routine, Bradbury sent a summary of his progress to Tony Boucher: "I'm 75 pages into the first-draft of the screenplay, which looks fine and seems to be making Reed happy. . . . Where my original story ended with the two people going into the plaza to meet the mob, my screenplay goes on for at least 70 to 80 pages beyond that encounter, which I won't discuss now, but which, I assure you, I am absolutely fascinated and happy with, in outline, and which should write well when I come to it."

By mid-July Bradbury had completed an initial long draft of nearly 180 pages. He provided Reed with progress samples weekly; once Reed saw that the first draft was progressing according to the outline, he simply offered general words of encouragement. He understood Bradbury's need to push through an emotional and uninterrupted "take" on the extended narrative before beginning a reasoned analysis. From mid-July through mid-August, Bradbury met with Reed more regularly to revise and cut.[4]

Bradbury's extension of the story was based on a single extrapolation: what if John Webb falters in his resolve to face death at the hands of the villagers? Is he really so different from the proud exploiters of the past? At the last moment he steers their steps toward the church in the square. The priest's parishioners have long since turned away, however, and without the strength of the people, he cannot offer sanctuary. He leads the Webbs back to the hotel, where they will begin the work of the lowest servants. By this point in the screenplay, Bradbury had developed new and complex interactions between Webb and Leonora, who has far more faith in humanity than her husband. He also developed fully articulated village characters to replace the faceless mob, and these people, more than the proud but broken John Webb, control the rest of the action and provide an effective frame for a feature-length film.

The dark and brooding police chief, intent on extending his control over the entire region, uses Leonora as a pawn to force Webb, an accomplished scientist, to create weapons; the priest and various townspeople, powerless but compassionate, risk their lives to help the Webbs escape. The power of the police chief fades as the old technology fails, but the future is uncertain—northerly winds cause birds to fall lifeless from the sky, portending the nuclear fallout that may follow. The people return to their church for the first time in years, and the Webbs set out by sea with other Americans, heading north into uncertainty. Webb's final observation reflects Bradbury's growing certainty during this period in his career that Mankind will provide its own salvation. "Do prayers work?" Leonora asks as they set sail. "Men work," her husband replies. "And when they work very hard, *very* hard and well, it's the same thing as prayer."

Reed made it easy for Bradbury to believe in his work, and, perhaps more significantly, to believe in his director. This attitude came through from Reed's early days as a stage director; shortly after his working experience with Bradbury, Reed stated his guiding premise in a long interview with journalist W. J. Weatherby: "I think it is the director's job—as in the old theatre—to convey faithfully what the author had in mind. Unless you have worked with the author in the first place, you cannot convey to the actors what he had in mind nor can you convey to the editor at the end the original idea." As an independent director, Reed had more latitude to choose works that interested him personally. Bradbury's story attracted him both as a work of fiction and as a subject of international interest. This last factor was crucial, for the production companies he depended on for financing and distribution considered international interest to be an essential predictor for financial success.

Bradbury's uninterrupted mornings in his secluded Piccadilly office reinforced his natural tendency to work early in the day. During his afternoons, evenings, and weekends, Bradbury found himself in a different world entirely, and this contrast no doubt contributed to his overall creativity. As the weeks passed, his expanding world of social and professional contacts in London filled some of these open hours. British-born Joan Harrison, who had produced his first two episodes of *Alfred Hitchcock Presents* the previous year, was living part of the time in London. She had met the popular British mystery writer Eric Ambler while producing one of his stories, and they were now married. Bradbury struck up a friendship with Ambler and renewed his earlier friendship with Jeanie Sims, who had been John Huston's London secretary during Bradbury's 1953–54 *Moby Dick* screenwriting assignment. She now worked for Huston's former associate director Jack Clayton, who was just entering his best years as a film director and producer in his own right.

Jeanie Sims's flat was a natural gathering place for many of London's actors, and Bradbury enjoyed a number of evenings there. Leo Genn, who had played Melville's Starbuck in *Moby Dick*, would recite passages of Bradbury's beloved Kipling for him.[5] These encounters were great fun, as was his renewed friendship with Jack Clayton. Through Carol Reed, he met Academy Award–winning art director Vincent Korda, who had worked with Reed on Graham Greene's *The Third Man*. Bradbury was unfortunately unable to meet Greene, who had originally encountered his stories through his cousin, the Hollywood expatriate Christopher Isherwood. Greene's recommendation of Bradbury to Carol Reed had made the entire screenwriting trip possible, but he was not done promoting him; that summer, Greene persuaded his Scandinavian publishers, Norstedt and Soners Forlag, to bring out the first Swedish editions of Bradbury's work—*Fahrenheit 451* and *The October Country*.[6]

Jack Clayton and Jeanie Sims introduced Bradbury to John and James Woolf, whose highly successful Romulus production company had recently produced Clayton's award-winning film, *The Bespoke Overcoat*. During Bradbury's two months in London, Romulus executives nearly closed a deal to extend Bradbury's story "No Particular Night or Morning" into a feature film. This was one of the intriguing dark science fiction stories that had found its way into *The Illustrated Man*: What if the isolation of interplanetary space travel leads a crewman to deny the reality of the world left behind? No morning, no night, no Earth—just the void of deep space. Romulus wanted Fred MacMurray to be featured in the film adaptation, and word-of-mouth speculations on the project soon surfaced in the American press.[7] But science fiction was a rare film commodity in Great Britain, and the venture never materialized.

Bradbury was also able to spend time with his British publisher Rupert Hart-Davis. Like Berenson, Hart-Davis had become a trusted correspondent who would receive some of Bradbury's most personal views on art and life. Beyond the motion picture scene, and perhaps best of all from Bradbury's perspective, there were the constant discoveries of literary London. Bradbury made a pilgrimage to Dickens's memorial in Westminster Abbey and visited the sturdy Tudor confines of the Old Curiosity Shop. He passed through Baker Street quite often and promised Tony Boucher, a fine genre critic and writer of mysteries, to "breathe your name in the sacred surroundings."[8]

There were many museum afternoons and theater evenings with Maggie, and Bradbury absorbed this cultural milieu with Falstaffian gusto. The eccentric architectures of Sir John Soane's neoclassic townhouse museum enchanted him—in years to come he would use Soane's 1827 cross-sectional floor plan as his stationery letterhead. The museum contained the sarcophagus of Pharaoh Seti I; late in life, he sometimes suggested (with a wink) that he'd like to be buried there. Beyond London, their day-trips included Warwick Castle, Oxford, and Shakespeare's Stratford-upon-Avon.

Other adventures now beckoned, however. Bradbury finished his first settled version of *The Rock Cried Out* screenplay on Friday, August 9, 1957. After reviewing the extended adaptation with Carol Reed, they agreed to resume work on a production schedule in Los Angeles over the winter, when Reed planned to visit the Hecht-Hill-Lancaster offices. There they also hoped to finalize Reed's intention to make a short film of Bradbury's companion story "The Highway" as a prologue to the feature film itself. On August 17, Bradbury and his family set off—by ferry and rail—for Italy and their long-deferred reunion with Bernard Berenson.

18 Berenson at Sunset

Through his weeks with Sir Carol Reed in London, Bradbury was able to achieve the next milestone in his screenwriting career—to adapt his own fiction for film under the encouraging guidance of a legendary director who proved to be both mentor and friend. But even greater satisfaction awaited, for now he could at last return to Florence for a final visit with a cherished friend and mentor—the eminent Renaissance art historian Bernard Berenson, who was now 92 years old. Bradbury knew that only the salary and expense-paid life of an overseas screenwriting job would permit the return visit to Villa I Tatti that Berenson constantly urged him to make.

He had almost earned his way back to Florence a year earlier, in 1956, when the cash-strapped Bradbury asked his agents at Famous Artists to survey films scheduled for European production in the coming months. Immediate interest in Bradbury came from Copa Productions, an independent company formed by producer Ted Richmond and screen star Tyrone Power. Richmond wanted Bradbury to write the screenplay for *Lorenzo the Magnificent*, a biopic of the Renaissance Tuscan prince scheduled for location production in Florence. Here was a chance to work in Berenson's world, just a few miles from Berenson's villa, but the price was too high.

He greatly admired Power, but he confessed his equally great aversion to Richmond in a July 1956 letter to Berenson: "*Lorenzo the Magnificent*... was owned, I found, by a producer whose main occupation in life seems to be keeping his shoes shined, his pants pressed to a razor-edge, his cigar lighted, and his diamond ring polished to a brilliance that would blind the eye of mortal man. Since I could not imagine embroiling myself with such a personality—and with a vision of the *Laocoön* in my mind—I withdrew from the scene."

The imposing *Laocoön* sculpture group in the Vatican, a representation of the mythological moment when Troy's high priest Laocoön and his sons are killed by Poseidon's sea serpent for arguing against the Greek gift of the Trojan Horse, offered a more modern caution for Bradbury. He would later tell Berenson that he had come to see the *Laocoön* as the "almost blind eating and casting out, devouring and moving on" of commercialized art and literature.[1] It would take another year, and an author-oriented director like Carol Reed, to lure him back to an international film venture. Finally, in mid-August 1957, fully satisfied with *The Rock Cried Out* screenplay, Bradbury set out from London with his family for Italy.

They spent two weeks touring Rome before setting out for four nights in Tuscany. This time Rome had provided the major cultural discoveries, and the brief stay in Tuscany centered on Berenson himself. Nicky Mariano sent Berenson's car for Bradbury and Maggie on the 5th, but this time their destination was not the nearby Villa I Tatti. It was a hotter season than their first visit, and they found Berenson and Nicky in the higher altitudes of his summer home, the more intimate Casa al Dono in Vallombrosa. The delight of the reunion was tempered by the very obvious evidence of Berenson's decline. In his 1961 UCLA interviews, Bradbury recalled how Berenson resented the inevitable visual consequence of the reunion: "He resented, of course, that we could see the fact that, finally, time was catching up with him."

Nevertheless, Berenson was able to take one slow turn through Casa al Dono's woodland gardens, offering a final word of caution that demonstrated his clear understanding of Bradbury's rising popularity and the temptations that awaited his return to America. Berenson's words lingered in his mind for many weeks, and he soon shared them with his Doubleday editor Walt Bradbury: "I cannot help but remember Mr. Berenson's taking my arm and walking with me through the woods outside his mountain house a few weeks ago, cautioning me not to be affected by 'gold or glory.'"[2]

This simple fatherly platitude nevertheless resonated like the earlier words of encouragement he had received from such intellectual luminaries as Christopher Isherwood, Aldous Huxley, Gerald Heard, and Bertrand Russell: "[C]oming from him, once again they made me feel everything was worthwhile."[3] It was a spoken admonition, and would be followed by fewer and fewer written words as Berenson's letters diminished to short notes and cards prepared by Nicky. By contrast, Bradbury's side of the correspondence continued to flow across the Atlantic in great waves of creative speculation and self-examination.

He went on in these letters to present his views on the nature of literary criticism, and he did so with more detachment than he could ever muster in his letters to his agent or his editors. Here he was speaking to his intellectual father, and the words were more insightful than strident. In these final letters he spoke to Berenson about his unexpected and unwanted role as a spokesman, of sorts, for science fiction among mainstream readers and about his more welcome but equally unexpected role as a lay spokesman for American Space-Age aspirations in the aftermath of the Sputnik scare. And he talked about the new voice he was finding in nonfiction prose—the voice of a writer who could talk, with conviction and enthusiasm and persuasion, about the art of writing.

On September 7th, the Bradburys boarded an overnight train for Paris. This was not just a final sightseeing destination before embarking for home—the four days and nights in Paris had far-reaching implications for Bradbury's career. On the evening of the 10th, they dined with one of Bradbury's dearest friends—Madame Man'Ha Garreau-Dombasle, an accomplished author whose husband was a distinguished French diplomat and longtime advisor to Charles De Gaulle. A most improbable friendship had grown from a chance meeting on the shores of Mexico's Lake Janitzio a dozen years earlier. Bradbury and Man'Ha met on a midnight boat ride to the island village of Janitzio for the candlelight observances ushering in the Day of the Dead—November 1, 1945.

Their mutual passion for writers and writing made them natural companions through the night's excursion, but they parted at dawn—Man'Ha, with her daughter, returning to Mexico City and Bradbury, with his friend Grant Beach, continuing on his three-month journey collecting masks for the Los Angeles Art Museum. Bradbury did not even know her name, and he never thought he would see her again. That afternoon, however, as he crossed an intersection in nearby Patzcuaro to shop for masks, a limousine pulled over; Man'Ha called to him, introduced herself, and gave him her card. And then, quite simply, she changed his life forever. First, she suggested that he and Beach should stop in Guanajuato to see the famous catacomb of mummies—an experience that resonated through his writing for decades. And then she made him promise to write and tell her all about his rising career as a writer.[4]

Their friendship would last until her death in 1999, at the age of 101, but by 1957 she had already endowed Bradbury with a lifetime of encouragement and a priceless introduction to the French literary establishment. Her own literary standing was indisputable; as early as the 1920s, Man'Ha (originally Germaine Massenet) was known for contributions to literary magazines and French translations of the poetry of Rabindranath Tagore. Her 1936 novel Sati led Benjamin Peret to identify her with the Surrealist movement, but the Second World War would extend her influence across French literature. When France fell to Germany, her husband, Maurice Garreau-Dombasle, was finance attaché to the French embassy in Washington, D.C.; he allied himself with De Gaulle, and became the Free French representative to the United States. Man'Ha subsequently supported exiled French writers in America, including André Breton, Saint-John Perse, and Jules Romains. Later in the war, when Maurice became De Gaulle's ambassador to Mexico, she befriended the lyric and Surrealist Mexican writer Octavio Paz.

She followed Bradbury's publishing milestones closely and found a kindred element of Surrealism throughout his best work. It's likely that French Surrealist writers, including her friend André Breton, author of the movement-defining *Surrealist Manifesto* in the 1920s, were initially led to Bradbury's fiction by Man'Ha even before the long-delayed French translations of *The Martian Chronicles* and *The Illustrated Man* reached print in 1954. The Bradburys had briefly visited Man'Ha in Paris during their first journey to Europe that year, and the chance to reprise that visit during the late summer of 1957 was almost as important as their return visit to Berenson. Dinner on September 10th was followed by a chauffeured excursion with Man'Ha to Versailles the next day. That evening, Man'Ha and other literary figures joined the French press at a cocktail party hosted by Denoel, Bradbury's Paris publisher, in honor of the new French edition of *The October Country*.

Parisian newspapers carried reports of the event, announcing Bradbury's recent film work with Sir Carol Reed as well. Thanks to Man'Ha and Denoel, Bradbury's reputation as a major imaginative writer was spreading among the French intellectual community. A review of *The Martian Chronicles* by Michel Carrouges and a broader review of Bradbury's fiction by Michel Deutsch were beginning to establish a Surrealist reputation for Bradbury in France.[5] These critics found Bradbury's creative hallmarks—his haunting dream-logic, his reverie-based exploration of man's deepest feelings, and his appropriation of Space-Age machinery without any reference to scientific logic—to be richly surreal; here was an unstructured, almost intuitive, but nevertheless extremely creative form of Surrealism that would be highly regarded by many (but certainly not all) French critics. The Denoel celebration marked the beginning of a canonical process that would place Bradbury, along with Faulkner and Poe, among the major figures in French rankings of American literary masters. Late in life, this process would culminate in France's highest literary honor—Commander, French Ordre des Arts et des Lettres.

On September 12, 1957, Bradbury and his family sailed for New York from Le Havre on board the SS *United States*. Before leaving Paris, he was reminded that this trip, as well as much of his working life, had been spent in the company of women. Half a century later, he would recall this incident in a private interview: "I was walking along the street in Paris one night, along the Champs-Élysées. . . . I heard some little high heels tapping beside me. I looked over, and here this woman of the night was walking beside me. I began to laugh, and this woman went, 'Monsieur, why are you laughing?' I said, 'Because, back in the hotel I have one wife, one nurse, three daughters; at home I have three female aunts, three female cousins. The last thing I need is one more woman.' She laughed, and she said, 'Good enough.' So she walked me to the end of the Champs-Élysées, and we said good night."[6]

19 | The Unforeseen

The last days of Bradbury's European itinerary offer a subtle indicator of his accelerating drift away from his colleagues in the world of science fiction. In mid-August 1957, a letter from British science fiction magazine editor Ted Carnell had found its way to 144 Piccadilly. The letter contained a final and rather persuasive attempt to convince Bradbury to attend the 15th World Science Fiction Convention (WorldCon) in London, scheduled for September 6–9 at the nearby King's Court Hotel. In many ways, Carnell was the editorial dean of British science fiction, and even though most of Bradbury's science fiction stories had found their way to the more literary British *Argosy* rather than his own genre magazines, he had maintained a cordial relationship with Bradbury for some time. Carnell offered the prospect of BBC television coverage and the opportunity for live studio interviews—something that would never happen at American genre conferences of that time.

The main attraction for Bradbury would be more personal, and Carnell knew it: "[I]t would be a great honour for all of us if you could manage to drop in during the Convention, if only to meet some of your old friends—Arthur Clarke is flying in from Ceylon; John W. Campbell Jr. as Guest of Honor [*sic*] is flying over; Forry [Ackerman] will be coming over on the special charter plane bringing a further 55 Americans. We don't stop there—others coming by sea."[1] John Wyndham, now at his peak as a master in the tradition of Bradbury's beloved H. G. Wells, was serving as WorldCon president, and he very much wanted to meet Bradbury for the first time.

But Bradbury was already preparing to depart London for Rome and his subsequent Tuscan rendezvous with Berenson, and the very weekend of the WorldCon he would be in Paris preparing for his literary reception the following week. Many of the attendees would be disappointed by this near miss; those who knew how near he really was to the WorldCon would have been annoyed, or worse, given his election to the board of the Writers Guild of America (West) that fall. His Parisian reception wasn't until the following Wednesday, and a younger Bradbury might have made a solo weekend trip across the short distance to London; any private lack of enthusiasm for the WorldCon would remain masked by his more immediate desire to minimize the stress of travel for Maggie and the girls.

The Bradburys debarked in New York on the morning of September 17, 1957, planning to stay for a week. The schedule allowed Bradbury and Maggie an evening out with Gilbert Highet and his wife, the novelist Helen MacInnes. Highet, who spent much of his high-profile career at Columbia University as a promoter of the Humanities in mass culture, had been won over to the merits of science fiction and fantasy largely by discovering the poetic and metaphorical richness of Bradbury's stories. They had become fast friends, and the four went out for Bradbury's first viewing of Disney's *Twenty Thousand Leagues under the Sea*.[2] In a few years, Bradbury would write the introduction to the popular Bantam edition of Verne's masterpiece, but during this trip through New York Bradbury's most significant encounter involved the media's increasing ability to distract him from his storytelling roots.

His interview with John Wingate on WABD television's *Night Beat* show offered a glimpse of the self-confident and somewhat dominating media personality that he would soon become. This was a new mask for Bradbury, and it made an impression on New York–based documentary film producer Alex Haberstroh, who was engaged in negotiations with John Fulton to supply actual rocket launch footage for Bradbury's proposed *Report from Space* television series. The week after Bradbury's appearance on *Night Beat*, Haberstroh sent his impressions to Fulton, noting that he was "unprepared for his fabulous candor . . . such as being *glad* that McCarthy is dead, and his belief that his concepts of God and religion are *larger* than those held by today's organized religions. This was like good fresh air to me, having heard so many, many statements calculated to avoid 'unnecessary offense.'"[3]

Bradbury had certainly earned the right to criticize McCarthy's legacy—his 1952 "Letter to the Republican Party" and the 1953 publication of *Fahrenheit 451* had been courageous acts at the height of McCarthyism, but his *Night Beat* comments went where few would follow. In a similar way, his conviction that religious leaders would eventually have to accommodate the Space Age had surfaced as early as his 1951 *New York Times* interview with Harvey Breit, but by 1957 his expression was less nuanced in ways that left him vulnerable to out-of-context quotation. The *Night Beat* interview, aired in the last days of the Dumont network, was not widely viewed, but it was an indication of things to come. Depending on his mood and audience, Bradbury was evolving into a speaker who could be motivational, polarizing, openly controversial, or—at times—all three.

He now spoke openly on more personal topics as well. His wonderful working relationship in London with Sir Carol Reed, so different from the stressful months with John Huston three years earlier, may have prompted his first public criticism of Huston. The August 31, 1957, issue of London's *Picturegoer and Film Weekly* parlayed a Bradbury interview into a larger retrospective titled "Huston Brings Out the Worst." On October 14, the *New York Post*'s Archer Winsten, who had interviewed Bradbury during his recent New York stopover, published Bradbury's detailed recollections of his falling-out with Huston under the title "Ray Bradbury Disillusioned." This was certainly not front-page news; although Huston was a high-profile director, there were far more critical commentaries in print. But Bradbury's comments were out of character; he had settled these very personal matters in his own mind more than a year earlier. The lead paragraph in Burt Rainer's *Picturegoer and Film Weekly* article was perhaps too close to the mark: "They say that John Huston . . . brings out the best in actors. Some people he works with seem to think that he brings out the worst in them."

These subtle shifts in Bradbury's public persona raised few eyebrows as he prepared to make the long rail journey home with his family. But Bradbury's sense of continuity in his professional and personal life was about to vanish in unexpected ways. The Unforeseen visited his personal life first; a call home to his mother provided the first news that his father had been hospitalized for two weeks with appendicitis. In recent years the enigmatic Leo Bradbury, a rugged outdoorsman who hid his passion for reading almost as much as he hid his love for his younger son, had begun to show affection in unspoken ways. His mother had not wired her son about the surgery for fear of worrying him, and in a largely unreasoned attempt to make up for lost time he took the next available train from New York, leaving Maggie, his three daughters, and their governess to follow him home to Los Angeles on the original railroad booking.

Bradbury found that the strong man who never took help from others was desperate for his son's return, and he immediately moved his father out of the veteran's hospital to more private accommodations in the Santa Monica hospital. But Leo's localized symptoms of appendicitis masked a more serious case of peritonitis, and he suffered a stroke that soon proved fatal. His father seemed unable to communicate, but Bradbury's two-a-day visits were rewarded with a few final whispered words: "I went to visit him one night, and I leaned over him, and he said two things. One, his lips moved, and I said, 'Are you trying to say, 'I love you'?' He said 'Yes.' And then he said—his lips moved again—and he said, 'I want to die.' He'd had it. He'd been sick for six weeks. . . . This talk of releasing your family to death—it's easy to talk about, but you can't do it when it comes time. . . . I went away destroyed by the whole thing."[4]

He took one healing insight from his father's deathbed, and by December 1957 he was able to share his considered thoughts in a letter to Berenson: "I did not understand my father, yet this lack of comprehension contributed in a strange sad way to my love for him in the last weeks. Not being able to reach him on one level, the verbal, I sought and found other ways just as meaningful, for I know now, what I have always guessed and half-known, that a touch or embrace, is a language, too, and my father knew this."

Bradbury now had to face a new phase of life within his own household as well. Maggie had long since taken on the responsibilities of parenting for their three daughters, and on this basic level the stress had been accumulating for years. It had surfaced briefly when their second daughter Ramona was born in 1951, and for a time Bradbury wrote his fictions long into the night within the detached Clarkson Road garage. Stress returned in late 1953, during the long winter nights in Dublin when she could no longer bear to see John Huston drive her husband close to despair over the *Moby Dick* script. She had learned to bear the burden of parenting, but the Huston experience had shown her something that she could not bear forever—the ways in which Hollywood quite possibly threatened to change her husband in other, less obvious, ways.

By the summer of 1955 Bradbury was deeply committed to the world of television, and his agents on both coasts had to handle the complicated dynamics of his rising media prominence. These ventures soon had unexpected consequences—for each project that was produced, many others fell by the wayside, and the lack of time to write new stories seemed to propel him deeper into the sideshow world of television and film adaptations. In early 1957, his return to motion picture studio work signaled a new level of risk, and the delightful cultural adventures of a second trip to Europe could not mask the danger. As they returned home, Maggie realized that there was no end in sight—further work on *The Rock Cried Out* would mean more months in the Canon Drive suites of Hecht-Hill-Lancaster, one of the most prominent and high-pressure independent production companies in the business.

Even if he didn't buy into the lifestyle at Canon Drive, Bradbury was perhaps too close to this world to see how it might be changing his personality. But Maggie was an excellent judge of character, and she couldn't miss the way her husband was beginning to overextend himself and, to some extent, to reinvent himself as a visionary but somewhat intolerant creative writer. Much of this played into his natural optimism and desire to make his own breaks, but his recent *Night Beat* interview was an indicator that being Ray Bradbury was becoming a difficult proposition. There were times, both in Rome and again after returning to Los Angeles in September 1957, when she was not sure that she could bear up. In the end, she found a way.

But Bradbury never saw that these private tensions at home might be the result of anything more than the unequal burden of parenting. He never believed that the consequences of rising fame could affect those closest to him, and on the surface he felt that he could ward off such consequences by simply confessing his sins. A few weeks earlier, Berenson had warned him away from the temptations of gold and glory; but when he related Berenson's words to Walt Bradbury, he added a telling corollary: "I have always been able to resist, on innumerable occasions, gold; but I'm afraid I'm basically predisposed toward a soupçon, if not a tureen, of glory."

Within days of his return, two more unexpected events tested his faith in New York publishers and West Coast television producers. On October 4, 1957, Russia launched Sputnik, the first artificial Earth orbital satellite; the following day, the U.S. Naval Research Laboratory confirmed the satellite's radio signal during four passes by Sputnik *over* the United States. For most Americans these events marked the beginning of the space race, but for writers like Bradbury, who had been pushing for space exploration in the media as well as in their own fictions, there was an even greater sense of urgency. Bradbury's very emotional response was amplified when he discovered that Doubleday's hardbound edition of *The Martian Chronicles* was now out of print. Doubleday had time to exercise their reprint clause, and with the Bantam mass-market paperback still selling well, there seemed to be no need to hurry—until now.

On October 19th, Bradbury sent Doubleday's Walt Bradbury an emotionally charged request to bring out a new edition of the *Chronicles*, noting how Sputnik was already changing how his work was being received: "A year ago, six months ago, speaking to audiences, I invariably mentioned my belief that we would be on the Moon in 10 years, on Mars in 25 years. Laughter always followed. This week, addressing the same sort of group one night, there was no laughter." But Bradbury was also fearful that the hard-earned credibility of veteran writers was now in jeopardy: "Already, Johnny-come-latelies are swarming into our field. They will borrow many of the ideas that I myself, or Heinlein or Sturgeon or you-name-him first introduced, and these late-comers will get all the credit, all the publicity, all the money, all the glory. Witness: Nevil Shute and *On the Beach*."

Bradbury was particularly sensitive about *On the Beach*, which offered a similar situation—American nuclear war survivors stranded in a foreign land—to his own earlier "And the Rock Cried Out," which he had just so painstakingly adapted to film for Sir Carol Reed. *On the Beach* was also being adapted for film and would prove to be a complicating factor in Bradbury's future negotiations with Hecht-Hill-Lancaster. Although he was talking to a trusted friend and advisor, he was explicit in his request that Doubleday release The Martian Chronicles if a new edition and a dynamic publicity campaign failed to materialize.

Walt Bradbury took no offense at the alarmist overtones of the letter and reassured his friend that the Chronicles remained a long-term priority at Doubleday. In the months ahead, Doubleday's efforts would fall far short of the desired outcome, but for the moment, and for many weeks to come, Ray Bradbury would be totally absorbed by a television show that had aired the night before Sputnik's launch. On October 3, 1957, the popular and critically acclaimed CBS weekly drama series Playhouse 90 aired a science fiction episode written by Robert Alan Aurthur—"A Sound of Different Drummers," featuring veteran film stars Sterling Hayden and John Ireland as "Bookmen" who destroy books in a dystopic world of the near future. The production was directed by John Frankenheimer, a leading figure in the 1950s golden age of television drama. It was a compelling and well-directed show, presented with minimal sets on a deep and darkened sound stage. It also had a number of striking parallels to Fahrenheit 451.

There had been harbingers. A week earlier, Bradbury was cautioned by a director he knew at CBS television who had seen a few moments of the rehearsal and thought that the show was uncomfortably close to Fahrenheit. Bradbury did not take this too seriously; he had a long history with CBS television and had seen five of his stories or original teleplays presented on network shows. In fact, the CBS series Rendezvous was already working on a half-hour production of "The Magic White Suit" scheduled for 1958. But on Sunday evening he began to receive calls from East Coast viewers who had already seen it and from his friend Bob Kirsch, a Los Angeles book review columnist who told him to turn on Playhouse 90 to see the end of the West Coast broadcast.

Many more calls came in that night and on the morning of October 4th, Jack Sher, a screenwriter who had successfully pressed three plagiarism suits, called to suggest the potential damage to the stage version of Fahrenheit 451—a project that had never been far from Bradbury's mind since his first attempt for Laughton two years earlier. The 4th was a Monday, and Ben Benjamin wasted no time calling the head of the CBS business office. It was apparently not the first call in to CBS; Benjamin reported that their lawyers were already reading Fahrenheit. CBS soon provided Aurthur's script for "A Sound of Different Drummers," and within a week scheduled a kinescope viewing for Bradbury at the studio. Bradbury detected minor overtones of Brave New World and 1984 in the show as well, but he was now firmly convinced that major conceptual and plotting elements were taken directly from Fahrenheit 451.[5] He asked Ben Benjamin to have Famous Artists agency lawyer Harry Sakolov prepare a suit for damages.

But Sakolov delayed action, and in late October Ben Benjamin urged an increasingly anxious Bradbury to be patient for the time being. On November 6, 1957, Congdon advised setting a deadline with Famous Artists for legal action, but he also explained the complicating factors that Bradbury had so far either ignored or minimized: "One has to be aware that Famous, or any agency for that matter, does a tremendous amount of business with CBS, and they are not equipped to think entirely from your point of view, as would an attorney." Bradbury reluctantly accepted the realities of the situation, but never fully understood why Famous Artists could not take sides in what he considered a clear case of plagiarism. When his November 15th deadline passed, Bradbury turned to Gerson Marks and Sandford Carter, partners in a private legal firm that had some experience with this kind of action.

Congdon provided Marks with a fully documented paper trail of the 1952 and 1955 negotiations for the "Fireman"/Fahrenheit properties. The 1955 negotiation with Television Playhouse was crucial, since Aurthur, as the show's story editor, had participated in the discussions. Meanwhile, Bradbury prepared a detailed outline of the similarities between his novel and Aurthur's teleplay. He also prepared another synoptic outline identifying the distinct differences between Fahrenheit and the dystopic worlds of Huxley's Brave New World and Orwell's 1984. This proved to be a smart move, but a painful one; eventually, the CBS defense team would try to tear down Bradbury's credibility—and ultimately fail—by attacking the originality of Fahrenheit itself.

Bradbury hoped for a swift resolution through a settlement or, if necessary, a trial. But Marks was stonewalled by the CBS lawyers, who soon turned the case over to legal representatives of the network's insurance company. This new defense team continued to deny any resemblance between Fahrenheit 451 and "A Sound of Different Drummers," and rebuffed all discussion of a settlement. But the mounting stress was already evident in Bradbury's correspondence, emerging full-blown in an October 1957 letter to Rupert Hart-Davis: "I hope the plagiarism business can be settled soon, for I hate to sicken my life with a situation that verges on the psychotic if you allow yourself to dwell on it. I hate to suspect the worst of anyone. It has been a shock to see this wanton use of my material in front of 20 million people, which destroyed our TV rights and endangered our stage and film rights." He had no way of knowing that he would have to live with this burden for nearly four years.

Early in the new year, the Unforeseen struck one more time; on February 4, 1958, Bradbury learned that his longtime friend and mentor Henry Kuttner had died. It was an untimely death—he had been just four years ahead of Bradbury at Los Angeles High School—and the unexpected heart attack shocked Bradbury into admitting just how little he really knew about the man who had shaped his early writing discipline more than any other friend. "I never really understood Hank," he wrote to Congdon, "for he was a very quiet and reticent man, rarely social. Our meetings over the years, save for a few times, were those of student and teacher. He was one of the most thoughtful people I have ever known, and by this I mean a thinking man."

On this point, Bradbury's memory proved imperfect; the wartime letters he had received from Kuttner offered equal parts guidance and friendship, often including the combined wisdom of Kuttner and C. L. Moore, his wife and writing partner. As he told Congdon, Kuttner had been his "best and most consistent teacher." There would have been no argument from Leigh Brackett, who critiqued more of Bradbury's stories during the war years, for she had also profited from Kuttner's advice in prewar days. But now Brackett and her husband, Ed Hamilton, were the only Golden Age writers who remained close friends. He still had warm relationships with many other writers and fans from the old days, but he had read hardly any science fiction since the mid-1940s; contact was limited to occasional conventions, publishing events, and related correspondence.

Hank Kuttner was special, however; Bradbury had persuaded Congdon to represent his quiet friend during his final years, and now he lobbied hard for a chance to pull Kuttner's short fiction together in a unified collection free of the many pseudonyms that had limited public appreciation of his true stature in the field. It would take nearly two decades, but Doubleday's *The Best of Henry Kuttner* would carry a Bradbury introduction. Privately, however, it was the shared creativity of the Kuttner-Moore team, so different from Bradbury's fixation on going it alone, that both mystified and fascinated him. "They were an astounding marriage; one I've often admired, in my own ego and selfishness. They held hands and worked the same typewriter, something I could never do."

20 | Dreams Deferred

During the fall of 1957, Bradbury returned to Hollywood with one of the finest screenplays he would ever write. Sir Carol Reed fully intended that *The Rock Cried Out* would be his next picture, but he had to rely on the willingness of Hecht-Hill-Lancaster and United Artists to work it into their production plans. Unfortunately, the prospect of expensive location shooting in Mexico made the project problematic for H-H-L. Lancaster nevertheless picked up the option on *The Rock Cried Out* before the end of 1957; he shared Bradbury's hatred of racial prejudice and social injustice, and some of the other properties he and Hecht had acquired pushed back against the long-standing racial intolerance toward the Black community (*Take a Giant Step*) and Native Americans (*The Unforgiven*). Bradbury's exploration of how white Americans might react to the leveling consequences of atomic war had intrigued Hecht and Lancaster enough to invest in the development of the screenplay.

But the H-H-L films released from 1957 through 1959 would not be able to match the success of earlier times. *The Bachelor Party* and *The Sweet Smell of Success* were box office disappointments. The Academy Award–winning *Separate Tables* and *The Devil's Disciple* won critical praise but earned little. Bradbury felt that *Season of Passion*, the last film to be produced under the Hecht-Hill-Lancaster name, best exemplified the process of decline. While in England, Bradbury and Maggie had seen the stage play under its original title, *Summer of the Seventeenth Doll*. They walked out after the second act: "It was just a shoddy, boring, maudlin, banal exercise in not very good writing." But before Bradbury returned from Europe, H-H-L had purchased the property for $300,000 and would eventually spend another fortune on Australian production.

During the winter of 1957–58, Bradbury tried to interest H-H-L in taking an option on *The Martian Chronicles*, but even the added leverage of Sputnik and the accelerating space race failed to generate any significant interest. The big three were most comfortable with dark and unforgiving realism, and Bradbury found that the films developed during his time at H-H-L generally failed to culminate in a purgative release of tension. His sense of Aristotelian catharsis was self-taught and clearly more intuitive than methodical: "The writer, the artist in any society at any time is in the business of releasing tensions, of observing people and seeing that at a given time, they need to laugh, or at a given time, they need to cry. It is the shuttling back and forth between these two tensions that is really needed."[1] These words, spoken almost contemporaneously with the events, ran strongly against the harsh realism he had seen in screening *The Sweet Smell of Success*: "You come out of the theater feeling defeated by life. You feel that all the villains of the world are waiting outside the theater for you."

His overt criticism of H-H-L's investments in risky properties and large production budgets was not unnoticed: "I always felt they thought of me as a cuckoo who came out of the clock occasionally and struck the hour and went back. I was that odd-ball who lived upstairs at Hecht, Hill and Lancaster. Every time I went into a room with Jim Hill he sort of looked at me, and I just sensed I'd never work for these people again. We got on very well. It was very polite, but Harold Hecht always kind of sidled off. I felt that they just didn't figure me at all. They didn't understand me." Occasionally, they acknowledged the broader world of writing that he came from. In December, Hill accepted an inscribed copy of *Dandelion Wine* with an explicit acknowledgment of the divide: "I never quite get over the thrill of knowing an author first hand who really writes books." Hill also relayed a long transatlantic conversation with Sir Carol Reed confirming that the director's enthusiasm "remains unabated."[2] But the early months of 1958 passed without any decision about production for *The Rock Cried Out*.

Reed returned to Los Angeles in February 1958 to discuss production schedules. He sensed the corporate lack of commitment for Bradbury's screenplay, and before returning to London he found (or generated) interest from Kirk Douglas in the possible purchase of the property from H-H-L. Douglas and his Bryna production company had a long history of interest in Bradbury's *Report from Space* television project, and during the first week of April three cable calls with Reed in London brought Bryna very close to a commitment for *The Rock Cried Out*. Arrangements were made to bring Reed back to Los Angeles in June for script conferences in preparation for an early 1959 production schedule in Mexico.

The close connection between Lancaster and Douglas, who would soon share top billing in *The Devil's Disciple*, played in Bradbury's favor; H-H-L was now willing to make a breakeven sale of *The Rock Cried Out* script to Bryna. He wrote to Congdon on April 2, 1958: "I'll have a whole year to take my time, cut the script when I feel like it, and rewrite scenes. A good way to go about it." He returned to H-H-L in June 1958, still unsure if Bryna and Reed would be able to find backing in time to beat Stanley Kramer, who was going ahead with his own nuclear holocaust survival drama—Nevil Shute's *On the Beach*.

Congdon soon developed a backup plan; during June he met with Otto Preminger in New York and showed him a copy of Bradbury's script of *The Rock Cried*

Out. Bradbury cautioned Congdon that Preminger could only produce and would have to accept Sir Carol Reed as director. Preminger agreed to this condition, but never warmed to the script and declined it. Congdon found strong interest from the Dino de Laurentiis production group, but again failed to win a commitment. Meanwhile, Bradbury's hopes for the Bryna option advanced significantly when he ran into Kirk Douglas at H-H-L in mid-June, during his first week back in harness; Douglas, who was just leaving for England to film The Devil's Disciple for H-H-L, confirmed Bryna's continued strong interest in The Rock Cried Out and promised to resume discussions with Carol Reed while in London.[3]

Despite Kirk Douglas's enthusiasm for The Rock Cried Out and press reports of a production race with Stanley Kramer's time line for On the Beach, Bryna's producers could not go ahead without a distribution contract from a major studio.[4] Furthermore, Twentieth Century–Fox's Island in the Sun was already out, and that very successful adaptation of Alec Waugh's Caribbean novel directly addressed many of the controversial postcolonial subjects that The Rock Cried Out confronted. Sir Carol Reed was still fully committed to Bradbury's screenplay, but without a distributor there was no chance to arrange a Mexican production schedule for 1959. In mid-October 1958 Reed made a last-ditch effort to interest Columbia Studios in the project before heading to Cuba to begin work on Our Man in Havana, but to no avail. Bradbury and Reed would continue to solicit interest from Hollywood and foreign producers for years, but The Rock Cried Out would remain one of Bradbury's most significant stillborn creations.

Bradbury was also very close to a deal with Bryna for his science fiction television series and had captured the interest of veteran film star James Mason to portray Captain Black, one of his Martian Chronicles expedition commanders.[5] In early April 1958, Ben Benjamin had Bryna on the verge of committing to a feature film expanded from Bradbury's television script of "—And the Moon Be Still as Bright," the fourth and final tale of first contact in The Martian Chronicles. This script had long been projected as the first episode for the Report from Space series that producer John Fulton was handling, and now Bryna wanted to expand the adaptation into a feature-length film designed to sell a potential sponsor on the television series without investment in a pilot episode.

But such a film would take a long time to develop, and the burden of finding a sponsor for Bryna's first television venture fell to the Music Corporation of America, which provided Fulton's agency representation for the series. Without a sample half-hour pilot, however, MCA was unable to find a sponsor—even though Bradbury had now committed stories from both The Martian Chronicles and The Illustrated Man to the project. Bradbury had seen this kind of interest wax and wane for more than a year, and by June 22, 1958, his comments to Congdon revealed that the complicated freelance producer relationship with John Fulton had become a bit tiring: "Much foolish activity again. Flurries, trumpets, entrances, exits, alarums, excursions! Bah!" The quality of the television series was his main worry, as he noted in an August 10th letter to Congdon: "I want to do the show, yes, if it can be the best damn thing I can get on film; I'd work my heart out for that. But when I tune in the old idiot-box at night, my heart whelms up with doubt."

By the time he parted ways with Fulton, CBS had already decided on two new pioneering shows that would knock Bradbury's concept out of contention for the foreseeable future: William Lundigan's *Men into Space* series and Rod Serling's *The Twilight Zone*, which had gotten the green light for a pilot after a successful prototype episode, *Desilu Playhouse*'s "The Time Element," earned good reviews and substantial fan mail during the fall of 1958. Bradbury masked his disappointment in the various newspaper interviews he gave on the future potential for science fiction in prime-time television; he would have to wait another quarter-century before his own series would finally reach television audiences.

: : :

Bradbury's other *Martian Chronicles* project fared no better. By the spring of 1958 his complex contracts for a musical adaptation, which involved Hollywood composer Leonard Rosenman and New York producer David Susskind, also slowly collapsed.[6] Susskind saw a strong potential for humor in some of the eccentric characters and ironic scenarios found in some of the *Chronicles* chapters, but Bradbury was convinced that the darker elements of loneliness and man's unrelenting desire to dominate the new frontier required a more operatic kind of musical approach. In retrospect, Bradbury would boil it down to categorical examples: Susskind wanted Frank Loesser's *Guys and Dolls*, Bradbury wanted Lerner and Loewe's *Carousel*. "You're going to have an opera, almost an opera here, in the best tradition of *Carousel*. There's just no other musical I can think of that approaches it."[7]

There was always a sense of mutual respect between the two men, but Bradbury felt that here, just as in his relationships at Hecht-Hill-Lancaster, Susskind regarded him as odd and somewhat enigmatic. Bradbury wrote it off as simply an unfortunate creative pairing and worked with Congdon to arrange a termination by returning half of Susskind's $1,500 advance. He continued to work with Rosenman, however, and by June 1958 Bradbury had teamed up with veteran television and screenwriter Sid Carroll to develop the book concept of the *Martian Chronicles* musical. This collaborative project continued, off and on, through the rest of 1958 and 1959, but eventually the creative process itself proved to be the greatest obstacle.

Bradbury even wrote a song so that he could understand how music advances story action. He came to think of the interwoven processes of scene description and song lyric composition as a form of creative shorthand: "The hard thing to learn is how to condense and still not give away too much of the plot in the writing of the scene, so that you don't leave enough room for the songwriter." Bradbury had always felt that a talented writer could adapt to any form of performance literature, but for the time being he decided that "this strange medium of musical drama" required a natural talent that, at least in his case, could not be taught.

There would be other disappointments in the final years of the 1950s. John Houseman, who secured rights to two Bradbury stories for the very literate *Seven Lively Arts* television series, was never able to bring these properties to production.[8] But the biggest disappointment involved his high hopes for a new Doubleday edition of *The Martian Chronicles*, which might finally display his settled intention for the contents. He had asked for the deletion of "Usher II," the restoration of "The Fire Balloons," and the addition of "The Wilderness" and "The Strawberry Window" to the original mix of Doubleday's first edition story-chapters.

Seven years out from original publication, Bradbury felt that the way men of God might face an alien world ("The Fire Balloons"), an original *Chronicles* chapter unwisely pulled just before publication, had new relevance now that manned space flight was no longer a dream of the far future. "The Wilderness" and "The Strawberry Window" would enrich the pioneering spirit that was largely limited to the short bridging chapters of the first edition. But Doubleday executives would not approve a change in content or even a new typesetting; Bradbury would have to settle for a new dust-jacket painting and an introduction by Clifton Fadiman, who managed to extend the annoyingly persistent myth that Bradbury mistrusted science rather than the government leaders who control it.

21 | The Great Wide World

The national alarm over Sputnik, the shock of the *Playhouse 90* plagiarism, and the tragedy of his father's death all happened during the first three weeks of October 1957, just a matter of days after his late September return from Europe. There had been very little time to take in the reviews of *Dandelion Wine* or to consider what the book might mean for his career. Robert Bowen, writing in the September 7 issue of the *Saturday Review*, came through in a big way, praising the essential truth of Bradbury's small-town world as the best since Mark Twain, a work of "real literary merit." The September *Harper's* magazine review praised the moral insights and Bradbury's privileging of human values in an age now largely controlled by technology, yet found the book too sentimental and "unbearably cute" to ring true. Basil Davenport's *Book-of-the-Month Club News* review found the same sense of wonder evident in Bradbury's earlier books, effectively presenting a powerful sense of "the evanescence of things, and the power of memory to keep them alive." Favorable reviews also appeared in the *Chicago Tribune*, the *New York Herald Tribune*, the *San Francisco Chronicle*, *Kirkus*, and the *Library Journal*.

But in Great Britain, *Dandelion Wine* signaled the beginning of the end for Bradbury as a widely popular author. British critics had been impressed with the mastery of image and poetic intensity of his science fiction, but they were less inclined to appreciate his very American brand of nostalgia. The London *Tribune* reviewer suggested "it might have been easier on the reader if he had been just a little less Bradbury and not striven so much for effect." The *Times Weekly Review* noted archly how "No unkind intrusion of cynicism or even honest realism troubles the sun-drenched little Eden of *Dandelion Wine*," and how perceptive scenes were often "muffled by cotton-wool sentimentalism." For the Manchester *Guardian's* Patricia Hodgart, the lyric intensity was not unlike Dylan Thomas, but the theme was overshadowed by grotesque characterizations. The October 20, 1957, Sunday *Times* of London was kinder, and the *Telegraph* put *Dandelion Wine* on a level with the best of Walter de la Mare, but the major British reviewers who had weighed in favorably on his science fiction titles were silent or subdued.

In time, Bradbury offered his most illuminating reflections to Berenson. In his very long letter of February 28, 1958, Bradbury reflected on how the American success of his largely autobiographical *Dandelion Wine* led him to look back on his own lifetime of reading. In these passages Bradbury offered one of the first major statements on the duality of his reading life:

> When I look back upon my adolescence it can best be illustrated by the ravening appetite one had for certain books. It was really a process of devouring certain authors whole and entire. It was true of childhood, too. It was literary cannibalism at full-pitch. I ate Jules Verne, fingernails, top-hat, and all. I made meals of Poe, Tom Swift, H. G. Wells, and later, Thomas Wolfe, John Steinbeck, Willa Cather, and many others. The point is, it was a hunger over and above any immediately rational explanation. I simply needed to be fed, my taste ran wild, I ate the food that sustained me. Later, my taste, my hunger, was refined. But there is still in me the raw excitement and admiration for magicians, runaway balloons, fireworks, dragons, castles, monsters, that filled me in those days.

But he also told Berenson how the British reviews of *Dandelion Wine* had been negative for the most part, "the first time in all my years of publishing that I've had such a terrible reaction to a book from any country anywhere." This too was a matter of taste, and he extended his metaphor of consumption to this new experience:

> [T]hese gifts from my subconscious, the gifts from any artist's subconscious are then displayed to the world for breakfast, lunch and dinner. The world eats sparingly or eats well. If the artist is lucky, the world comes back for seconds. The gift given is the gift wanted. The gift offered to the U. S. in my *Dandelion Wine* seems to have been the most desired. . . . But now we find ourselves in England, a country where I did not grow up, where I was not born or shaped in any way. They do not hunger for my book, they find me all sticky marmalade and no bread. What can I do about this? Nothing, of course. . . . If you can look straight in the face of one who finds sustenance elsewhere, and accept it, you are well on your way to a long and adjusted life.

Bradbury was developing a perspective to deal with the deferred dreams of film and television, a perspective that he described for Berenson as "a kind of philosophy for any artist so he can live comfortably in the world." He could express the root metaphor to Berenson with a candor that would never appear in his public writings:

Well, it seems to me that while there is a small core of aesthetic and critical inquiry in the world, toward which an artist may cast a glance on occasion, the world itself is this almost blind eating and casting out, devouring and moving on. . . . We are then part of this great earthworm (block that metaphor) that eats tonnages of swill every day, and with it a few vitamins (I consider myself a vitamin) with which to sustain the brain in its head as well as the one in its tail. . . . Occasionally a writer finds himself popular not only with the Big Maw but with the critics and reviewers who trot beside the Idiot Beast. It doesn't happen often. I've had a little taste of it.

Through the experiences of his two extended sojourns in Britain and continental Europe, Bradbury was learning to navigate the turbulent boundaries between the arbiters of intellectual and popular culture. He now had firsthand experience with the art of the Renaissance, the neoclassical and romantic periods, and modernity, and he was forming an aesthetic around the more fantastic, sublime, impressionistic, and surreal genius of certain innovative favorites. He was fascinated by texture, by contrasts of light and dark, and by subjects that crossed over into dream and reverie. By the late 1950s he was beginning to categorize art by his own very impressionistic and surreal standards, and developed classifications that had little to do with rational analysis at all.

For Bradbury, the aesthetic impulse had always centered on bringing beauty into everyday life. His domestic sense of beauty as an everyday pleasure was certainly in line with his now fully formed passion for Renaissance and nineteenth-century romantic art, where beauty of form dominated. Architectural forms caught in dreamlike perspectives appealed to him regardless of period, and this explains his great passion for Piranesi's finely executed views of roman ruins, his more haunting imaginary prison vaults known as Carceri d'Invenzione, and Joseph Michael Gandy's paintings of Regency London fused into surreal romanesque decay.[1] As a writer, Bradbury has often been classified as a neoromantic, but Gilbert Highet may have offered a more discerning distinction when he described his good friend as a neoclassical fabulist.

Bradbury's European travels had also led him to John Martin's powerful Old Testament paintings of Heavenly wrath, as well as Martin's striking architectural fantasies. A magazine purchased from a store on Rome's Via Veneto in 1957 opened up the fantastic worlds of Doré and Grandville to him.[2] His love of the engravings of Bewick and Hogarth, the anatomical abstractions of Bracelli's *Bizarie*, the nightmares of Fuseli, the elemental passions of Goya, the romantic subtleties of Turner, the light and dark contrasts of Tintoretto and Rembrandt, and the earlier Renaissance innovations in form and perspective had all resulted from firsthand encounters in the great galleries and museums of London and continental Europe.

These great discoveries simultaneously framed and validated his views on the modern and contemporary movements. He embraced the impressionism of Renoir and Monet, and the postimpressionism of Seurat and Toulouse-Lautrec. He liked some of the early-twentieth-century innovators, where there was still beauty of form—Matisse's women in rooms, and his sense of design, which would in fact provide the weapon Bradbury used to criticize the avant-garde in "The Watchful Poker Chip of H. Matisse." He liked Picasso's classical and Blue periods, especially the café paintings of 1901–2, but his appreciation of Picasso's Cubism came more slowly.

Bradbury could not abide Abstract Expressionism or the underlying premise that beauty should have no representational context. He disliked Jackson Pollock and barely accepted De Kooning. This view was not simply a reflection of Berenson's very public hostility to the modernists, but rather a more visceral and deeply personal resistance to a world where beauty is no longer the center of art, where one can no longer build an identity around the beauty of the human form. To a large degree this instinctive view predates the influence of Berenson in his life; in *Fahrenheit 451*, Bradbury has Clarisse McClellan tell of a time before abstract art, when pictures "even showed people."

He would never have anything positive to say about the Museum of Modern Art, and this overarching dismissal of Abstract Expressionism, Minimalism, and much postmodernist art would anger many critics. He would add fuel to the fire by constantly breaking the divide between low and high distinctions of art. His lists of favorite artists would mingle such names as Botticelli, Doré, the Pre-Raphaelites, Rackham, Dali, and Braque with the polished comic strip renderings of Hal Foster and the best science fiction and fantasy art of Chesley Bonstell, Frank Paul, Howard V. Brown, Hubert Rogers, H. W. Wesso, and Elliot Dold. The careers of fine arts book illustrators like Joe Mugnaini and Rockwell Kent, both admirers of Bradbury's stories, also helped him break down the traditional distinctions.

Hollywood had an inevitable impact on this process. Charles Laughton was now a major influence on Bradbury's aesthetic development and in some ways was beginning to replace the distant Berenson. Unlike Berenson, who remained a beacon of the High Renaissance to his last days, Laughton easily negotiated the tensions between intellectual and popular culture in ways that validated Bradbury's own wide-ranging enthusiasms. This aspect of their relationship was never more apparent than in Bradbury's very public defense of Disneyland, which by 1958 was drawing fire from such critics as Julian Halevy in the Nation. Bradbury countered Halevy (who felt that the park was no more a place for children than Las Vegas) with his own editorial letter in the Nation, placing Laughton at the center of his defense: "I did better than take a child on my first visit, I accompanied one of the great theatrical and creative minds of our time, Charles Laughton. I've never had such a day full of zest and high good humor. Mr. Laughton is no easy mark; he has a gimlet eye and a searching mind. Yet he saw, and I found, in Disneyland, vast reserves of imagination before untapped in our country."[3]

Here was a preview of the kind of highly emotionalized judgment that Bradbury would publicly level at those who could not abide the wide-ranging potential of the human imagination. He conceded Disney's mistakes in a forgiving way, but he had no such forgiveness for those like Halevy who scorned Disney's attempt to raise illusion and wonderment out of its carnival origins. His judgment on Halevy's imagination had a magisterial air of finality: "He will never travel in space, he will never touch the stars."

Bradbury could be just as passionate about high culture discoveries; his great love for the romantic composers now extended to include the influential Hector Berlioz, whose work he had first encountered in London, through a 1954 Covent Garden performance of The Trojans. His great passion for the composer opened through the delightful back door of Berlioz's fiction. In 1956, he discovered Evenings with the Orchestra, a round of twenty-five stories told during successive evenings in the orchestra pit by musicians who are bored to death by the mediocre scores they must perform. One story told of a future society where music controlled all life activities. Bradbury was fascinated by the rare combination of musical and lyric prose genius and grew to appreciate the nonconformist spirit of his compositions and arrangements, as well as the great entertainment of his stories; in later years, he visited the grave of Berlioz in Paris.[4]

He responded to his broadening experience in the world of art with the wonder and enthusiasm of the self-taught, a characteristically Bradburyan response to art and literature that endeared him to many critics and aggravated others to distraction. His boundless joy with these long-anticipated discoveries recalls "Cora and the Great Wide World," first published in America in The Golden Apples of the Sun—just six months before his first European adventure in 1953. Illiterate and isolated in a remote rural community, Cora depends on the letters her nephew writes for her to bring the Great Wide World to her mailbox. But when her nephew returns home at the end of summer, she cannot read the mail or answer it. Gradually, her connection to the world is broken forever.

Bradbury had subsequently gathered a new harvest of golden apples from his European travels of the 1950s. His taste in visual art was now clearly defined by example, and he would soon begin to champion his own personal pantheon in prefaces and articles of his own. But Berenson was gently dying, and within three years Laughton would follow him to the grave. As the decade neared its end, it was not clear if Bradbury would need another mentor to focus his emerging views of art and aesthetics. All he knew for certain was that he had found the Great Wide World; to lose it would be unbearable.

22 | *The Dreamers*

Bradbury's original 1957 contract with Hecht-Hill-Lancaster included an option for one or two more screenplays involving unspecified company properties. In mid-June 1958, with the production fate of *The Rock Cried Out* still undecided, H-H-L exercised that option and put Bradbury back to work on *The Dreamers*, a recent novel by Roger Manvell, a BBC film critic best known as director of the British Film Academy and chairman of the Radio and Television Writers' Association in Britain. *The Dreamers* took up, but in a very different way, some of the same controversial issues of racism in the postcolonial world that Bradbury had examined in *The Rock Cried Out*.

Bradbury was instantly attracted to the thematic issues of *The Dreamers*, but his enthusiasm focused on the structural and situational parallels he found with one of his favorite motion pictures—the 1945 Ealing Studio film *Dead of Night*. The series of tales brought together for *Dead of Night*, ranging from the unsettling to the terrifying, center on a country house where the guests tell their tales in turn. They are all linked to the recurring nightmare of one guest, an architect who knows that the nightmare will eventually kill him if he can't discover who (or what) is projecting the dream. Bradbury soon established *Dead of Night* as the model for two unproduced anthology films of his own—first with the stories he had brought together in 1947 for his *Dark Carnival* collection, and later for the science fiction stories he had loosely linked together in 1951 to form *The Illustrated Man*.

Manvell's novel told a similar tale. Simon & Schuster's dust-jacket summary for the American edition of *The Dreamers* pinpointed how the first 40 pages of the novel captivated Bradbury: "Five different inhabitants of a small English village have the same dream, in succession. The first is made physically ill by it till she describes it to the second and finds herself relieved. But the second then has the dream—carrying it a few steps further into horror—and is made even more seriously ill by it, till she confides it to her husband. So it goes, the dream becoming progressively more nightmarish, the dreamers progressively more ill, until at last one of them—a beautiful divorcée—is found apparently dead of sheer fright."

The Dreamers echoed the enthralling scenes from *Dead of Night*, and more. All the books that Bradbury had read on the nature of violence, the darkness hidden within the human soul, had led almost inevitably to his encounter with *The*

Dreamers. All his reading on sensation and on psychoses, the criminal case studies that Leigh Brackett had given him, his reading on the Salem Witches, his reading of Fredric Wertham's three books, and finally his encounter with Bronowski's *The Face of Violence*, seemed to culminate in this subtle, almost actionless fiction, centered on what Manvell referred to, late in the novel, as "the evil within."

But before Bradbury could begin to build a treatment or an outline, he would have to deal with a fundamental structural problem that he had never encountered before as a screenwriter—the terrifying progression of the dream plays out in the first 40 pages of the novel, leaving the rest of the tale to the actions of two outsiders who solve the deadly mystery and help the victims purge the powerful evil that yet resides within them. There was only one course open: "I had to rewrite the novel before I could do the screenplay, actually. I did a good job, I believe, of reconstructing the novel in cinematic terms, because the author, unfortunately, gave away so much at the beginning of his novel that people simply wouldn't sit in a theater and watch it, if they knew everything ahead of time. You simply have to spread these things out and delay certain types of information so that you have some suspense framework working for you."[1]

A number of distractions took him away from any significant work on *The Dreamers* through much of the summer and on into the fall of 1958. Ben Benjamin and Bradbury spent long hours responding to Twentieth Century–Fox's interest in extending "The Illustrated Man" into a feature film. With Benjamin's guidance, Bradbury asked for $75,000 based on a first-draft screenplay, an option for subsequent drafts, and rights to the story if production went forward. This was not out of line for a novel-length work, but Fox executives may have found this proposition too risky for an undeveloped story property and declined. Bradbury was nonetheless surprised by the rejection, having been encouraged by the resources Fox had committed to their latest science fiction horror film. He relayed his frustration to Congdon, noting that "20th threw up their hands in horror, in spite of foreseeing a $4,000,000 gross on their $390,000 investment on *The Fly*."

After much consideration he turned down MGM's request that he script a big-budget production of *The Four Horsemen of the Apocalypse*. In early August 1958, he confided to Congdon that he used the impending birth of Alexandra as a graceful excuse: "I told them with the advent of the new baby I will have my own Four Monsters shaking the house and making deep sleep seem worth consideration." Privately, however, he was stressed by the inconsistent quality of studio offers he was receiving. His continuing success with *Alfred Hitchcock Presents*, the occasional screen credits with other dramatic and adventure television series, and his ever-widening circle of Hollywood acquaintances made this kind of uneven industry prominence inevitable.

His increasing celebrity status had its compensations, especially when he could work with people he respected. In December 1957, on the board of the Writers Guild of America (West), he served as master of ceremonies for the ACLU banquet celebrating the 166th anniversary of the Bill of Rights. This event was highly publicized—Bradbury introduced two-time Nobel Laureate Linus Pauling, who was petitioning for a nuclear test ban. During the fall of 1958, he worked with actress Jean Simmons, Robert Nathan, Clifford Odets, Norman Corwin, Groucho Marx, and other literary and Hollywood figures to honor poet Carl Sandburg, who had turned 80 earlier that year.

But he had not had a motion picture screen credit in the two years since the release of *Moby Dick*, and on August 10th he expressed his disgust with the quality of most of these offers in a note to Congdon: "In the last six weeks, I've turned down some magnificent chances to do screenplays free or nearly free for 'friends' who were appalled that I was letting the great opportunity slip through my ignorant fingers. As I believe I pointed out to you before, I'm first rate in the office to these people, but fifth-rate with their bankers. I would like to close up the gap, someday." That same week, he and Maggie changed their home telephone number.

Finally, by late October 1958, Bradbury could focus once again on the challenge of adapting *The Dreamers* for Hecht-Hill-Lancaster. He had now spent nearly two years of his professional life working for months at a time within the luxurious Hecht-Hill-Lancaster complex at 202 Canon Drive, and he would spend a large part of the next year in his office there. But he was still an outsider, and he used a whimsical, Roald Dahl–style extended metaphor to convey this sense of strangeness to Don Congdon:

> Just a note to let you know I am imprisoned in this Chinese Fortune cookie factory and am stuffing this message in the next confection that goes into the oven and thence to you!!!
>
> Don't need help now. All goes well. . . . John Huston arrived yesterday to liven things up with his own production here. Lancaster is flexing his muscles, Jim Hill is drinking quietly on the side, Harold Hecht is ebullient as ever, running in and out with original El Grecos and Picassos under his arms. . . . I am writing treatment pages to fill in all the material Roger Manvell conveniently, and with malice aforethought, left out of his book. I am enjoying this, really, and am sure I will do a fine script. No ego here, I just feel that way about the property. . . .
>
> The baker is coming now, so must stuff this in cookie and run!!! Yes sir, Mr. Hill, no, sir, Mr. Hecht, maybe, Mr. Lancaster!

John Huston's presence was tied to Lancaster's starring role in The Unforgiven, a Hecht-Hill-Lancaster property that was finally filmed and released in 1961, well after the other partners had parted ways. But Bradbury nonetheless was able to focus and work through these distractions; now that he had committed to deconstructing Manvell's premature exposure of the story line, he began the process of restructuring. Three years later, he would describe the root metaphor in his UCLA interviews: "It was then up to me to create a string of beads. That's what you're doing when you're writing a screenplay of varying colors and sizes. You start out with a little microscopic pea and work up to the grand diamond at the end of the string that flashes most and means most to everyone. It's not easy to do."

He profited from the easy way that Marvin Borowsky, his assigned producer, listened and responded to his evolving screen treatment for The Dreamers.[2] But Borowsky was not appreciated at H-H-L, and he left before the end of 1958. Bradbury was retained, and on January 5, 1959, he continued work at H-H-L with a new advisor, writer-producer Frank Davis. Bradbury was relieved to find that Davis did not intend to interfere with his own writing and feel for The Dreamers, and they established a good working relationship. By the third week in January, Bradbury finished his second treatment and began work on the actual screenplay.[3]

In Manvell's novel, the deadly nightmare in this small English village has a target: Dr. Morgan, who had been a medical officer in British East Africa until his strong bias against the tribal peoples accidentally results in the death of a witch doctor's beautiful wife. The magic man has followed Dr. Morgan back to England and starts the dream on its way through the village. Morgan barely survives, but not before his lover falls into a near-death state within the dream. Dr. King, a Black Anglo-African physician who has studied the darker magic, is quickly able to link the dreamers to Dr. Morgan's past, and initiates a race against time to find the assailant and turn the dream back on him before Dr. Morgan's lover dies.

Bradbury knew that he had to delay Dr. Morgan's early and relatively easy revelation of both his racial hatred and the tragic African origins of the revenge dream. For his screenplay, Bradbury had Dr. King work far deeper into the process of exorcising the dream (with near-tragic results) before he is able to unmask Dr. Morgan's secret. This strategy also allowed Morgan and the other dreamers a heightened awareness of the need to face the evil within—evil that allowed the dream to gain traction in their individual lives. Consequently, the dreamers all bear a greater responsibility in confronting the would-be killer; in his screenplay, Bradbury moved this confrontation into the story's root metaphor—the abandoned manor house at the center of the deadly dream. With Dr. King's help they succeed in destroying the magic man, but they also learn that they must achieve a more compassionate sense of humanity in the new postcolonial world.

The second draft of Bradbury's script was complete by April 1959, but by that time Hecht-Hill-Lancaster was beginning to come apart. Their Academy Award–winning film version of *Separate Tables* (1958) would represent the high-water mark of H-H-L's power and influence among independent filmmakers. Most of the films released after *Marty* and *Trapeze* were not moneymakers and couldn't offset the mounting debts with United Artists over unproduced properties and operating expenses. As a result, the company was dissolved in the summer of 1959. Hecht, who had discovered Lancaster, would work with him again, and Jim Hill would remain in film production for many years as well. At last, Bradbury was able to escape the intoxicating world of 202 Canon Drive.

In the end, luck broke Bradbury's way; his submission of *The Dreamers* won him back his rights to *The Rock Cried Out*. He was now free to work directly with Sir Carol Reed, who continued to line up potential production and distribution partners. In 1964 *The Rock Cried Out* would attract the interest of Paul Newman, who wanted to direct and change the setting to Africa. Bradbury insisted that Reed would direct, but encouraged Newman to take the lead role. Still later, Bradbury received an offer from the King brothers and Edward Dmytryk who wanted it to be set in India. But Bradbury didn't know these cultures in the way he knew Mexico, and he declined. In spite of periodic interest, neither of Bradbury's Hecht-Hill-Lancaster screenplays were ever produced.

There were other transitions during his final months with H-H-L. In the fall of 1958, the Bradburys made the decision to sell the Clarkson Road home they had lived in for nearly a decade. It had cost only $11,000, but the recent construction of a nearby interchange for Interstate 10 raised property values significantly and made it possible to purchase a much larger home in the affluent Cheviot Hills neighborhood, situated midway between the Twentieth Century–Fox and MGM studios. The new home on Cheviot Drive was barely a mile from Clarkson Road; it would remain the center of his personal life for the rest of his career.

23 Dark Carnivals

Doubleday expected the unpublished *Summer Morning, Summer Night* Illinois novel, now free of the nostalgic and sentimental elements that Bradbury had novelized and published as *Dandelion Wine*, to be the next book—a Green Town sequel, set a year later in the summer of 1929. But Bradbury was instead beginning to transform his unsold *Dark Carnival* screenplay into the novel that had been peeking out of its various incarnations since 1945. Congdon was impressed with the evolving screenplay and at Bradbury's urging he submitted it to Doubleday for review. Walt Bradbury felt confident with Bradbury's command of the material and prepared a two-book contract for a new short story collection and a novelization of the *Dark Carnival* screenplay.[1] During 1958 and 1959, he would fashion a first-person draft, "Jamie and Me," with a Huck Finn–Tom Sawyer blend of narrative structure. He worked at this approach in fits and starts until the end of 1959, when he transformed the story line one last time into a third-person narrative of Jim Nightshade and Will Halloway, set in Green Town but with characters and a 1932 time-line distinct from the Green Town adventures of *Dandelion Wine*.

During 1959, another dark carnival began to shadow his career in ways that he would not begin to suspect for decades. In June, the Federal Bureau of Investigation established a background file on Bradbury based on information gathered by the FBI's Los Angeles Division. The report found no evidence that he was ever a member of the Communist Party, which was not at all surprising given his background. He was raised in a conservative working-class family and wore the sunflower pin of a Landon Republican in high school. Bradbury had never had any sympathy with communism and despised Stalin; the idealism of his late teens centered on the Technocracy Movement, which played well in some conservative circles.

A residuum of this idealism led him to vote for third-party candidate Henry Wallace in 1948, but he generally voted for Democratic candidates on through the 1950s. His 1952 "Letter to the Republican Party" published in *Variety* and the *Nation* was not even cited in the FBI report; the letter's anti-McCarthy stance had appealed to the generally liberal readership of the *Nation* and the largely L.A.-centric entertainment world reached by *Variety*, but it was only a more eloquent variation on many bitter postelection editorials. There was a bit of ego beneath the eloquence, and the few Los Angeles columnists who responded to it—most notably in the *Mirror* and the *Examiner*—were dismissive.[2]

Even though he sometimes worked in the carefully watched world of the film industry, Bradbury was primarily a freelance fiction writer and spent little time around screenwriters who were blacklisted or suspected of communist leanings. Maggie, as well as his agent Don Congdon, shared his confidence that the major writing markets would not turn away from him if he continued to couch his larger social criticisms in the speculative worlds of science fiction and fantasy. His active membership in the ACLU, which drew support from a fairly broad range of liberals and moderates, raised no eyebrows in Washington. During the mid-1950s, the relatively low level of controversy around Bradbury even attracted offers from those who wanted to deflect or at least minimize their own problems with the blacklist.

Bradbury would later recall that director William Wyler, who had wanted him to adapt Jessamyn West's *The Friendly Persuasion*, sent his brother, producer Robert Wyler, to ask if Bradbury would front the script written by Michael Wilson, who had list troubles because he had taken the Fifth Amendment during his HUAC appearance in Washington. Bradbury refused to take credit for the script, arguing on ethical grounds and also because he found Wilson's work to be excellent. Other voices silently seconded Bradbury's opinion—Wilson received no screen credit and his Academy Award nomination was disqualified, but his screenplay was honored with an award at the 1957 Screen Writer's Awards banquet. Years later, Bradbury would participate in the Writer's Guild restoration credit to Wilson for *The Friendly Persuasion*.[3] Another writer, whom Bradbury described as the "eleventh man" among the Hollywood Ten, approached him with a direct appeal to front a script, again to no avail. Bradbury was very sympathetic, but he felt—perhaps naïvely—that anyone confronted by McCarthy should simply set out the facts in a press conference and appeal to public opinion rather than plead the Fifth Amendment in front of McCarthy.[4] Naïve or not, that would certainly have been Bradbury's course of action if he had ever been summoned.

For a time, the federal government was more concerned with Soviet interest in Bradbury's major works than they were with Bradbury himself.[5] Using French literary agents as intermediaries, Russian representatives approached Congdon about publishing Bradbury translations in early 1956; Congdon steered clear, but he was certain that the Soviets would find a way around conventional Western contracts. Sure enough, during Bradbury's September 1957 stay in Paris, a journalist gave him a copy of the first Russian edition of *Fahrenheit 451*; he would later tell Tony Boucher what else the journalist had discovered: "F.451 sold 500,000 copies in Russia before they found it really criticized them, too. Now, on the black-market, it smuggles for high prices."

On his own, Boucher had already discovered (albeit thirdhand) U.S. government opposition to Russian attempts to publish *The Martian Chronicles* and *The Illustrated Man. Fiction,* Boucher's French edition of *The Magazine of Fantasy & Science Fiction,* contained this editorial commentary: "[T]he American State Department opposed the publication, reasoning that these works were in danger of giving a distorted and unfavorable view of the American way of life. Who was it who said that poets are more to be feared than revolutionists?" Boucher's Paris editors cited only a "serious source," but regardless of the veracity Western authorities could do little with Soviet publishing policies, which often allowed the relatively small fees paid for magazine serialization to cover subsequent book publication by the state-owned periodicals.

In the end, however, it would not be the State Department, but rather a single FBI informant, who persuaded the FBI to open a file on Bradbury out of a concern for national security. There was no shortage of conservatives in Hollywood, and there were writers in and beyond the industry who felt that science fiction offered an easy route for subversion. Bradbury's well-known anticensorship stories were more concerned with the death of the imagination than they were with any narrow political stance, but others—most notably "Carnival of Madness," revised for *The Martian Chronicles* as "Usher II"—were critical of any government that tried to regulate literature. Yet no specific political agenda ever emerged from Bradbury's body of work, and the informant's case actually rested on a single word that Bradbury had spoken in a public forum nearly five years earlier.

That public moment was, in many ways, inevitable. After his return from Europe in 1954, Bradbury began to take a more active role in the Writers Guild of America (West). Collectively, the members of WGAW attracted a great deal of government surveillance, and this became painfully and publicly apparent during the August 1954 general meeting of the Guild. A vote to deny membership to past or present Communist Party members (and anyone who had taken the Fifth Amendment during Congressional hearings) was easily defeated in a secret ballot vote. After a discussion among the leadership, it was decided to revote by a public show of hands. Bradbury and a few others objected to this procedural violation and voted again to defeat the measure, but many others reluctantly supported it to avoid the appearance of being soft on communism. During the second vote, Bradbury rose and shouted "Cowards!" His outburst was described in *The Hollywood Reporter,* along with the ironic announcement that "henceforth," the WGAW would follow *Roberts' Rules of Order.*[6]

The informant added a bit to the account for the June 1959 FBI report, asserting that Bradbury had actually yelled "Cowards and McCarthyites," and noted that Bradbury had also been highly critical of the House Un-American Activities Committee in an earlier talk to a local writers group. The report further noted that Bradbury had subsequently signed an advertisement in two Los Angeles newspapers (the *Times* and the *Mirror*) opposing the continued investigative activities of the HUAC. But the FBI was apparently more interested in the possibility that science fiction's spreading paperback popularity, fueled in part by America's post-Sputnik interest in the accelerating space race, masked an antigovernment stance nested in the futuristic fictions of certain popular writers. Bradbury's early stand against McCarthyism in the WGAW meeting simply made it easier to group him with a number of writers to be watched. No value was seen in him as an informant, and no interview was scheduled. He would therefore remain ignorant of his FBI file for the rest of the twentieth century.

The confidential FBI report was prepared just as Bradbury was enduring one of the worst moments of his public life. The glacially slow progress of his *Fahrenheit 451* lawsuit against CBS and Robert Alan Aurthur had been a constant distraction in the back of his mind since the winter of 1957–58. The United States District Court in Los Angeles ordered CBS to file a response to Bradbury's complaint by October 15, 1958, but the actual trial was not scheduled until mid-May 1959. As the trial progressed through the final week of May 1959, Gerson Marks's prosecution of the case on behalf of Bradbury centered on Aurthur's familiarity with *Fahrenheit 451*. There was plenty of evidence that he valued *Fahrenheit* as a dramatic property, including the 1955 NBC negotiations to secure *Fahrenheit 451* for the network's *Television Playhouse* series.

Robert Alan Aurthur had been involved in those negotiations on behalf of NBC. He was story editor for the series and worked with fellow writer Bernie Wolfe and producer Gordon Duff during the acquisition phase. On the stand, Aurthur maintained that he had acted only as an associate producer, primarily as a telephone intermediary with Don Congdon. He also held fast to his contention that he had never read the novel, even though he had a stake in the dramatic potential of all the stories considered for the *Television Playhouse* series. Bradbury's lawyers could only establish that Aurthur read exhibit 16, Wolff's act-by-act summary of the technical challenges involved in adapting *Fahrenheit 451* for television.[7]

But the defense strategy was far more emotionally hurtful than anything that Aurthur said on the stand. Defense lawyers incessantly pounded Bradbury with accusations that *Fahrenheit 451* was the real culprit in the case; they maintained that Bradbury's dystopic vision of the near future was no different than Huxley's *Brave New World*: both novels presented societies where compassion and creativity were replaced by technological wonders and constant cascades of superficial entertainments for the eye and mind. Furthermore, the defense maintained that Fire Chief Beatty, Bradbury's false prophet, was no different than Huxley's Mustapha Mahon or Orwell's O'Brien. Robert Alan Aurthur was sworn to tell the truth, but the defense team had no such obligation in mounting their more general defense of "A Sound of Different Drummers." This assault on Bradbury's integrity was simply an accepted legal strategy, but it was also one of the most heartbreaking paradoxes of the human soul that he would ever encounter.

The following week, Judge Leon Yankwich found in favor of the CBS defendants, but he relieved Bradbury of the burden of paying the defense attorney's fees. Marks and his partner, Sanford Carter, knew that the chances of a successful appeal would be slim in most cases, but the clerk of the court advised them off the record that this case might have better odds. Bradbury asked Marks to file the appeal, but the emotional stress was evident in his next letter to Congdon: "I won't let myself be built up again. This has been the unhappiest month in my life, mainly because it has shown me a side of myself that I don't enjoy seeing. It has made me nervous, lousy company, mean, high one moment, low another."[8]

Bradbury's fictions had generated a great deal of media interest for almost a decade, but the CBS plagiarism suit offered a painful reminder that he had relatively little to show for his constant and time-consuming efforts to develop and sell television projects. With the prospect of his own *Report from Space* series now nearly dead and *Fahrenheit 451* tied up in litigation indefinitely, Bradbury turned to a new show whose originator had already sought his input—Rod Serling's *The Twilight Zone*, scheduled to premier in the fall 1959 lineup of CBS productions.

Screenwriter John Gay, who had worked with Bradbury on the Hecht-Hill-Lancaster screen treatment for *White Hunter, Black Heart*, introduced him to Rod Serling sometime in 1958. By this time, Serling's reputation was secure as a multiple Emmy Award–winning writer of realistic television drama, but he was increasingly frustrated by the creative restrictions he was encountering. Fantasy and science fiction offered a way to effectively insulate social criticism from the full effect of these restrictions, and he sold CBS on the concept even though he had no experience with this kind of writing. He turned to Bradbury for advice on source material and writers and received a guided tour through Bradbury's home library. Serling left with borrowed copies of work by such Hitchcock favorites as John Collier and a recommendation to hire some of the younger writers that Bradbury had been encouraging.

In July 1959, Bradbury sent Serling a script based on his 1951 space exploration fantasy "Here There Be Tygers," but he held back from becoming the major contributor to *The Twilight Zone* that Serling had hoped he would become. Although he was enthusiastic about the potential advances that this show could make in television drama, Bradbury was also sensitive to the possibility that his own prominence as a genre pioneer in television might be diminished. In all, fifteen television productions for various network programs carried Bradbury credits (as writer or story source) during the 1950s, but the general public knew almost nothing of the dozens of unproduced single-story scripts or the far more significant *Bradbury Showcase* and *Report from Space* series concepts that almost made it into production long before *The Twilight Zone*'s 1959 debut.

Nevertheless, Bradbury needed an emotional rebound from the disappointment of the *Fahrenheit 451* plagiarism trial, and during July 1959 he agreed to submit two more scripts for the series. His ambivalence came through in his July 18th letter to Congdon: "Since he himself admits it is going to be a 'Bradbury' type series, I might as well get fringe benefits. It's always possible someone may think Rod is some step-son or other I dropped along the way. Better this than, some years from now, people asking me if Serling is my teacher and master, eh?"

: : :

More than a year would pass before the appellate court responded to Bradbury's appeal filing in the *Fahrenheit 451* case. In the meantime, he began to reassess his relationship with the Famous Artists agency, where Ben Benjamin and others had looked after his Hollywood interests for the better part of a decade. He still had confidence in Ben, who had usually respected Bradbury's desire to avoid screenwriting during the mid-1950s even when the agency had multiple offers lined up. But the agency now had a number of new faces, and Bradbury sensed an aggressiveness that he could not abide; as he observed to Don Congdon, "some of these new people would make me feel cornered in an open field. They would be willing to sell a TV series just to sell a series."

This growing sense of mistrust had deeper roots—Famous Artists had not been willing to engage its own lawyer against CBS in the *Fahrenheit* case, and Bradbury had not forgotten that disappointment. These agency frictions paralleled his growing frustration with Doubleday's reluctance to increase the budget for promotion of his hardbound editions. He felt, rightly or wrongly, that his hard-fought escape from the Doubleday science fiction logo and the broader market appeal of *Dandelion Wine* merited such an investment in his future, especially given the ever-increasing Bantam paperback royalties that Doubleday shared equally with Bradbury.

The seeds were sown for major changes in his professional relationships—by the early 1960s, he would break with Famous Artists and leave Doubleday for Simon & Schuster. He would work with other editors and other agencies, but he would never be as close to an editor or screen agent as he had been to Doubleday's Walt Bradbury and Ben Benjamin at Famous Artists. Don Congdon—the one element of continuity in his professional life—had been his sole counselor during the late 1940s, and during the early 1960s he would assume that role once again.

Part IV

"Cry the Cosmos"

The month I turned in the *Martian Chronicles* script, late in the summer of '65, we had our first photographic assays of Mars. And the studio said, "There's no life on Mars, so let's not shoot the film." How stupid! I mean, that's all the reason to do it, if there's no life there—*we're* the life, aren't we?

—RB, 2005

24 | Medicines for Melancholy

During the spring of 1959, Bradbury's ever-growing passion for the performing arts provided yet another diversion from story and novel writing—the one-act Irish plays that he had been working on intermittently for many months. These had evolved from his largely unpublished file of Irish stories and story ideas inspired by his seven months in Ireland during 1953–54, writing the *Moby Dick* screenplay for John Huston. His daily encounters with the common speech of the Dublin shops and city entertainments still echoed in his mind. In late December 1958, he told Congdon how one Dublin voice in particular welled up from his memory as he composed these highly romanticized one-act plays:

> I used to walk through the rain from the Royal Hibernian Hotel up around to a little candy and magazine shop near a theatre in Dublin, so I could talk, but mainly listen, to an old lady there who had harps for vocal chords and the sweet wisdom of pure intuition in her selection of words. The woman was a poet, or seemed so to me, but I imagine, all languages, in the hands of proper people, heard by foreigners, become magical. If I have any of the lilt of the Irish in my stories about them, it comes from my nights in the candy-shop chewing Cadbury's Milk Flakes and listening to Edna St. Vincent Millay's great-grandma, or driving out to Kilcock and back 4 or 5 times a week with Mike, my driver, one way, and Nick, my village chauffeur, coming back. They both breathed blarney and barley.[1]

Bradbury briefly considered gathering his five Irish stories into a collection to be titled *As I Was Walking through Dublin City*, but dramatic adaptation soon became the greater temptation. His trips from Dublin out to John Huston's Courtown House had led him to a cozy pub in nearby Kilcock, and the tales set in this enchanting locale provided the best starting point. The first two stories-into-drama, *The Great Collision* and *A Clear View of an Irish Mist*, began as teleplays during the summer and fall of 1958. Bradbury wrote these at his Hecht-Hill-Lancaster office, working on *The Dreamers* screenplay in the mornings and his Irish one-acts every afternoon.

On Christmas Eve he showed them to Charles Laughton, who was now back in Los Angeles after a long series of engagements in London. Bradbury had written them without Laughton's input; he also refrained from rereading his beloved Sean O'Casey while adapting the plays, but as he told Congdon, he was nonetheless determined to catch the spirit and humor of Sean O'Casey's *A Pound on Demand*: "It's one of the most hilarious half hours in stage history if put in the hands of real actors who savor the whole thing. It's delicious. I suppose, in a way, that's why I've done these plays. I haven't, at any time, consciously imitated O'Casey; I have, in fact, stayed strictly away from his plays during this time, for fear of taking on too much coloration. I wanted, mainly, to imitate his driving zest and the irrefutable illogic of his lovely characters."

He couldn't help envisioning Laughton playing his publican Heeber Finn as a transplanted Yorkshireman among the Irish, and told Congdon how he'd "love to see people like Barry Fitzgerald and Thomas Mitchell and Arthur Shields water their mouths over roles like these." Bradbury often let his imagination leap far beyond the bounds of show business realities, and usually Congdon or Ben Benjamin could restrain these impulses before Bradbury showed his naïveté in more public ways; in this case, however, writer-producer Sy Gomberg offered an unexpected way to test the dramatic potential of the Irish one-acts.

Bradbury had known Gomberg since his first extended studio work at Universal in 1952. Sometime in 1958 he told Gomberg that his enthusiasm for the new Irish plays was matched by his uncertainty of their quality. Gomberg was having some actors over one evening that week and persuaded Bradbury to bring his new one-act scripts so that his guests could walk through a reading to see if the plays had potential. Veteran screen actors James Whitmore, Strother Martin, and Arthur Franz quickly put Bradbury at ease and soon proved the entertainment value of these light pieces. The one-act structures, and his ability to portray the Irish temperament and speech patterns, forged a breakthrough for Bradbury as a dramatic stage writer.

In January 1959, Bradbury found interest in the Irish plays from noted film and stage actor Dan O'Herlihy and one of MGM's television directors, Roger Kay. Bradbury's old friend Paul Gregory, now working independently from Laughton, also showed interest.[2] Meanwhile he had posted a new Irish play, *The Anthem Sprinters*, along with the other two one-acts to Don Congdon during December 1958, but Congdon was cautious about circulating them with Broadway producers. He sensed a great interest in Bradbury within the New York theater world, but he had also observed that Irish plays usually found a life off-Broadway. By the end of March he had answers. Emmett Rogers, producer of *No Time for Sergeants*, loved the writing and passed the plays on to actor Tony Perkins, who was already an enthusiastic Bradbury fan, for a possible summer 1959 New York run. But Rogers shared Congdon's reservations about the subject matter and ultimately declined. At this point Mary Frank, producer of the award-winning *Tea and Sympathy*, offered to take on the three one-acts as a single play for Broadway.

Frank formed a production partnership with director Windsor Lewis, husband of stage and screen star Barbara Bel Geddes, and quickly finalized a contract with Bradbury and Congdon. Bradbury pulled the one-acts together as *The Anthem Sprinters* and tried to refine the new three-act on through the summer of 1959. Frank and Lewis came to the West Coast for working sessions, and they allowed Bradbury all of the creative license he wanted. Strangely, however, he discovered that their encouragement, so different from the almost unbearable pressures he had found working for John Huston, produced the opposite effect on his work. In fact, the wide-open permissiveness of Frank and Lewis turned out to be incredibly destructive to the Irish play, which now included an inquisitive American journalist and a love interest.

When Mary Frank sent *The Anthem Sprinters* out to veteran New York playwrights for advice, the consensus was that the original one-acts were superior as self-contained works. Three years later, Bradbury reflected on this discovery in his UCLA interviews: "So it's better, I think, in any work of art . . . that at a certain point, you must leave it alone. At a certain point, you must leave a novel alone. A painting, at a certain point, you must leave alone. That means you leave the flaws in it. You leave the badness in with the goodness, even in writing a play." By the end of the summer of 1959 the project had reached an unproductive end, and the partnership was amicably dissolved.

Bradbury had indeed obscured what he called "the raw goodness" of these original Irish one-acts by prematurely merging them, and he had learned a valuable lesson in the process. The restored originals of these plays would have the liveliness of O'Casey's one-act masterpiece, moments of audacious and irreverent debates in the spirit of George Bernard Shaw, with a dash of sentimental piety from G. K. Chesterton. They were great local entertainments, but they could never be more. Bradbury would have to turn back to his more universal subjects to fashion plays that could reach New York and other Eastern audiences.

Film and television writing had already bled off the creative concentration he had formerly devoted to short fiction and degraded his many attempts to produce original novel-length fiction as well. Now the playwright's craft was about to tip the balance in favor of performance art, changing the course of Bradbury's career forever. It was all a matter of confidence, and the readings by James Whitmore and his colleagues provided all the confidence he needed to go forward. His widening circle of friendships in Hollywood added a personal sense of magic to the process. In earlier times Sy Gomberg had brought Bradbury into Gene Kelly's circle of family and friends; now James Whitmore became a good friend as well and would star in Bradbury's first stage production—an adaptation of his award-winning 1946 radio play *The Meadow*, performed at the Huntington Hartford Theater in March 1960. Bradbury also met the well-read Rod Steiger at Sy Gomberg's gatherings, and they too became close friends for life.

As a writer, he had now worked with or had come to know such first-tier Hollywood figures as Fritz Lang, John Huston, Alfred Hitchcock, William Wyler, David O. Selznick, James Wong Howe, Lazlo Benedek, Edward Dmytryk, King Vidor, and George Cukor. Through King Vidor he met Sam Jaffe, and for a time he joined the circle of friends who spent Sundays with Jaffe and his wife Bettye Ackerman; she would later star in Bradbury's "The Jail" during the 1962 season of *Alcoa Premiere*. At the Jaffe luncheons he would refine his ideas on art with Edward G. Robinson, whose distinguished acting career overshadowed his accomplishments as an art collector. Here he also began an enduring friendship with Zero Mostel.[3] What always began by meeting Bradbury the writer soon turned into respect for Bradbury the oral storyteller, a man who was now comfortable and entertaining in casual conversation with Hollywood's elite.

: : :

Bradbury's explosion into the world of stage drama coincided with a second wave of success with the *Alfred Hitchcock Presents* television series. His third episode, "Design for Loving," aired November 9, 1958, and was the second Bradbury tale produced from a Bradbury script. It was based on "Marionettes, Inc." (1949), featuring an inventor who builds an automaton in his own image so that he can lead a secret life away from his unsuspecting wife; he will eventually be disposed of by his own creation, who has grown all too fond of both wife and home. "Special Delivery," an original Bradbury teleplay in the tradition of Jack Finney's "Body Snatchers," aired during the fifth season on November 29, 1959.

Hitchcock taught his producers and directors how television differed from film; Norman Lloyd, who would produce, direct, and even act in Bradbury episodes, recalled Hitchcock's brief summation of the principal distinction: "Remember, it's a close medium."[4] Bradbury's lifelong love of large-scale special-effect films, as well as his encounters with Renaissance masterpieces during his European experience, helped him understand just what Hitchcock meant. By the spring of 1959, he began to discuss the limitations of television in newspaper interviews:

> Television will always be a minor art until it gets a bigger screen. An entertainment medium must have size. The artist always creates symbols bigger than man himself, but in TV the viewer is bigger than the image. When you see

reproductions of Da Vinci or Michelangelo in an art book, you say, "That's interesting." But when you see it "in person," huge and majestic, the walls fall in on you! The same thing applies in TV. "King Kong," for instance, is a well-constructed picture and a masterpiece in its field—but you cannot see it properly on TV, you must see it on a large screen.[5]

Ironically, his big screen ventures were not as successful. In spite of the ongoing appellate court action on the Fahrenheit case, Bradbury was discussing his well-traveled screenplay for his popular Collier's story "To the Future" (adapted as The Fox and the Forest) with both the director and the producer of the very subject of his lawsuit—Playhouse 90's "A Sound of Different Drummers." Such was the nature of Hollywood, and such was Bradbury's deep fixation with adaptations of his work during these years. Director John Frankenheimer, who had never been involved with Aurthur's script, was not part of the plagiarism case. Martin Manulis had produced the Playhouse 90 episode for CBS and was a defendant in the suit, but he was head of his own production company at Twentieth Century–Fox studios and knew of Frankenheimer's strong interest in The Fox and the Forest property.

In September 1960, Manulis read the original story in a copy of The Illustrated Man sent on by Bradbury; he found it more than interesting, but not as a motion picture. Other Twentieth Century–Fox producers had shown interest in a version of this screenplay as early as 1952 and again in 1958, and it would remain one of Bradbury's best unproduced screen properties. Meanwhile, a television offer to script Jack London's classic story "To Build a Fire" for CBS came even closer to production. Bradbury completed a full treatment, but the network ultimately paid him off without picking up the option.

These media disappointments were counteracted to some degree by the February 1959 publication of his new Doubleday story collection. The best fantasies he produced in the mid- and late-1950s came together in A Medicine for Melancholy. The title story, supplied at the last minute by Bradbury, invoked the enchantment of medieval romance to prove that love from the proper stranger can cure many maladies that puzzle the coldhearted physicians of any age. The now-familiar poetic prose carried through in the stronger stories—Michael Malone's review in L.A. Magazine praised his engaging style as a "mixture of Chaucer, Turgenev, and de Maupassant."

As usual, Bradbury had Doubleday send copies to the major writers who had inspired him. This time he included the aging Somerset Maugham, whose midlife memoir, The Summing Up, had influenced him greatly at the end of his high-school years. Maugham, now 85 years old and quite frail, wrote twice, noting the Poe-esque qualities of "The Town Where No One Got Off" as well as Bradbury's unique gifts as a writer. There were other little gems throughout the collection, including "The Strawberry Window," a post-*Chronicles* tale of Mars that centered on the pioneering habit of bringing a little bit of home along to a new world, and "A Scent of Sarsaparilla," which captured all the attic smells and reflections and textures of past things through a series of marvelous self-contained prose-poems.

"The Day It Rained Forever," featured as the title story for the variant contents of the British edition, was honored as Bradbury's fourth appearance in Martha Foley's *Best American Short Stories* anthologies. It would be his last appearance in this series, but for the moment all he knew was that the new collection was not marketed as aggressively as Bradbury had hoped, especially after generally good reviews. Walt Bradbury used his influence to mount a belated advertising campaign in April 1959, but later that month he resigned to take a new editorial post with the Henry Holt publishing house. Bradbury and Congdon were now more concerned than ever that the advertising allocations for his books would remain limited by the large author and title list that Doubleday maintained. In terms of publishing, the future seemed unclear.

Even with the satisfaction of publishing *A Medicine for Melancholy*, Bradbury's attention remained, for the most part, directed at stage and screen. Charles Laughton was still interested in the idea of an illustrated *Dandelion Wine* and offered advice on Bradbury's new idea of a picture-and-poem book for "Icarus Montgolfier Wright" as well. He spent a lot of time talking with Laughton, and during the late winter and spring of 1959 these conversations turned more and more to Shakespeare and *King Lear*. Laughton was preparing to take the title role for the hundredth anniversary season at Stratford-upon-Avon in June; he would share his approach to the play, using Bradbury, and at times Christopher Isherwood and Elsa, as sounding boards.[6]

These conversations took Bradbury to a new level of understanding of Shakespeare. He knew Shakespeare's gift of language, both by direct study and through Melville's appropriations of it in the pages of *Moby Dick*; but now he learned the subtleties of Shakespearean characters as well. Directly or indirectly, Laughton led him to Wilson Knight's influential study *The Wheel of Fire*, which reinforced and extended the poolside lessons at Laughton's home. Laughton had enriched Bradbury's understanding of Shakespeare, George Bernard Shaw, and Shaw's amicable opponent, G. K. Chesterton—reading passions that would restore his soul at crucial times for the rest of his life.

25 | Escape Velocity

In October 1958, exactly a year after the tiny Soviet satellite Sputnik attained orbital velocity, the United States seemed ready to leap ahead in the space race and break free of Earth's gravitational attraction entirely. The attempt at escape velocity would mean nothing, however, if the vehicle failed to engage the gravitational field of the moon, or—worse still—if it simply fell back into an unintended (and ultimately unstable) Earth orbit.

The wonder of orbital space flight had already moved humanity farther into the future than any development in recorded history, but for Bradbury and many others, it was only a prelude. A successful and guided escape from Earth's gravitational pull was, symbolically, the first step to the stars, opening out into the dreams of scientists, writers, philosophers, and anyone who asked the ultimate questions about Mankind's destiny. For Americans, the magic number was 23,860, rounded upward and forever imprinted in the nation's collective consciousness as 24,000 miles per hour.

Bradbury was quick to take up the standard for these aspirations and made the most of Doubleday's 1958 reissue of The Martian Chronicles. He was now on a new trajectory that allowed him to promote his long-held vision of a new start for the human race. For this reason he continued to read the nonfiction of Willy Ley—a favorite science writer from his teenage years—and even Wernher von Braun, who had begun to write lightly fictionalized scenarios for the first space missions. Bradbury had already purchased the 1956 Ley and von Braun collaboration, The Exploration of Mars, with its captivating interior art by Chesley Bonestell. Lunar explorations would provide the first step to other worlds, however; portions of von Braun's First Men to the Moon appeared in 1958 and 1959 issues of This Week magazine, complete with realistic color art by Fred Freeman. Bradbury secured the hardbound edition of this work as well and kept both of these volumes among his most cherished books for the rest of his life.

His own speculations about the first lunar mission reached print even earlier than von Braun's; barely six weeks after Sputnik's launch, Dorothy Townsend's "Bradbury Sees Moon Conquest in 10 Years" was featured in the November 21, 1957, Los Angeles Times. But Bradbury barely addressed the technological capabilities that fascinated Ley and fairly consumed von Braun; his interest was in the human factor and how space would affect man's heart and soul. On August 22, 1958—his 38th birthday—the *Los Angeles Times* "Family" magazine insert featured a color cover photo of Bradbury and a lengthy interview-based article by his good friend Dick Donovan. He was not afraid to be candid with Donovan, who had written one of the first *Martian Chronicles* reviews in 1950, and this openness was apparent in the title: "Ray Bradbury Pities Unprepared Humans Who 'Must' Explore Space."

Donovan offered an early journalistic paraphrase of Bradbury's conviction that the inevitable death of Earth and its sun, combined with the more immediate fears of self-inflicted nuclear annihilation, made it essential that humanity embark as soon as possible on the final adventure into the Cosmos and thereby assure relative immortality. It was by no means a unique perspective, but Bradbury's outspoken commentaries on the social consequences of space exploration and colonization were reaching a wider reading audience than most of his peers and had done so throughout most of the 1950s. In early January 1960, Bradbury penned his own feature, "Writer Takes a Long Look into Space," for the *Los Angeles Times*. Here, he focused on interplanetary flight and the prospects for life on Mars, and before the year was out he would publish his first space article for a national reading audience—*Life* magazine's "A Serious Search for Weird Worlds."

At the same time, Bradbury was exploring a parallel line of thought involving the religious consequences of space travel. He had explored the storytelling possibilities of this nexus in such late 1940s stories as "The Man" (Christ persecuted across Earth's interstellar colonies) and "The Fire Balloons" (priests among the first colonists of Mars). But his summer 1957 European travels triggered a more ecumenical interest in these possibilities. He was intrigued by the ceremonial magnitude of a "private" audience he had experienced at Castel Gandolfo, where the rapidly aging Pius XII greeted and blessed an open-air crowd of perhaps ten thousand. The following year, as Pius declined through his final illness, Bradbury purchased *Guide for Living*, an English anthology of the Pope's addresses.

In these pages Bradbury learned how the dying Pope had served, as a young boy, under the tutelage of the prominent priest-astronomer, Fr. Lais, in the Chiesa Nuova. During the last decade of his papacy, Pius XII hosted and addressed numerous scientific conferences on such subjects as natural science, astronomy, and the exploration of outer space. Bradbury was profoundly affected by the unprecedented words spoken by Pius at the 1956 Congress of the International Astronautical Federation: "If until now man has felt himself to be, so to say, closed in on the earth, and has had to be content with fragmentary information which came to him out of the universe, it seems now that he is being offered the possibility of breaking this barrier and having access to new truths and new knowledge which God has spread in profusion throughout the world."

The publication of the groundbreaking papal addresses led Bradbury to step up the tempo of his speculations. His November 1959 comments for "TV and Science Fiction" fully capture this new intensity: "And how about religion? . . . When space travel is widespread the impact on religion could be as provocative as the Darwinian theories. And space psychology—how will the psychologists prepare us for space travel? And how about the sociopolitical ethics of dealing with creatures up there, on Mars, for instance?" It was only a matter of time before NASA's Mariner program would eliminate Bradbury's "for instance," which was based on the creative line of Martian storytelling and scientific extrapolation he had inherited from his childhood reading of H. G. Wells, Percival Lowell, and Edgar Rice Burroughs; but as the new decade dawned, he was already exploring a new book project that reached far beyond the Red Planet.

In early March 1960, Bradbury sent Congdon a book proposal titled *God on Tomorrow Morning*, described as "a collection of short stories about the Space Age, God, and Man in the coming half-century." It was to be a collection of stories by other writers, introduced by three of his own tales. The *précis* paraphrased his recent comments on Darwinian parallels, and went on in fanfare style: "In the last twenty years, a good body of writing has appeared in science-fiction, justifying God's ways to Man and Man's ways to God once he makes his most insolent excursion toward the stars."

His précis was clearly intended to help Congdon sell the concept, but his choice of contents demonstrated a fairly narrow reading of more recent humanistic science fiction. There were no stories by such early masters of this form as Kuttner, Simak, or van Vogt—in fact, no science fiction of the 1940s at all. His surviving list of fifteen titles were all published in the 1950s, mostly in the few genre digests that he still occasionally read: *If, Infinity Science Fiction*, and the *Magazine of Fantasy & Science Fiction*, and Ballantine's *Star* anthology series of new stories. He planned to lead off the anthology with three of his own tales of religion taken out to the stars, including "The Fire Balloons" and "The Man."

He would circulate this concept, sometimes with Don Congdon but often on his own, throughout 1960 and 1961. This multivolume project, along with his plan for a boy's collection of his own Space-Age stories, were manifestations of his ever-increasing need to chronicle and inspire America's reach for the stars. Bradbury found strong interest from Bantam's Oscar Dystel and Hiram Hayden of Athenaeum, less interest from major trade houses. His Space Library concept would never find a publisher, but, as he confided to Congdon, his inner fire never diminished: "I feel I would be dreadfully sad and disappointed if someone ran off with 'My' space age. It is a dreadful thing to have such a proprietary interest in an Era that does not really belong to me, but to everyone, but nevertheless there it is. I am irresistably [sic] drawn into and made part of this Time."[1]

This impulse fueled Bradbury's successful effort to achieve a metaphorical escape velocity in his own professional life—his departure from Doubleday, the house that had launched his rise to major market publishing. The trouble seemed to center on the long-awaited Dark Carnival novel, which neither Walt Bradbury nor his successor, Tim Seldes, really wanted in the first place; it represented too much of a throwback to his genre work. Walt Bradbury, in particular, sensed his friend's tendency to form little islands of security around his early success in dark fantasy, and he had been advising against it for years.

Bradbury's dissatisfaction with Doubleday had also been growing for years and really centered on promotion and the perceived reluctance to turn any significant portion of Doubleday's substantial revenue from the Bantam paperback editions into advertising. Congdon and his client evaluated the advantages of various potential publishers during the winter and spring of 1960, including Random House, where Bradbury felt that his more prominent titles could find an enduring hardbound status within the Random House Modern Library series. But above all, a personal relationship, very much like the one he had enjoyed for so long with Walt Bradbury, would be essential; Bradbury felt that Random House, or any other potential publisher, would have to supply a "somewhat fanatic editor who knows how to pet a porcupine-s-f writer."[2]

Alfred A. Knopf had had his eye on Bradbury for more than a decade, and he assigned Stanley Kauffmann, recently hired away from Ballantine, to lead the negotiations. Bradbury had worked closely with Kauffmann on the final revisions to *Fahrenheit 451* and *The October Country*, but he may have felt that the sheer size of the Knopf empire, so similar to Doubleday's, would lead to the same kind of problems. He pulled back from Knopf at the last minute, leaving Kauffmann to explain the loss to his publisher.[3] But Bradbury had already made up his mind to leave Doubleday and made his intentions known to Tim Seldes during July 1960.

If the firm's editors were disappointed, they didn't show it; "Doubleday, as I imagined, did not panic for the exits when they heard the news that the flea was packing his tiny trunks and leaving," Bradbury wrote to Congdon on July 24, 1960. He would move his future fortunes to Simon & Schuster within a few weeks, returning to Doubleday only to publish his two collections of stories for young readers, *R Is for Rocket* (1962) and *S Is for Space* (1966). He shopped these collections aggressively with his new Simon & Schuster editor, Bob Gottlieb, and elsewhere, but since the stories were combed out of his earlier Doubleday collections, it was easier in the end to keep these specialized collections there as well. Ironically, these titles, lightly Bowdlerized (with Bradbury's consent) to reach the school markets, would represent his greatest success with libraries in hardbound format.

: : :

Bradbury's years of work on the Dark Carnival novel entered its fullest phase of development just as the final break with Doubleday was playing out. In early April 1960, Bradbury sent off a 377-page first submission to Don Congdon under the title he had finally settled on: *Something Wicked This Way Comes*. The Dark Carnival was now the referent, framed within the ominous words of Shakespeare's three weird sisters as they await the coming of Macbeth. It was the perfect title, even though the bulky typescript remained in a somewhat rough state. Bradbury had allowed the carnivalesque play of his material—the predatory carnival, returning periodically down through time to trap the souls of various lonelies and dreamers of the small midwestern town—to overcome conventional narrative plotting.[4] The author himself almost seemed to be entrapped with the rest of the town, and his cover letter to Congdon made it plain that he knew it: "Half the book is first draft, half of it second. Much of it is a bit too long, some of it is too short. Some of the characters sort of wander off, here and there. . . . The texture at the end is a bit too thickly populated with incident, and, I guess you'd say, symbol. Later I'll decide what goes, what stays."

At this stage Bradbury planned to cut about 50 pages, but he felt that the book was essentially in the form that he wanted to see in print. Most of all, he needed Congdon to understand that this submission would require his agent to, initially, look beyond the roughness: "The main thing, which I'm sure you're prepared for, is that perhaps never before in the last 13 years, have I sent you a story or a book manuscript in quite this almost-but-not quite born state. As you read, I know you will mentally cut some of the more florid metaphors which always encrust my first and second drafts. Sometimes I give myself, on a single page, 4, 5, or 6 similes which, by the fifth draft, dwindle down to one or two really good ones, for proper emphasis."

Bradbury's summer 1960 expansions outweighed his cuts, however, resulting in a new 425-page typescript that needed further work. He was now having second thoughts about his title, which he considered "artsy-craftsy"—his shorthand for too allusive and intellectual. After considering a number of other titles centering on characters or episodes within the novel, he wisely decided to retain the title allusion to Shakespeare.[5] It was a novel about the choices for good or for evil, after all, and the title allusion to Shakespeare helped focus the positive magic of the book on the town library, where the final struggle of the novel begins in earnest.

Work on *Something Wicked This Way Comes* would be intermittent throughout the rest of 1960 and on through the summer of 1961. On July 12, 1960, the day after sending Congdon the second draft of the novel, Bradbury and his lawyers left for San Francisco to prepare for an appearance before the U.S. Court of Appeals, Third District. This was the culmination of a yearlong process to see if the Court would review the decision against Bradbury in the U.S. District Court concerning his *Fahrenheit 451* plagiarism suit against CBS. On Friday, July 15, 1960, after only an hour with the appellants, the three-judge panel conveyed their preliminary opinion that the case was worthy of review.[6] The time and money spent the previous year assembling the appeal case now seemed worthwhile, but six months would pass before the appeal would be argued in court.

While Simon & Schuster's Bob Gottlieb reviewed the second draft of *Something Wicked This Way Comes*, Bradbury decided to use this latest version of the novel to promote the earlier *Dark Carnival* screenplay version. By the fall of 1960, he had the screenplay under review at Twentieth Century–Fox, and the draft novel under review at Columbia Pictures. These were risky moves, but there was a reason behind his sudden desire to press so hard for a *Something Wicked* film deal—word was out that director George Pal was planning to purchase film rights to Charles Finney's 1930s novella, *The Circus of Dr. Lao*.

His good friend Charles Beaumont was scheduled to write the *Dr. Lao* adaptation and asked Bradbury to drop the idea of circulating the new novel version of *Something Wicked* among the major Hollywood studios. Beaumont went so far as to call Congdon about his fears, prompting Bradbury to suggest to Congdon that Beaumont was simply exhibiting his usual "bad case of nerves." Bradbury preferred to move ahead and let his new novel help sell the screenplay version, for he knew very well how the distinctions between two vaguely similar works could be blurred in Hollywood:

> [I]f you tell a producer, in general terms, that *Lao* and *Something Wicked* are both novels about a carnival/circus that comes to a small town and changes people's lives, the producers are going to jump in one of two directions. It is doubtful that both projects can be made in the same year. No matter if *Lao*'s circus is not designedly evil and my carnival *is*. No matter if very little happens to the Arizona townspeople in *Lao*, and much happens to the characters in my Illinois town.[7]

Beaumont's driven nature did not diminish the fact that Bradbury considered him a first-rate talent, and he told Congdon in the same letter that he would accept a deal where Beaumont would script a new version of *Something Wicked* if *Dr. Lao* lost out in the competition.[8] This option proved unnecessary; Beaumont would add his own creative stamp to the basic story of *The Circus of Dr. Lao*, moving it even further away from Bradbury's more deeply humanistic novel of good and evil. MGM's *The Seven Faces of Dr. Lao* premiered in 1964; over time, however, Bradbury's *Something Wicked This Way Comes* would have far greater long-term prominence as a novel than Finney's odd and loosely constructed tale.

: : :

The political conventions of the summer of 1960 also engaged Bradbury's attention. He had actively supported both of Adlai Stevenson's presidential campaigns of the 1950s, but John Kennedy's candidacy seemed to present new horizons for the Democratic Party. Kennedy's effectiveness in the first presidential debate was not lost on Bradbury, and he conveyed his surprise to Congdon the next day: "Am I crazy, or did Kennedy do a fine job last night on TV, opposite Nixon? It's the first time I've felt optimistic about the Nov. election. If Kennedy can do this three more times, in the TV debates, the independent voter cannot help but be swayed. We'll see."[9]

Bradbury's very public stance against McCarthyism had drawn him more fully into the ACLU camp during the mid-1950s; by 1960, his firm opposition to nuclear proliferation had led him to join the Committee for a SANE Nuclear Policy and add his signature to open letters published in support of weapon test bans and nuclear disarmament. Like many, he could do this while still maintaining a vocal and active distrust of the Soviet Union that, like his hatred of war, occasionally came through in his fiction as well as his nonfiction prose.

But each NASA rocket launch, successful or not, was pulling Bradbury toward another kind of activism. The various unmanned missions had a wide range of purposes, but they all advanced the reliability of the lifting rockets that would soon take man into space. Bradbury's deepening interest in the underlying technological challenges led him to attend UCLA's public lecture series on "Peacetime Uses of Space," which considered international jurisdictions in outer space, the possibilities of space-based telescopes, and the uses of atomic power in space exploration.

In early January 1960, Bradbury took a significant step beyond UCLA's public lectures when he was selected as one of thirty-seven influential Californians to participate in a five-month, ten-lecture series on the "Impact of Scientific Change." Bradbury listened to a number of distinguished scientists speak on such topics as "The Conquest of Space." The *Los Angeles Times* reported that the lecture series class included business leaders, lawyers, physicians, film producers, and other "men of means." Bradbury, who had never attended college at all, was the only literary author. The public library had been his classroom and had inspired him to become a writer; now, his interactions with an increasing number of men of science, business, and government would help him formulate the more specific visions of the present and the near future that he would bring to the interviews, lectures, and nonfiction essays that would divert more and more time away from creative writing.

The nation's slow but steady progress toward manned spaceflight also brought renewed interest from Hollywood; MGM arranged to bring Bradbury on board to adapt The Martian Chronicles for a major film, but a writer's strike kept him out of the studio until midsummer 1960. He hadn't had a studio office since leaving Hecht-Hill-Lancaster the year before, and writing at home had become a mixture of delight and distraction. The four Bradbury daughters now ranged in age from 11 down to 2, creating a complex domestic dynamic that had long since spilled out into the neighborhood. "Summer is here," he wrote to Congdon in late June. "How do I know? I now have nine daughters. Five of them belong to other people on the street, and the color of their hair and eyes shift from hour to hour."[9] Maggie bore the brunt of all this activity, but Bradbury had always enjoyed taking the girls to swim. Nevertheless, as he confided to Congdon, "MGM will seem paradise."

26 | Martian Odyssey

When it came to marketing his own work, Bradbury was willing to take long shots that his Famous Artists agents were not always willing to initiate. In late 1959, Bradbury approached veteran independent producer Julian Blaustein, who was in the midst of developing a succession of MGM films, with an unexpected proposition—a major studio production of The Martian Chronicles, using the expensive three-camera Cinerama process to create panoramic vistas of the planet Mars.[1] The two men had known each other for years; Bradbury almost certainly met him in the spring or fall of 1952, when they were both working for Twentieth Century–Fox. At that time Blaustein had just produced The Day the Earth Stood Still, a well-made 1951 Fox release that had, under Robert Wise's gifted direction, clearly transcended genre boundaries.

Their paths probably crossed again in 1958 over at MGM, when Bradbury turned down an offer to adapt The Four Horsemen of the Apocalypse—a film that Blaustein would eventually produce for the studio. A November 6, 1959, Variety magazine review of Blaustein's The Wreck of the Mary Deare, and his special-effects success with the most expensive water sets that MGM had ever built, prompted Bradbury to renew his efforts to film a big-budget production of The Martian Chronicles; perhaps now, with the producer of The Day the Earth Stood Still as an advocate, he would be able to secure a studio contract.

Bradbury was persuasive, and Blaustein was persuaded, but there was currently no place in Blaustein's schedule for the Chronicles; much would depend on Bradbury's ability to write a viable treatment and script. At this point, however, Bradbury was focused on securing a contract, for he knew that a science fiction project would encounter some degree of opposition at MGM. Studio head Sol Siegel was the main obstacle; he had been at Twentieth Century–Fox during Bradbury's frustrating ten-day stint trying to adapt Jack Vance's "Hard-Luck Diggings" in early 1952, and he was directly responsible for releasing Bradbury before he could finish adapting Kurt Siodmak's "Face in the Deep" for Fox later that year. During the same period, MGM had been even more dismissive of Bradbury's work; in 1952, Siegel's predecessors at MGM turned down a John Houseman and Vincente Minnelli plan to produce The Martian Chronicles before it ever got past the discussion stage.

But MGM had subsequently filmed *Forbidden Planet*, a picture that producer Nicholas Nayfack had asked Bradbury to script. Sometime in 1955, still recovering from his exhausting months with John Huston and wary of new studio entanglements, Bradbury had declined the offer, but there were no hard feelings at MGM. In January 1960, Ben Benjamin negotiated a contract that would pay Bradbury $10,000 for a detailed outline or screen treatment of *The Martian Chronicles*. MGM could then exercise options on a Bradbury screenplay; in the event that the film went into production, Benjamin and Bradbury were negotiating for postrelease profits that would potentially bring the total payments (that is, from treatment to release) to $100,000. Predictably, the negotiations did little to ease the tensions between Bradbury and the studio head. On January 26, 1960, Ben Benjamin described the situation to Don Congdon: "Sol is far from certain that he wants to do this and I must confess it is difficult for Ray to understand this. Sol is being very wary, and by so doing seems to antagonize Ray."

Bradbury had high hopes that Blaustein would be able to smooth the waters, but a writer's strike kept him out of the studio until July 1960.[2] This delay had no effect on his optimism or his sense of destiny. More than a quarter-century earlier, in 1934, a 13-year-old Ray Bradbury had spent his first day in Los Angeles trying—unsuccessfully—to walk the ten miles from downtown Los Angeles to the MGM Studio complex. By 1960, the studio was a relatively short and effortless downhill bicycle ride south along Motor Avenue from the Cheviot Hills home he had purchased the year before. Maggie now had the family's only driver's license and a car; in the afternoons, she would drive down to MGM and rescue both husband and bicycle from the uphill ride home.

He soon discovered that he was learning more about characterization in the studio than he ever had as a storywriter. He commented at length on this strange irony in a July 29th letter to Don Congdon:

> Fascinating thing about working on *The Martian Chronicles*. Eleven years ago, whatever knowledge I had about characterization was pretty intuitive, and hidden from myself. While a great lot of my character knowledge is still pretty much touch and go, play by ear, I can do more "thinking" about them now and going through the book I've had to sit down and work out a real background for each of the characters I did in sketch form so long ago. Most of the captains in *Chronicles* have no real past. Spender, also, when you come down to it, was an Idea in motion. It has been really fascinating to figure out what I was up to, and also to let my current subconscious run free with old subconscious devices and people. I am, in a way, riding happy piggy-back on the younger writer who did the book.

He was indeed beginning to look back at that young writer he had once been, and this distancing process was accelerated by his parallel sense of growth as a screenwriter. Bradbury had spent most of the last seven years refining his screenwriting talents and learning—largely by trial and error—how to write for the stage. He was now beginning to develop a rationale to explain his versatility in ways that masked his real problem—finding time to write the short stories that had made him famous.

During July 1960, Bradbury generated a great deal of background character analysis, but his long-standing reliance on subconscious inspiration—so crucial to his early years as a fiction writer—would prove less effective in the more structured world of screenwriting. The danger was implicit in the somewhat mystical explanation he offered Don Congdon: "I now have 18 pages of character analysis which will go back on file into my subconscious against that day or hour in the coming months when I'll need it in the screenplay. No sooner do I 'know' a thing than I try to 'forget' a thing, a very important part of writing, I feel. To know a thing too obviously can put you out of joint. But to recognize and put into shadow the materials you need makes for a relaxed approach to coming problems."[3]

Bradbury's intense emotional identification with his characters surfaced again when he sent his first draft of the treatment to Blaustein on August 9, 1960: "All of my short stories and novels have been done the same way I do my screenplays—I guess you would say I let my characters have their heads. . . . [O]nce I set all of the characters on their feet, in The Martian Chronicles, they will fill in the holes and smooth out any bumps that may at first be apparent in such a brief thing as a treatment." He was clearly uncomfortable with the concept of a treatment, and was perhaps too eager to jump ahead into the script: "[A] treatment is always a little too intellectual and cold, and I want a chance to let my people act warmly and excitingly together."

During the rest of the summer and early fall Bradbury worked through a 160-page draft (and a subsequent 100-page draft) of what he referred to as a "screenplay-treatment." Unfortunately, he had little interaction with Blaustein, who was in production with two other films. As late as October 30th, Bradbury was still optimistic that the film would be made using the highly expensive magic of the Cinerama process, but without the guidance of a producer, his work could not proceed.[4] Late in the year, MGM diverted him to write the voice-over narrative and consult on the final editing for Samuel Bronston's production of King of Kings. That work was enjoyable for the most part, but by February 1961 he realized that he was at an impasse with the Chronicles.

Ben Benjamin read a conflated 180-page version and found it to be a "beautiful and poetic narrative," but he also felt that it was neither a treatment nor a screenplay. Benjamin, always sanguine and usually supportive, wrote a private and rather critical analysis to Don Congdon:

> Ray has just not dramatized, or shown in a step-by-step progression, how this picture will look on the screen. His description and dialog is beautiful, but the things that he passes over in the script in the main are the things that are crying for dramatization. I don't mean by this that it was entirely narrative, but many of the things he did dramatize, cried for much more heightening.
>
> Doing a treatment . . . is really a job of carpentry. A studio head like Sol Siegel is not interested in reading poetic dialog. What he is looking for is how the picture will visually appear on the screen. He knows in most cases that the writer can write. His question, and that of most producers in a studio, is can the writer construct. Unfortunately, Ray has not demonstrated this in the treatments he has done.
>
> Ray understands this—though he is somewhat bewildered by it all because I am sure that he feels that a lean and spare progression of scenes which builds to a climax is really not writing in the true sense, and I guess it isn't, but when you write for the screen you have to follow certain rules.

Bradbury remained more interested in the mystery of the process than the rules, and his letters to Congdon focused only on the mystery:

> I've begun to know the difference between story-page, theatre-page, and screen-page, a fascinating thing to watch the cogs in my mind ease over into new functions, to change gears and use slightly different languages. On the short story page, images to be read and summoned up by the mind; on the stage, images to be heard and shaped as echoes; on the screen, direct images to be seen, but always masking some small element of mystery, so you give the viewer a chance to supply echoes and shapes with his own imagination. Fascinating, fascinating. I think a writer can really grow by learning from each to strengthen the other.[5]

The engaging metaphors did not obscure the fact that this self-analysis was an oversimplification of a very complicated process, and his evasiveness continued into the series of UCLA Oral History interviews that he undertook during the spring of 1961. In these interviews he made a more focused statement about the greater need for compression in film than in the novel or stage drama:

> On the screen that same moment of truth that occurs in the other two forms has to be pared way down because you can't say anything twice on the screen.

You can say a thing twice on the stage; in fact, we have to because people may have forgotten; but, on the screen, you've already hit them so hard with the truth, visually, that you can't repeat. The mind remembers visual things much more quickly than it remembers a thing in a novel or a thing on the stage. So, you have to hit people again and again in a novel, and you have to hit them quite often on the stage, but you hit them only once on the screen.[6]

But execution was another thing entirely. These comments were made as his time at MGM drew to a close, and they masked the great problems he had encountered trying to maintain any sense of objectivity with The Martian Chronicles. In earlier years, Bradbury had been working from the slightly distanced perspective of another writer's work when he prepared the Moby Dick screenplay for John Huston and The Dreamers for Hecht-Hill-Lancaster. He could talk about compression very easily in the abstract, but it was harder to bring the process effectively to bear on his own work.

Ben Benjamin was not alone in his analysis; none of the other agents at Famous Artists thought that the hybrid treatment-script was on the mark, and neither did anyone at MGM. Bradbury's confidence was further eroded by his lack of contact with Blaustein, whom he had counted on for advice and guidance. In reality, there was little basis for such an assumption; he had pursued Blaustein and MGM from the beginning, and the original option contract represented a speculative commitment rather than the full commitment of resources that an in-house project might enjoy. In mid-March 1961, Bradbury sent Congdon an update that reflected the realities of the situation: "I am leaving MGM until sometime in May. Blaustein is so busy with his other films, I figure I have seen him a total of one hour in the last 8 months. Not even a lunch in all that time. The entire experience, in retrospect, seems rather sorry. But I kept waiting, putting off, rationalizing, hoping."[7]

But he did stay on at MGM for the time being. By early April 1961, however, it was clear that the script had no chance of being picked up under the existing option agreement; MGM would pay the contracted $10,000 for the treatment, but the studio wanted another screenwriter to carry on. Ben Benjamin tried to negotiate a new deal that would allow another writer to step in but would still require MGM to pay Bradbury according to the original agreement even if he wasn't continuing as screenwriter. Given the studio's growing uneasiness with the Chronicles, such a deal was out of the question.

In mid-April, Bradbury's spirits were boosted when Richard Brooks, who had written and directed the recent Academy Award–winning Elmer Gantry for United Artists, expressed interest in becoming producer-advisor for Bradbury and the *Chronicles*. But Bradbury's support higher up in the studio hierarchy was waning fast, and nothing came of this possibility. Bradbury's only victory was a psychological one—he was able to challenge studio policy and had his name typed into the working script. It was as close as he would get to producing *The Martian Chronicles* at MGM.

: : :

The brief interval of work on MGM's *King of Kings* allowed Bradbury to extend his knowledge of postproduction editing and established long-lasting friendships with some of the studio's finest off-screen talents. During October and November 1960, he was assigned to adapt a sequence of voice-over narrative bridges from the Gospels of the New Testament; this involved working with the distinguished film editor Margaret Booth and Harold Kress on the final positioning of the narrative, and with legendary composer Miklós Rósza on the background soundtrack for the narrative sequences. This work would prove to be satisfying and productive—in fact, the narration represented Bradbury's most productive contribution to a feature film since his adaptation of *Moby Dick*.

The creative dynamics were actually very similar. He had successfully transferred the biblical and Shakespearean overtones of Melville's classic novel into his *Moby Dick* screenplay, and the confidence he had developed during that process had not diminished during the intervening seven years. For *King of Kings* he would provide essential bridges from the gospels and would do so fairly quickly; Philip Yordan's script provided the underlying continuity, and director Nicholas Ray had already completed most of the shooting schedule. Bradbury's internal scripting was sequenced into the soundtrack at the appropriate points by Rósza, who recorded a working version with Bradbury's voice dubbed into the orchestral performance. Orson Welles, who had performed Bradbury's adaptation of Father Mapple's sermon for *Moby Dick*, recorded the final edited version of *King of Kings* narration.

Bradbury confided to Bob Kirsch how his experience differed from that of other, more famous, crossover writers: "I'm learning all about the business from the ground up, which is what every writer ought to do. I feel more fortunate, actually, than people like Faulkner or Fitzgerald, who worked here but who never got into the intestines of the technology to see what made it go there."[8] But Margaret Booth's masterful postproduction editing encountered some problematic scenes, and Bradbury was inevitably drawn into the creative aspects of this process.

His outspoken nature, and the fact that he was a contract writer who had less on the line than the full-time editorial staff, made him the perfect unofficial negotiator when producer Samuel Bronston wanted to diminish or even remove the role of Judas from the final release cut (Judas was reinstated). But Nicholas Ray was already preparing to direct 55 *Days at Peking*, Bronston's next big-budget picture, and reshooting even minor scenes for *King of Kings* would be a tough proposition. This situation hardly deterred Bradbury; he had relatively little postproduction experience on any film, but the scene descriptions in his 1953–54 preproduction *Moby Dick* script for John Huston (as well as his impressive 1952 treatment for Universal's *It Came From Outer Space*) revealed an instinctive gift for visual dramatic effect.

In the end, none of his recommendations were accepted, but they nonetheless reveal a great deal about his screenwriting creativity. One wonders how *King of Kings* might have been enriched by the shot he wrote to follow Pilate's fateful decisions: the brutal Barabbas and the brutalized Jesus, one moving to freedom, the other to the Crucifixion, exchanging glances as they pass. Bradbury's greatest disappointment centered on MGM's refusal to replace the brief concluding scene of the Great Commission with Bradbury's more finely textured and imaginative version. Longtime Knopf editor Bernard Smith, now a producer at MGM, had tipped off Bradbury that the original 1-page conclusion was just about locked in. His alternative conception was not biblically accurate, but it was emotionally striking. Late in life, he recalled the proposed scene during a private interview:

> I wrote a scene in which Simon called Peter is out in the sea and they have the pulling in the net and the fish in the net, what have you. And the disciples and Simon pull into the shore, they walk along the shore, and they see an apparition by a bed of coals. And on the bed of coals, these fish are being baked. They're not quite sure who it is, because Doubting Thomas wonders who it is. And Christ lifts his hand into the light, and from the wound on his wrist, blood drips onto the fish and onto the coals. And he says, "Take of these fish and feed thy brethren. Take of my message, and move through the cities of the world and preach my testament." So the sun is beginning to rise, and we know that it's Christ's ghost there by the fire, but it's the supper after the Last Supper. . . . The last supper is on the shore, with the fish. He feeds the disciples . . . and then he says to them, "Take of my message," and he walks up the shore.
>
> Well, the sun is rising and, as we often see on the highway, you stand at a certain angle and the vibrations of the heat on the sand make a mirage of the city beyond the hill, or the hill beyond the hill. So as Christ walks up the shore, if your camera is down in the sand looking up, when you walk away, no matter what direction you're going in, you're going uphill because of the camera angle. So he's walking up the shore, and the further he gets up, the

heat of the day shimmers him. . . . And that's the Ascension. I wanted to do it in such a way that you believe it. . . . Christ's footprints are left in the sand, and the wind blows the footprints away. And that's the second Ascension. And then the disciples do what Christ said, move out in all directions to preach his words to the world. So they move out in a great circle, along the shore, in three or four directions, and their footprints are left in the sand. And they blow away, and that's the end of your film.[9]

Bradbury's fictionalized doubling of the Last Supper and the Resurrection is not scriptural, but it is visually powerful—and memorable—in the mind's eye. He wrote both short and long versions of this scene, and sent them directly to studio head Sol Siegel, asserting his firm conviction that "it is very important to give the film a dramatic 'coda' of emphasis and some dramatic intensity."[10] Bradbury's proposed scene was rejected, but it nevertheless reveals evidence of his emerging passion for revisionist cinema, a tendency to write film reviews (and even book reviews) that analyze by contrasting the actual work of art with an imaginary alternative. More than once, he would end his reviews with a variation on the signature line, "I go now to re-write the Book of Job."

Bradbury's voice-over narration for *King of Kings* enriched the final viewing experience, but he received no screen credit when the film was released.[11] Bradbury's connection was further obscured when Orson Welles refused his own screen credit—MGM paid him for the voice-over recording, but declined Welles's request for an additional sum to use his name. Nevertheless, Bradbury had advanced his reputation with the major studios, and this achievement served as prelude to the next plateau in his film career: cofounding the Screen Writer's Film Society in 1961. He had no inkling that this pioneering venture, which led to the founding of Director's Guild and Actor's Guild film societies, would have more impact in Hollywood than any of the scripts he would write for the next twenty years.

27 | "Cry the Cosmos"

On May 15, 1961, television and film director Roger Kay asked Bradbury to write a new version of his *Dark Carnival* screenplay for review by United Artists. This request suddenly brought to the surface all of the pent-up frustrations of his various Hollywood disappointments, right up to the recent impasse at MGM. Two days later he sent a short letter to Kay declining the proposal and briefly expressing his more far-reaching decision to cease writing screenplays. But Bradbury's 2-page unsent draft of that letter, written within hours of his meeting with Kay, offered a far more emotional statement of his decision:

> I have had six or seven experiences now, all of them winding up brutally or bitterly, with many groups of people. I know now I am not cut out to be moving through the world, the business world, or the artistic world, attempting to work with others. I should have faced this long ago, instead of smiling, agreeing, and hurting people with promises that could never be kept. . . . Call this weakness, call this even, if you wish, paranoia, but I flee the financial as well as the artistic marketplace of cinema, TV and stage. This seems sane to me.

He clearly found himself in the frame of mind that had shaped his earliest success in fiction. That frame of mind had been sparked by his 1944 reading of Ayn Rand's *The Fountainhead*; now, nearly two decades later, similar emotions surfaced:

> I know my place is in hiding out, retreating, being a hermit, and writing short stories and novels, so I never have to see anyone or have any advice about my work. I know I am my own best advisor and can go on for the rest of my life being happy, working alone. The ten months at MGM have capped this, along with my name being taken off *King of Kings*.
>
> I see the pattern now that I could not recognize in myself. And it was my creative intuition which threw monkey wrenches into the machinery again and again over the years, for I only thought I wanted to work with people. I was kidding myself. I have never needed anyone nor will I ever need anyone, as long as I stick where I belong, in the safe small quiet hidden world of short stories.

His renewed determination echoed the working method of Rand's isolated but brilliant architect Howard Roark of *The Fountainhead*, an aspect of the novel that interested him far more than Rand's philosophy when he first read the novel in 1944. This ideal, along with his natural inclination to go his own way, had fueled a decade of quality story writing, but since 1954 he had gradually drifted away from his storytelling focus as Hollywood relentlessly beckoned. Here was a glimmer of the old resolve, a chance to get back to the kind of edgy, tightly constructed, and stylistically unique stories that he had written in the old days. But the unsent draft also noted how he would continue to write stage and screen adaptations of his works—privately, for himself. And eventually this temptation would once again lead to his undoing as an original teller of tales.

This creative crisis point came just as he was realizing that there would soon be no more mentors in his life. In far off Tuscany, Bernard Berenson had gently faded away and died at his beloved Villa I Tatti in late September 1959. In America, and perhaps also in Italy, Berenson's passing was overshadowed by the sudden death of Mario Lanza on the same day. Lanza's media tributes and obituaries pushed Berenson out of most of the stateside newspapers; at 94, Berenson was, in a way, a man of the last century—older than the great Caruso, whom Lanza had famously recreated in film. Berenson had really lived his life across the three-hundred-year arc of the Italian Renaissance, and he had made the art of that age come alive for Bradbury.

Charles Laughton was also nearing the end and would begin to decline into his final illness within the next two years. For a time Bradbury reached out to the aging Pulitzer Prize–winning poet Robert Hillyer, beginning a warm correspondence that continued from September 1959—nearly the day of Berenson's death—to Hillyer's own death in 1961. They had a mutual interest in the Hollywood crowd that gathered in the 1930s around Gene Fowler, whose biography of John Barrymore had reminded Bradbury of his abiding fear of the end that fate held in store for those who lived only for the fame of Hollywood. On January 9, 1960, he confided that fear in his second letter to Hillyer: "I was always touched and saddened, reading Fowler's book about Barrymore, to realize that these were all children, fantastic, wild, irresponsible children, all hurrying to bed, all rushing headlong toward the eternal comforts of the grave." Bradbury told Hillyer a remarkable story of his 1942 encounter with one of these doomed celebrities, the artist John Decker:

> I was in John Decker's art gallery a few days after the death of Barrymore, and Decker, entering from his living quarters in another part of the building, somehow took me for a friend, or at the very least an acquaintance . . . it was early in

the day but he was well into his third or fourth martini, I estimated, . . . Decker took me by the arm and led me into a small room where he opened a double set of doors in the wall, behind which hung a sketch of Barrymore made within moments after his death. Standing there and looking at Barrymore's profile, and the profile of Decker next to me as he stared at his sketch, I realized that within a short time Decker too would be dead, and dead in much the same way Barrymore died . . . of being the strange and frantic child, panicking at life and itching after darkness. I have rarely had such a huge irony acted out for me . . . for Decker bore quite a physical resemblance to Barrymore. If I recall correctly, Decker was dead about two years later. [ellipses Bradbury's]

This almost breathless account of seeing both the past and the future in men's faces, spit out between ellipses points, went farther than he had ever gone in his letters to Berenson. These letters to Hillyer sometimes exhibit a hint of desire for a mentor to replace those he was losing, but at the same time he felt uneasy about the process; his next words to Hillyer were, "Good God, I don't know why I've told you this." The rapidly aging Hillyer remained a good correspondent for another year, yet he was already fading from Bradbury's life faster than Berenson had.

Bradbury was now in his fortieth year, and the time of mentors had passed. He was beginning to draw his inspiration from the Cosmos, and from the men who explored it through their writings or actions. In mid-January 1960, almost on the eve of the first manned space flights, *Life* magazine's editor in chief Ralph Graves lured Bradbury into the role of an essayist with an exclusive assignment to write about "Life on Other Worlds." The commission of $2,500 came with expenses paid and files of research materials, an arrangement that cushioned his return to a kind of prose that ran counter to his naturally emotional and spontaneous mode of writing.

Bradbury was convinced that his friend Loren Eiseley would be the best source of advice and was somewhat disappointed when Eiseley could offer only the example of similar essays he had written on related subjects. Fortunately, *Life*'s bundle of research materials offered a basic structure, and Bradbury was able to follow that structure with a growing sense of confidence. The Project Ozma radio telescope in Green Bank, West Virginia, had recently upstaged the approaching manned launches with its new mission to search the heavens for signals emanating from interstellar civilizations; from this starting point, Bradbury worked with articles by Project Ozma's Frank Drake, Cornell's Philip Morrison, and a half dozen other astronomical authorities to write about planetary environments in our solar system and beyond, and the kinds of life forms that might evolve on these alien worlds.

The final article, re-titled for effect as "A Serious Search for Weird Worlds," appeared in the October 24, 1960, issue of *Life* magazine. Although Bradbury's engaging style was obscured by long passages of quotation and paraphrase from the experts, and by the somewhat obvious pen of *Life*'s copyeditor, the article was well received by mainstream readers. But the few paragraphs that glistened with genuine Bradbury style revealed evidence that Bradbury's uneasy sense of continuity in the Cosmos was about to reach a breaking point. This struggle was deeply internalized, but it was, at its essence, very simple: How could he square his conviction that we live in a universe with no beginning and no end with his instinctive (but so far ungrounded) sense of a Creator?

There had been hints of this private debate in some of his correspondence. More than a year earlier, on March 3, 1959, he had closed a letter to his London publisher Rupert Hart-Davis with this strange benediction: "God love you and Ruth. And when I say God, I don't mean a namby-pamby anthropomorphic God, I mean all the powers, forces, gravities, and wonders of the universe; may they let you pass with little friction, and send you easily, happily, and excitingly on your way." His disaffection with Man-in-God's-image echoed down from his sporadic late-teen writing notes of 1939–40, but so far the evolution of his beliefs had stalled with his elemental observation (most notably in his 1952 *Nation* article, "Day after Tomorrow") that Man will be his own salvation, avoiding (with luck) self-annihilation and evading (through spaceflight) the ultimate death of the sun and subsequent destruction of Planet Earth. These observations begged an ultimate question, and Bradbury's ripeness for an answer blossomed in the final two paragraphs of his *Life* magazine essay:

> The dust which once flew in the voids, the stuff of the sun, the mineral trash of Earth, has reared itself up in our time to become man—to speak in tongues, to put forth hands and, with one of its billion-year-developed senses, to see those beckoning stars. That dust which came down through cycles of destruction and rebirth now desires to seek other dusts, to know what further shapes strange suns and gravities may have given them.
>
> In our time this search will eventually change our laws, our religions, our philosophies, our arts, our recreations, as well as our sciences. Space, the mirror, waits for life to come look for itself there.

What are these cycles of destruction and rebirth? The ambivalent relationship between life and death had fascinated him all his conscious life. Like many of his peers, he had long since embraced a Space-Age purpose for Humanity, a quest for the stars that provided meaning without the need to guess at any greater mysteries; now he had reached the point where he wanted an existential answer that did not simply dismiss the notion of a creator as irrelevant. It was at this point, sometime in 1961, when Bradbury purchased a copy of the first English-language edition of *The Saviors of God*, by Nikos Kazantzakis.

This series of "Spiritual Exercises," written in 1923, are sometimes dismissed as darkly atheistic, but Bradbury was instantly attracted to them. He certainly knew of Kazantzakis, who had lost the 1956 Nobel Prize for Literature by a single vote. He may have known that Kazantzakis defied ideological labels in much the same way that he himself had defied political, philosophical, and genre labels as a writer. But he could not mistake the affinities in their styles, bridged masterfully through the new translation by Kimon Friar. The Shamanistic tones of Walt Whitman (a Bradbury favorite) echoed here, suggesting an ascending life force common to all matter. But the direct inspiration for Kazantzakis was not Whitman, but Henri Bergson, a philosopher that Bradbury, in spite of his lack of postsecondary education, had already read in part. As early as the mid-1940s, Bergson's concept of time and reality had informed Bradbury's earliest novella-length story, "The Creatures That Time Forgot" ("Frost and Fire"). But Kazantzakis had actually studied with Bergson in the early years of the twentieth century, and *The Saviors of God* turned on a crucial Bergsonian principle that Bradbury had not yet examined: the concept of the life force, or *élan vital*.

Kazantzakis's spiritual exercises led to the Bergsonian conclusion that, in Friar's introductory words, "Man himself is only one manifestation in the long, evolutionary, upward progress of mysterious and vital forces—perhaps the finest yet evolved in the history of earth, the most capable of spiritual refinement, yet certainly not the last or the best possible." And it was this life force, taken back out to the universe, that would restore, in Kazantzakis's own words, the God "buried in our matter and in our souls." Spirit, constantly making and unmaking matter, was the force that Bradbury had been looking for, presented by Kazantzakis in the chapter titled "The Relationship between God and Man": "It is not God who will save us—it is we who will save God, by battling, by creating, and by transmuting matter into spirit."

Man must renew and strengthen the "deathless Cry" of the universe, said Kazantzakis, and Bradbury celebrated this discovery in his next major article for *Life* magazine. During the summer of 1962, shortly after the first half-dozen Russian and American manned space shots, *Life* planned a special issue on "The Take-Over Generation," featuring articles by and about the up and coming Americans who were about to "take over our destiny." This issue, published on September 14, 1962, featured a "provocative" article by Bradbury titled "Cry the Cosmos." It opened with a Kazantzakian transmutation of matter into spirit: the ancient elements of earth, water, air, and fire, thundering to life in a rocket launch—basic atomic structures brought together and transformed into new energies for a cosmic purpose.

There was a new tone to Bradbury's richly metaphorical catalog of the technologies that would take humans into space, and his pivotal definition of our relation to the Cosmos exploded with the spirit of *The Saviors of God*:

> For ultimately a Human Being, though we fondly think so, is not a shape at all. It is not a creature all torso, head and limbs. Neither is it a cylindrical shape with gills. It is not a color. It need have nothing to do with size or place of habitat. Above all, humanity is an Idea, a concept, a way of doing, a motion toward light or dark, a selection between the will to destroy and the will to save. The more times such selection tends toward the Good, the more human we say that thing is becoming. We must seek ways to know and encourage the good in ourselves, the will toward light, in order to recognize it and encourage it on other worlds.

Within a week of publication, his editors telephoned Bradbury three times with news that "Cry the Cosmos" had received the best reader reaction of any *Life* article in years.[1] Bradbury naturally saw his science fiction, especially the early stories gathered into *The Martian Chronicles*, *The Illustrated Man*, and *The Golden Apples of the Sun*, as his own Kazantzakian "spiritual exercises," the perfect vehicles for evangelizing a cosmic purpose for the human race. "Cry the Cosmos" also reenergized his conviction that science fiction was entering the cultural mainstream. Later in the year, at the UCLA Conference on Cultural Arts, he appeared on a panel with Aldous Huxley, who speculated on the dominant literary movements of the future. Bradbury quickly interposed that science fiction would soon subsume the traditional literary genre forms and define the mainstream literature of the next century.

Bradbury's first encounter with Kazantzakis was life-changing, but he did not blindly adopt the doctrines of *The Saviors of God*. In a very real sense, Kazantzakis had simply triggered a conscious realization of insights that had simmered at the subconscious level for more than a decade. Glimpses of the life force surfaced in his 1947 O. Henry Prize–winning story "Powerhouse," where the wonders of the electric power grid reflect the self-sustaining life force of the star-filled night sky: "for every light that was put out, another could come on . . . what seemed like death was simply a ceasing of power at one small point, while light and life were reapplied in another room a few miles distant." There were also elements of *The Saviors of God* that he simply could not accept. In his copy, he crossed out Kazantzakis's admonition not to pity the generations that had suffered and died without hope; the language of the Bible echoed in Bradbury's stories and his screenwriting, and he would always privilege the universal concept of Love as the greatest of all virtues even as his settled beliefs led him elsewhere. Love was the central concept instilled in his midwestern Baptist upbringing, and it would be the last word spoken as he was laid to rest.

Bradbury would remain convinced that the other mysteries of the universe—its size, its origins, and its fate—were ultimately unknowable, even to those future generations who would reach the stars. But he now had the last major insight that would inform his view of the Cosmos for the final fifty years of his long life. As he began to take the measure of Mankind from a Kazantzakian perspective, he continued to take the measure of himself as a writer. He also began to measure himself against the boy who yet remained an essential part of his imaginative process. On August 22, 1960, in the midst of his existential quest for the creative impulses of the Cosmos, he pondered these comparisons in a letter to Don Congdon:

> I am forty years old today. Jesus God. The irony is, I still feel like the boy who woke up summer mornings in Illinois thirty years ago. Hell, it's a collaboration between him and me still, anyway, his early delights, and my later wisdoms knocking together and coming out in stories. It's not a bad combination, and it has been a good life. I wouldn't mind a few more years at it, God Willing, as the Irish say.

He would, indeed, continue to have the luck of the Irish. Between his two *Life* magazine appearances, his seemingly endless plagiarism suit against CBS finally played out. The three judges of the Ninth Circuit Court of Appeals had decided to read Robert Alan Aurthur's *Playhouse 90* teleplay and *Fahrenheit 451* before ruling; in January 1961, the Appellate Court delivered a 2:1 reversal in favor of Bradbury. A CBS request for rehearing was denied on March 23, 1961, ending Federal court action at this level. CBS then announced their final gambit—a filing with the United States Supreme Court. Bradbury had Marks publicly announce their willingness, in spite of the potential financial burden, to file as well.

He had called what turned out to be a bluff hand by CBS; when they realized that Bradbury would not back down over the Supreme Court filing, the insurance advisors recommended a settlement, which was reported in the Hollywood tabloids on August 4, 1961. Bradbury collected $25,000, which he split evenly with Gerson Marks for his four-year prosecution of the case.[2] He also had the satisfaction of a private meeting with the CBS lawyers, who were required to bring the check to Marks's law office. The conversation was brief, and Bradbury did all the talking.

28 | In the Twilight Zone

The August 1961 resolution of the *Fahrenheit 451* plagiarism case came just as Rod Serling and producer Buck Houghton were acquiring Bradbury's "I Sing the Body Electric!" script for the third season of *The Twilight Zone*. In a very real sense Bradbury's decade-long effort to establish his own television series had paved the way for *The Twilight Zone*, but this was completely unknown to the viewing public. Bradbury's enthusiastic engagement with a grateful Rod Serling during the show's development could not fully counterbalance his private sense of frustration that the first science fiction and fantasy television series was developed by a writer whose award-winning television writing career centered on realism.

Bradbury's path to a *Twilight Zone* episode was long and, at times, contentious. In early April 1959, CBS purchased a *Twilight Zone* option on "Here There Be Tygers," a 1951 story that centered on a marvelous Bradbury conceit: a strange planet that turns dreams into reality, providing everything that Earth's first survey team could imagine or want. The exploitative desires of one crew member awaken the planet's full volcanic fury, and the expedition decides, like medieval mapmakers faced with stories of enchanted lands, to leave this world beyond the edge of the star charts. One crewman, a wistful dreamer, stays behind, and finds an Edenic paradise beneath the projected illusion of planetary violence. Bradbury's script was promising, but the required special effects seemed too expensive for the production budget, and the option was never exercised.

During the summer of 1959, Bradbury promised Serling another script, but he apparently refrained from submitting anything else for a year and a half. This hiatus was largely the result of a complex dynamic that was evolving around the two principal members of Serling's core writing team, Charles Beaumont and Richard Matheson. Long-term friendships extended this group to include William F. Nolan, George Clayton Johnson, and a few other Hollywood writers. Nearly all of them had, in various ways, been influenced or even mentored by Bradbury, and now most of them wrote in close association with Serling and his new television series.

Under his agreement with CBS, Serling had to write 80 percent of the scripts. Many were original stories, while others were credited adaptations. He relied on Beaumont and Matheson, and eventually other writers, to script the remaining episodes. Serling was an undisputed master of mainstream realism, having received numerous Emmy awards and nominations during the 1950s as a writer for some of the major 60- and 90-minute dramatic television series of the day. The first 36-episode season of *The Twilight Zone* earned him an Emmy as well, but he was already encountering unexpected pushback from established writers in the very genre field where he was now a pioneering writer/producer.

For years, Serling had felt free to draw inspiration from the moods and basic situations explored by other writers, both past and present. His focus had been on the human factor, and his character-based adaptations and original teleplays went generally unchallenged on creative grounds. Genre fiction was new territory, however, and he soon found what he considered to be an overdeveloped proprietary instinct within the science fiction and fantasy field. The debate centered, more or less privately, among those writers who wrote for him, and others who were close to them and were therefore most likely to study the development of the series with the most scrutiny. On December 4, 1960, in the early weeks of the second season broadcasts of *The Twilight Zone*, Charles Beaumont spent an afternoon presenting a shocked and bewildered Serling with his concerns, and those of his fellow writers.

Beaumont was his closest writing colleague, and was perhaps the most creative talent Serling would ever work with. He had the strongest reputation for loyalty and integrity within Serling's slowly expanding circle of writers, and was more concerned than the others by what he perceived as unacknowledged idea borrowings. He presented Serling with a list of stories by other writers—and even some of his own stories—that he and (presumably) others felt had been the unacknowledged sources for some of Serling's *Twilight Zone* teleplays. These similarities were not, for the most part, deeply invasive; even Beaumont conceded that there were two sides to the argument, and as this more or less private debate continued over the next few years, it was often hard to see more than a general influence at work in many of the stories under discussion.

Serling's first-season teleplay for "The Lonely," broadcast on November 13, 1959, offers a prime example of the deep proprietary feelings that Serling found so bewilderingly outré among his colleagues. In this original teleplay, Serling's protagonist is a condemned convict on a deep-space prison asteroid, who is provided with a female android companion. He grows to love her over time, but when he is eventually pardoned, there is no weight allowance for her aboard the rescue ship; the ship captain realizes that she must be destroyed or the former prisoner will never leave his prison. During their December 4 meeting, Beaumont's dissection of this very moving story stunned Serling: Beaumont concluded that Serling had cobbled the story together from Bradbury's "The Long Years" (human doctor with android family marooned on Mars), Beaumont's "Mother's Day" (prison asteroid), and Bill Nolan's "Joy for Living" (a female android's doomed quest for human affection).

Serling studied Beaumont's script-by-script analysis, but could not concede that his work went beyond normal bounds of influence and inspiration. Within twenty-four hours he had refuted Beaumont's analysis in writing;[1] it was a difficult letter to write, but he nonetheless respected Beaumont for bringing his concerns directly to him to answer. That same day, he wrote an even more difficult letter to Bradbury, for he knew that Bradbury shared some, if not all, of Beaumont's views, and had chosen to brood rather than clear the air.

Bradbury's reservations about Serling's teleplays went back more than a year, and began with a preview showing of the pilot episode, "Where Is Everybody?" A man awakens in a state of amnesia, and finds that the town around him is abandoned. Car engines are still warm, appliances are running, just as if the people had suddenly left moments before he awoke. But this world is simply a hallucination, and he revives to find that he has been in an isolation experiment to see if he could endure prolonged space travel. Bradbury was reminded of his own *Martian Chronicles* story "The Silent Towns," where one of the last Martian colonists returns from the hills to wander through the recently abandoned settlements left behind when the threat of war back home sends everyone back to Earth.

There were really very few similarities between these story lines, but Bradbury's reaction shows the deep influence of the other writers within the circle he shared with Serling. Several were with him at the preview, and from this point on they reinforced his growing mistrust of Serling's originality as a relative newcomer to science fiction and fantasy writing. The main complaint among this group of writers was that Serling had read too much fantasy and science fiction too quickly and could not keep track of the interplay between original and borrowed ideas.[2] Bradbury himself came to this conclusion shortly after "Where Is Everybody?" was broadcast on October 2, 1959. He would always maintain that Serling realized an unintentional borrowing when his wife Carol, who was reading *The Martian Chronicles*, pointed out some similarities between the pilot episode and "The Silent Towns." By Bradbury's account, Serling made at least two phone calls of apology and offered to pay for the rights, but never followed through.

Oddly enough, in his letter to Bradbury of December 5, 1960, Serling never mentioned the pilot episode at all. Instead, he explained his frustration with what he perceived to be the obsessive turf battles over originality in his new genre home, using the complicated accusations over "The Lonely" as a case in point. But he spent the greater part of his letter defending his script for "Walking Distance," another first-season show that Bradbury seemed to find even more invasive than the pilot episode. Serling's response was based solely on Beaumont's analysis from the previous day's meeting, but he knew from the dynamics of friendship that the claims originated with Bradbury himself.

"Walking Distance," broadcast on October 30, 1959, bore all the hallmarks of quality that carried over from Serling's award-winning realism of the 1950s. His best scripts for *The Twilight Zone* presented an eloquent and appealing sense of nostalgia, with tight dialogue that nevertheless had strong emotional impact. In this episode a big city businessman seeks rest and rejuvenation in a trip to his small hometown. As he walks into town from the service station where he has left his car, he passes back in time and discovers his parents, his childhood home, and even the boy he had once been. Events make it clear that he must walk back out of town and return to his own time, and he reluctantly agrees that he must not warn his younger self of the harsh grown-up world that awaits.

In a very real sense, "Walking Distance" reflected the best of what Serling and Bradbury had in common—character-driven stories that examine the large and small philosophies of life, past, present, and future. But Bradbury's complex envy and mistrust of Serling was triggered once again, this time by Serling's use of a small-town carousel to suggest the protagonist's transition back into the world of the present. This metaphor seemed too close to the carousel at the heart of his nearly finished *Something Wicked This Way Comes*, a device out of time that alternately aged or regressed its riders.

Serling only *implied* the temporal shift, by means of a quick dissolve from his childhood carousel into a spinning hi-fi phonograph disk playing music in the big-city world of the grown man. But Bradbury's long creative development of his dark carnival carousel, as well as his passion for writing stories about similar encounters with our older and younger selves, fueled his displeasure. Beaumont had pointed out to Serling that Bradbury's original had already been adapted for television and broadcast in 1954 as "Merry-Go-Round"; this was, in Bradbury's mind, where Serling would have seen it.

In his letter Serling maintained his total ignorance of Bradbury's forerunners, noting how a recent visit to Binghamton, New York, where he had grown up, revealed the true catalyst: the now-condemned Recreation Park merry-go-round that he had loved as a child. Serling's summation touched on the very reasons he had wanted Bradbury's participation in the *Twilight Zone* series: "If there is a similar mood in this piece, Ray, I can neither affirm nor deny that that mood came in part from your writing. I admit and quite frankly that I've always been impressed by your sensitivity and your honesty. If there was any sub-conscious carry over of mood, I'm sure you would agree that this could well be coincidental and certainly not overt."

Serling's position carried the day, and Bradbury chose not to dispute the sources of "Walking Distance" any further at that time. Bradbury had been careful, for the most part, to keep his criticisms of Serling to the small circle of writers that had gathered around Beaumont and Matheson. Ironically, this may have served to aggravate the situation, for Beaumont's driven and often tortured creativity colored his observations about his own work as compared to the work of others. Bradbury had already seen this tendency when Beaumont worked himself up over Bradbury's *Something Wicked This Way Comes* screenplay, which seemed to threaten his own chances to script *The Circus of Dr. Lao*; at the time, Bradbury simply described Beaumont's concern to Congdon as "one more example of Chuck's ability to panic when someone drops a teacup."[3]

Bradbury did not share Beaumont's total proprietary obsession with the work in hand: "Every job is uppermost to him, everything in life, seized on, is, in the moment, most important." He knew this was a key to Beaumont's creative genius, and he shared the impulse to some extent; but Bradbury also knew that a writer has to be able to let go of his creation at some point. "There is always tomorrow, there are always other projects and ideas. Chuck hasn't discovered this yet. I don't believe he thinks he will wake up tomorrow morning, alive." Nevertheless, Bradbury's ambivalent attitude toward Serling was complicated by Beaumont's somewhat overreaching claims that Serling borrowed too freely; it all seemed to confirm and magnify his own problem with Serling, and he avoided direct confrontation entirely.

There are few secrets in Hollywood, however; Serling had heard rumors of Bradbury's displeasure even before Beaumont's accusations, and in Serling's mind the greater fault was Bradbury's for leaving it on a slow burn for so long. It was clear to both men that a meeting was in order, and within a few days of receiving Serling's December 5th letter Bradbury met with Serling to clear the air. In person, Bradbury's warmth and great good spirits could always mend the consequences of his anger, and Serling's genuine admiration made it possible to rejoin efforts to secure a Bradbury story for *The Twilight Zone*. He confided to Bradbury that network pressures had led him to offer his resignation, convinced that the series would be canceled anyway. *The Twilight Zone* was renewed for a third season, but Serling no longer carried the pressures (or title) of executive producer.

Within a week, Bradbury sent Serling a script based on a yet-unpublished story, "A Miracle of Rare Device." On December 13, 1960, Serling responded with thanks and some positive comments, along with upbeat suggestions to streamline the character interactions. Bradbury's engaging tale of two Arizona desert drifters who discover an ever-changing cityscape mirage led to a strong script, and on May 8, 1961, Serling and Houghton acquired it for the series. But it languished in preproduction, and, like the effects-heavy "Here There Be Tygers," the episode was never filmed.

Serling's subsequent comments suggest that, in the case of "A Miracle of Rare Device," the problem centered on dialogue rather than special effects. In later years, Serling reflected on this challenge: "Ray Bradbury is a very difficult guy to dramatize, because that which reads so beautifully on the printed page doesn't fit in the mouth—it fits in the head. And you find characters saying the things that Bradbury's saying and you say, 'Wait a minute, people don't say that.'" It was a knock that Bradbury had heard before in Hollywood, although, as his success with scripting for Hitchcock indicates, not all of the television directors he worked with felt this way.

But as Serling and Houghton prepared for season three, Bradbury broke the deadlock over "A Miracle of Rare Device" by offering a swap-out with a new script based on another one of his unpublished tales. "I Sing the Body Electric!" was the story of a widower who purchases an electric grandmother to care for his three grieving children. The plot had its origins in his never-ending readings in psychology; during the 1950s, he had read that children sometimes respond to the death of a parent with bitterness and a sense of abandonment, and he wanted to see if the robotic grandmother, fully equipped with nurturing emotions and instincts, could heal the anger and fear emanating from the only daughter, the youngest of the three children.

The arrangement was finalized on September 12, 1961, but during October the first attempt to film the episode was not successful. Houghton arranged to have most of the scenes reshot during February 1962, and this attempt proved much better. Nevertheless, the process caused more strain in the Serling-Bradbury relationship. The reshoot required a short-notice request for Bradbury to revise the script; Bradbury told Congdon that the call had come the night before shooting resumed, just as he was in the midst of difficult revisions to *Something Wicked This Way Comes*: "I asked them why they hadn't asked me to do the revisions some time during the 8 previous weeks, and they merely shrugged and toed the floor."[4]

Most of the complexities of revising and reshooting "I Sing the Body Electric!" were eventually worked out, but one very short editing cut in the May 18 broadcast version proved a lasting disappointment to Bradbury. It eliminated the crucial moment when the electric grandmother, played to great effect by Josephine Hutchinson, reveals her mechanical nature to the children. There is no loss of continuity, but for Bradbury the cut diminished the essential difference between human and automaton on which the story hinges. The fact that he had invited a number of friends to his home for the broadcast only served to magnify his disappointment. He felt that he should have been consulted, and this more than any other incident convinced him that he could not work any further on the series.[5]

This disappointment came only a few months after the broadcast of an episode that seemed closer to a Bradbury story than any other in the entire Twilight Zone series. "Nothing in the Dark" had aired earlier that season, on January 1, 1962. An old woman, living in the basement of a condemned tenement, is certain that she can keep Mr. Death from crossing her threshold. She concentrates her vigilance on the gruff demolition foreman outside her door, never guessing that the handsome but wounded young man she has rescued from the street is, in reality, Mr. Death. He gently shows her that, in the words of Serling's closing monologue, "there is nothing in the dark that wasn't there when the lights were on."

This episode seemed very close to "Death and the Maiden," a Bradbury story first published in the March 1960 issue of The Magazine of Fantasy & Science Fiction. Bradbury's old woman endures the same terror as well as the same unexpectedly blissful revelation, and the tight focus of the situation made these similarities seem all the more like a "lift" to Bradbury. There were, to be sure, differences in plotting; his old woman lived in a rural cabin, and the more isolated environment allows Mr. Death, posing as a young lover willing to respectfully romance her, the opportunity to talk his way into her fortified home.

"Nothing in the Dark" was indeed very close to his own work, but then so was the young writer, George Clayton Johnson. It was his second Twilight Zone script, and, like the older Beaumont and Matheson, he had been influenced by Bradbury. But unlike the other writers, Johnson had participated in Bradbury's writers' group and had recently finished coscripting Bradbury's short animated feature for Format Films, Icarus Montgolfier Wright. This creative dynamic had already entered the Twilight Zone—Johnson always acknowledged Bradbury's hand in the final scene of his first episode, "The Four of Us Are Dying."

Even before "Nothing in the Dark" aired, Bill Nolan cautioned Johnson about the strong parallels with Bradbury's "Death and the Maiden." But Johnson's ability to challenge the old woman differently, in a more claustrophobic urban setting, with the decoy element of the gruff foreman, and with the different means of entry for Mr. Death, allowed for some degree of creative leverage. Bradbury's closeness to Johnson persuaded him not to pursue the similarities, but the situation brought back all the old feelings about Serling's series.

Bradbury was beginning to vocalize his feelings again, but he did not approach Serling with them; on May 13, 1962, both men interacted with apparent warmth as science fiction panel participants at the Seattle World's Fair. But just a week earlier, when his Bantam paperback editors wanted to use Serling's name as a publicity boost, Bradbury firmly vetoed the opportunity: "Rod is a Johnny-Come-Lately, who will come and go and be forgotten in the s-f field; his greatest strength, and I wish he would realize it, lies in the sort of powerful realism he did for *Playhouse 90*. I wish he would go back to that and leave the s-f to us guys who know how to do it . . . meaning myself, Chuck Beaumont, Heinlein, and others."[6]

Bradbury's frustration with "Nothing in the Dark" and then his disappointment with the editing of "I Sing the Body Electric!" needed only a small spark to ignite a final explosion. That spark was provided by a member of the editorial staff at *Los Angeles* magazine. In early September 1962, Bradbury was in the magazine's offices working on the draft of an article. One of the younger staff members knew the Serlings, and for a few minutes the conversation turned to the *Twilight Zone* series and its host. Bradbury sensed that he was being drawn out; the questioning went on and on, and it was only later that he realized that the exchange may have been a probe to see if there was a story to be had for publication. On September 12, the tenor of Bradbury's comments was relayed to Serling, and the exchange of letters that followed opened both new and old wounds.

Their final written exchange took less than twenty-four hours. On the 13th, Serling wrote to dispel any notion of plagiarism concerning the pilot script for "Where Is Everybody?" A comparison of the two plots bears out Serling's contention; it's likely that Serling's original telephone calls in the fall of 1959 had been motivated by his desire to keep Bradbury, truly one of his favorite science fiction and fantasy writers, interested in writing for the series.

But Bradbury was fixated on the telephone conversations, which short-circuited any rational thought about the creative distance between the two stories. On September 14, his response centered on that memory: "The old question still remains, why, after all this time . . . didn't you buy the story from me that you absolutely promised to buy? I didn't ask you to promise, I didn't insist, I told you it wasn't necessary. Yet finally, after some days of thinking it over, you called and insisted on buying the story and said you would contact my agent immediately. Three years have gone by, and no call" (ellipsis Bradbury's).

He also cited the Johnson script of "Nothing in the Dark," feeling that this more recent incident signaled a pattern of unacknowledged creative borrowings throughout the series. He also made it clear that he felt totally ambushed by the *Los Angeles* magazine staff; the encounter seemed far more than a naïve and unfortunate line of questioning by a young staffer who didn't understand the consequences of her words. The older editors had followed the game as well, and for a long time Bradbury broke off his relationship with the magazine. In closing, he acknowledged his own bad judgment in not speaking directly to Serling, but his final comments showed the unbridgeable divide that, from Bradbury's perspective, would always remain:

> As for our friendship, it is, of course, now officially over. I'm sorry I was a hypocrite, but I actually thought I could get over all the bugging things, and that we might finally come to some peaceful equilibrium. It seems that is not fated to be. I can only hope and promise no one will, in future, ask me about the *Twilight Zone*. I will try to keep my mouth shut. But if it opens, you can be sure I will try to tell the truth and not lie.

For his part, Serling did not want a break; Bradbury was one of the authors who had inspired his own move into the field—the author who had also inspired the other principal writers on his staff. In terms of mood and engagement, *The Twilight Zone* was not far distant from Bradbury's perennial October Country. That was, in essence, the problem. Serling no doubt could have credited certain writers with the original ideas for some of his scripts, ranging from his own circle of writers back through such inspirational sources as Chekhov's "The Bet" (adapted as "The Silence"). But few charges were brought during the five-year run of the series; in the case of Bradbury's work, even the need for acknowledgment in Johnson's "Nothing in the Dark" does not rise to the level of plagiarism. In his own scripts, Serling often did capture the wistfulness and nostalgia of a Bradbury tale; as Marc Zicree has noted, Serling made no secret of it in such wish-fulfillment stories as "Walking Distance" (Dr. Bradbury) and "A Stop at Willoughby" (the Bradbury account).

Bradbury's fundamental wariness of Serling was not so much based on notions of plagiarism as on his firm belief that Serling did not have a true feel for the genre he was pioneering on television. There was also an underlying element of envy, but it was based on his own truly groundbreaking work in television, and the many disappointments he had experienced along the way. Serling's high-pressure dealings with Hollywood took a similar toll on his own psyche, making him hypersensitive to Bradbury's talk around town. In the coming decades, the quality science fiction and fantasy concepts that eventually reached the airways would be few and far between; but both men had, in their very different ways, made possible nearly all that would follow.

29 Something Wicked This Way Comes

For a time, Bradbury followed the course of action he had set out so forcefully and privately in the spring of 1961—he went back to writing new fiction, short and long, avoiding interactions with others as much as possible. At first, the intensity of this resolve even led him to back away from an honor he had sought for years, and finally won. In early 1961, he was asked to participate in the Bread Loaf Writers School at Middlebury College and immediately proclaimed his excitement to Don Congdon: "I have accepted an invitation to spend two weeks at Bread Loaf from August 15th to the 30th this summer, lecturing with and standing alongside of Robert Frost, Howard Nemerov, John Ciardi, and others. This is an old, old dream come true, an adventure I've always wanted."[1]

Unfortunately, his great disappointment at MGM over The Martian Chronicles screenplay changed everything. During the following weeks he canceled his participation in the Bread Loaf residency, after the program brochures that included his name and biographical note were already printed. But this unexpected burst of sacrificial self-discipline also had its compensations; he was now able to take up the stalled third draft of Something Wicked This Way Comes without the temptation of major film work or the distraction of Bread Loaf. On April 10, 1961, he informed Congdon that he was now back at work on the novel, noting that he had already "come up with fresh insights into the character of the two boys, which is all important, especially in differentiating them throughout the first sections of the novel." This was a flaw that Congdon had reacted to in the first submission, and he saw the latest breakthrough as a sign that Bradbury had at last fully turned back to the work in hand.

In September 1961, Bradbury would face the first true test of his ability to avoid new Hollywood demands. His upcoming adaptation of Stanley Ellin's "The Faith of Aaron Menefee" for Alfred Hitchcock Presents brought him once again into occasional contact with Hitchcock himself, who was considering a film about nature turning on Mankind. After initially considering Fredric Brown's novel The Mind Thing, an August 1961 newspaper article about a localized attack by frenzied seabirds in Capatolla, California, prompted Hitchcock to turn instead to Daphne du Maurier's short story "The Birds" as a potential film project.[2] After considering other writers, he asked Bradbury to adapt the story.

Bradbury immediately relayed his dilemma to Congdon: "Main trouble is he wants me immediately, and, of course, my novel calls piteously to me to get on to the end and get the manuscript off to S&S." It was apparent that, as usual, Bradbury was simultaneously attracted and repelled by the offer; he was literally thinking it through as he wrote to Congdon, drifting from characteristic metaphor into an uncharacteristically cryptic shorthand: "Here I stand in the plenteous rain with nary a spoon nor a drinking cup. Am also guilt-ridden by hidden self who declared, earlier in summer, no more films for rest of year." Could he make the hard decision, or was there a third way?

In a risky move, Bradbury tried to satisfy both demon and Muse by asking for an eight-week delay, citing his in-progress work for Hitchcock's television show. Hitchcock would eventually film *Marnie* before turning back to "The Birds," but at the time he was keen on the du Maurier project and reluctantly turned to another writer. This came as a great relief to Congdon, who knew that Bradbury needed to produce a sustained work of long fiction if he were to continue to develop as a major presence in American literature.

The novella-to-short-novel triumph of *Fahrenheit 451* masked a fact that discerning fans and critics had seldom addressed in print. As the years passed, Bradbury remained at risk of joining Edgar Allan Poe as one of the only storytellers with an enduring international reputation who had not also become a successful novelist. In the fall of 1962 Bradbury finally broke through this barrier with the publication of *Something Wicked This Way Comes*. Ironically, the most insightful review of this dark fantasy emerged from a prominent science fiction article—a major 2-page literary feature by Anthony Boucher in the *New York Herald Tribune*. In "The Eerie Ebb of Science Fiction," Boucher (writing under his familiar *Tribune* byline "H. H. Holmes") took full measure of the postwar boom-and-bust cycle of the genre and addressed the central question: "why is science fiction itself such a negligible element in American publishing?"

Boucher could attest to the consistently limited readership base for science fiction and hope that the race for the moon (and the ever-increasing range of mass-market paperbacks) would eventually carry science fiction into mainstream literary prominence. But his roll call of the major practitioners ended with an observation that succinctly captured the increasingly publicized paradox of Bradbury's prominent role in this history: "The one writer whom the mainstream critics have consistently recognized as an ambassador and almost as a symbol of S.F. has been Ray Bradbury . . . yet it can be (and often has been) argued that Bradbury never really wrote science fiction at all—rather, poetic fantasies on themes from the future."

Boucher's long article culminated in a review of *Something Wicked This Way Comes* that balanced praise for the power of the narrative fantasy with a concise statement of its limitations as allegory: "Bradbury's good and evil are simply and unsubtly conceived, as is the final defeat of Darkness by Love and Laughter. The novel lacks distinction as an allegory; and its beings, both human and supernatural, lack the complexity that could bring them fully alive." But the true triumph of this first novel from an established storyteller was the sustained combination of suspense, invention, and what Boucher called "the small horrors of magic" that Bradbury was finally able to extend into long fiction without relying on the original armature provided by a short story idea. Bradbury's "The Black Ferris" of the late 1940s—transformed into a nightmare carousel during the long years of novel development—merely provided the central metaphor for the dark powers of Evil. The extended structures of the novel itself, perhaps overly long but ultimately effective as sustained narrative, clearly define the last great breakthrough of Bradbury's writing career.

British readers and critics continued to be divided about Bradbury's departure from science fiction. The London critics had not cared very much for *Dandelion Wine*, and *Something Wicked* also received mixed reviews in Britain. Two years earlier, his good friend and publisher Rupert Hart-Davis, always uneasy with the science fiction label, defended the kind of light and dark fantasies that were becoming the standard Bradbury fare. His comments show just how tired he was of the critical debate over one of his favorite authors: "I abominate science fiction. . . . Bradbury is a man of poetic imagination who uses gadgetry to liberate that imagination."[3]

But Bradbury's shift to fantasy cost him one of his most influential admirers within the British literary world. Kingsley Amis, a strong champion of *Fahrenheit 451*, came down hard on Bradbury in his *London Observer* review of *Something Wicked*: "Deprived now of the discipline provided by science fiction and its pressures toward reality and reason, Mr. Bradbury has plunged bald-headed into a kind of Californian Gothic, with echoes of James Purdy and the Dylan Thomas of 'The Map of Love.'"[4] In far more subtle ways, however, *Something Wicked This Way Comes* exhibited Bradbury's mastery of a most chilling form of terror. Anthony Boucher was on the right trail when he suggested that the novel evoked the moods of Charles Williams, a mythopoeic fantasist and close friend of both C. S. Lewis and J. R. R. Tolkien. Bradbury had in fact read and been greatly affected by Williams's masterpiece, *Descent into Hell*.[5] The dark narcissism and chillingly casual disregard for humanity that emerges in Williams is reflected in Bradbury's carnival masters, Cooger and Dark.

The long-awaited first novel extended Bradbury's reputation as a myth-maker, a fabulist who was not afraid to experiment in new forms. But *Something Wicked This Way Comes* also suggested that he could find sanctuary, a safe zone for his creativity, by returning to the forms of dark fantasy where he had first made his mark on American literature. His post–*Fahrenheit 451* experiments in form and genre had moved with limited success from occasional story collections to a largely hit-and-miss pattern in television and no success at all in the exhausting motion picture endeavors he had undertaken since 1957. Repeating the remarkable success of his *Moby Dick* screenplay had so far not translated into a single motion picture production, and these efforts had contributed to the marked decline in his production of short stories. The new novel would become a capstone to the incredible creativity of his first two decades as a writer, but could he continue to grow and develop? In his *Herald Tribune* review article, Boucher's brief refinement of this essential question would prove to be right on the mark: "[O]ne has the impression of an intensely creative mind still uncertain, as its owner approaches his middle years, of the precise nature of its creative powers."

: : :

In early 1962, the final revisions of *Something Wicked This Way Comes* coincided with Bradbury's return to regular television work. Predictably, his renewed interest in teleplays came through his established relationships with Hitchcock and his principal producers, Joan Harrison and Norman Lloyd. Besides his one-off scripts for *Steve Canyon* ("The Gift," 1958) and *The Trouble Shooters* ("Tunnel to Yesterday," May 1960), and the single episode ("I Sing the Body Electric!" 1962) that resulted from his complex relationship with *The Twilight Zone*, Bradbury's success in television from 1956 through 1964 derived in large measure from his association with *Alfred Hitchcock Presents*.

For the seventh season, Lloyd convinced Bradbury to adapt Stanley Ellin's "The Faith of Aaron Menefee." He had rarely adapted the work of other writers for film, and never at all for television, but Bradbury provided Lloyd with a fine teleplay of Ellin's story, which centered on a fanciful mix of faith healing and crime. The episode aired on January 30, 1962, followed barely a week later by his original teleplay for *Alcoa Premiere*, "The Jail." This was not a Hitchcock show, but Lloyd and Harrison were engaged to produce one episode and they asked Bradbury for an original story. To this point, "The Jail" was only a concept that Bradbury had dictated into a tape recorder eight years earlier: If minds could be transferred between bodies, then executions would no longer be necessary; the minds of the condemned could be transferred into the bodies of elderly derelicts, thus becoming harmless wanderers for the few short months or years left to them. The derelict's mind, worthy or not, would gain the criminal's vigorous body.

The Writers Guild of America nominated "The Jail" for a WGA Television–Radio Writers' Award.[6] Bradbury's strange twist on mind transfer, and the emotional impact provided by the dialogue and plot, made for an excellent speculative drama, but ABC received enough complaints about violating the sanctity of the human soul that "The Jail" was never rerun on network television. All in all, however, the success of these two teleplays during the 1961–62 viewing season provided a rare moment of satisfaction with his Hollywood fortunes, and coincided with an even more significant off-camera milestone for Bradbury—the founding of the Screen Writer's Film Society.

Bradbury struck a chord with many Writers Guild of America (West) members by suggesting that screenwriters had little time to see foreign films, experimental films, or refresh themselves on the classic mainstream or genre films that had inspired many of them to take up the craft in the first place. He joined forces with the expatriate British writer Ivan Moffat and, with administrative support provided by WGAW Executive Director Michael Franklin, enlisted other writers to help find a theater home for the Guild's nascent Film Society. Val Davies, president of the Academy of Motion Picture Arts and Sciences, pledged the Academy's Theater on Melrose Place for twice-monthly Sunday evening screenings from October through December 1961.[7]

Similar experiments had failed in the past, but this time more than 500 Guild writers joined. The promise of a convenient and reliable venue, and the opportunity to have a say in the selections, had made all the difference. The wish list was impressive, with the membership favoring such foreign films as La Dolce Vita, Breathless, Seventh Seal, Wages of Fear, and a number of more elusive titles; Among American films, only Chaplin's Limelight made the top ten. But securing screening rights proved a bit difficult at first, and the fall lineup, which included The Great War (Italian), The Joker and The Testament of Orpheus (both French), and Fate of a Man (Russian), did not please everyone. Bradbury's hand was evident in these selections—he was already an admirer of Sergei Bondarchuk, who starred in and produced Fate of a Man, and his fascination with Cocteau's stage and screen work (as well as the appearance of Picasso in the film) drew him to The Testament of Orpheus in spite of its significant structural flaws.

Oscar-nominated film screenings at the Academy Theater required the Guild to find an alternate home from January through most of April 1962. The Director's Guild, which already screened films on an irregular basis in the Guild's theater on Sunset Boulevard, provided the temporary venue, and the addition of the influential film historian Arthur Knight to the Film Society leadership significantly raised the Society's ability to secure prerelease screenings of major American films. *To Kill a Mockingbird* was the first 1962 screening, and *The Miracle Worker* and *Advise and Consent* soon followed. Together, Bradbury, Knight, and to a lesser degree Moffat were able to establish a fairly popular mix of new foreign and American releases along with an increasing number of classic films that had long been consigned to late-night television.

Bradbury encountered many of the important new foreign films of the 1960s in this improbable venue; like his acting company, he found himself manager and virtual proprietor of an imaginary world and spread both his enthusiasm and influence across a broad cross section of his peers. But not without occasional resistance; objections to such experimental films as *The Balcony*, *The Trial*, and Cocteau's *The Testament of Orpheus* led Bradbury and Knight to prepare a coda in the spring of 1963: "These selections, while studded with more conventional films, suggest the fundamental aims of the Society—to broaden the writer's awareness of what is happening in the world of motion pictures."

It soon became clear that they weren't in the business of running "easy, popular films" or presiding over chatty social events. Bradbury maintained that how a film is viewed is just as important as the film itself. Some would be irritated by his view that the theater is a temple; his friend Christopher Isherwood would leave the Society in 1964 after one of Bradbury's more intemperate admonitions to remain silent during the showings. Yet the Society endured largely because of the core membership of serious colleagues that the founding leadership nurtured from the start.

His friendship with Arthur Knight represented the greatest personal dividend for Bradbury. Over the next quarter-century he would often guest lecture in Knight's USC film classes. As the 1960s progressed, Allen Rivkin, president of the Screen Branch of the WGAW, joined the Film Society's leadership team and reinforced Bradbury's established pattern of trying new things to keep the Society's reputation as a significant opinion-generating force both within and beyond the American film industry.

: : :

His converging moments of success with television, the Film Society, and the long-awaited *Something Wicked This Way Comes* were punctuated by moments of great personal sadness. Charles Laughton, Bradbury's last true mentor, was dying; he collapsed on tour early in 1962 and was eventually brought home to Los Angeles, barely aware of his surroundings during the final long months of his life. Even as he declined, his Hollywood presence lived on through such 1962 feature film releases as *Spartacus* and *Advise and Consent*. *Spartacus* was, in fact, a living memory for Bradbury—Laughton had brought him onto the Roman Senate set to meet the cast, including Sir Lawrence Olivier.[8] Over his career, Laughton had won an academy award for Best Actor and was nominated twice more—the last time, along with his wife Elsa Lanchester, for the 1957 film *Witness for the Prosecution*. Many great names were concerned about his final illness, which was spreading rapidly from the original diagnosis of kidney cancer.

Yet Bradbury, who was not a Hollywood insider at all, found himself singled out at times to help Elsa deal with the final months. On August 6, 1962, he wrote to Congdon about his latest visit: "His wife called me to the house last week; I spent several hours with her and unless there is a miracle of remission, which *does* happen once every ten thousand times, his chances for survival are limited. It was a strange sad day . . . for I realized that with all their fame and money, here were the Laughtons depending on someone, really, who is a comparatively new friend . . . a situation which flabbergasts, unsettles, and touches me, by turn. I have nothing but good thoughts of Charlie . . . though he has always groused about money, and I have heard much from others . . . still I can only judge by my own experience, which was excellent" (ellipses Bradbury's).

Laughton died in mid-December 1962, and Bradbury could not bring himself to attend the funeral. Elsa understood, noting how much Charles had hated funerals too (he never attended them). "I remember his graciousness with me," he wrote to Congdon on the 19th, "his thoughtfulness about my own creativity when I was working on the operetta with him, . . . and the private performances of Shakespeare he often gave for me to prove a point he wanted me to learn." Bradbury would continue to visit Elsa and even brought her to performances of his plays over the years, but the loss of Charles left a great sadness in the relationship. He steered her away from one biographer who was intent on exposing the complexities of the Laughton household, but in the end he could not convince her to filter the images that reached the public eye. It was an unrealistic wish, but one that Bradbury felt strongly about concerning those friends who had led dark and secretly stressful lives.

His desire to privately comfort and protect the off-trail lives of certain friends was already a Bradbury hallmark, and the deep history of this impulse was beginning to surface in his more recent fiction. Around the time of Laughton's death, Bradbury considered gathering these new tales as *The Fire Walkers*, "a collection of stories about The Others." Here were the "collectors," those solitary "Lonelies" who joined him at the Hollywood studio gates in the late 1930s, determined to touch the hands and secure the autographs of movie moguls and film stars. Here also was "The Great Man Dies," a telling of Laughton's final days. Two others,

"The Cold Wind and the Warm" and "The Better Part of Wisdom" had evolved out of his 1953–54 sojourn in Ireland, where he had once discussed Irish views on homosexuality with a Catholic priest. "The Haunting of the New" described an Irish manor house that literally burns from sexual excesses of all kinds that go on within its walls.

The three Irish stories were tales of compassion and sentiment, written to illustrate Bradbury's evolving sense that differing lifestyles should be met with tolerance and acceptance: Villagers slowly come to accept the exotic band of gay writers who stumble into Heeber Finn's pub ("The Cold Wind and the Warm"); an Irish grandfather accepts his grandson's male companion ("The Better Part of Wisdom"); and the manor house, rebuilt, shuts out all the aging lovers, who must learn to grow old gracefully ("The Haunting of the New"). "The Long After Midnight Girl," however, attempted to return to the darker worlds of Bradbury's earliest fiction: a Los Angeles ambulance team recovers the body of a beautiful young girl who has hanged herself, discovering to their shock that the victim is really a male transvestite. The medics' chilling sense of Otherness is swallowed up by compassion—no matter what the circumstances, heartbreak was the real cause of death.

The stories he intended for The Fire Walkers had ambivalent roots in his imagination; when he submitted "The Haunting of the New" to Congdon, his cover letter announced "More surprises from the old 'subcon.'"[9] For the most part they were based on his observations of real lives extended into the fantastic— sometimes darkly, but almost always with compassion. On a thematic level, these stories also highlighted Bradbury's growing impulse to adapt traditional wisdoms to an increasingly relativistic world. But they were gently written, reflecting the changing times in American culture, and that lack of tension and emotional power stood in contrast to the hard-hitting stories of racial injustice and poverty that Bradbury had pushed through to publication in less tolerant times. Bradbury tried to bolster the collection by adding two closely related and very powerful stories from earlier decades, "Interval in Sunlight" and "The Next in Line," which together portray an estranged couple vacationing in Mexico—the wife perhaps suspecting, but not really consciously aware, that her self-absorbed husband is letting the heartbreaking poverty and terrifying superstitions of the people slowly kill her.

Even with the novella formed out of the two Mexican masterpieces, The Fire Walkers would be a risky proposition. The other stories, with such tantalizing titles as "Hunka," "Who Put Out the Fire on Fire Island," "The Monk," and "The Woman at the Bottom of the Spanish Steps," are known today only through discarded fragments. His homage to Laughton was put off, perhaps because of his concern for Elsa (he would later substitute another English friend, Gerald Heard, writing about Heard's final lonely days in his 2008 story "Last Laughs"). The Hollywood autograph seekers were relegated to nostalgic essays and small moments in his later detective novels. Don Congdon, who felt that Bradbury's best story collections had wide-ranging contents, recommended against publishing The Fire Walkers, and Bradbury turned instead to plans for his first fully retrospective story collection—a project that would eventually become, in 1965, The Vintage Bradbury.

Something Wicked This Way Comes was, in many ways, a culmination of his early achievements in dark fantasy and paved the way for Bradbury to showcase some of his best weird tales through new media adaptations. There was no longer any need to decline further work for Alfred Hitchcock, and in 1964 he would see two tales adapted for the extended format Alfred Hitchcock Hour. Writer James Bridges earned an Emmy nomination for his adaptation of "The Jar," but Bradbury wrote his own teleplay for "The Life Work of Juan Diaz," a recent story of a Mexican villager who provides more effectively for his impoverished family as a displayed mummy than he ever could as a living man. "Juan Diaz" was the culmination of many good Mexican tales based on his 1945 road trip through Mexico, and together the story and the teleplay provided closure to his most terrifying memory of that journey—the mummies of Guanajuato. Bradbury stories had premiered on Hitchcock's first television season and would help close out the final season of this remarkable series run.

30 Out of the Deeps

For most of 1962, through the stress of his final break with Rod Serling and the delights of writing "Cry the Cosmos" for *Life* magazine, Bradbury was deeply involved with refining the dark fears that fairly exploded out of his final drafts of *Something Wicked This Way Comes*. His renewed focus on prose narrative, uninterrupted by major outside commitments, brought other benefits as well—in 1962 he published eight new stories, more than he had published in a single year since 1957.

But he also felt the deep tidal pull of his most significant media achievement—his 1953–54 screenplay for *Moby Dick*, the film that had brought him all the opportunities (and perils) that accrue when an established writer finds sudden success in Hollywood. His complex working relationship with director John Huston had left him incapable of fully letting go of the subject; by the early 1960s, the whale and his pursuers welled up once again in Bradbury's imagination as a deep space odyssey titled *Leviathan '99*. Bradbury would always give the impression that this project first emerged as a radio play that evolved over the next half-century into a longer stage play, an opera libretto, and eventually into a novella. But early drafts of the novella predate the mid-1960s radio play; in fact, these pages originate in 1961–62, and they echo the sublime awe and fear of evil that he was simultaneously trying to perfect in *Something Wicked This Way Comes*.

Bradbury first spoke of the Leviathan concept sometime early in 1960, when Jay Richards, one of the only new agents at Famous Artists that he could warm to, introduced him to a new television production company planning to launch an hour-long show dedicated to presenting what Bradbury later described for Congdon as "classics in modern dress." The deep impact of John Huston and the *Moby Dick* experience prompted him to take the show's premise a step further: "I suggested that I do *Moby* as a space-story, laid in the future, with Ahab a captain of space, searching for a white creature somewhere out beyond. If done correctly, it could be fascinating. I've had the idea for some years, since my days in Ireland, when I got to brooding over Ahab and my own science-fiction."[1]

Leviathan '99 thus began as a way to reappropriate *Moby Dick* from John Huston. In concept, it is pure but sincere Melvillean homage, a direct transfer of Ishmael's story from the southern seas to the sea of space. By April 1962, with *Something Wicked This Way Comes* finally finished and in proofs, he developed a narrative outline of the Leviathan plot for Bob Gottlieb at Simon & Schuster. Bradbury's sense of the frontier tradition, so apparent in *The Martian Chronicles* a dozen years earlier, surfaced again in his first draft opening of *Leviathan '99*: "[W]e would have Ishmael's arrival at the town of Independence, Missouri, which has become a rocket port, for it was from there that the old covered wagons moved out into the wilderness of America in the pre–Civil War days. Symbolic then of mankind moving into the star wilderness, the Independence rocket port is central to the American motion into space. It is here that our Ishmael goes to sign on the space craft instead of a ship of the sea."

Bradbury knew the dangers of such a creative homage to Melville and his language, and he made that clear in closing the outline he sent to Gottlieb: "I don't for a moment claim this won't be a dangerous exercise. Unless I bring it off at the top of my form, it could severely damage my reputation and career. If I do bring it off, even then there will be some who would just as soon I rolled over and died as touch their beloved Ahab." But this strange novel concept gave him a chance to experiment freely with the "wild ideas and half-poetries" that had lurked around the edges of his creative sensibilities for a quarter-century, and his many months in Ireland shaping the *Moby Dick* screenplay had offered a structure for release. "I've spent a lot of time with the Pequod in the last nine years, and think and hope and believe I am ready for the adventure."

Gottlieb counseled against writing in Melville's style and urged a more subtle narrative. Bradbury countered that any imitative elements would "dissolve away" in revision: "The essence of Melville is what I'm after, the spirit, not the style itself. And gradually even the essence, of course, will suffer a sea-change from brine to meteor-dust, from island coral to mineral fire sifting in space. Melville will give me my transfusions, but I must, finally, live for myself. His symbols will be transmuted."

For a time "Cetus I," the White Comet at the center of his early draft fragments, held his creative attention. His initial time line began with the next return of Halley's Comet in 1986, causing perturbations in the outer solar system that would bring the vast planet-killing Cetus I to the inner planets in its wake. By 1999, Bradbury's Ahab figure, blinded by an earlier encounter with the comet, is back on its trail with bionic optics that provide "more than enough special sight to pursue his white beast which was born ten billion miles deep in eternity, which came out of the dark like a messenger of God to strike and run." Over time, *Cetus* would become the Captain's pursuit ship, and the White Comet would be renamed "Leviathan." The space-time setting, pushed forward a century into the future, also advanced outward into interstellar space; wisely, Bradbury left his Captain unnamed.

The year is 2099, and Bradbury's Captain turns the crew of the starship *Cetus* away from exploration to destroy Leviathan. The major elements of Bradbury's *Moby Dick* resurface in direct transfer: Ishmael Hunnicutt Jones ships out on the *Cetus* with his Space Academy roommate Quel, a spidery telepath from the Andromeda galaxy. The Captain's motivation: revenge; the crew's motivation: the black diamonds buried in the comet's stony heart. There is no pretension of subtlety here—the work has intensity and beauty because it celebrates and extends Melville's poetic style and rich metaphors, and it's not surprising that Bradbury first wrote it as prose narrative. But Melville's prose is not always successful, and Bradbury would eventually discover that his appropriation of Melville's language was better suited for radio—a medium he had not worked in since the 1940s.

: : :

Even before work on this ocean-of-space tale lapsed, Bradbury's fascination with the nineteenth century's other great fictional sea captain resulted in a significant nonfiction publication. The creative spark for this new project emerged from his discovery that Jules Verne had read Melville's masterpiece before fashioning his own Captain Nemo. In the spring of 1961, an offer from Bantam Books provided an irresistible opportunity for Bradbury to write an introduction for a forthcoming Bantam edition of *20,000 Leagues under the Sea*.

Bradbury's passion for Verne's fiction was now in full bloom; he would always say that he had read Verne as a boy, mixed in with his earlier Depression-era passions for Edgar Rice Burroughs and other great romancers. He no doubt browsed Verne in the public libraries of his youth, but his real reading came later, when he was already a professional writer. His 1955 *New York Times* story-essay, "Marvels and Miracles—Pass It On," had been a speculation on how Verne might view the world fifty years after his death; this had been a somewhat self-conscious exercise, a trying out of nonfiction writing for major-market popular audiences. But the mid-1950s Disney film adaptation of *20,000 Leagues under the Sea* had captivated him, and by 1961 his good friend Ray Harryhausen had animated a feature film adaptation of Verne's *The Mysterious Island*, which included a return of Nemo to Verne's work. Bantam could offer only $500 for Bradbury's introduction (the new Anthony Bonner translation required a full share of the projected royalties), but Bradbury nevertheless accepted with enthusiasm.[2]

By September 1961, Bradbury had completed "The Ardent Blasphemers," a compelling but highly off-trail introduction for *20,000 Leagues under the Sea*.

Through carefully selected passages from Verne and Melville, Bradbury developed a detailed comparison of the very different madnesses that consumed the darkly misanthropic Nemo and the monomaniacal Ahab. The authors, rather than their characters, were the "ardent blasphemers" of Bradbury's title; despite their very different cultural origins, Verne and Melville represented the values that would distance Man from God and dominate the next century of world history: "Verne accepts the natural world and would ask all men to accept its secret ways and join in making themselves over nearer to the hidden heart of this secret. . . . Melville cannot accept and with Ahab rages at the blind maunderings of a God he cannot comprehend."

For Bradbury, these were also the choices facing the highly polarized postcolonial world in the second half of the twentieth century, and his extended metaphors formed a compelling analogy: "Ahab's ship pursues an unpursuable God. . . . Nemo's ship pursues men to remind them of their wickedness, to improve it, or be sunk." He was able to lead his two mad captains to the central question of the modern age, the ultimate uses of Mankind's marvelous but terrifying new technologies:

> Ahab might explode a hydrogen bomb to shake the foundations of God.
>
> But in the fright-flash of illumination, at some distance, we would see Nemo re-perusing notes made in mathematical symbols to use such energy to send men to the stars rather than scatter them in green milk-glass and radioactive chaff along the shore. . . .
>
> The logic that informs Nemo can well build us homes on far planets circling more safely placed suns. Like Nemo we may well find we need not destroy the horrific whale of reality, we may lurk inside it with machineries, plotting our destinies and going our terror-fraught ways toward an hour when we can lie under those stranger suns and bask easy and breathe light and know peace.

And with a simple closing command for "Portholes tight! Periscopes down!" Bradbury concluded his Space-Age take on an enduring classic of the sea. This work, and his subsequent *Life* magazine essays celebrating the rewards and challenges Mankind would face in outer space, would represent some of his best prose of the 1960s. But the most significant consequence of "The Ardent Blasphemers" was purely serendipitous. The new Bantam edition of *20,000 Leagues under the Sea* quickly caught the attention of Tom Scherman, a 22-year-old California artist and model-maker. Scherman's enthusiasm was no passing fancy; his passion for Disneyland's Nautilus exhibit and his skill as a modeler would lead to a distinguished career with Disney's Imagineers.

Scherman had contacts with some of the planners involved with designing the United States Pavilion at the World's Fair, and he urged them to read "The Ardent Blasphemers" and secure Bradbury's talents for the pavilion's audiovisual concept planning. Bradbury did not yet know Scherman, who would become a good friend, but he soon encountered the consequences of Scherman's actions. In late June 1963, two U.S. Pavilion planners from New York unexpectedly showed up at Bradbury's home and asked him to write a 20-minute narration for the American exhibits.[3]

This invitation had a double gratification, for one door into planning for the World's Fair had already opened and, just as quickly, closed. In early January 1961, the manager of the Styling Staff Activities at General Motors met with Bradbury and asked him to develop a concept for the Fair's GM exhibit. The GM planners didn't balk at Bradbury's monetary demands for both the concept and subsequent consultant's fees. The prospect of this project raised his spirits during the first two months of 1961, as his final frustrating days at MGM were beginning to wind down. It seemed he would return to the same Long Island meadows where he had experienced the 1939 World's Fair, and he shared this enthusiasm in a January 14 letter to Congdon:

> This is the sort of thing, really, I am cut out for, from a lifetime of elation and excitement about them. I thought I would die before I made it to Chicago in 1933 to see the fabulous exhibits. I thought I would drop dead before I saved enough money to come to New York in 1939. Jesus God, if I could really come up with an Idea that GM would accept, wouldn't it be great for all of us, in 1964, for me to come back and take us all through the acreage?

But this cherished opportunity had suddenly vanished in mid-March 1961, when GM decided to go in another direction with their exhibition planning. More than two years later, Scherman's urging and Bradbury's subsequent high-profile "Cry the Cosmos" article in *Life* magazine had convinced the U.S. planning team to engage his talents for the Fair. He would eventually write a narration representing the entire nation to a world audience, and he would work hand-in-glove with the exhibit's Cinerama film planners, some of whom had worked on the visuals for the Fair's famous 1939 precursor. In one sense, this was yet another distraction from fiction writing, but it went a long way toward fulfilling his growing need for recognition as a chronicler of America's past and present, a storyteller of our possible futures.

: : :

His projection of Melville's and Verne's nautical masterpieces into the ocean of space had first emerged just as a sea change occurred in American politics. He had been frustrated with the occasional disconnect between Democratic words and actions in the early 1950s, the threat of McCarthyism not withstanding. Now, however, he had high hopes for the new Democratic administration, and he shared these hopes with Congdon on January 20, 1961: "I can hardly believe this day has come—the day of Kennedy's inauguration. . . . I hope, somewhere down the line, to be part of this democratic four years. I'm sending all of my books to Kennedy, through Arthur Schlesinger Jr., who is a s-f fan, with the word that if there is some way, in the coming years, for me to help dramatize the Space Age, I would be delighted (hell, what a weak word) to try my hand at it."

But one of the greatest disappointments in the early days of the American space program occurred within a few short months of the Kennedy inauguration. A sobering Russian victory in the space race came on April 13, 1961, as Major Yuri Gagarin returned from the world's first successful orbital flight. This did nothing to help Bradbury's increasing sense of isolation and stalemate at MGM, where he still maintained a fast-fading presence. "The Russians are aloft and here am I, grounded, at MGM," he wrote to Congdon that same day. "Jesus H. Christ . . . better I have an office in the San Diego Zoo."

In spite of these setbacks, Bradbury had already found another way to bring his cosmic vision to the screen. Ever since its 1956 publication, Bradbury had sensed the visual possibilities of "Icarus Montgolfier Wright," an allegorical tale that demonstrated how Mankind's reach for the stars built on the earlier paradigms of flight: The night before the first manned lunar mission, the pilot astronaut dreams about the historical and mythological pioneers of flight, and how he now shares their collective dream. Bradbury had experimented with a verse adaptation illustrated by Joe Mugnaini before George Clayton Johnson, a young writer who sometimes attended Bradbury's writer's group, suggested a short film illustrated by limited animation sequences of Mugnaini paintings.

The words were Bradbury's, carefully bridged and adapted to fit the new series of Mugnaini paintings by Johnson. The small studio Format Films was immediately attracted to the project and secured financial backing and distribution from United Artists.[4] Well before the film was completed, Bradbury realized that this adaptation would be the best way he could contribute to the new administration's promise to reach the moon by the end of the decade.

Bradbury's bridge to the White House indeed proved to be the distinguished historian Arthur Schlesinger Jr., who was appointed a special assistant to the new president in 1961. Bradbury began to correspond with Schlesinger almost immediately, yet he waited more than a year to follow through on his resolution to send books to the new president. In April 1962, with the film adaptation of *Icarus* nearing completion, Bradbury finally felt confident enough to send two complete sets of his books to 1600 Pennsylvania Avenue—one set autographed to Schlesinger, the other inscribed to President and Mrs. Kennedy.

He even tabbed the stories most relevant to the administration's new Space-Age initiatives, including "Icarus Montgolfier Wright"; his covering letter to Schlesinger also summarized his new *Icarus* film, the recent international stage and screen interest in his books, and his upcoming panel appearance at the Seattle World's Fair—an event that would nearly overlap with the president's scheduled appearance at Seattle's National Conference on the Peaceful Uses of Space.[5] Bradbury's point was that he could help the administration in ways that the technocrats and scientists could not: "There are many people who know the facts about the various projects headed toward space. There are only a few who interpret, aesthetically or otherwise, our entire purpose in Space."

Schlesinger had already read all of Bradbury's books in paperback but was grateful to have a hardbound set; he conveyed the other hardbound set to the president, along with the comment that Bradbury was "carrying on the tradition of H. G. Wells in combining social comment and human emotion with fantasy of the future." It was all very gratifying to the young man who had never gone to college and encouraged him to take the next logical step. On September 5, 1962, with the Format Films adaptation of *Icarus* completed, Bradbury proposed a White House screening of the film: "I believe it is a film we could show the world in order to indicate our aesthetic drives and interests at this time, as well as our political motives." He also suggested meetings with the president to determine if he should script a series of similar films for the government. This was a reach, of course, but Bradbury was encouraged by the fact that his Hollywood friend George Stevens Jr., who was now Director of Motion Picture Services for the United States Information Agency in Washington, frequently interacted with Schlesinger's staff.

In late October 1962, the White House screening of *Icarus* was unexpectedly delayed by the nine days that came to be known almost immediately as the Cuban Missile Crisis. On October 25, Schlesinger, working at the United Nations during the height of the crisis, sent a message to Bradbury that the screening had been rescheduled for the following Monday, October 30. That weekend witnessed the most critical moments of the crisis, if not the entire century, yet all this passed behind the scenes; incredibly, Schlesinger and George Stevens went ahead with Monday's White House screening of *Icarus*, which was well-received (Stevens held a second screening at the USIA before sending the 35-mm print back to Bradbury). President Kennedy, still deeply involved with the international situation, was unable to attend in person, but sent a personal letter of thanks.

For Bradbury, who had remained at home in California, Kennedy's letter had more impact than the crisis or its aftermath. He had written of such apocalyptic scenarios in his fiction, his nonfiction, and his public addresses for more than a decade, and the initial impact of this unexpected nuclear standoff shifted almost immediately in his mind to a cautious confidence that sanity would prevail. "The first day, I was rather stunned," he wrote to Bob Gottlieb on Halloween, "and then I began to think again of the fact that parties and policies no longer run the world but, to quote the old familiar 'things are in the saddle and ride men.' So the atom bomb controls, in the final analysis, both Kennedy and Khrushchev, whether they like it or not. To look into the face of Annihilation can be satisfying only to a mad man. Luckily, neither is mad."

Icarus Montgolfier Wright was now part of the White House pledge to reach the moon before the end of the decade, and this endorsement compensated for the commercial scheduling challenges that faced any short-subject Hollywood production. Format Films had little say in the marketing of *Icarus*, and the United Artists distribution strategy often frustrated Bradbury. In January 1963, Bradbury sent the film to NBC news anchor Chet Huntley, who arranged an invitation to appear on the *Today* show; the offer fell through when Bradbury couldn't break his fear of flying. An unexpected Academy Award nomination for best animated short subject soon made it all worthwhile, but this honor also reawakened his abiding ambivalence about aesthetic recognition. His disdain for the critics and their awards had become, for the most part, a way to defend his creative subconscious—as well as his increasingly conscious ego. But the Oscar nomination jolted his perspective, and in mid-February 1963 he described the impact to Congdon: "I thought that such things as Awards were beyond and away and locked outside me. But, Jesus God, no. I am grateful for this experience if for no other reason than it knocks down one more barrier, one more stupid prejudice. We do like it when people pay attention, even when it is people . . . who we often make fun of."

31 Machineries of Joy

During the 1963 Oscar ceremonies, the 1962 short subject Academy Award went to *The Hole*, an independent production that focused on the fear, described from a working-class perspective, of an accidental nuclear war. Bradbury had sensed that *The Hole* would win out over *Icarus*, given the nuclear brinksmanship that had so recently played out over the Cuban Missile Crisis. Bradbury and Joe Mugnaini, whose artistic genius had been the true star of the film, gave the much-coveted admission passes to their teenage daughters, dropped them off at the event, and watched the Oscar ceremonies from a nearby bar. Nevertheless, the nomination had provided a significant capstone to his first decade as a Hollywood writer.

The lessons that Laughton had imparted to Bradbury over the last seven years of his life applied more to the stage than to screenwriting. The stage had been the first love of both men, and Bradbury's first insights into handling directors and actors had come through observing and listening to Laughton. He didn't have to handle veteran producer and actor John Houseman, whom he had known for more than a decade when Houseman was finally able to bring some of Bradbury's one-acts to UCLA during the 1961–62 season. Seeing the plays performed, initially by his distinguished actor-friends at Sy Gomberg's home, and now by UCLA's drama students, provided the confidence Bradbury needed to explore professional performances.

Bradbury secured a rent-free contract from Lucille Ball for the Desilu Playhouse for August 1962 performances for a one-act production of *Way in the Middle of the Air*.[1] This adaptation of a *Martian Chronicles* story-chapter (the migration of Black American settlers to the Martian colonies) had its roots in a concept he had pulled together for producer Paul Gregory in 1955. At the Desilu Playhouse, Bradbury found his actors among the resident acting company; he also found a great deal of guidance from Tracy Roberts, a veteran of New York's legendary Actors Studio who had become a much sought-after director and acting coach.

With a contract extension approved for 1963, Bradbury undertook his most ambitious dramatic challenge so far: an evening of three one-acts based once again on his own stories—the whimsical medieval fantasy "A Medicine for Melancholy," his very contemporary "The Wonderful Ice Cream Suit," and the futuristic cautionary tale, "The Pedestrian"—presented under the overarching title *Yesterday, Today and Tomorrow*. Tracy Roberts produced and directed *The Wonderful Ice Cream Suit*, the most natural adaptation of the three. Bradbury was greatly impressed by Charles Rome Smith's direction of *The Pedestrian*, and asked him to double up and direct *A Medicine for Melancholy* when film and television actor John Hoyt, who was also performing in the play, wasn't able to continue effectively as director. The groundwork laid in these productions led Bradbury to retain the directing talents of Smith and form his own acting company, The Pandemonium Players, for the following season. The 1964 trio of plays, produced at the Coronet Theater on La Cienega, would establish the working dynamic that Bradbury would carry through in successive seasons and many small-venue theaters for more than forty years.

By contrast, Bradbury found himself completely unable to control his fortunes throughout his experience with the London stage, where he came close to participating in one of the early seasons of the Royal Shakespeare Company. Peter Hall, one of Britain's most prominent stage managers and producers, had combined with the directing talents of Peter Brook to found the RSC as a popular theater that included an experimental theater component. During 1963, the A. D. Peters agency, which had long represented Bradbury's British interests for Congdon, generated enthusiasm from Peter Brook for several of the one-acts, including *The Veldt* and *The Wonderful Ice Cream Suit*.[2] Plans for a Royal Shakespeare run of several Bradbury plays seemed to be finalized when Brook, who was still trying to put the RSC on firm financial footing, began to rework the experimental program for the 1963–64 season. Brook's schedule narrowed to a monthlong run in London at the Aldwych Theatre for *The Veldt* only and then dwindled to just a few days across a variable schedule of dates; in the end, Brook and Hall decided against running the Bradbury plays at all.

The missed chance was incredibly frustrating for Bradbury, at times causing stress with Margaret Ramsay and the other A. D. Peters Agency representatives who were trying to make sense out of the Peter Brook negotiations. But Bradbury managed to restore his spirits by applying a time-tested literary allusion: "[G]ood luck with all the Ramsay-were-the-Borogroves and the Peter-Brook-Outgrabe, in London," he told Congdon on January 21, 1964. "I oft have the feeling you and I are peering through a rather strange mirror at our agent-friends there in Muddle-Upon-Thames, and I'm not at all sure who is on *which* side. I *believe* we are in open air, and *they* are under glass, but would not want to bet on it."

: : :

In spite of the significant new distractions of the professional stage, Bradbury managed to pull together a new story collection, *The Machineries of Joy*. This was another wide-ranging collection, not easily categorized, and there were editorial challenges over the contents. Simon & Schuster's Bob Gottlieb soon joined his British counterpart, Rupert Hart-Davis, in expressing doubts about the Irish stories that were slipping into the more recent collections. They were beautifully told tales that sometimes faded out into dialogue-rich anecdotes, and there was a degree of stereotyping that was beginning to set some editors, critics, and even readers on edge. Congdon remained enthusiastic, but he was also focused on coaxing *any* new stories out of Bradbury's growing file of unsent story drafts. When Gottlieb gently questioned the Irish stories in the new collection, Bradbury brought in the usual suspects to blame:

> As for the Irish stories, I feel they should remain in the book to make it a richer mixture. One of the troubles I've had over the years with snob critics and snob readers is them running up on stage while I'm playing the harp and crying out, "Sure, but can ya play the tuba?" I then play the tuba. "Sure," cry they, "but can ya play the oboe!?" I play the oboe. "Piano!" cry they. Piano. "Now," they say, "would you mind letting down the sandbags and putting up the curtains, and take a few tickets while you're at it. . . . ?" I do all this. And, having done it, am still, in some quarters, patted on the head, no better than Dr. Johnson's dog.[3] (ellipsis Bradbury's)

With the exception of the weird-tales showcases he had fashioned for *Dark Carnival* and *The October Country* and the science fiction focus of *The Illustrated Man*, Bradbury had the enviable problem of producing story collections that opened out across his wide range of science fiction, fantasy, and (occasionally) realism. He wanted editors who would willingly join the parade, and he expected Gottlieb to be no different: "So, as in the case of *A Medicine for Melancholy*, I think it is best to have both frontal, backal, sidal, and topal attacks on the reader. Let us be rocket men, let us be sea creatures, let us be Irish, and let us be dogmatic priests bewildered by the whole damn affair."

Irish priests, in fact, stood at the core of "The Machineries of Joy," the new collection's title story, and represented the most engaging but most direct assault on the men of God who might still balk at Man's swift progression into the heavens. "It's the Lord's space and the Lord's worlds *in* space, Father. We must not try to take our cathedrals with us," the California pastor tells the dubious Irish priest. The collection had started out to showcase fifteen of the stories Bradbury had published in magazines since early 1960. One of these, "Death and the Maiden" (the tale that would cause so much concern among the *Twilight Zone* writers), came from the *Magazine of Fantasy and Science Fiction*; twelve represented big dollar sales to the *Saturday Evening Post* and *Playboy*, two magazines where Congdon could command top dollar prices. The collection was rounded out by five older stories, the strongest of which was "And So Died Riabouchinska," the ventriloquism crime story that was the basis for his first *Alfred Hitchcock Presents* sale in 1956.

: : :

The contents of *The Machineries of Joy* came together just as Bradbury was entering a very dynamic phase of Hollywood negotiations. Over the winter of 1962–63, he had to evaluate and sometimes counter offers on a half-dozen properties. His long residency at MGM netted an offer to adapt *The Greatest Story Ever Told* (he convinced director George Stevens to sign their mutual friend, the poet Carl Sandburg, instead). He was also asked to rewrite MGM's troubled *Mutiny on the Bounty* script in midshoot, but he declined when the studio fired his great friend, director Sir Carol Reed. Twentieth Century–Fox executive Walter Wanger wanted Bradbury to write an original screenplay for their budget-breaking *Cleopatra*; Bradbury was tempted by the chance to work with two friends, director Rouben Mamoulian and set designer John De Cure, but he was wary of adapting classic stage drama to film. He declined, suggesting that Wanger already had two great writers at hand: William Shakespeare and George Bernard Shaw.[4]

More than ever, his focus centered on adapting his own works. During November 1962, he planned a production venture for *Something Wicked This Way Comes* with his good friend Laslo Benedek, whose film directing credits included *Death of a Salesman* and *The Wild One*. They scouted various Hollywood sound studios, but were unable to secure an agreement for a large-scale production.[5] This adventure naturally rekindled the torch he carried for a *Martian Chronicles* film, but he wasn't at all sure that his agents at Famous Artists were up to the challenge. In fact, a break with Ben Benjamin and Famous Artists had been building since the fall of 1957, when the agency's lawyers opted not to represent Bradbury's *Fahrenheit 451* plagiarism suit against CBS. It would have been a clear conflict of interest, but Bradbury had never liked the fact that the agency represented networks as well as writers.

There was nothing that the agency could do about this, or about the higher standard that Bradbury's circulating adaptations were held to because they emerged from genre subjects like horror ("The Veldt," *Something Wicked This Way Comes*), science fiction ("The Veldt," "The Fox and the Forest"), and fantasy ("The Wonderful Ice Cream Suit"), or were simply considered too controversial ("And the Rock

Cried Out"). As a consequence, Ben Benjamin and the other agents often did not cast a wider net with these properties, and this was really at the heart of Bradbury's dissatisfaction. He had played his own hunches in contacting such high-profile producers as Julian Blaustein for the *Chronicles*, the Mirisch Brothers for *Something Wicked*, and even the legendary producer-director team of Sam Spiegel and Sir David Lean, fresh off their success with *Lawrence of Arabia*.

Unrealistic? Perhaps, but Bradbury had often made his own breaks with publishers and producers, and his triumph with John Huston and the *Moby Dick* script had originally seemed just as much of a long shot. He couldn't abide anything less from his Hollywood agents, and in late March 1963 he told Ben Benjamin that he would end his twelve-year association with Famous Artists. In mid-April, he began a new agency relationship with two old friends who were associated with the General Artists agency—Malcolm Stuart and Ingo Preminger, brother of producer Otto Preminger. He wasted no time in taking advantage of Ingo's excellent European film connections, directing him to send his "Wonderful Ice Cream Suit" script to Federico Fellini in Italy.[6]

The first true test of his new agency relationship would center on the *Martian Chronicles* film adaptation that MGM had relinquished nearly two years earlier. Once again Bradbury made first contact, but this time he acted on impulse rather than frustration. On May 8, 1963, he saw *To Kill a Mockingbird*, a film destined to earn eight Academy Award nominations (and winning two) at the following year's ceremonies. It was directed by Oscar nominee Robert Mulligan and produced by Alan Pakula, who had been interested in "The Veldt" and some of Bradbury's other science fiction stories for several years. Bradbury was deeply affected by *Mockingbird*'s small-town setting of earlier times. "A lovely, lovely film," he told Congdon. "What Pakula and Mulligan could do for *Dandelion Wine!*" But Pakula's interest still centered on Bradbury's science fiction subjects; when Bradbury contacted him a few days later, the discussions began to turn quite naturally to "The Veldt" and *The Martian Chronicles*.[7]

A shift away from "The Veldt" was made easier by Gene Kelly, who had come back into Bradbury's life in early May to pursue a film anthology of Bradbury science fiction stories (including "The Veldt") with MGM. He had always enjoyed Kelly's friendship and enthusiasm for his work; even though nothing came of this project, it allowed Bradbury to focus his conversations with Pakula and Mulligan solely on the *Chronicles*. Mal Stuart pursued the negotiations with intensity, and by early June 1963 he had brokered a favorable deal. Bradbury began work in late July, while the contract details were still being worked out. His task was to develop a completely new script, quite distinct from his MGM product, and the first week of work focused on developing what he called a "step-outline" of the material. This interaction went very well, and on August 12 he began to compose the new screenplay.

Bradbury was deep into his new *Chronicles* script by November 22, 1963, a day when he was scheduled to meet with Alan Pakula to discuss his progress. A week later, on December 1, he described that fateful day in a letter to Don Congdon: "I arrived at his office to find that the President had been shot. I felt the manuscript turn to ash in my hand. I carried it away with me, when, after a long wait with Alan, we heard the announcement, final and brutal, of the death of the President. . . . I went my way, to come back some other day on business that now was of no importance."

Bradbury was convinced that his richly imaginative subconscious, so essential to the highly original ideas and lyrical prose of his best stories, was just as traumatized as his waking mind: "I have never had the two aspects of the human mind so vividly and sadly illustrated for me as in watching my own reactions to this dread passage of time. You think you are done with this? The Subconscious says, no, no, for I have given you this, and again this. And you find that on the fourth day the hurt is worse, and the tears still start forth, and you want like unholy anything to be back on the early morning of the 22nd so you can run out yelling and warning the world what is going to happen. But Time Machines don't work, and you wind up being 'disturbed.'" For once, Bradbury's creative time machine impulse for a second chance, often sent out in his fiction to save great figures as well as everyday people from a darkly looming fate, seemed to fail him; instead, he poured all of his cathartic reactions into the letter to Congdon:

One man decided to hold an Election. One man did. All by himself, he dared to vote for everybody. And so . . . Election Day, November 22nd, is over, gone, done, and one man has revoked the ballot for 180 million Americans, put our President in the earth, and given us the most brutal and terrifying and frustrating week in the history of our own lives, anyway. . . . But, damn it to hell, our generation has been shoved under the earth suddenly. It may not come again, this sort of time for our generation to have this power in these few short years before fifty. There was a special pleasure in having one of us in the White House. . . . The power that will come to our generation later, and it must come, won't be quite the same, will it, when it falls into older sadder hands?

At this point Bradbury felt guardedly optimistic about Johnson's unexpected rise to the presidency, but that would change as the Vietnam conflict began in earnest. This greater trauma was still ahead, however, cloaked in an uncertain future that Bradbury no longer wanted to imagine: "My Time Machine is set for 'Now' from here on, and will move only Ahead, moment by moment." As the somber new year approached, he would turn back to his stage plays, his new *Martian Chronicles* screenplay, and possible screen options for *Something Wicked This Way Comes* and "The Wonderful Ice Cream Suit," and a few—a very few—new stories.

A day or two after unburdening his mind to Congdon, Bradbury handed in his first 150 pages of the refashioned *Chronicles* to Alan Pakula. The two men began work again on December 3, 1963; over the next few weeks, Pakula was impressed with the great passion and clarity of vision for the project that Bradbury exhibited in his notes and discussions.[8] For his part, Bradbury felt that he had definitely made the right choice for a producer-director team, and looked forward to the time when Pakula and Mulligan would be able to seek major studio backing for the final script. Quite a bit of work remained, however, and Bradbury knew it.

His 1960–61 MGM script had carried through elements of his 1950s television series concept, surrounding the key chronicle of Captain Wilder's fourth expedition discovery of a dying Martian civilization ("—And the Moon Be Still as Bright") with other *Chronicles* story-chapters and three unrelated space tales ("The End of the Beginning," "Kaleidoscope," and "The Rocket"). That first screenplay had become Wilder's story, and the story of others like him, who made the sacrifices to reach Mars before the entire colonial enterprise collapses back on a war-torn Earth, damned by the darker side of the same technologies that had taken Mankind into space. The old MGM script was still a planetary saga, offering little more than a glimpse of the greater Cosmos as the remnants of humanity find a second chance as the new Martians.

The new screenplay he was writing for Pakula and Mulligan eliminated the sidelight drama of Wilder's personal life and the unrelated space stories of the earlier screenplay. In place of this material, Bradbury brought in *Chronicles* story-chapters such as "The Martian" and "Night Meeting," stories of further contact with surviving Martians. As British film scholar Phil Nichols notes, these new elements reveal the Martians as reflections of ourselves, a new script element that sets the stage for a daring new episode: a lost city, a fully automated relic from the most advanced period of the dead Martian civilization. Here was another of Bradbury's fascinating machineries of joy, and perhaps his most intriguing one; it emerged fully formed as a story within the script, almost completely free of scene and shot descriptions. The lost city is a vast desiring machine, allowing Captain Wilder and his fellow explorers to experience their greatest aspirations—or their most terrifying fears.

Wilder is given his greatest dream: the immediate conquest of deep space, and colonization of the stars. But he pulls back from the dream just before it consumes him, knowing that he and those who follow him will have to earn their way beyond the confines of the solar system. The city, outmaneuvered, destroys itself and the others who cannot break away from their obsessions, but not before Wilder gazes into Mankind's far future. Here was the broader vision of Bradbury's 1962 "Cry the Cosmos" essay in *Life* magazine, carried even further by laying out a specific path to the stars. The original *Chronicles* tales of nuclear war on Earth, and the closing consolation of humanity's tenuous toehold on Mars, were replaced in the new screenplay by Bradbury's articulated Wellsian vision of a far grander cosmic destiny.

Refining the new screenplay, as well as finding a studio to back the production, took time. By July 1964, the Pakula-Mulligan team had a commitment from Universal for the *Chronicles*. The studio announced plans for a big-budget production that revived Bradbury's dream for the original concept: a ten-million-dollar film (Universal's biggest price tag since *Spartacus*) presented in the big screen Cinerama process. Gregory Peck, who had won his Academy Award under Robert Mulligan's direction in *To Kill a Mockingbird*, entered a verbal agreement to take Captain Wilder's role.[9] With Bradbury still working through his second draft of the script, studio enthusiasm was based primarily on the Pakula-Mulligan track record in Hollywood; clearly, a final contract would depend on Universal's reaction to the final script.

On November 23, 1964, a year and a day after Kennedy's assassination, Bradbury found himself working in offices that Alan Pakula maintained at Warner Brothers, one of the few major studios where he had not worked before. He found a sheet of Jack L. Warner's stationery in his desk, and promptly typed a letter to Congdon on it, noting that he admired Warner (as well as independent mogul Sam Goldwyn Sr.) for not relinquishing his authority to the New York executives who now controlled much of the film industry. He also respected Warner Brothers for their tradition of good storytelling and reflected on this grand history in an ellipsis-filled reverie:

> There is a certain air about a studio like this . . . memories, I imagine, of the best all around films made by any studio. . . . Warner films hold up over the years . . . when you think back on the product of the thirties and early forties . . . not the musicals, no, strangely enough . . . but all of the Bogart films, all the Bette Davis films . . . all of the Huston films made here . . . Edward G. Robinson, James Cagney . . . they were story tellers and told their stories well. . . . *Robin Hood*, with Flynn, is still a damned fine all around jolly adventure . . . anyway, I have respect for any studio that respects story telling . . . and my nostalgia for the place is based on this story-telling background which was their symbol until a few years ago.

Bradbury continued to urge his screenplay along on "its Juggernaut way through space," but he remained unable to bring it all together as he worked feverishly through the fall and early winter on the Los Angeles stage production of *The World of Ray Bradbury*. His final mimeograph was ready by April 11, 1965, but he could not shake off an uneasy sensation of looming rejection. On May 4, Universal did indeed reject the project; Bradbury's analysis, expressed in his May 5 letter to Congdon, was that Universal expected another *It Came From Outer Space*, an original Bradbury screen story that was a solid 1953 moneymaker for the studio. He knew that this kind of terror science fiction was no longer A-budget material, but he hadn't been able to convince the studio that the *Chronicles*, re-fashioned into an inspirational glimpse of humanity's deep-space destiny, could define the new Space-Age aspirations of the movie-going public. That honor would eventually fall to his friend Arthur C. Clarke and *2001: A Space Odyssey*.

In November 1965, Alan Pakula took out one last extension on his option, but Bradbury began to sense, as he had at MGM with his first *Chronicles* script, that his producer had reservations about the final long draft of the new screenplay. Gavin Lambert, who had written both the novel and screenplay for Pakula and Mulligan's recent film *Inside Daisy Clover*, was called in to revise Bradbury's screenplay. Predictably, Bradbury was not willing to lose control, especially when no studio was involved; even before the extended option expired, Bradbury began to look elsewhere for a producer. He first thought of Twentieth Century–Fox's Elmo Williams, a Bradbury enthusiast, but Williams was fully engaged with running European operations for the studio. François Truffaut, who had spent four years on *Fahrenheit 451*, also declined the *Chronicles* screenplay in its present form.[10]

"Nothing can be given, ever," Captain Wilder said when the lost city of Mars offered him the stars. "I must earn, I must take." Even Bradbury never fully grasped how close he had come to making the *Chronicles* the Space-Age film he had wanted to make since his first days at MGM. He thought the climactic lost city episode was a good story, but not a great one; besides, he was exhausted by the five years spent on his two *Chronicles* screenplays.[11] By this time other more promising Hollywood ventures beckoned to Bradbury; he sold the lost city segment to *Playboy* as a new short story, and filed away the now greatly diminished screenplay with all the disappointments that had gone before.

Ray Bradbury (left) with Alfred Hitchcock (center) and composer Bernard Herrmann, on the set of Hitchcock's *Torn Curtain*, winter 1965–66, just before the break that ended years of Hitchcock-Herrmann collaborations. Bradbury stories were adapted for various Hitchcock television shows from 1956 through 1964; two later episodes were scored by Herrmann, as was François Truffaut's film version of Bradbury's *Fahrenheit 451*. Courtesy of Universal Studios Licensing LLC. Bradbury's presentation copy from the Albright Collection; courtesy Donn Albright and the estate of Ray Bradbury.

Bradbury, at work in his home basement office, mid-1960s. By this time he had taken a Wilshire Boulevard office that he would use for the next two decades, but he continued to maintain an active writing presence at home throughout his life. Photograph by Ray Hamilton. From the Albright Collection; courtesy Donn Albright and the estate of Ray Bradbury.

Bradbury in his basement office at home, circa mid-1960s. The theater lobby poster above his head carries his screenwriting credit. His collection of primitive masks, and masks from his various stage productions, can be seen in the background. From the Albright Collection; courtesy Donn Albright and the estate of Ray Bradbury.

Ray and Maggie Bradbury, circa 1963–64, with daughters (clockwise, from top left) Susan, Ramona, Alexandra, and Bettina. Charles Laughton's wife Elsa Lanchester always referred to the children as "the four graces." Journalist Oriana Fallaci was impressed by the sagacity of these four animated "summer blondes": "A lot of Father's books are used as school textbooks, you know." Portrait courtesy of the estate of Ray Bradbury.

"The theater is no place for realism." Bradbury's assertion appeared in Gerald Nachman's *New York Post* feature on October 8, 1965, the day *The World of Ray Bradbury* one-acts opened in New York. Bradbury poses in front of his Los Angeles home with lobby cards for two earlier 1964–65 Los Angeles runs of his one-act plays. From the Albright Collection; courtesy Donn Albright and the estate of Ray Bradbury.

Bradbury escorting Charles Laughton's widow, Academy Award–nominated actress Elsa Lanchester (right), into a performance of his *Wonderful Ice Cream Suit* one-act plays, spring 1965. Maggie Bradbury (center background) and her husband remained close to Lanchester for the rest of her life. Photograph by Julian Davis. From the Albright Collection; courtesy Donn Albright and the estate of Ray Bradbury.

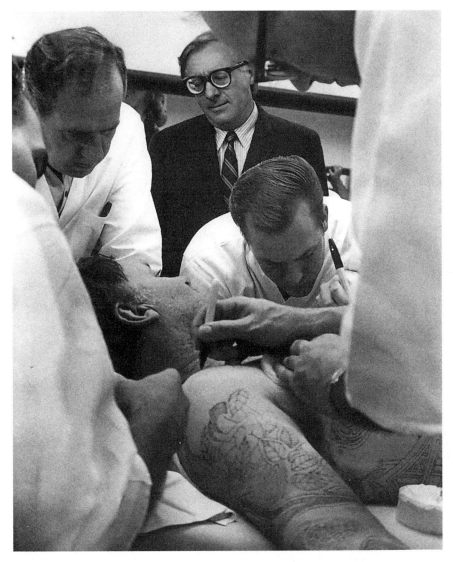

Ray Bradbury framed by studio makeup artists applying vegetable dye tattoos to Academy Award–winning actor Rod Steiger on the first day of shooting for the Warner Brothers–Seven Arts Production of *The Illustrated Man*. Steiger's long friendship with Bradbury played a part in his decision to accept the title role. Photograph by Floyd McCarty. Licensed by Warner Bros. Entertainment Inc. All rights reserved. Bradbury's presentation copy from the Albright Collection; courtesy Donn Albright and the estate of Ray Bradbury.

"[W]e will build those starcraft . . . and head for stars so far away they are impossible to imagine." Always the dynamic speaker, Bradbury engages his audience during Caltech's 33rd Annual Seminar Day, Winnett Center, Pasadena, May 16, 1970. His speaking presence at Caltech began in 1956 and continued through the first decade of the next century. Photograph by Floyd Clark. Courtesy of the Archives, California Institute of Technology.

Arthur C. Clarke (left) and Ray Bradbury share a private moment of levity during their Caltech debate on "Mars and the Mind of Man" in Ramo Auditorium, Pasadena, November 12, 1971. This friendly debate with astronomer Carl Sagan and planetary scientist Bruce Murray occurred on the eve of the Mariner 9 orbital rendezvous with Mars. Photograph by Floyd Clark. Courtesy of the Archives, California Institute of Technology.

Part V

If the Sun Dies

Don't let us forget this: that the Earth can die,
explode, the Sun can go out, will go out.
And if the Sun dies, if the Earth dies, if our
race dies, then so will everything die that
we have done up to that moment. . . . Let us
prepare ourselves to escape, to continue life
and rebuild our cities on other planets:
we shall not be long of this Earth!

—RB, 1964

32 A Backward Glance

Although Bradbury's attempts to find financial backing for his new *Martian Chronicles* screenplay staggered on intermittently through 1966, any real chance of bringing the *Chronicles* to the screen as the defining film about space exploration ended on July 30, 1965, with the publication of what the *Los Angeles Times* and many other newspapers headlined as the "most remarkable photograph of the age." A sequence of unprecedented photographs from Mariner IV included a July 11 image that revealed firm evidence of a heavily cratered Martian surface completely devoid of canals or artificial features of any kind; this did not preclude hidden evidence of past life, but for the moment it led the Caltech science team in charge of the data to conclude that Mars was essentially a dead planet, more closely resembling the moon than the geologically dynamic Earth.

Bradbury would live to see later photographic missions and unmanned landers reveal significant evidence of past dynamism on and just beneath the surface of Mars, but the Mariner IV evidence persuaded many that Mars had none of the internally generated geological features of a life-bearing planet. For Bradbury, both the general and scientific comments were shattering: President Lyndon Johnson was "a little bit relieved" that the images showed no evidence of intelligent life; more to the point, Dr. Robert Leighton, Caltech's lead investigator for the photographic objectives, conceded that "the search for a fossil record does appear less promising if Martian oceans never existed." Almost overnight, Hollywood interest in *The Martian Chronicles* evaporated.

But even without the magical endorsement of Hollywood, Bradbury's Mars had significant and compelling Earthbound themes that had already made it a paperback and library favorite with nearly a million copies in print. So far, Doubleday had refused Bradbury's long-standing plea to reconfigure the *Chronicles*, but in late 1963 Time, Inc. published a new edition that restored "The Fire Balloons" (a late deletion from the original 1950 Doubleday text) and added "The Wilderness," a story that Bradbury had added to the 1953 British Science Fiction Book Club edition. Since the British editions all lacked "Usher II," the new Time edition represented the first truly complete 28-chapter edition to reach print. The series editors moved quickly on the new edition, and Bradbury was thrilled to discover that they had already secured an introduction by one of Britain's most eminent scientists—Fred Hoyle, Plumian Professor of Astronomy at Cambridge University.

Hoyle was not a fan of pulp science fiction, but he felt that the authors who transcended the genre boundaries did so by exploring what was rapidly becoming the most crucial issue of the late twentieth century—environmental responsibility:

> *The Martian Chronicles* breaks ground at exactly this point. To throw the environment into clearer focus, the author has used Mars in place of Earth, but the problems are those of Earth, and the people are to a great degree terrestrial people. Ray Bradbury encloses us in a hall of mirrors that mercilessly reflect our way of life, distorting to emphasize more urgently faults in ourselves and in our civilization. With stealthy strokes he lulls us into smug self-satisfaction and then ruthlessly thrusts our faces against "the whole crooked grinding greedy setup on Earth."

Beyond the cautionary relevance of the individual fables, Bradbury's unique style contributed to the enduring power of the overall work. Fred Hoyle, well on his way to becoming a science fiction author of some distinction, echoed the earlier comments of such fellow countrymen as Christopher Isherwood and Aldous Huxley concerning Bradbury's poetic style: "The fantasies woven around the planet Mars captivate our senses with the haunting reality of their delicate imagery, and into this enchanted spun-glass world the author pushes us with all our clumsiness and picnic litter. Only the rare few can appreciate the beauty; only they have understanding. This is the poet speaking, speaking in a new medium."

With the exception of a good teleplay by Richard Matheson (unevenly translated by NBC into an often-tedious 1980 television miniseries), *The Martian Chronicles* would prosper through the rest of the twentieth century without the help of Hollywood. Bantam's sturdy paperback, often "Permabound" for school and public libraries, would be reprinted more than eighty times by the end of the twentieth century. But Hoyle's commentary in the new edition would represent the last major commentary for some time to come. There were no subsequent printings of the Time edition; in fact, there would be no other new editions for a dozen years and no commercial editions for nearly two decades. Only Bantam's mass-market paperback soldiered on, but that, as it turned out, would be enough.

: : :

Perhaps because his production of new stories was at an all-time low, Bradbury felt ready to showcase his first truly retrospective story collection; it was only natural that Congdon and Bradbury would turn to Random House and its long tradition of Modern Library and Vintage compilations of literary masters. His earliest known table of contents, dated April 5, 1963, included twenty-five stories gathered from nine books, followed by his popular *Life* magazine essay, "Cry the Cosmos." Contents shifted as Bradbury and Congdon successfully negotiated the Random House contract with Jim Silberman during April and May 1964. With the exception of four story-chapters from *Dandelion Wine*, which were grouped under that heading in midvolume, the final selection of twenty-six stories mixed genres and source collections. "The Illustrated Man," which had not appeared in the 1951 story collection of that name, and in fact had never appeared in any Bradbury collection, was slipped in without fanfare. The collection was published as *The Vintage Bradbury* in August 1965.

There had been very little dispute over the contents, but behind the scenes a great deal of trouble had erupted over the volume's introduction.[1] Both Bradbury and Congdon convinced Random House to discard the introduction they had commissioned from George Plimpton, which was framed within an imaginary tongue-in-cheek dialogue between Plimpton and a fictitious devotee of Sci-Fi. When Plimpton published the rejected introduction in the *Washington Post*'s "Book Week" section, his title allusion (to Samuel Johnson, no less) gave away the gently patronizing tone of the entire essay: "Small Science and Less Technology: A Close Dialogue with a Science Fiction Addict on the Problems of Ray Bradbury."

Bradbury suggested that Random House use his own essay, "How to Keep and Feed a Muse," as the introduction, unless Jim Silberman could persuade Gilbert Highet to write one. Highet, still one of the nation's leading popularizers of the Western literary canon, readily agreed. The new introduction followed up on Highet's various earlier efforts to place Bradbury's talents within the major Western literary tradition, and provided what Bradbury considered the perfect frame for *The Vintage Bradbury*. In this important essay Highet captured all of Bradbury's strengths and weaknesses; he saw him as that rarest of writers, a spinner of original and poetic fantasies who "enlarges rather than degrades human life."

A limited hardbound printing was issued for libraries, but Random House pulled back from a precontract promise to reissue *The Vintage Bradbury* as a Modern Library title. This may have prompted Bradbury to explore the possibility of a more comprehensive retrospective along the lines of Penguin's Viking Portable Reader series. An undated but detailed outline for "Kaleidoscope: A Ray Bradbury Reader" survives, revealing Bradbury's most complete assessment of his best works from this period of his life. The genre-based contents include four of his published essays on writing capped with "Cry the Cosmos," thirty-six stories (including four as-yet unpublished ones), two one-act plays, four poems, and two substantial excerpts from *Something Wicked This Way Comes*.

Bradbury's title page had a handwritten glimpse at the categories that filtered through his mind as he reviewed the hundreds of stories he had written by this point in his career, annotated in the familiar associational drill that had always aided his subconscious focus on particular kinds of stories: "The Weird, The Fantastic, The Irish, The Future, The Past, The Vampires, The Marionettes, and The Murderers" (subtitled "Suspense"). But the contents of the "Bradbury Reader" followed a collection-by-collection chronology that he would adapt for his two later one-hundred-story retrospectives, *The Stories of Ray Bradbury* (1980) and *Bradbury Stories* (2003). The "Bradbury Reader," however, offered a more intriguing mix of short and long fiction, drama, poetry, and essay than would ever reach print. The concept pulled from too many volumes and articles involving too many publishers, however, and "Kaleidoscope: A Ray Bradbury Reader" was never realized in print.

As the broader retrospective concept of a Bradbury reader fell by the wayside, the 1950s EC graphic adaptations of his early horror and science fiction stories made their way back into print. William M. Gaines, the original publisher, partnered with Ian Ballantine to publish a two-volume set in mass-market paperback form as *The Autumn People* (1965) and *Tomorrow Midnight* (1966). Bradbury's backward glance focused more intently, however, on the Doubleday titles that no longer had hardbound editions in print: *The Golden Apples of the Sun* and *A Medicine for Melancholy*. By the mid-1960s Walt Bradbury, now back at Doubleday, convinced the house to bind these two books together in a single hardbound edition. Walt Bradbury came up with the title, based on the 22 tales in each of the original collections, of *Twice-22*;[2] The new combined edition was published in both trade and book club issues in 1966.

: : :

During the mid-1960s he also returned to Melville and attempted once again to lure Ahab into the galactic seas of *Leviathan '99*. The novel-in-progress of 1962 languished until he realized that a radio adaptation would provide a shorter path to completion, thus allowing the novel to fully emerge from his unpredictable "subcon" in its own time. This option began to surface in October 1963, when NBC Radio's vice president of programs Robert Wogan negotiated a reading of Bradbury's "The Fog Horn" on the nationally syndicated "Monitor" program. Wogan had been urging a "Monitor" series of Bradbury stories ever since Bradbury's well-received "Monitor" interview with host Frank McGee during the author's 1962 trip to New York. An NBC tape recording of the show soon reached Bradbury, who was impressed with Basil Rathbone's reading. The intense but low-key Rathbone remained the best-known cinema incarnation of Sherlock

Holmes, and his presentation of "The Fog Horn" revealed the potential that a distinguished reading voice could bring to *Leviathan '99*. Other projects, as always, intervened, but by the late winter of 1965 Bradbury had secured the interest of his friend and mentor Norman Corwin to produce.

Corwin was a legendary figure in broadcasting, a chronicler of the home front during World War II and a pioneer of postwar historical and literary specials on network radio. But he was now semiretired in Los Angeles, and negotiations with the East Coast NBC offices were tricky. In his New York heyday, Corwin had encouraged and provided dinners when a younger Bradbury came east to sell his Martian stories in 1949; now, in 1965, Bradbury used his own influence to secure an appropriate fee and use of NBC's Los Angeles radio studios for Corwin to produce *Leviathan '99*.[3] But progress on the radio play was disrupted by countless other projects and remained unfinished until August 1966. The project finally foundered when revenue-starved NBC radio required that the *Leviathan* script be carved into 3-minute snippets broadcast between commercial breaks; as far as Bradbury was concerned, that ended further negotiations.[4] He would eventually find sustained interest from the BBC, where a well-received 1968 London broadcast was headlined by his good friend, Christopher Lee.

Lee was already well-established as a genre star, fronting a number of Hammer's horror films in England, but his prolific career included mainstream features; Lee had worked for John Huston in *Moulin Rouge*, and Bradbury met him in London through Huston during the spring of 1954. Lee's interest in Bradbury's work crossed genre lines, and he was always alert for a chance to work with a Bradbury adaptation. After the BBC *Leviathan '99* broadcast, Lee actively sought to purchase Bradbury's script for Roger Manvell's *The Dreamers*, intending to bring this subtle British masterpiece of dark fantasy to film.[5] Rights to *The Dreamers* now resided with United Artists, but Lee was never able to make the deal; what was probably Bradbury's best screenplay remained in obscurity, unproduced.

For Bradbury, his most significant backward glance would center on his renewed efforts to bring *Fahrenheit 451* back into a hardbound edition. By 1966, the long-awaited release of Truffaut's film adaptation of *Fahrenheit 451* provided the leverage that Bradbury would need to bring out a hardbound edition of the novel. Ian Ballantine's small hardbound first printing of 1953, released simultaneously with the mass-market paperback issue, had served its short-term purpose of bringing the novel to the major bookstores and reviewers; it had long been out of print, but the approaching release of the film persuaded Simon & Schuster's Bob Gottlieb to push through a new hardbound edition, complete with the two original companion stories that had by now dropped out of successive issues of the Ballantine paperback.

These were also the years when *Fahrenheit 451*'s mass-market paperback was finally beginning to approach the impressive long-term sales records of *The Martian Chronicles*, *The Illustrated Man*, and *Dandelion Wine*. Truffaut's forthcoming film, as well as the great popularity that Bradbury's other titles enjoyed with the Teen Age Book Club, led Ian Ballantine to add *Fahrenheit 451* to the Bal-Hi series of Ballantine titles marketed to high schools and the broader young reading markets. This would require what Ballantine called a "specially edited edition"; on June 6, 1966, Ballantine sent Bradbury an explanation of the concept, a marked copy of the proposed changes, and an assurance that the "adult" or regular trade edition paperback would remain unchanged.

The Bal-Hi "edition" was really a modified reissue of the first-edition type-setting; at about one hundred points in the text, words and phrases containing profanity; references to God; or references to insanity, drinking, or sexuality were removed or modified. Bradbury gave tentative approval pending Congdon's okay, but it's not at all clear that Bradbury gave considered thought to the Bal-Hi text. He simply referred to it as the "corrected copy of F.451" when he returned it on June 10 and seemed far more concerned with other projects in his cover letter.[6] Bradbury had resigned himself to these kinds of editorial impositions for Doubleday's *R Is for Rocket* in 1962 and more recently for the 1966 publication of *S Is for Space*, companion story collections aimed at juvenile readers. Above all, he wanted to extend the availability of his work for young readers and school libraries; if this was the way to bring young readers to *Fahrenheit 451*, then so be it.

But this was not a story collection, conceived and assembled specifically for young readers; *Fahrenheit 451*, a book about the importance of preserving unmediated literature and great ideas in an age of multimedia wonders, was now systematically altered in significant ways. In 1973, the censored text was accidentally transferred to successive printings of the commercial text; for the next five years, no one could buy an unexpurgated copy of *Fahrenheit 451*—and no one realized it. By 1978, when a class of Missouri high-school students and their teacher asked Bradbury why their Bal-Hi text differed from the text of older store-bought copies, Bradbury had long since forgotten that he had actually been part of the approval process. He was, in a very real sense, "seeing" the effects for the first time; he added a cautionary coda to a new 1979 restored Ballantine edition and to the many editions that would follow.

33 Stops of Various Quills

Although *The Martian Chronicles* screenplays and refashioning of his classic works loomed large throughout the early 1960s, these projects by no means dominated his imagination. During those same years, he was extending his creativity into a wide range of new genres and cultural activities; many of these projects remained unpublished or unproduced, yet the publicity surrounding all of them greatly advanced his presence across the entire spectrum of American popular culture.

A young man from the windswept solitude of the Edwards Plateau, not far from San Antonio, Texas, provided the spark that would illuminate a new creative horizon for Bradbury. Clinton Lenoir, a Rice University student, wanted desperately to discover the essence of creative writing. Perhaps it was the intensity of the young man's pursuit of insight, but this letter struck a chord that hundreds of similar inquiries had not vibrated. Bradbury had, from time to time, offered written critiques of new work by young writers and had occasionally presented glimpses of his writing philosophy in the pages of the professional periodical *Writer*. But Lenoir wanted him to bring those isolated observations into sharper focus; Bradbury's half of their 1961 correspondence resulted in three letters that began the process of reshaping all that he had said before, in his articles and in his countless lectures to writing groups. In 1962, the San Antonio Public Library published Bradbury's letters to Lenoir in a slim pamphlet titled *The Essence of Creative Writing*.

There was more of a reflective tone here than had surfaced in Bradbury's three major essays for *Writer*: "The Joy of Writing" (1956); "Zen and the Art of Writing" (1958); and "How to Keep and Feed a Muse" (1961). He had been moving in this direction with the last essay, which probed deeper into the working of the subconscious than he had done in his other public statements. In "How to Keep and Feed a Muse," Bradbury used the simplest metaphors to good effect: "[W]e stuff ourselves with sounds, sights, smells, tastes, and textures of people, animals, landscapes, events, large and small. . . . This is the storehouse, the file, to which we must return every waking hour to check reality against memory, and in sleep to check memory against memory, which means ghost against ghost, in order to exorcise them, if necessary."

Lenoir's quest had been prompted by a Bradbury story his mother had read to him in the late 1940s. It really didn't matter to the boy that "I See You Never" had been a *New Yorker* story, or that it had won a place in the *Best American Short Stories* volume for 1947; what mattered was that it was a true story of the human heart. It was the short, simple tale of an illegal Mexican migrant worker removed by federal agents from the loving family that had taken him in. Lenoir and his mother had just experienced the same heartbreak, and as the years passed he wanted to know how Bradbury could create stories that could evoke remembrance, reflection, and healing in ways that so many readers found compelling. The young man probed deeply, and Bradbury began to analyze his own process more consciously than ever before. He would later tell Lenoir's mother that "Clinton had set me to thinking, on paper, about certain aspects of life and how they applied to a life-art: literature."

In the midst of these exchanges, Bradbury began the long series of interviews that culminated in an even broader biographical reflection on his life as a writer. The UCLA Oral History program interview transcript ran to more than 550 typed pages, and Bradbury quickly discovered that his earlier letters to Lenoir had opened his own mind to deep reflections for the UCLA interviewer. "I shall always be grateful for his gift to me, of myself, which is the best we always do for one another, anyway," he observed to Lenoir's mother. "He turned me back to my resources as I hope I turned him back to his."

The UCLA interviews became a continuation of this turning back and reflecting; in these sessions, conducted during the spring of 1961, Bradbury offered his views on the importance of a daily writing schedule, how to write from the true emotions of the heart, and how to avoid the pitfalls of writing for commercial gain or intellectual status. These were lessons already laid out to some extent in his trio of *Writer* essays, but Bradbury went on with extensive commentary on writing for stage and screen, and on the role of the creative writer as a social and political critic. The fabric of these comments was held together by hundreds of personal reflections, and as a whole the UCLA interviews represent Bradbury's closest coherent approach to autobiography—a genre of writing that he found far too self-conscious and challenging to attempt on his own.

In early September 1963, Bradbury received word that his young friend from the high plains of Texas had died shortly after a tragic accident. "I wept the other day, for a boy I had never met," he told Lenoir's mother; in the same letter he described the UCLA interviews to her, and how Clinton had inspired his entire approach to this project. Still unfamiliar with the institutional restrictions on an oral history text, Bradbury planned to publish it someday and prepared a page dedicating it to the memory of Lenoir. It remains today an archival artifact, however, unpublished and undedicated, open to on-site researchers only. But the Lenoir letters and the UCLA interviews together led Bradbury to consider the concept of a unified discussion of his views on writing; eventually, he would gather his first three *Writer* articles, along with a dozen subsequent pieces, in the form of an essay collection that many writers and students know today as *Zen in the Art of Writing*.

The evolution of this collection took decades, but a parallel broadening of Bradbury's nonfiction writing had more immediate consequences. His abiding love of visionary architectures, fired by boyhood encounters with science fiction art and the great Chicago and New York World's Fairs of the 1930s, finally exploded into print during the mid-1960s. The catalyst was public transportation in the Los Angeles region, where the loss of the grand old streetcar lines had accelerated an inevitable transition into chronic traffic congestion. The ghost of his beloved Red Car and Yellow Car lines, and the creative example of Disneyland's monorail, culminated in Bradbury's "Los Angeles: The Promised and Re-Promised Land," which appeared in the July–August 1963 issue of *American Home*. He advocated a pylon-mounted monorail system, following what was left of the center island right-of-way for the old Red Car line.

His article appeared only in the California edition, but it attracted unexpected support from the entire Curtis Publishing Company. During July, the company president, along with the editors of *American Home* and its venerable companion, *The Ladies Home Journal*, flew out from Philadelphia and arranged a full-scale promotion involving city officials and Walt Disney himself.[1] This event marked the beginning of Bradbury's long and ultimately unsuccessful campaign for a regional elevated monorail system. Other doors would open, however; he would soon find himself a creative consultant for Disney and his successors, and eventually a consultant on many of the regional mall projects designed by the noted California architect John Jerde. Dozens of articles on urban development would follow, opening out into a significant new range of creative nonfiction in his canon.

Bradbury was a more marginal player in urban planning than he was in the space program; with the exception of his work for Disney, his influence was never really felt beyond the Southern California region. Nevertheless, his value as a creative inspiration was beginning to cross disciplinary boundaries, and during the spring of 1964 he was asked to address the School of Architecture at the University of Southern California. As he told Congdon, Bradbury was not surprised that his method was equally relevant in the visual arts: "[T]he rules of creativity apply wherever you put them down. You either love what you are doing or don't love it. I teach love, jumping up and down, yelling with excitement, intuitive thought, proper hates . . . but you've heard all this before."

His narration text for the forthcoming New York World's Fair required a different kind of writing altogether, but it afforded Bradbury the chance to reach a far broader audience.[2] The U.S. Pavilion planners made it easy for his Muse to respond; they wanted something along the lines of his "Cry the Cosmos" article in *Life* magazine, this time blending a story of America's past achievements with the nation's future aspirations in Space. He finished an 18-page script by the end of July 1963 and sent a copy directly to the White House in hopes that President Kennedy would see and approve it. The White House mailing, and even the narration itself, were very self-conscious acts; at the time, it wasn't clear in his own mind whether he really cared about the underlying nature of his service or was merely reaching for another moment of public recognition.

He was soon forced to answer this question by the sudden tragic death of the president. On December 1, 1963, he expressed his surprisingly deep emotions to Don Congdon: "[N]ow I find I cared a very great deal indeed, and was looking forward to meeting him in April when he was supposed to open our Pavilion at the Fair. A very silly, superficial, and personal thing, of course, but now that it has been taken away, along with so much else that was of greater meaning, I find the Pavilion itself of very little importance right now." But his work on the narration was nearly done, and he knew that in time his enthusiasm and pride would return.

Bradbury's final narration text reflected the influence of his good friend Norman Corwin, who had defined the midcentury network radio documentary tradition in America. Here were the native peoples and their lands, the westward migrations of the Old World settlers into and across these lands, presented with a full view of what was achieved in forging a new nation, and what was lost in the process. The poetic prose was intentionally skewed toward the Whitmanesque, showing grand vistas of lands and waters, catalogs of people and events. The pace was rapid and concise, reflecting the lessons Bradbury had learned writing cinematic scene descriptions and voice-over narration in Hollywood.

The context, however, was pure Bradbury. He designed his story around the primal elements of the environment—the combined wilderness of land, sea, and sky—and then fused them to celebrate America's newest and most ambitious dream: "From Canaveral to California you mix the elements of raw mythology. From chemistries of Earth, fused with Air, you strike forth . . . fire!" (ellipsis Bradbury's). The image was right out of his 1962 "Cry the Cosmos" article in *Life* magazine, and the closing pages of the new World's Fair narrative was infused with the same Kazantzakian views of the Cosmos that were emerging more and more frequently in his public talks and interviews: "Looking back from Space, you will see your Birthplace, Earth, the old wilderness, dwindle as the Human

Race reaches for the stars, for eternity, and for possible survival and immortality in the next billion years. Man, God made manifest, goes in search of himself."

Bradbury, by way of Whitman, Corwin, and Kazantzakis, spoken by the familiar voice of veteran Hollywood actor John McIntyre, reached many of the fifty-one million people who attended the World's Fair. Even as this triumph reached its international audience, Bradbury continued to worry about the effectiveness of the exhibition itself. Over the winter between the 1964 and 1965 World's Fair seasons, he offered conceptual refinements to the designers, never dreaming that his own narrative would be targeted for revision by Lyndon Johnson's White House.

Early in 1965, the same U.S. Pavilion executives who had celebrated Bradbury's narrative now called with a request to cut his concluding Space-Age visions and replace them with a salute to the Great Society—a core feature of Johnson's recent landslide election. Bradbury declined in the strongest terms, prompting a visit by the director and his staff. Bradbury held firm, maintaining that the Age of the Rockets provided a far more compelling inspirational mythology: "Let these be the torches held high to excite the young people to do the job which will in turn build your Great Society. . . . [A]dd more Space materials to the entire U.S. Pavilion and send the kids out, blazing with excitement to conquer new worlds."[3]

It was, perhaps, only a matter of semantics, but Bradbury was being fiercely loyal to his long-established notion of art. "You've got to find the right symbol," he told students at Pasadena City College a year later. "We must lie to ourselves beautifully with our new mythologies. That is the function of art. It is a way of beautifully lying—containing many wonderful truths. You don't start with that banal title. . . . It's going to grow out of our excitement, with poetry and with art and with photography and all the things you're going to go out and change as individuals and make that Great Society which can be named after it is made."[4] This, in essence, is what he told the Pavilion director, and his World's Fair narrative remained unchanged.

: : :

The major published interviews that would both clarify and obscure various aspects of his long career began with "A Portrait of Genius: Ray Bradbury," in the December 1964 issue of *Show*. To no one's surprise, Bradbury told his *Show* interviewer that Jules Verne was his favorite science fiction writer: "a writer of imagination, moral fibre, and good humor who inspires as he writes. He makes one proud to be a human being." Whether it was there or not, Bradbury saw an anticipation of Kazantzakis in Verne's literary vision: "In an age which has often bankrupted its fund of ideals, Verne, from another age, calls out to better goals and warns man not to worry so much about his relationship with God, but rather to see to his kinship with other men. Would that there were more like him writing today."

Indeed, Bradbury still had a firm grip on his further intentions for Jules Verne's Captain Nemo. There had been hints in "The Ardent Blasphemers," Bradbury's audacious introduction to Bantam's 1962 edition of *20,000 Leagues under the Sea*, that he would have to return to the brooding complexities of Nemo and refashion him for modern times. Bradbury had noted that, in the final pages of Verne's novel, "hope lives on after Nemo, when, either through remorse or inadvertency, he puts his ship down into the maelstrom. We are unsure of his death." Verne himself had closed with hopes that if Nemo still lived, the wonders of the sea he so loved might transform him from a wrathful judge of Mankind's disregard for life into a scientist focused on peaceful exploration.

Bradbury considered this a most sublime possibility, suggesting a natural consequence in the final pages of his introduction: "And in that sublimity lies hope for Nemo and his American nephews, the boys who have grown to manhood and machinery since." Almost immediately Bradbury had conceived *Nemo!*—a concept for a novel based on just such a Bradburyan conflation of Verne's nineteenth-century Captain and the Tom Swift tradition of latter-day American fiction. *Nemo!* would be an even riskier proposition than *Leviathan '99*, however, for now Bradbury was operating in the exciting but shallow waters along the margins of young adult pulp fiction and popular romance. Bradbury's modern-day explorers revive Nemo from the frozen coffin of the *Nautilus* and witness his transformation from a secretive and bitter scientific recluse into a gifted explorer intent on the salvation of Mankind. Nemo designs a microscopic *Nautilus* to carry miniaturized surgical teams inside the human body, as well as a new spaceship *Nautilus* to carry explorers to the stars.

Random House had shown some interest in the Nemo concept as early as the summer of 1963, but Congdon was unable to win a firm commitment. Bradbury's July 1964 trip to New York for the World's Fair provided an opportunity for face-to-face negotiations over the novel, which he now saw as the first of a series of books—perhaps juveniles—following Nemo's odyssey through the stars. By late May, Trident Press (representing Pocket Books) and New American Library were interested in the project.[5] Ed Doctorow of NAL proved to be the more earnest negotiator, and the July trip eventually led to a $10,000 contract with NAL and an excellent 10 percent commission on the paperback royalties. Bradbury received $5,000 on signing, with the remainder due on delivery of the novel.

But the outline that burned so bright in Bradbury's mind failed to transform into a novel, and the 1965 submission date passed without any significant progress on the text. Once again, the main distraction involved media adaptation; this time the stage, rather than the silver screen, was the main obstacle, as Bradbury spent much of 1964 and most of 1965 immersed in one-act stage adaptations of his stories. Given the combined value of Verne and Bradbury in the popular imagination, NAL editors could afford to be patient—until the 1966 premiere of the Twentieth Century–Fox film *Fantastic Voyage* and the subsequent novelization by Isaac Asimov.

The film's miniaturization of a surgical team and their voyage through a patient's bloodstream was very similar to the climactic technological adventure that Bradbury had planned out for his modern-day Captain Nemo, and in September 1966 NAL used this unfortunate development to offer an amicable termination of the contract. The answer was as intriguing as it was frustrating; he patiently explained his habitual deference to the timing of his subconscious sources of creativity: "*Nemo!* hasn't been finished, mainly because it wasn't *ready* to be finished, whatever that may mean. I do not intend to be obscure about this, but the fact is my mainsprings are hidden from me." He would return the advance if necessary, but he fully intended to take up the novel the following spring. "The work *does* get done, but always at a time my subconscious chooses." He had always subordinated the rational act of revision to the subconscious act of creation, allowing his hidden mind, in effect, to control the sequence of topics; this method had been key to his early success, but now it was becoming a way to deflect an ever-increasing range of deadlines.

Bradbury dropped the surgical adventure that seemed so close to the *Fantastic Voyage* premise, and his subconscious failed to respond to what remained of the novel. He never wrote more than a few short, sketchy chapter drafts for *Nemo!* and eventually returned NAL's advance. Yet his reaction to the possibility that others had borrowed his ideas was surprisingly calm. He remembered that he had shown the *Nemo!* concept to producers at Fox in 1963, before he ever sent it to NAL, and had interacted with one of the original *Fantastic Voyage* story writers at about the same time. Much time had passed, however, and he had little recollection of his studio discussions at all: "[I]t is all too vague, and there is no use getting paranoid on it. It must be forgotten."

34 | *The World of Ray Bradbury*

As Bradbury moved deeper into small-venue, experimental stage adaptations of his stories, it became apparent that his approach to playwriting was far from the avant-garde, or even the mainstream Modernist stage. In 1962, he had summarized his views while judging an evening of UCLA student performances of one-act plays by Tennessee Williams, Samuel Beckett, and Eugene Ionesco. Producer and actor John Houseman (who had spent a decade trying to land Bradbury for television and film) moderated the panel and was no doubt surprised by his friend's commentary.

Bradbury's words were, to say the least, controversial—he began by declaring the plays "intellectual horse manure," and followed up with a rationale couched in a hard-hitting metaphor that became a recurring image in subsequent interviews: "You want me to wet my finger and put it in a light socket and electrocute myself with realism. Even if it hides behind some of the masks of Ionesco and Beckett, it's really realism, you know. I won't do that. I will build a light bulb and screw it in the same circuit, and make light with the same electricity. But I refuse to die for you. . . . I don't want happy endings. I want unhappy endings that help you live."[1]

Paul Newman, who had developed strong interests in directing Bradbury's star-crossed screenplay of *The Rock Cried Out* and playing Montag in Truffaut's *Fahrenheit 451*, worked hard to lure Bradbury into the harsh realism of the modern stage. During February 1964, Newman urged Bradbury to read the plays of Harold Pinter, but Bradbury's response was true to form; he quickly filed his verdict in a letter to Don Congdon: "I have just finished *The Caretaker*, and it is an actor's dream . . . why? Because the cup is empty and the actor must fill it up with his own soup or wine. No wonder actors love Pinter. He is so numb, so hollow, so devoid of ability, he lets the actor take over and have a field day holding the whole goddam thing up. And people, seeing his plays, marveling at the actor, praise Pinter. Well I refuse to praise Pinter to please Paul."[2]

This kind of private reaction would become public more and more often throughout the rest of Bradbury's career. The point was often blurred by the bluntness of the commentary, but there was usually an insight that merited exercise in a public debate. In later years Bradbury would come to respect Pinter as a screenwriter, but he could never warm to his stage plays. He found Newman great company and a stimulating conversationalist, but he could not abide the acting school that Newman, among others, came to epitomize: "I see now what the Method people are up to, they are would-be writers and to hell with the Word. Well, sir, to hell with them, sir, is my answer." His emotional responses to contemporary realism, and in particular to the Theatre of the Absurd, previewed his emerging confidence in confronting the arbiters of literary taste: "At long last, the flat statement comes easier to me. For years I ran in fear of intellectual excoriation if my opinion diverged from their norm."

It was a war he would never win in print, but he might win it on the stage itself. The greatest challenge centered on control. Bradbury had spent a decade chafing at the limitations imposed by television and motion picture producers; he found more room to experiment during his two years with the Desilu Theater, but even here the productions never seemed to reach the level of success that he hoped for. In 1964, he formed his own Pandemonium Production Company, secured a five-year contract for the Coronet Theater, and hired the proven talents of director Charles Rome Smith to put on a trio of new Bradbury one-act plays. He stepped away from the attractions of The Wonderful Ice Cream Suit and the Irish one-acts, with their sentimental and nostalgic celebrations of the past; instead, he decided to risk everything on three somber and often dark visions of the future adapted from three other Bradbury tales: "The Pedestrian," "The Veldt," and "To the Chicago Abyss." The whole was more than the sum of the parts and was presented as The World of Ray Bradbury.

The plays opened on October 14, 1964, drawing unity from the interrelated themes and strong performances by Harold Gould in both The Pedestrian and To the Chicago Abyss. Gould's performances hinted at the distinguished television and film career to come, but The World of Ray Bradbury gained a life of its own. Even the overly optimistic Bradbury, who had expected only a two- to four-week run, was amazed to see the show sustained for an incredible eighteen weeks, closing on February 14, 1965. The weekly schedule of seven shows cost Bradbury $20,000 to produce, but he essentially broke even. The favorable reviews also won a commitment from Claude Giroux, the president of Allied Arts Pictures, to back an off-Broadway New York run in the spring.

Reviews were generally favorable throughout the Los Angeles run. Bradbury had carefully enhanced the unifying themes of the original stories—what John McLaughlin, writing for the Nation, called "the loss of human values to the machine" (The Pedestrian, The Veldt) and the legacy of consumerism and mediocrity in a postapocalyptic world (To the Chicago Abyss). Bradbury had given The Pedestrian a dramatic life by introducing a second actor who could be lured from his TV by the solitary title character to enjoy—if only for a moment—the sights, smells, and sounds of the forbidden sidewalks and greenways. Harold Gould's strong performance gave the dark world of To the Chicago Abyss that hint of hope that Bradbury required, by proclaiming, through his memories of the long lost "junk of a race-track civilization," that the "mediocre must be, so that most excellent fine can bloom."

After the final curtain, Bradbury hosted what he called a "beer-pretzel and champagne party" on stage with friends. Norman Corwin was there, along with Sir Carol Reed. Claude Giroux was also there and announced his commitment to start rehearsals in April for the New York production. For Bradbury, the small stage of the Coronet provided the perfect venue for celebration: "what a fine place to have a party, at the very heart of the theatre itself." The next day, his account of events for Don Congdon offered a glimpse of the true depths of his identity with the world of the stage:

> [T]his is where I have belonged since I was ten. It took a long time and a very long way around from doing magic tricks then, and appearing in amateur theatricals, to a night like last night when you say to yourself, I really belong. This theatre is as much my body and my flesh as my own body and flesh are. How fortunate to be one of those who really knows his place, finds it, and tries to tend it well and make it vital.[3]

He now felt familiar enough with the dramatic stage to accept an invitation to write a retrospective essay on the Los Angeles theater season for the most prominent annual in the field—the Burns Mantle Yearbook. He wrote for The Best Plays of 1964–1965 volume, surprising no one by altering the traditional review narrative form to fit his own distinctive style of nonfiction prose. With only touring revivals for competition in the large Los Angeles venues, he focused the review on his own recent success with the three one-acts of The World of Ray Bradbury, and his follow-on run of three plays centered on The Wonderful Ice Cream Suit.

In a sense, he was once again crusading to overturn the status quo, in this case trying to celebrate the potential for original drama beyond the traditional dominance of the New York stage. His thesis centered on the fact that in the midst of "the excitements, terrors, delights, and despairs of our robot era," his one-acts were the only ones "dramatizing man's conflicts with his machines and his hidden self." Bradbury's essay showed how much he regarded his own productions as establishing an alternative to the often darkly brooding Theatre of the Absurd, and how much he was looking forward to his first chance to see his plays produced on a New York stage. That chance would come very soon, and with great disappointment.

Although Giroux was first and foremost a filmmaker, his enthusiasm for experimental theater convinced Bradbury to hand over production and financial control in order to bring *The World of Ray Bradbury* to New York. It was an acceptable risk; his Pandemonium Players opened another trio of plays at the Coronet in early March and would not be involved with the New York production at all. Giroux agreed to take on Charles Rome Smith as director, and Bradbury felt that this would ensure a significant degree of continuity with the successful Los Angeles run. The cautious Giroux eventually moved the opening back to the fall 1965 season, leaving Bradbury blissfully unaware of the disaster to come.

The underlying problems with *The World of Ray Bradbury* were apparent to the more discerning critics of the Los Angeles production. In the *Nation*, John McLaughlin found that the production privileged stagecraft rather than action or dialogue. Bradbury implicitly conceded this danger in conversation with McLaughlin, noting that among the lessons learned was "to trust the word. . . . You've got to believe in your own language." Nevertheless, Bradbury had great faith in Smith as a director and in the sound effects of John Whitney (a veteran, like Bradbury, of the New York World's Fair exhibition teams). Bradbury's longtime collaborating artist Joe Mugnaini had prepared excellent background graphic projections, and the work of all three of these men carried over to the New York production that opened on Friday, October 8, 1965, at the Orpheum Theater.

By the time Bradbury arrived in New York for the opening weekend, Giroux had already drawn his ire for treating Smith as an outsider and placing him in very poor lodgings. Bradbury also felt that George Voskovec, a talented film and stage actor, was not right for the parts that Hal Gould had played back home. But the real problems emerged through the weekend as the major media reviews came in.[4] Some of the brief notices were positive, but most of the full reviews were critical. The influential *Village Voice* found the characters corny, the situations contrived, and the dialogue preachy. The *New Yorker* liked Voskovec, but considered the whole evening equivalent to "pay television." UPI's Jack Gaver couldn't recommend it; Taubman's *New York Times* review credited Bradbury's humanist qualities but declared that his "playlets are not particularly theatrical."

"There's nothing more frightening than opening night," Bradbury would recall nearly forty years later, "when the critics come up the aisle in a phalanx of bitterness and bile, heading to the exit to kill you in the lobby."[5] But he would always blame Claude Giroux for the failure of the New York production. On Monday, after the major reviews reached print, Giroux and his coproducers closed the show. Bradbury was certain that the shortcomings could have been worked out over the course of a few more performances and felt that Giroux had killed his wondrous dramatic child in its cradle. But Bradbury's acclaimed mastery of the short story did not always carry over into his stage adaptations; George Oppenheimer, in his review of the New York production for *Newsday*, noted that *The World of Ray Bradbury* was "more story than play": "It is easier to evoke fantasy and fear on the printed page than on the visual stage."

For Bradbury, the year couldn't end soon enough, and his backward glance at 1965 offered little to celebrate. His attraction to experimentation in the performing arts had proven, once again, impossible to suppress, and for nearly two years he had been drawn back to long stints of full-time work on stage and screen projects. The Los Angeles run of *The World of Ray Bradbury* had been an exciting and critically successful experience, proving that he could mount an alternative, small-venue theater in the very shadow of the national and international touring companies. But this success failed to generate a revenue stream for future productions, and the jump to New York had proven disastrous by nearly any standard of evaluation. The *Life* magazine publication of his Hemingway homage, "The Kilimanjaro Device," was a true high point, but it would be the only story he would publish during 1965.

This was the first time since 1941, his first year as a paid professional, that only one Bradbury story reached print. Yet he remained optimistic, and his end-of-year letter to Congdon expressed his resolve within a new metaphor of time:

> I can see now that from here on it will be a waterfall of days and each must be grabbed onto and worked with as well as possible. I am getting more and more touchy about giving my time to people. Once I squandered it horribly, now I refuse again and again to go to lunch with anyone. I want that time to write, or walk and think about things, or go off to a book store, gallery, or what have you. I am going to ride the waterfall my way. So, too, I am more afraid of working with people than ever before.

At age 45, he now saw time passing with the speed and elusiveness of a waterfall. Occasionally, his accelerating sense of time, along with the public commitments that more and more frequently broke into his resolve for solitude, distorted his ability to plan his future milestones as a teller of tales. At the end of 1965 he believed that he had published almost enough stories over the last two years to contemplate a new collection, but in reality there were only four; for the rest of his career, his newer story collections would have to be fortified by much older uncollected tales from the 1940s and early 1950s. These often revealed the old Bradbury hallmarks, such as the twist ending and an effective touch of terror, but they were the remainders of an earlier time—a time that had already been captured so effectively in such timeless collections as *The Illustrated Man*, *The Golden Apples of the Sun*, and *The October Country*.

35 | If the Sun Dies

Bradbury published only four rather sentimental and anecdotal stories in 1966, placing them in a range of specialized entertainment magazines that included *Cavalier*, *McCall's*, and *Playboy*. He could command (thanks to Don Congdon) excellent rates, but it was clear that he was continuing to move away from short fiction narratives; film negotiations remained a constant background pulse, and by now the play had indeed become the thing. Lines and stanzas for new poems came to him more and more frequently, swallowing up yet more precious moments of creativity. His speeches, even more than his stories, now became forges for tempering his settled views on issues of the present and the future.

He was now speaking at major college events more frequently than he was lecturing classes or seminars; more often than not, his presentations would open with blunt political statements that were usually insightful and occasionally outrageous, but always thought-provoking. His April 1966 address to the Pasadena City College Convocation began with a jeremiad against the established intellectual magazines that he had enjoyed so much as a young writer, disappointed that the *New York Review of Books*, *The American Scholar*, *Harper's*, *The Atlantic*, the major literary reviews, and even *The Nation* seemed to have left the essential responsibility for social criticism to *Mad* magazine and other humor periodicals.

Here again, his instinctive need to give popular culture its due would create controversy in intellectual circles: "I am a trash heap of the mediocre that has made itself excellent," he told the Pasadena students and faculty. "I am full of so much junk, and yet I make use of this junk because I can pull from it the symbols of our time that represent us as a mass of people trying to be individual." He would always champion the individual, criticizing the marginalization of Native American cultures and the economic or educational disadvantages endured by Black and Hispanic Americans. Bradbury was dead set against the Vietnam Conflict and was blunt in his criticism of President Johnson and Defense Secretary McNamara; when he returned to Pasadena in February 1967 to address the annual Freshman Dinner at Caltech, he referred to the president as "the Uriah Heep of America," an edgy allusion to the scheming antagonist of *David Copperfield*.[1] In Bradbury's mind, Vietnam in particular, and Johnson's highly manipulative and untrusting nature in general, far outweighed Johnson's socially progressive role in issues such as racial integration and voting rights legislation. But in all these campus addresses, he would eventually home in on creativity and problem-solving in the Space Age, claiming with some justification that "We are science fictional children of a science fictional age."

His more specialized public addresses turned more often to the challenges facing a society where, he felt, new novels were empty of ideas, and the ubiquitous television screen had abandoned quality dramatic programming for superficial entertainments. Bradbury's December 1966 address to the American Society of Cinematographers showcased the effective emotional impact of his public speaking as well as his emerging eloquence as an apologist for the motion picture industry. Following the method he had used to preach the literary merits of science fiction, Bradbury struck at a similar rhetorical question whenever he spoke on the cinema: "It's a popular medium; how can it be any good at all?"[2]

For this particular audience, he used many of his old anecdotes of his days roller-skating from theater to theater in 1930s Hollywood and accounts of the combination of luck and talent that brought him to the attention of midcentury directors like John Huston and Sir Carol Reed. But Truffaut's adaptation of *Fahrenheit 451* had just come out, and Bradbury was now able to elevate the aesthetic context of his commentary. He did this in the best way he knew—by drawing on his European travels and his firsthand encounters with the great art of the Old World.

Bradbury's two European encounters with Renaissance art had changed his approach to fiction, and not always for the better, but he was now able to describe meaningful analogies of scale between the great canvasses and the possibilities of the silver screen to portray the grandeur of the heavens: "That's the problem with the Space Age—we're always holding it in our lap. It's like the Italian Renaissance—until you go to Italy and you see a real Botticelli, which is as big as any one of these walls here, or your first Tintoretto or a Rubens or a Fra Angelico. When you see any one of those paintings, it holds *you* in its lap."

There were risks with this approach, and sometimes Bradbury would go over the top. His discussion of the wide-screen, three-camera Cinerama process offered a prime example: "We all know that Michelangelo invented Cinerama 400 years ago—didn't he? With that huge ceiling you can lie on your back in the chapel and stare up at this 'new way' of looking that Michelangelo gave us. It took us 400 years of messing around with technologies before we finally put the thing on the screen." The image risks absurdity, but the conviction gave a serious context to a daring analogy. The High Modernist critic might scoff, but the analogy formed a meaningful bridge for a broad range of lay readers and listeners trying to imagine why scale was so important to the cinema.

Such observations on the creative potential of film paralleled his attempts to refine his settling views on the Cosmos. The Italian writer Oriana Fallaci's 1964 interview with Bradbury, published two years later in *If the Sun Dies*, revealed how his reading encounter with Kazantzakis had settled down into an articulate view on the nature of things. Fallaci was already a well-known international journalist and author—attractive, flamboyant, ambitious, but also compassionate and deeply concerned about the Space-Age challenges facing Mankind. Her new book emerged from many conversations with NASA astronauts, engineers, and scientists, but she began with two chapters based on two days of interviews with Bradbury in his own home.

Although these taped conversations had to bounce back into English from the Italian first edition of *If the Sun Dies*, the American text nevertheless documents how Bradbury eloquently reprised fifteen years of philosophical commentary: his celebration of technological wonders, his displeasure with the misuse of these wonders, and his dual purpose as both a preventer of futures and a designer of creative alternatives. But Fallaci's reservations about the space program, compressed into a single phrase about Mankind's "headlong leap into the void," triggered Bradbury's most compelling statement of the Cosmic imperative:

> Don't let us forget this: that the Earth can die, explode, the Sun can go out, will go out. And if the sun dies, if the Earth dies, if our race dies, then so will everything die that we have done up to that moment. Homer will die. Michelangelo will die, Galileo, Leonardo, Shakespeare, Einstein will die, all those will die who now are not dead because we are alive, we are thinking of them, we are carrying them within us. And then every single thing, every memory, will hurtle down into the void with us. So let us save them, let us save ourselves. Let us prepare ourselves to escape, to continue life and rebuild our cities on other planets: we shall not be long of this Earth!

Here was well-traveled ground, but Bradbury went on to map out the further conclusions that Kazantzakis, and the Kazantzakian appropriation of Bergson's élan vital in *The Saviors of God*, had brought to his view of Religion and the Cosmos:

> There's no point in searching for God elsewhere, because God is ourselves, and I don't accept the idea of God as something superhuman, transcendental, something incorporeal playing with his toys, stars and men. I don't accept the idea of God as something far removed. I see God as something that grows

and expands through senses and thoughts, that wants to be mortal in order to die and be born again, and wants to move on, to push ahead with the human race, to spread and expand it throughout the whole cosmos! God is this flesh, this voice.

In his mind, Western religions would have to embrace this view or collapse. Even as a child, Bradbury had balked at the notion of Original Sin, and therein lies the root cause of his search for another way. This dissenting impulse was, of course, already well established in his fiction; "The Fire Balloons," found in some American editions of *The Martian Chronicles* and all American editions of *The Illustrated Man*, tells us how Father Peregrine could discover no evil on the Red Planet, nor any concept of sin. But Fallaci pursued the point, asking Bradbury if a spiritual or moral imperative of *any* kind pervaded the universe and its life forms.

It was a most revealing moment, for Bradbury could not see the way through his abiding sense that neither Mankind, nor any other sentient race, would ever be able to overcome the visceral fear of Otherness. This was the theme of his original screen treatment for the 1953 Universal film *It Came From Outer Space*, and it would surface in more than a few Bradbury stories. It seemed to Bradbury that the realization that Humanity is an idea that transcends form would not govern our actions until our far distant descendants have left the human form behind. He saw no hope for our age, where racial tensions, class wars, and the legacy of economic exploitation cast long shadows on into the foreseeable future.

If the Sun Dies—Bradbury's central rationale for space travel—had given Fallaci's book its title, but there were distortions around the edges of the published text. She was an effective practitioner of the New Journalism, framing her narrative of Chapters Two and Three entirely around the interplanetary dynamics of the Bradbury family: four animated daughters of varying ages and the mother, all summer blondes. Maggie was clearly the Primum Mobus, constantly tugging at the four minor planets and her great, self-absorbed Jove. Certain side observations, and even some of Fallaci's own reactions to Bradbury's comments, seem a bit fictive at times, but the core quotations—transcribed from tape—all ring true to Bradbury's maturing way of expressing his views on the Cosmos and our part in it. It was, on balance, a most revealing interview.

Yet it was not the accumulating interviews, speeches, poems, or stage plays alone that diverted him from his old concentration on storytelling; these more public forums of speech and performance art also drove him further into the world of fame. He had been somewhat self-deprecating in his earlier observations on the effects of cultural prominence and had by and large restricted such comments to his private correspondence. But when his "Film and the Space Age" lecture to the American Society of Cinematographers was published, his opening lines—intended to compliment his audience—were psychologically telling: "I think this is the first time in my life that I've been really in awe of a group of people. I have a fantastic ego and I'm not easily humbled."

Early in his career, his ego was apparent only in his compulsion to speak out beyond the pages of his creative works. During the early 1950s, he knew that his strength as a freelance writer would prevail even if his comments about Mc-Carthyism might close doors in Hollywood or keep him from selling stories to certain magazines. His broad-based audience appeal continued to increase, but the FBI file initiated in 1959 created another audience that he wasn't even aware of. His file slowly grew throughout the 1960s, as his speaking opportunities increased and his commentary grew more strident—an inevitable consequence of growing fame and the heightening social and political tensions of the times.

His public comments concerning Vietnam and the Johnson administration had not gone unnoticed; when an FBI reporting error inadvertently triggered an update on his file in 1968, the new report noted his opposition and listed the rather tame arts and community organizations he had joined to demonstrate against the Vietnam Conflict. An FBI interview seemed justified, but his out-spoken ways raised concerns that an interview would only fan the flames; this risk, and perhaps his increasing service to the NASA space program, persuaded the FBI to close his case; the proposed interview was not initiated, and Bradbury would not learn that his FBI file even existed for another thirty-five years.[3]

36 | Truffaut's Phoenix

Bradbury's most significant cinematic milestone of the 1960s—Universal Studio's 1966 release of François Truffaut's *Fahrenheit 451*—originated six years earlier, when producer Raoul Lévy recommended the book to Truffaut over dinner in August 1960. The themes and the plot of the novel aligned with Truffaut's passion for books and promised the kind of personal engagement he required in all his film projects. In February 1962, shortly after the acclaimed release of *Jules and Jim*, Truffaut wrote to Bradbury and suggested a meeting in New York. He was considering a joint French and American venture with Paul Newman in the role of Montag—ideas that suggest he was at least contemplating, at this earliest stage, an English-language film. He and Newman would meet at Argentina's Mar del Plata film festival in late April 1962, where both received awards (Truffaut for *Jules and Jim*, Newman for *The Hustler*). Truffaut stopped in New York en route to Buenos Aires and met with Bradbury in Don Congdon's office during the second week of April.

Bradbury was still an Earthbound traveler, however, and every rail trip from Los Angeles to New York was a major undertaking. But there were already good reasons to make the trip—a chance to talk to Arthur Penn about his three-act Irish play *The Anthem Sprinters* and the opportunity to see *Something Wicked This Way Comes* through the final press stages with Congdon and his new publisher, Simon & Schuster. He juggled his lecture schedule and managed to arrive in New York on April 11, and soon found himself in an enjoyable but complicated conversation with Congdon, Truffaut, and Truffaut's interpreter Helen Scott.

In spite of his enthusiasm, Bradbury entered the conversation burdened by his seven-year history of disappointments with *Fahrenheit*—the failure of his stage script for Charles Laughton, the long court battle with CBS over the *Playhouse 90* plagiarism case, and the longer history of near misses with television and film possibilities. He initially countered Truffaut's proposal with the possibility of adapting stories from *The Martian Chronicles* and related tales from *The Illustrated Man* as an anthology feature. At the end of the day, Congdon and Bradbury felt that they had secured the science fiction anthology feature in return for a promise to sell Truffaut the rights to *Fahrenheit 451* as a second feature film. Bradbury and his family were invited to the south of France later in the spring, where he expected to work primarily on the *Chronicles*-based project.

Truffaut, however, thought that he was free to make an offer for *Fahrenheit* without the encumbrance of the space stories anthology project; when he fully realized the misunderstanding, he wrote to Bradbury explaining how the constantly accelerating achievements of the space race made an outer space exploration film problematic; furthermore, the expense of such a production would delay *Fahrenheit*, which in Truffaut's mind was a far better candidate to become the first major European science fiction film. Bradbury was still reluctant to take on a screenwriting role for *Fahrenheit 451*, and by July 1962 both men were satisfied with a rights-only contract for $40,000; as much as he and Maggie would have enjoyed aspects of another sojourn in Europe, his increasing commitments to stage adaptations, promotion of his new novel, plans for a new story collection, and an ever-expanding range of nonfiction writing commitments did not really allow for another script commitment.

Truffaut was also engaged in the first comprehensive book-length study of Alfred Hitchcock's films. He arranged to interview Hitchcock in Hollywood for four days in mid-August 1962; after the last interview on August 19, he and Helen Scott had a few days to meet with Bradbury and extend the friendship that was already beginning to form. Maggie Bradbury's command of French was a key factor, enabling them to take Truffaut out alone to see more of the Southern California culture than he had seen before.[1] His great respect for the author of *Fahrenheit 451* now blossomed into an enduring long-distance friendship that the slow and exhausting process of filming the novel would not diminish.

The *Fahrenheit 451* contract was an expensive gamble for Truffaut's relatively small production consortium, Les Films du Carrosse, and he hoped to get the project underway by the end of 1962. Truffaut immediately began work on a French-language production; Oskar Werner, who had proven his worth in *Jules and Jim*, agreed to take on Captain Beatty's role. Two scripts fell short of the mark before Truffaut and Jean-Louis Richard developed a third during the summer of 1963. A final collaboration between Truffaut and Claude de Givray resulted in the fourth and final version by the fall of 1963. Truffaut now envisioned a story-driven film without major stars, produced in French, with the intriguingly aesthetic title *Phoenix* indicating the protagonist's rebirth within the flames of a dying world.

Most European producers considered science fiction to be an American genre, and firm financial backing seemed unobtainable until independent American producer Lewis Allen proved willing to take on the film. But the final path to filming *Fahrenheit* did not appear until Allen first tempted Truffaut with *Bonnie and Clyde*. Truffaut was, for a time, suspended between choosing the one film over the other, but as events slowly took *Bonnie and Clyde* to director Arthur Penn, Truffaut turned back to *Fahrenheit 451*. Allen relieved the financial pressure on Les Films du Carrosse by purchasing the *Fahrenheit* rights for $34,000 and Truffaut's script for another $30,000. By the beginning of 1964, it seemed as if filming could go ahead in the fall; the French script of *Phoenix* had once again transformed, by virtue of the Anglo-American backing, into *Fahrenheit 451*. It would be Truffaut's first English-language film, and the effects he had in mind would require him to venture into color production for the first time in his career.

Throughout 1964, Allen arranged potential studio options in Stockholm (Truffaut's preference), Toronto, and London. But there still remained the question of securing distribution, and this would unexpectedly add another year to the preproduction saga. Allen had lined up a tentative deal with Universal until, in the fall of 1964, Sam Spiegel brought in a strong counteroffer involving Columbia Pictures that promised to significantly expand the scope of the entire project. Spiegel had produced such blockbuster films as *The Bridge on the River Kwai* and, most recently, *Lawrence of Arabia*. Now, he offered his Horizon Pictures and Columbia distribution resources to transform *Fahrenheit 451* into a much larger production with major actors in every role. During the winter and spring of 1965, an array of potential casting options expanded the projected budget from just under a million to three million dollars. Allen assured Bradbury that the expanded scope of production was sustainable: "we will get all of the advantages of Spiegel's promotion and distribution when the film is completed."[2]

Bradbury, having sold the rights, was never involved with these decisions, and even Truffaut was kept out of the negotiations, but throughout 1964 and much of 1965 Allen kept Bradbury updated on the bewildering parade of casting possibilities. These included Jean Seberg or Jane Fonda for the young Clarisse, and Oskar Werner, Sterling Hayden, or Robert Ryan for Captain Beatty. Paul Newman turned down the starring role twice, leaving Terrence Stamp as Truffaut's choice to play Montag. During the Columbia negotiations Sam Spiegel also strongly favored Stamp, who he felt was the next Peter O'Toole or Albert Finney. He also apparently considered a Richard Burton and Elizabeth Taylor combination before casting differences led Spiegel to pull out in June 1965. But Lewis Allen quickly revived the Universal deal and secured MCA, Universal's European division, for production in London, beginning in January 1966.

Bradbury was not silent during the casting wars and made his preferences clear to Allen during the spring of 1964.[3] He thought highly of Stamp's performance in *Billy Budd*, but considered him absolutely wrong for *Fahrenheit 451*: "he is far too young, too immature, and therefore would be, I think, unbelievable, as Montag. . . . It should be a man in his middle thirties, to whom the knowledge of his book-burning sins would come as a more stunning and dreadful blow." Bradbury was also unimpressed with the Seberg and Fonda options for Clarisse, and he was strongly opposed to the choice of Sterling Hayden for Captain Beatty.

The reasons had nothing to do with Hayden's acting, which he had always enjoyed. Bradbury preferred actors he knew, and felt that Kirk Douglas or his good friend Rod Steiger were better suited to the role; but the choice also opened old corporate wounds: "Hayden played in the plagiarism of *Fahrenheit 451* which appeared on CBS-TV some years ago, though, of course, he played the Montag character. As you recall, I took the case all the way to the Supreme Court, won, and was paid off. Just one more reason why I wouldn't want Hayden in *your* version." Bradbury envisioned Steiger's wife Claire Bloom as the best choice for Clarisse, and his friendship with both actors prompted an even more romantic scenario: "For that matter, I would prefer Steiger for *Montag*! Please think of him for that role, also. Steiger as Montag, and Robert Ryan as the Fire Chief, wouldn't that make for powerful casting?????"

Bradbury was never able to convince Truffaut to drop Terrence Stamp from the film, but Stamp left the cast for reasons no one could have foreseen. In August 1965, Truffaut accepted Lewis Allen's suggestion that Julie Christie be cast as both Clarisse and Montag's wife Mildred. Truffaut visited her on the Madrid set of *Doctor Zhivago* and was impressed by her talent, personality, and command of spoken French. Stamp felt upstaged, and when Truffaut could not convince him to stay with the project, he convinced an uneasy Oskar Werner to shift from consideration for the Captain Beatty role into a firm hire as Montag. Pressure from British Actors Equity led Truffaut to seek a British actor as Captain Beatty. On November 19, 1965, Allen asked Bradbury for last-minute suggestions, but on January 11, 1966, Truffaut moved ahead on his own to hire Cyril Cusack, who had impressed him in *The Spy Who Came in from the Cold*. Shooting began two days later at Pinewood Studios.

Bradbury chose to maintain his distance as Truffaut worked through the increasingly stressful weeks of production. Truffaut and Werner had radically different perspectives on the role of Montag, and their formerly warm relationship completely disintegrated very early on in the filming schedule. Truffaut enjoyed working with Julie Christie and found the largely British crew very satisfactory even though he still felt a great disadvantage in his lack of facility in spoken English. He would later reflect on the impact of his limitations on the translation of the original French script, his screen direction, and his limited ability to evaluate the effectiveness of the English dialogue.

Truffaut remained conscious of the creative debt he owed to Bradbury. His first entry in his *Fahrenheit 451* journal, serially published in both French and English issues of *Cahiers du Cinema* during and just after production, clearly acknowledged the debt: "In point of fact, this film like all those taken from a good book half belongs to its author, Ray Bradbury. It is he who invented those book burnings that I'm going to have such fun filming, which is why I wanted colour. An old lady who chooses to be burned with her books rather than be separated from them, the hero of the film who roasts his Captain, these are the things I am looking forward to filming and seeing on the screen, but which my imagination, tied too firmly to reality, could not have conceived by itself. . . . Ray Bradbury comes to my aid, providing me with the strong situations I need in order to escape from the documentary."

His *Fahrenheit 451* journal also held darker surprises. As a leader of the New Cinema, Truffaut was not inclined to accept heroes or authority figures. On January 21, 1966, he wrote: "One very unfortunate thing of which I had not thought at all is the military look of the film. All these helmeted and booted firemen, smart, handsome lads, snapping out their lines. Their military stiffness gives me a real pain. Just as I discovered when I was making *Le Pianiste* that gangsters were for me unfilmable people, so now I realize that I must in future avoid men in uniform as well." Universal's lawyers inflicted similar pain, directing Truffaut not to burn on screen any books that remained under copyright protection. He ignored this directive, without consequences.

But eventually, the books themselves, which Truffaut had so carefully chosen by title and author from a number of London bookstores and flea markets, restored Bradbury's magic to the set. On March 9, he described a series of special moments: "The subjects of films influence the crews that make them. . . . [R]ight from the start of *Fahrenheit 451* everybody on the unit has begun to read. There are often hundreds of books on the set; each member of the unit chooses one and sometimes you can hear nothing but the sound of turning pages."

Truffaut finished editing the film in July 1966, and at last Bradbury could see how Truffaut had interpreted his work. He came down to Universal for a private screening on August 31, just as Truffaut, an ocean away, was preparing for the Venice Film Festival's jury viewing—*Fahrenheit 451* had been selected by the festival director as the British entry for 1966. Two hours after his first viewing, Bradbury cabled Truffaut before posting a longer letter that same day. Although he had not given way to Truffaut's request to visit during filming in the U.K., or his even stronger plea to attend the Venice Festival, their shared vision elicited birth metaphors in Bradbury's cable ("How rare are such twins") and in his letter: "I was very nervous at the studio, for it was like having a baby."

Later that week Bradbury arranged to see it again with a small group of friends and family. His old friend Fritz Lang, whose silent classic *Metropolis* had been such an early influence on Bradbury's dystopic vision of the urban future, was critical of the closing metaphor and its sidelights—the Book People, Truffaut's use of the incidental snowfall, and Bernard Herrmann's score.[4] Bradbury countered by declaring that Truffaut had captured the essence of the novel through his tight focus on the books-as-character throughout the film. He expressed a more detailed reaction to Don Congdon a few days later: "I believe it is a fine film, quite moving, and, in the aggregate, excellent. I think it will cause much talk, be damned by some, be praised by many." Truffaut's New Cinema aesthetic seemed refreshing, almost enchanting, after what Bradbury had experienced on the production side of Hollywood, but he did notice Truffaut's intentional suppression of the novel's emotional core: "The film is a trifle cold, which works well most of the time. I would have liked the relationship between Montag and the strange girl next door to have been somewhat warmer. Nevertheless, it is a first-class experience, and one that we will all be pleased about the rest of our lives."[5]

It had taken four years for *Fahrenheit 451* to emerge from Truffaut's initial French-language concept of *Phoenix*, but even as an English-language production (his first and last), it was truly an international film and was received with varying degrees of success from country to country. Truffaut was pleased by the Scandinavian and Finnish enthusiasm for the film, but he was clearly concerned that American audiences would be critical of the way that he had played down the potential for a romantic component in Montag's awakening and therefore would not empathize with the way that he had directed Werner's portrayal. Truffaut would fly to New York for events connected with the November 10 opening at the Plaza Theater, but neither he nor Lewis Allen could persuade Bradbury to come East for the premiere.

There is, of course, nearly a half-century of Bradbury's published and spoken commentary on the production, but he never really distanced himself from the film—at least not enough to make a summative critical statement unobscured by emotion. The two most insightful comments came from critics who were, to varying degrees, associated with Bradbury. Arthur Knight's review was colored by his close association with Bradbury, both personally and through their combined leadership of the Writer's Guild Film Society, but Knight kept his focus on a fundamental ambiguity: "The resultant film is highly original, thought-provoking, and at the same time distressingly superficial. The dangers that lie ahead are not from the book-burners, but from those who may direct them; and somehow *Fahrenheit 451* never gets around to this."

George Bluestone, who corresponded and met with Bradbury and spent a great deal of time on location with Truffaut, got to the central departure from the novel that limited the power of the film—Montag's lack of passion on screen, and the resulting lack of motivation for his awakening. This was at the heart of Truffaut's dispute with Oskar Werner, who wanted to bring out the romantic awakening that Clarisse sparked in Montag's character. Throughout filming, Truffaut steadfastly maintained his position that the books were, collectively, the film's central character; this proved to be a magnificent gamble, but one that Truffaut ultimately lost at the box office.

In spite of mixed feelings about the exhausting *Fahrenheit* experience, Truffaut had no reservations about working with Bradbury again. Bradbury had found Truffaut, like Sir Carol Reed before him, to be a director who privileged authors—therefore, a director he could trust implicitly. Bradbury lost no time in suggesting more collaborations. On October 9, 1966, a month ahead of the American release of *Fahrenheit*, Bradbury sent Truffaut *Les Foire des Tenebres*, the French edition of *Something Wicked This Way Comes*. By early February 1967, Truffaut had read it: "It's a beautiful book and I was particularly impressed with the subtle handling of the adolescence theme."

In the end, however, the complexities he had encountered in financing and adapting *Fahrenheit* may have driven his final decision; on February 6 he told Bradbury that *Something Wicked* did not fit in with his current plans. But Bradbury remained optimistic that he would work with Truffaut again, and in June 1967 he offered Truffaut his mixed animated/live action concept for "The Picasso Summer," an expansion of his short story "In a Season of Calm Weather." What if an American tourist on the Riviera, coming across an old man drawing large abstractions in the sand, realizes that the artist is Pablo Picasso? Could he save the art before the tide comes in? Could he ever find Picasso again? On June 28, 1967, Truffaut, acting perhaps more out of regard for Bradbury than for the project itself, sent his friend a detailed analysis of the very formidable challenges this project presented. Bradbury was also holding out for an English-language film; Truffaut, who felt that his lack of a command of English had worked against him all through the *Fahrenheit 451* project, regretfully declined "The Picasso Summer."

One final hope remained—Truffaut had not forgotten the stories-into-film concept they had discussed nearly five years earlier. In a February 6, 1967, letter to Bradbury, he proposed "going back to our old and initial idea: an omnibus sketch film based on five or six of your short stories, to be directed by myself and four or five of my friends." This would be contingent on Universal's sense of *Fahrenheit 451*'s box-office success and the amount of freedom his colleagues would have in creating a French-language film. This was stunning news for

Bradbury—Truffaut's revised concept for the omnibus was very much in the tradition of the multiauthored, collaboratively directed 1945 Ealing classic *Dead of Night*, the concept that Bradbury had always felt so perfect for his *Dark Carnival/ October Country* tales.

This time, though, the stakes were even higher. Truffaut was talking about the science fiction treasures of *The Martian Chronicles* and *The Illustrated Man*, and such a venture would have taken Bradbury's film history down quite a different path with some of his best-known science fiction; potentially, such a project could have made up for fifteen years of Hollywood disappointments and avoided the decades of disappointment that were to come. But Truffaut was never able to carry forward on this dream, and soon the time had passed; the director sensed that he could only make so many films in the prime of his career, and he moved on to projects closer to his heart. Once again, Bradbury could only look down the road not taken.

37

A Colder Eye

Esther Moberg Bradbury died in November 1966, at the age of 78. Tiny houses and apartments had been the extent of her world since the second decade of the twentieth century, and she did all she could to keep her family within it forever. Two of her four children had died in infancy: Skip's twin Sam in 1918, during the great Influenza epidemic that had nearly carried off Esther as well; and baby Elizabeth, discovered cold in her crib one morning in February 1928. Bradbury would later observe to Don Congdon how "Mom would have been glad if Skip and I had stayed home, learned to knit and sew, and helped her with the wash. By the time Dad died, she had him doing most of the feminine stuff around the house and out beyond . . . washing . . . shopping . . . etc." (ellipses Bradbury's).

Bradbury's father had died in 1957, and late in life, his youngest son had begun to see how much the quiet man had loved his children. But there was far less to know about his mother, and he was uncomfortable when Skip had her cremated and consigned to burial with their father whenever the mortuary had "time and inclination." In early December 1966, Bradbury decided to make his first solitary trip to the gravesite, recording his thoughts in a private written note:

> The boy who truly loved his mother is buried deep under all the years when that love was tested and somehow failed because mother withdrew, neither understanding her husband or her sons. Poor lost girl, who was she? We know so little of each other, but I know even less of her. I will send a ten year old boy to the graveyard to put flowers on her grave. I will return a 46 year old man, bewildered at the fact of buried love dug up and for a moment exhibited in the cold December light.

These time-traveling thoughts harkened back to the happiest times in Waukegan, when he and his mother would listen to the Chicago Cubs radio broadcasts as they played their day games at Wrigley Field during the late 1920s and early 1930s. He remained within that little family group until 1947, sleeping in the same bed with his brother Skip until he was 27 years old and Skip was 31. Each son eventually raised four children, but no one in the extended family was ever very close to Mother Bradbury; the full magnitude of her withdrawal came to him now and would haunt him from time to time for the rest of his life.

Her death culminated a year of increasing stress as he tried to secure a studio contract for *Something Wicked This Way Comes*. In its earliest form—The *Dark Carnival* screenplay of the 1950s—this novel predated his *Martian Chronicles* scripts; with virtually no current studio interest in the *Chronicles*, Bradbury's dark carnival once again took center stage. The intensity of Bradbury's passion for filming this novel overcame logical thought at times, and this had an impact on some of his most enthusiastic Hollywood supporters. Twentieth Century–Fox's Elmo Williams, fully occupied with running the studio's European operations, reluctantly turned down Bradbury's plea to produce the film in the fall of 1965. Bradbury continued to apply pressure until Williams's wife Lorraine interceded, noting the strain on her husband: "you seemed to clinch your teeth around his interest in *Something Wicked This Way Comes* and never let go."[1]

At times Bradbury described the various players as if they were pieces on a chessboard—even when he held the players in high regard. In the space of twenty-four hours during February 1965, three proven talents came to discuss projects: Sir Carol Reed (still trying to find a way to film *The Rock Cried Out*), the distinguished Italian actor and director Vittorio Gassman (interested in staging Bradbury's plays in Italy and New York), and director Blake Edwards, who had never lost interest in filming *Something Wicked*.[2] In earlier times, Bradbury's reaction would have been ebullient, but all he could muster for Congdon was a brief reportorial summary.

There was no fault in a colder eye (some of the filmmakers and stage impresarios who approached him deserved little more), but his great disappointment over the *Chronicles* screenplays made him overly cautious with Blake Edwards, who came back with another strong offer for *Something Wicked* in late November 1965. Bradbury considered it seriously; for reasons he could never fully explain to Congdon, he felt that Edwards was better at straight drama than he was with his highly successful comedies. But he became cautious after viewing *The Great Race*, which was, as he told Congdon, "a dreadful picture."[3] Bradbury would only write a screenplay for Edwards that followed "absolutely down-the-line from the book"—a virtual impossibility for *Something Wicked*, given the special-effects technology of the day.

But Bradbury's reluctance was also based on a far older problem: Samuel Goldwyn Jr. still held an option based on Bradbury's original *Dark Carnival* teleplay and screenplay concept of the mid-1950s. Given the increasing interest in

Something Wicked This Way Comes as a film property, Bradbury really had no choice but to buy back Goldwyn's $20,000 option; in the fall of 1966, he wrote the first of four annual $5,000 checks so that he could, eventually, consider earnest offers with a free hand. But the unavoidable four-year moratorium on *Something Wicked* was only one of four Hollywood disappointments during the late summer and fall of 1966—disappointments that led to one of the more significant writer's blocks of Bradbury's prolific career.

In late October, Herb Alpert and the Tijuana Brass canceled plans to develop a feature film musical of *The Wonderful Ice Cream Suit*. An agreement for Bradbury to script the film had been evolving since May, with contracts ready to finalize since early July. The Brass was entering peak years of musical popularity and as negotiations dragged on Bradbury came to the conclusion that Alpert was not yet comfortable with the motion picture environment. Bradbury agreed on an amicable resolution that allowed him to keep $7,500 (10 percent of the full screenplay payment) to cover his work to date; nevertheless, the money could not compensate for the loss of time as he concentrated on his first attempt to enter the world of musical adaptation. He found himself unable to work on stories or other projects for much of the summer and early fall of 1966.

Bradbury knew that the Brass had stalled for time, but he blamed his new Hollywood agency, Ziegler-Ross, for missing the main chance to close this deal and two others that surfaced while the Tijuana Brass deal was in negotiation: a new query from Kirk Douglas, who was now interested in a feature film version of *The Illustrated Man*, and another from his old friend Mal Stuart, who presented MGM's new interest in a feature film of *Leviathan '99*. But his Ziegler-Ross agents did not pick up on either offer soon enough; interest cooled quickly on both before Zig Ziegler's associates got around to responding.

Even Bradbury knew that both the Kirk Douglas and MGM inquiries were little more than feelers and might not have panned out anyway; he said as much to Congdon, but years of near misses in Hollywood had made him extremely sensitive to the danger of delay. He had warned Ziegler of his unhappiness in June; by early November 1966, as all three of these opportunities dissolved, he was ready to find a new agency.[4] To be sure, some fault rested with the agency; but Bradbury knew too many of the industry's producers, directors, and actors on a personal level, and he sometimes tried to stay one step ahead of his Hollywood agents in ways that were often counterproductive. On some level, he probably realized this; Ziegler smoothed the waters, and Bradbury would stay with his agency for another decade.

: : :

His stage fortunes were also tenuous. He was still trying to recoup the money he had invested in the Coronet Theater plays of the previous two seasons; these debts, as well as *The World of Ray Bradbury's* 1965 New York disaster, led him to declare a moratorium on stage production.[5] Drama was in his blood, however, and in March 1966 he told Congdon that the earliest of his stage experiments was beckoning: "I have plopped back into work on *The Anthem Sprinters* three-act yesterday (Saint Patrick's Day, by God!) and I think I am finally licking a five year old problem, by re-arranging the sequence of some of the big scenes!"[6] During April, *Playboy* purchased three Bradbury tales for $9,000: "The Haunting of the New," "The Lost City of Mars," and "The Man in the Rorschach Shirt." A new season of plays seemed possible, but *Anthem Sprinters* was delayed until summer 1967 by the very complicated work involved with collaborating on a *Dandelion Wine* musical, with a score by William Goldenberg and lyrics by Larry Alexander.

It was a challenging experience for all involved, but the musical eventually met with a degree of success through the advice and influence of Burgess Meredith and Zero Mostel and actually played at New York's Lincoln Center in April 1967. These were concert readings rather than full-set productions, but the experimental theater venue was enjoyable for Bradbury, who trained out from the West Coast for the first Sunday performance on April 23. "I will, therefore, be the only sane person at the performance," he wrote Congdon a few weeks earlier, "for I know, from the past, how panicky and absolutely nuts people get in the days before an opening."[7] He remained in New York until May 8, working on various plans, including what to do with the Irish plays.

The Irish stories, brimming with comic anecdote and village humor, would always have a limited audience in dramatic form. Bradbury's underlying premise ("Life in Ireland is a great joke. If not, then we would all crack apart with crying.") ran the risk of offending the Irish-American community, but he never took the risk very seriously.[8] Nevertheless, he was frankly surprised when UCLA expressed interest in production of *The Anthem Sprinters.* Here was a rare chance to capture the intellectual and "in" crowd, he told Congdon ("Jesus forgive me for using those terms").[9] *Sprinters* finally ended up at the Beverly Hills Playhouse in October 1967, billed under the combined titles of the component parts: *The Great Collision of Monday Last, The First Night of Lent, A Clear View of an Irish Mist,* and *The Anthem Sprinters.*

It was a necessary tune-up before returning—under the overarching *Anthem Sprinters* title—to the familiar Coronet Theater in Hollywood, the scene of all the good times with the original Pandemonium Players back in 1964 and 1965. Now, in February 1968, the opening night audience response was reminiscent of the enthusiasm for *The Wonderful Ice Cream Suit* in 1965, counteracting the mixed newspaper reviews that were beginning to come in; the scars of the New York disaster with *The World of Ray Bradbury* were finally healing: "My skin is getting thicker," he told Congdon. "This time out, the wounds have cut shallow."[10]

Then, suddenly, ticket sales diminished significantly, and Bradbury closed the run after the March 24 Sunday evening performance. After nearly six years of stage productions, he had enough data to offer Congdon a good guess at the cause: audiences wanted science fiction theater from a Bradbury theater company.[11] The 1964–65 run of *The World of Ray Bradbury*, presenting three alternate views of the future, had been far and away the high point of his stage career so far. It took thirteen months of *Anthem Sprinters* rehearsals and performances, and yet another sizable monetary loss, to reveal that his beloved Irish plays, the works that had showed him he could write for the stage back in the late 1950s, would have to give way to a broader mix of Bradbury stories-into-drama the next time out.

He would round out the 1960s by producing new plays in Los Angeles: *Any Friend of Nicholas Nickleby's Is a Friend of Mine*, which brought Charles Dickens into childhood memories of Grandmother Bradbury's boarders, and *The Day It Rained Forever*, based on one of Bradbury's last enduring fantasy tales of the 1950s, where the old men of a dying desert town are revived when a lady arrives, playing her harp and bringing life-renewing rainfall. *Nicholas Nickleby* played at the Hollywood Actor's Studio West in August 1968, but *The Day It Rained Forever* (paired with *A Clear View of an Irish Mist*) marked Bradbury's return to New York's Lincoln Center experimental stage for a three-performance run as *Fire and Mist*. These February 1969 performances were directed by Bradbury's old friend Marvin Kaye, whose effectiveness with minimal sets and confined space overcame the venue limitations.[12] Such small theater settings, presenting a lesser target for mainstream critics, offered a sanctuary of sorts for Bradbury's very personal form of stage magic.

: : :

The various Bradbury stories that were transformed into stage, screen, and television successes during the 1960s, especially Truffaut's *Fahrenheit 451* and the Hitchcock television episodes, increased his standing in Hollywood, but the ongoing undercurrent of missed opportunities in his media adaptations moved closer to the surface in the late 1960s as several projects—concepts in which Bradbury had invested a great deal of his time and energy—became creative dead ends.

Jean-Louis Barrault, one of the major forces in the French postwar theater world, had been working for nearly a decade to write and produce a stage play of *The Martian Chronicles* in Paris. By the summer of 1967, Barrault had cut his very long adaptation to an hour and a half, a move that would accommodate his desire to feature the unrelated Bradbury one-act *The Pedestrian* as a curtain raiser for *The Martian Chronicles*. Barrault's stature in the French theater was significant, and both Bradbury and Congdon agreed to extend his option into the spring of 1968 without further payments if it would help get the show launched.[13] Yet fate intervened in a most improbable way just before production; Barrault had allowed college student activists to use his Orpheum Theater during the often violent student revolt and paralyzing strikes that threatened De Gaulle's government in May 1968. *The Martian Chronicles* sets were heavily damaged, but the French government also closed Barrault's theater permanently. By the time he was able to restart his career, hopes for a new *Chronicles* project were gone forever.

Bradbury and Congdon hoped that they had much more control over Harry Belafonte's very enthusiastic attempts to transform *The Wonderful Ice Cream Suit* into a musical for the New York stage.[14] Planning began in 1966, but contracts were not completed until October 1967 due to strong interest from producer Carl Reiner for a major motion picture studio production. But even after Reiner's competition for rights fell through, work with Belafonte moved very slowly. The versatile actor-singer could command major resources, but his schedule prevented development of a play script, or even the assignment of a writer-director and lyricist-composer. In late 1968, Congdon made such assignments a requirement of the last extension, but in the end Belafonte's other priorities, as well as his intention of making *The Wonderful Ice Cream Suit* into a political statement play, persuaded Bradbury and Congdon to walk away.

Even the prospect of Bradbury's final payment on Samuel Goldwyn's option control of *Something Wicked This Way Comes* would bring new and unexpected stresses. During May 1968, he sent Alfred Hitchcock a copy of the novel, but it didn't find a place in Hitchcock's production schedule.[15] In the spring of 1969, with the Goldwyn release in sight, Bradbury reopened discussions on the project with Walter Mirisch, whom he had known since the Mirisch brothers produced his screenplay of *Moby Dick* for John Huston. Mirisch had been interested in *Something Wicked* since the novel was published in 1962 and had been part of a proposal involving Blake Edwards some years earlier. But Bradbury had now moved on to a new list of directors, more of a wish list than a practical one. Along with possible names such as his old friend Jack Clayton from *Moby Dick* days, he included Sir David Lean and Robert Wise.

Mirisch knew that Edwards remained interested and apparently felt that this fact complicated Bradbury's desire for a director from the new wish list. Bradbury interpreted this news as unwanted interference from a director he was no longer interested in; his direct response to Edwards was full of anger and came close to the paranoia that he often joked about in his dealings with Hollywood. In response, Edwards pointed out that he had an active contract with the Mirisch production company and had been actively urging them toward just the kind of big-budget production that Bradbury had always wanted for this book. But hard words were exchanged on both sides, and friendship was restored only many years later. Clearly, the colder eye that Bradbury occasionally brought to bear in his Hollywood negotiations was, at times, unwise; nearly a decade would pass before serious offers on *Something Wicked This Way Comes* would bloom in Hollywood.

As these various triumphs and disappointments of the late 1960s played out, Bradbury had a different kind of encounter with death than he had ever experienced before. He had worked through the deaths of his mentors Bernard Berenson and Charles Laughton, but now he had to deal with the loss of one of the first significant writing talents he had himself mentored. Charles Beaumont, or Charles Nutt as he was then, came to him as a teenager in 1946, when Bradbury was in his midtwenties, to share their mutual love of comic and animation art. By the early 1950s, he was critiquing Beaumont's stories and witnessed his young friend's rapid rise to prominence in major market magazines, television, and film. Tragically, Beaumont began to age rapidly in his midthirties, exhibiting symptoms diagnosed as either early-onset Alzheimer's or Pick's disease. On March 27, 1965, Bill Nolan, who had ghosted a few final Beaumont scripts, told Bradbury that their friend had entered full-time care: "He still knows people, but even this will vanish soon." Beaumont died in late February 1967; after the service Bradbury dated his copy of "The Mass on the Day of Burial," adding his friend's name as well; he would keep Beaumont's missal with him for the rest of his life.

38 | The Isolated Man

In spite of his scheduled coverage of the Apollo program for *Life* magazine, the enduring prominence of both *The Martian Chronicles* and *The Illustrated Man*, and the growing respect accorded *Fahrenheit 451*, there was new concern in certain circles about the lack of new Bradbury stories. "The Lost City of Mars," published in the January 1967 issue of *Playboy*, proved to be his only new story for the entire year, and 1968 would mark the first time in his twenty-eight-year professional career that no new stories reached print at all. Some of the magazine and anthology editors were surprised to be offered Bradbury poems instead of stories; Harlan Ellison ended up without any work by Bradbury for his groundbreaking *Dangerous Visions* anthology in 1967, but Congdon's consistent hard-bargaining approach with anthologists only masked the real problem.

In September 1968, *Galaxy* magazine's Fred Pohl, a Bradbury friend and fellow writer from the prewar fanzine days, made one of his periodic requests for new stories. There was certainly a long history to draw on; Bradbury's "The Fireman," the early version of *Fahrenheit 451*, had appeared in the February 1951 issue. With almost no new stories in hand, Bradbury offered Pohl two poems—verse that had already appeared in what he called "Data Computer" magazines. A disappointed Pohl urged Bradbury to return to his roots as a short story writer, but Bradbury had long since rationalized his deep immersion in media adaptations as a fully justified step beyond the short story form that had made him famous. He sent Pohl a listing of sixteen science fiction and fantasy projects he had completed during the mid-1960s, but only five of these were stories, and only two of the stories had reached print. Nevertheless, Bradbury felt he had more than proved his point:

> I could go on. But the simple fact is, I have never given up SF, as you infer, or Fantasy. *The Illustrated Man* is now finished as a film. *The Picasso Summer* (fantasy) has just completed shooting with Albert Finney. And, of course, during the last year, I covered the Apollo Project for *Life* (SF-come-alive) and did a major article on it.
>
> In sum, Old Ray is still doing business at the same old stand. It's just some of the work is hidden until such time as it hits the stage or the screen. 1969 will

be a big year for my films with at least two pictures out at once, plus a third possible come Halloween of '69, plus a special on TV in June with Richard Harris. Nuff said.[1]

The touch of petulance in his response suggests an underlying uneasiness—perhaps generated by the very real possibility that the media productions he was now relying on almost to the exclusion of new short stories would, as in the past, leave him largely disappointed. In fact, the 1960s would slide into the early 1970s with a series of disappointments for Bradbury. Of the projects he cataloged for Pohl, his three far-traveling screenplays—*The Martian Chronicles*, *The Rock Cried Out*, and his adaptation of Roger Manvell's *The Dreamers*—represented his greatest investment of time and creative energy. They had all been funded by major production companies a decade or more earlier, but none of the three would ever be filmed. His new animated screenplay *The Halloween Tree*, so lovingly encouraged by animation legend Chuck Jones, would remain in limbo until Twentieth Century–Fox terminated animated productions, leaving Bradbury without a studio or a producer.

There were also disappointments in the wings for the other projects he outlined for Pohl. The Richard Harris television special never materialized. Bradbury had been encouraged by the successful BBC London production of his *Leviathan '99* radio play in May of 1968, but his determination to produce a stage version in Los Angeles resulted in a significant financial loss in 1972. *The Illustrated Man* would prove to be both a personal and critical disappointment in 1969, and the long-delayed release of *The Picasso Summer* in 1972 was deeply flawed by a series of production misfortunes and directorial indifference to the animated sequences that Bradbury and Wes Herschensohn had labored for nearly six years to preserve.

Picasso Summer had started out with great promise in December 1964, as Herschensohn warmed to the idea of structuring his film around Bradbury's "In a Season of Calm Weather": an American tourist, intent on finding Picasso during a Biarritz vacation, fails in his dream to commission his very own painting until, walking along the shore, he finds Picasso outlining an ephemeral masterpiece in the sand. All he can do is enjoy his new treasure until the tide takes it away. Through Herschensohn, Bradbury just might meet Picasso, whom he had been trying to contact, without success, since writing the story.[2] It looked for a while like Jean Renoir, another figure that Bradbury idolized, would direct. The three met in late 1964 or early 1965 to work on the concept, and Bradbury found that Renoir knew and admired his stories just as much as Bradbury admired the films of Renoir and the great impressionist masterpieces of the aging director's distinguished father, Pierre Renoir.

But Jean Renoir was retired, and his frailty discouraged potential MGM backers. By 1967, the Campbell-Silver-Cosby Corporation, a production team built on the close working relationship between Bill Cosby and his agent Roy Silver, closed the deal and began filming in southern France with the enigmatic French director Serge Bourguignon. Bradbury was not consulted as his script went through many changes, and Bourguignon's European footage ultimately proved unworkable; he was replaced by Robert Sallin, who reshot some of the European scenes before completing work on California's Catalina Island. Bradbury was greatly disappointed when Picasso, angered at some of the behind-the-scenes events on location, declined to appear in the film or compose for the animations; when Herschensohn's impressive stand-in animations were heavily cut during final editing in 1968, Bradbury lost all remaining enthusiasm for the project. The four-year wait for release, downgraded to a single CBS television late-night viewing, only added insult to injury.

In his project listing for Fred Pohl, Bradbury had gone so far as to include his narration text for the U.S. Pavilion at the 1964–65 New York World's Fair; this prose poem had indeed carried the characteristic Bradbury sense of cosmic purpose into the far future, but its great popularity at the Fair was now a fading memory for all but the most devoted attendees or cultural historians. For the most part, his efforts to bring similar dramatic presentations to life in museums and exhibitions would be largely stillborn. Only the Disney projects, just coming up on his horizon, would bring success in the decades ahead.

: : :

The 1968 filming and 1969 release of the Warner Brothers/Seven Arts production of *The Illustrated Man* should have been, along with Truffaut's *Fahrenheit 451*, one of the great achievements of the decade for Bradbury. In 1960, he had prepared a screen treatment for producer Jerry Wald, who targeted *The Illustrated Man* after surveying thousands of libraries for lists of the most often borrowed books. Wald negotiated an agreement with Format Films, where Bradbury's *Icarus Montgolfier Wright* was already in production as an animated short. *The Illustrated Man* would have been Format's first feature-length animated film, but the money never came together.[3]

Bradbury found no significant interest until the late 1960s, when director Jack Smight formed a deal with Warner Brothers for a live-action feature. Bradbury reserved the right to approve the male lead, but did not reserve script approval. Smight had just directed Rod Steiger in *No Way to Treat a Lady* and selected him from Bradbury's list. Steiger accepted, bringing Claire Bloom in as the enchantress who creates the curse of the future-telling tattoos; together they also formed the continuity of lead roles in the three stories from the original *Illustrated Man* collection that became the focus of the film: "The Veldt," "The Long Rain," and "The Last Night of the World."

Behind the scenes, however, Bradbury's isolation from the Warner Brothers/ Seven Arts motion picture production represented another deeply disappointing experience. He greatly admired the efforts of Rod Steiger and Claire Bloom, as they worked to modify and bring life to a script that Bradbury had not authored; but his direct interaction was largely limited to a few publicity photo opportunities with Steiger and his plaster template, which provided a frame of reference whenever the makeup crew touched up the Illustrated Man's vegetable-dye tattoos.

Even that was a chance encounter; Bradbury simply walked over from NBC, where he had attended a Harry Belafonte television rehearsal, and stumbled into the first day of shooting at Warner Brothers.[4] He remained an isolated figure through-out production work and beyond; a personal comment buried in his writing notes captures his sense of total exclusion: "Fascinating to suddenly remember that on the night of the cast party for *Illustrated Man* when it was all over and various groups went off for smaller celebrations here or there, neither the actors, the producer, or the director of the film invited the writer, Ray Bradbury, to join them. The film, now over, finished, done, was an act of God, all to itself. The writer, who was he?"

This brief third-person reflection, written in January 1972—more than two years after the film's release—hints at the effect that fame was slowly exerting on his personal feelings as well as his more public statements. Studio interaction was at times cordial, and his appearance at the cast party had provided a surface sense of accomplishment. Bradbury saw a screening of the film with friends and family in October 1968 and expressed initial satisfaction to Congdon.[5] But Bradbury always felt that Smight's decision not to ask Bradbury to script was ultimately destructive to the film, even if it was contractually legal. This frustra-tion, coupled with the film's somewhat disappointing critical reception, began to color his feelings in abiding ways. He felt that too many of the rich metaphors had dissolved away into cliché, and that each individual story segment gave away too much of the suspense too soon. This was probably inevitable in an omnibus story film, and Bradbury's summative impression reflects the challenge facing this kind of structure: "*The Illustrated Man* . . . is not a good film, but it has a lot of good stuff in it. Everything is there except the film."

Filming of *The Illustrated Man* coincided with the complex and tragic presidential election campaign of 1968, which proved to be a major decision point for Bradbury. His public criticism of President Johnson and the administration's Vietnam policy was not a cry against the Democratic party, which he had supported with varying degrees of enthusiasm since the 1952 election; but his voice had attracted Republican listeners. On March 30, 1968, Bradbury offered this response to a telegram that apparently came from Leverett Saltonstall, the recently retired liberal Republican senator from Massachusetts: "The announcement of the Kennedy candidacy has changed the entire political climate. Like many others, I find myself atop a fence. I cannot in all conscience make a further declaration at this time. I only know that Johnson must be thrown out of his job this year. I severely doubt that [Eugene] McCarthy can do. I distrust Kennedy but feel he has the available power to knock off Johnson. Until I can argue myself clear of my problems concerning these men, I must withhold opting for one or the other."

Bradbury's outspoken opposition to Johnson and the prosecution of the Vietnam Conflict was consistent with his far earlier opposition to the tactics of the House Un-American Activities investigations, his written and spoken cautions against McCarthyism, and his decades-long effort to secure public libraries from political and special interest pressures. He was perhaps most protective of the rights of Hollywood writers, and a 1963 article by William Trombley, "Don't Stick Your Neck Out: Politics in Hollywood," sparked the most succinct statement of his philosophy: "I have always believed, and still believe, the really brave man is the one who stands completely alone, unprotected, or, if you wish, unsullied by any group."

Although this editorial response was never published, it offered more than a hint of things to come: "Group Think, Left or Right, is nonsense. Most groups, left or right, are time-wasting tea parties." By the late 1960s Bradbury was moving away from active memberships in antinuclear, antiwar, or legal defense groups. Sometimes it would take just one perceived misstep to trigger the break. In June 1968, when the ACLU announced that the organization would guarantee the rights of Robert F. Kennedy's assassin Sirhan Sirhan, Bradbury considered it more an act of showmanship than principle and ended, for a time, his long-standing membership.[6]

He had felt most comfortable with Eugene McCarthy's vision, but as his candidacy faded Bradbury was willing to back Vice President Hubert Humphrey until he heard his nomination acceptance speech later that summer. Humphrey avoided a direct stance on the Vietnam Conflict, and this represented a crucial error in Bradbury's mind; he had felt the same frustration when Adlai Stevenson had not aggressively pursued an end to the Korean War in his 1952 campaign. In a preconvention interview with the *Daily Californian*, the student newspaper at Cal Berkeley, Bradbury predicted that the Democratic Party would end up electing Richard Nixon. He had remained with Stevenson in 1952, but this time Bradbury crossed over and voted for the Republican presidential candidate for the first time in his life.[7]

His most effective commentary that year was not aimed at national politics, however, but rather at the politics of filmmaking and film criticism. "Death Warmed Over" appeared in the January 1968 issue of *Playboy* magazine as a feature-length editorial opinion article on the horror film tradition in Hollywood, but it was really an explosion of frustrations from his decade-long attempt to bring his own history of horror cinema to television. In the early 1960s, he had managed to get his good friend, the influential film historian Arthur Knight, to defer his own plans for such a special so that Bradbury could go ahead with his proposal. James Mason was willingly recruited to host and narrate Bradbury's concept, which was to be broadcast with Mason seated alone in one of the great Hollywood movie theaters. All of these efforts failed to win backing, and Bradbury ended up staging his own imaginary theater-based narration in the pages of *Playboy*: "A ticket jumps with a cough of dust into my hand. All to itself, the theater door hushes open."

Congdon was frankly surprised that *Playboy*, whose editors had already published seventeen Bradbury stories as well as the famous 1954 reprint of *Fahrenheit 451*, would buy such a polemic essay.[8] Bradbury began with one of his best explorations of the grand superstitions and mythological traditions that gave symbolic shapes to death and inspired the great horror films of our time. But he quickly veered off into an indictment of the lack of imagination in contemporary cinema: "How much longer will American jackdaw intellectuals run about collecting reality, holding it up, declaring this to be the truth?" All the old Bradburyan rage against censorship and elitism came back, censorship imposed not by governments, but by society itself. For the first time in years, he raged in print against "the book-burning intellectuals who, like Dr. Spock, fear Batman without having seen him; Dr. Wertham, who finds murder under every comic book; and the librarians who won't allow the *Oz* books on their shelves."

He gave brief but heartfelt homage to the great horror films, inspired by Shelley and Stoker, Poe and Hawthorne, Kipling and Robert Louis Stevenson. He invoked the masterful terror of Val Lewton's films, where everything works toward a single moment of terror, where the monster is only suggested, never fully seen. He dismissed the harsh realism of *Who's Afraid of Virginia Woolf?* as well as the ephemeral immaturities of *The Monster of Blanket Beach* and *I Was a Teenage Werewolf*. He wanted films about the long dark night of the human soul restored to writers and filmmakers who could work between these two extreme approaches. It was a plea for balance between the rational and the dreamer in us all, the "fact collector" merged with the "secret creator." The edginess that was largely absent from Bradbury's newer stories had returned, finding new life, at least for the moment, in his nonfiction prose.

39 | A Touch of the Poet

By the mid- and late-1960s, Bradbury's poetic voice, long associated with his metaphor-rich prose fiction, was unmistakably emerging in verse. This impulse had its origins long before Aldous Huxley and Gerald Heard told him he was a prose poet in 1950. His 1930s high-school poetry class and poetry club experiences led to a number of unpublished poems in the early 1940s, but only a few of these showed potential beyond his early proclivity for examining the darker shades of life.[1] Gerald Heard, at the center of the Isherwood-Huxley group of Bradbury encouragers, was the first to direct Bradbury specifically toward poetry after reading his novella "The Fireman" in 1951: "One day, you know, I hope you'll publish poems—it is not merely a truly original invention that carries your writing into its own stratosphere—it is the rhetor's power of fusing an image with a phrase & in the natural flow of narrative. The metaphors . . . are . . . new associations, recognitions of likenesses unperceived before but fused for good after you have linked them. You could, I fancy, surpass Christopher Fry."[2]

He was rarely able to control and shape his verse in the ways that Heard envisioned, but by the mid-1950s he was beginning to show the diversity of subject and mood that would characterize the many poems that would follow. "Death in Mexico," a serious release of the emotion he had invested in the dark Mexican stories of the late 1940s and early 1950s, appeared in a 1954 issue of *California Quarterly*. He soon began a correspondence with the poet Oscar Williams, whose work he had read for more than a decade; Williams placed Bradbury's "A Dublin Limerick," a celebration of his best memories of Irish life, in New American Library's 1957 Mentor anthology, *A Treasury of Light Verse*.

Light verse is indeed the best way to characterize most of the poems that began to flow through his typewriter after 1960. Bradbury always preferred to date his great flood of poems from the publication of "All Flesh Is One: What Matter Scores?" in the December 14, 1970, issue of *Pro* magazine. He was encouraged to submit the poem by Don Anderson, an editor with *Sports Illustrated*.[3] Bradbury knew little of the subject, but he did remember his brother's magical moments playing semipro football for the Los Angeles Bulldogs and the pride that their father felt; verses had surfaced from these memories. The editorial encouragement he received for this poem ("I read it to my father," *Pro*'s editor later told him) boosted his confidence to the point that he began serious discussions with Knopf to publish a volume of his poetry. There was already a body of published poems ranging back through the 1960s, poems that had already captured the emotional release and celebration he wanted from his verse. "Harvest" (1962) and "What Age Is This?" (1963) offered the first evidence of this wave in print and are typical of what would follow through the next decade and more.

On September 9, 1964, Bradbury noted in a letter to Congdon that "I have been writing on the average of a poem a day every day now for some months. Some good, some bad, some better than good. A fine way to start the morning when I come in to sit down at the typewriter and get the juices flowing." Pages of typed and, more significantly, handwritten verse survive from this period; the large hand scrawl and widely spaced lines of the holograph pages contain short bursts of poetry, often disordered and incomplete, and suggest that verse may very well have been a preferred warmup for prose on a frequent, if perhaps not daily, basis. Less than a year later, the growing quantity of verse—and the fact that Congdon had caught him submitting some of it on his own—led Bradbury to ask his friend and agent for a significant indulgence:

> Yep, you're right, I submitted the poem "When Elephants Last in the Dooryard Bloomed" on my own. If you prefer, in future, I will send all of my poems to you for submission. However, I have been reluctant to do so, for poetry is such a strange and inconclusive field, I wanted to spare you time and trouble. Let's play it by ear. When I come up with an occasional brilliant poem, you'll see it, first. My other, merely genius, poems, I will submit on my own, okay? So much for today's outburst of outrageous ego.

In February and March 1966, Bradbury read his poetry over several evenings to audiences at Loyola University and was encouraged by the response. For the most part, publication remained confined to local and regional magazines, but Congdon was already circulating the better ones; during the summer of 1967, the *Saturday Review*'s poetry editor, the accomplished John Ciardi, declined "God, For a Chimney Sweep."[4] But over the next year Bradbury poems made it into two college literary journals, *Florida Quarterly* ("Dusk in the Electric Cities: and This Did Dante Do") and *Texas Quarterly* ("What Seems a Balm Is Salt to Ancient Wounds").

His verse began to appear in science fiction publications as well, including *Galaxy* magazine, where Fred Pohl's successor, Ejlar Jakobsson (another old editorial friend from the pulp magazine days), bought three Darwin poems to publish in the April 1970 issue. Harry Harrison took the Dante poem for his new Delacorte anthology, *Nova One*. These were not, by Bradbury standards, breakthrough moments. Some anthologists and genre magazine editors simply could not afford new or even reprinted Bradbury stories; even Harlan Ellison settled for "Christ, Old Student in a New School" for *Again, Dangerous Visions*, in 1972.

Bradbury had few illusions about his verse, and he spoke quite frankly to Congdon about the sheer wonderment of it: "It is really great to come to the time in my life when I can write a poem and then be able to read it and keep my lunch down. It has taken so many years to learn to write this way, intuitively, that now I am enjoying myself when the poems get published." On March 3, 1969, he told Congdon that he was intent on adding a poetry volume to his canon in 1970 or 1971. He had recently followed his trusted Simon & Schuster editor, Bob Gottlieb, to Knopf, a trade house that had long sought Bradbury, but the editorial review process there did not go through without opposition.

By the time that Bradbury submitted his selections in the fall of 1970, they included celebrations of past literary masters, homages to great discoverers, and intimations of Mankind's evolving place in the Cosmos. At least one Knopf editorial reviewer felt that the work reflected a nineteenth-century sensibility and style that stood no chance in a postmodernist world of new poetic talents. Some of the poems were certainly didactic, while others brimmed with excess emotion. But the better ones, like "Remembrance," were experience-centered, and sometimes had the conciseness of more mature verse. In the end, Knopf opted for publication—this was, after all, Ray Bradbury—and placed him under the skilled guidance of Nancy Nicholas, who would shepherd three volumes of Bradbury verse through to publication during the next decade.

But Bradbury's poems, like the screenplays and stage plays, had more sub-stantial consequences in terms of his overall body of work. He was pulled still further away from story writing, and his output diminished over the next four decades as he continued to work in these other, more vocal forms. The pattern is parallel in some ways to that of Robert Penn Warren, the only writer ever to win Pulitzer Prizes in both fiction and poetry; in his best short story, "Blackberry Winter" Warren's narrator offers a caution over poetry, "for poems are great devourers of stories." Warren's great second flowering as a poet, and his con-tinuing prominence as a novelist, extinguished his capacity for short fiction; in a similar way, Bradbury's other voices rechanneled the creative fires that had, for two decades, produced some of the most popular stories of the times.

: : :

Another kind of poetic sensibility had emerged through his stage musical of *Dandelion Wine*. Not surprisingly, the catalyst originated through his deep con-nections with Hollywood actors who also had strong ties to the New York stage. Burgess Meredith and Zero Mostel had been friends for the greater part of a decade; they were planning a New York repertory theater venture and encouraged Bradbury to develop his *Dandelion Wine* musical in the spring of 1966.⁵ "I have come up with an overall theme-conflict-structure idea which I believe will hold *Dandelion Wine* together as a musical," he wrote to Congdon in May. By midmonth he had a two-act structure in rough draft form. It would take almost a year to reach the stage, as Bradbury worked to integrate his refashioning of Green Town around the music and lyrics of William Goldenberg and Larry Alexander.

Billy Goldenberg was a gem to work with, but there was occasional tension between Bradbury and Alexander, who wanted to adapt the narrative text himself. Bradbury wisely allowed Alexander to try it, and fail at it, while he shaved his own ego by writing a song about the Lonely One—a much more enjoyable failure than Alexander's. The fast-paced magic of the finished musical would be very difficult to transfer to stage, and the best compromise was found when New York's Lincoln Center agreed to present a reading performance, with orchestra instead of a full-set acting production, during April 1967. Bradbury's finished adaptation was well integrated with the musical elements, but his innovative and psychologically revealing refashioning of *Dandelion Wine* controlled the entire work.

Here was the same glorious small-town summer of 1928 found in the novel, but the action of the musical was controlled by a completely new element—the interaction between young Douglas and an older Douglas ("Mr. Forrester"), looking back through time and memory to learn how to make his peace with the ghosts of the past: "Look . . . there are two special years in everyone's lives . . . when you're twelve you find things change, people get sick, people die. You cry inside. But somehow make do. Then, when you're forty, or thereabouts, the same kind of year happens" (ellipses Bradbury's). The central premise of the play soon emerges—if the man can work through that summer again with the boy, then he'll know how to live again.

The challenge centered on how to play out this new dynamic. Congdon suggested letting young Doug receive a gift of insight in return, but Bradbury knew that any revelation would have to follow the arrow of time forward: "So we have to face up to the old Time Travel problem of the invulnerable and unchangeable fact," he told Congdon shortly before the Lincoln Center opening night. "If Doug gets any new reward, this changes his older self. There's a paradox involved anyway, if we accept the Young Doug as real. He isn't, of course. We have been watching a memory all evening long. And how do you reward a memory? You can't. All the memory can do is reward your older self by changing position slightly so as to let you go by."⁶

Forrester makes his memory of young Doug realize what it must do: "And you never forgave that summer, this summer, for happening to you. You held on all your life. It's still there in your heart—*my* heart. And it's killing you—and that means killing *me*." Young Doug releases all the sorrow, and the older man learns to live again. Bradbury also increased the intensity of the musical by bringing in plot elements from "These Things Happen," the story of a schoolboy's crush on a beautiful young teacher who will die before her time. This sorrow, too, must be released along with the other sorrows of 1928.

The new musical *Dandelion Wine* offered healing through a form of reverie verging on self-hypnosis, a state of mind that Bradbury had often studied and sometimes succeeded in practicing for pain throughout his life. This clue leads to an even more intriguing psychological parallel: Forrester reveals his age as 38—the same age as Bradbury had been when, during the winter of 1957–58, he had to work through his own year of unforeseen events. A decade later, in 1967, the narrative of the *Dandelion Wine* musical emerged as perhaps the best adaptation of his own work that Bradbury would ever achieve on stage—more restorative than nostalgic, and far more poetic than sentimental.

Bradbury's increasing interest in verse, as well as his ability to reconfigure the poetic qualities of *Dandelion Wine* for the musical stage, brought satisfaction to a master storyteller who was no longer willing to bring his full creative powers to bear on original story ideas. But here, as in his screenwriting adaptations, he was never able to fully master these new forms of writing. He was not really interested in becoming a poet of great reputation; verse was simply another way of transmitting wisdom or recapturing an important moment of discovery from days long past. But stage adaptations of his stories were becoming the creative center of his world, and he was perhaps too close to these precious resurrections of his stories to understand why they were not often able to succeed beyond the small theater venues of southern California.

Don Congdon, however, worked close to the New York theater world and had interacted with it for his clients as long as he had been an agent. And he had the distance to critique Bradbury's plays far more effectively than their author. In the fall of 1968, when Bradbury unsuccessfully tried his hand at adapting his work for the increasingly popular presentation form known as Reader's Theater, Congdon took the opportunity to analyze the larger problems at play in Bradbury's stagecraft:

> You are a magician in the theatre, and your stories lend themselves beautifully to sleight-of-hand, double-images, and so on; but I think you are often overwhelmed with the spectacle and are not deeply enough involved with the conflicts that go on between your characters. . . . Too many of your stage adaptations permit the story to remain a statement of the short story situation.

This simply isn't enough to keep the attention and engage the emotions of the audience, because the success of a play usually depends upon the interplay of emotion between characters, right down to the line-by-line writing.[7]

Congdon knew that Bradbury already had the other gifts of a playwright; the plotting was strong, the text concise, and the stage direction sure-handed in most of his adaptations for stage. Bradbury had always assumed that any of his plays could be fixed through cutting, or by finding a more magical mix of metaphor and lyric prose. But Congdon had spoken to many of the professional theater people who attended various Bradbury plays, and the back-channel consensus was that he simply didn't "give the actors lines with which they can establish intimate emotional conflict."

Bradbury never really overcame this tendency to privilege metaphor over character interaction on stage. The *Dandelion Wine* musical, and the two other versions that would follow in the coming decades, were an exception. There was emotional depth here, and he would never forget the very positive personal reactions he received from the prominent stage figures attending the April 1967 Lincoln Center performances, including Anthony Quayle, Richard Rogers, and Agnes De Mille. Quayle's wife, the actress Dorothy Hyson, asked him, "What can I do to help this play go on forever?"[8] High praise, indeed, for a man who usually had to finance his own stage magic.

40 | "Christus Apollo"

Bradbury's renewed friendship with television and motion picture composer Jerry Goldsmith was one of the few positives to come out of *The Illustrated Man* film experience. They had first met when Goldsmith was scoring and producing broadcasts for *CBS Radio Workshop*, where two Bradbury stories were adapted for the initial 1956 season. Goldsmith's score for *The Illustrated Man* inspired Bradbury to approach the California Chamber Symphony, where he served as an advisory board member, to request that Goldsmith be commissioned to compose a cantata based on a long poem that Bradbury had been trying to sell, for at least three years, as "In This Time of Christmas." He would often describe it as his Christ-in-the-Space-Age poem, and in early September 1968, Goldsmith, already a multiple Academy Award and Golden Globe nominee, agreed to set it to music.[1] In the process, Bradbury would be able to use this new aesthetic dimension to make his final revisions to the poem. The following year he would close I *Sing the Body Electric!* with the final version, "Christus Apollo"—the first piece of freestanding verse to appear in a Bradbury story collection.

Bradbury's good friend and Chamber Symphony conductor Henri Temianka may have helped envision the large scale of the commission, which required an orchestral accompaniment for a narrator, mezzo-soprano, and choir. Goldsmith adopted a 12-tone dodecaphonic approach to the composition of what he realized was a very spiritual celebration of Mankind's first steps toward the stars. In the cantata's final form, Bradbury's narrator offers the initial point of departure: a brief celebration of the seven days of Creation leading into a "long Eighth Day of Man." The chorus then carries Bradbury's poem into the Ninth-Day world of the Apollo missions: "And the Ninth Day's sunrise | Will show us forth in light and wild surmise | Upon an even further shore." Narrator and chorus together describe Bradbury's vision of man restoring God to the Cosmos, suggesting the unity that informs the title that Bradbury had now settled on for both the poem and cantata forms: "Apollo's missions move, and Christus seek, | And wonder as we look among the stars | Did He know these?"

Late in the cantata, the chorus and the mezzo-soprano together give the Kazantzakian charge that Bradbury had modified for the Space Age: let Mankind go out to the Cosmos, following a divine inspiration but forging a new humanistic mythology, as "Christus Apollo." It seemed a timely secular inspiration, on the eve of Humanity's first orbital journey to another world. In this poem one finds perhaps Bradbury's greatest fiction, one that he was fully capable of believing.[2] The first public performance of the Christus Apollo cantata occurred on December 21, 1968, in UCLA's Royce Hall, with the narration read by Charlton Heston accompanied by the California Chamber Symphony. Heston's performance anticipated, by just four days, what the Apollo 8 crew would broadcast on Christmas Eve as they orbited the Moon, reading from a far earlier inspirational text: "In the beginning . . ."

: : :

Christus Apollo capped two years of lectures and articles that focused more and more on the approaching lunar missions. In his February 1967 address to Caltech's freshman class, Bradbury took the intellectual magazines to task for their slow response to the Space Age; during the 1950s, he had found little if any reporting in the New Republic, Harper's, the Partisan Review, the Atlantic, or even the Nation, which had published his 1952 article on the importance of science fiction. "What other fiction is there to write?" he told his Caltech audience. "You are science fictional children of a science fictional age, and from here on in, that's all it's going to be. All of our major problems are science fictional problems." This tendency to present controversial assertions as fact worked best in his Life magazine articles; the last of his three Space-Age excursions in Life, "An Impatient Gulliver above Our Roofs," was the most startling of all. The article appeared in the November 24, 1967, issue to celebrate the first unmanned Apollo launch on November 9.

The technology and science for "An Impatient Gulliver" was mortared into the picture captions by Life's research teams, leaving Bradbury free to focus on the impact of scale in the body of his article: "We Lilliputians have failed to tape-measure the very Gulliver who stands impatient above our roofs. We have watched with growing, if mild, contempt as our television tube squashed a 363-foot rocket down to meaningless inches, crushed it small in an electronic wine press." He hated how television limited the ability to perceive scale; now he described the launch of the Saturn V rocket and its payload as equivalent to "lighting a fuse to the Arc de Triomphe, firing the Statue of Liberty at the stars, or heaving the Sphinx to circumnavigate the moon." But the best part of this experience for Bradbury was the chance he had to meet and observe the Apollo astronaut team. When he was introduced to them, he saw a wave of recognition in their eyes; they knew his name, and shared his dreams.

Bradbury would win the Aviation Space Writer Association's Robert Ball Memorial Award for "An Impatient Gulliver above Our Roofs." This enjoyable phase of work with NASA and *Life* magazine played out as he began to gather stories for *I Sing the Body Electric!*—a collection that marked the beginning of his twenty-five-year relationship with the Alfred A. Knopf publishing house. In 1968, Bob Gottlieb left Simon & Schuster to take over Knopf, a house that had almost secured Bradbury nearly a decade earlier. In September, Bradbury also left Simon & Schuster for Knopf, with the understanding that Knopf would publish *I Sing the Body Electric!*[3]

This new story collection was now his first priority for Knopf; at this point he felt that "The Kilimanjaro Device," his *Life* magazine homage to Ernest Hemingway, would be the title story; it took Hemingway back in time to die before the crippling injuries of his later life that would destroy his creative powers and lead him to suicide. Don Congdon thought it a good choice, as "people will love it, and people will hate it." For a time, the story generated interest from Orson Welles and Rod Steiger for a feature film adaptation.[4] But just now, there were more important concerns—Bradbury realized that his lack of recent sales would have a significant impact on the collection and voiced his disappointment to Congdon on September 14, 1968: "I feel rather like I felt during the summer of 1948 or 1949, before I began to sell somewhat steadily to the larger magazines. I look at my stories and love them . . . and wonder why editors don't love them, too!" (ellipsis Bradbury's).

He sent in a group of nineteen stories to Congdon on December 19; these included a number of old published stories from the 1940s and 1950s that remained uncollected: "I, Mars" (re-titled "Night Call, Collect"), "The Women," "The Shape of Things" (re-titled "Tomorrow's Child"), and "The Tombling Day." These were among the best of the early science fictions and fantasies that had not been fused into *The Martian Chronicles* and *The Illustrated Man*, but there would be fewer and fewer of the old stories to feed into subsequent collections if his Muse continued to be diverted into adaptations for stage and screen. Indeed, these concerns would become an abiding reality; more than half of the stories in the seven collections he would publish during the rest of his long life would contain published and unpublished stories resurrected (and in many cases reworked) from the first very creative decade of his career.[5] In this sense, the new collection would be the last of his career to showcase more new stories than old.

Bradbury still considered using "The Kilimanjaro Device" as his title story until February 15, 1969, when he finally finished and submitted "I Sing the Body Electric!" The original unfinished story draft of the 1950s had been diverted into a 1962 *Twilight Zone* teleplay. The android grandmother, fashioned to restore a family devastated by a mother's untimely death, had become one of Bradbury's favorite characters; once the youngest child realizes that the grandmother cannot be taken by death and accepts the loving care and wisdom she is programmed to give, the family is restored. The story satisfied one of Bradbury's most urgent cautions about technology: learn about the machines we create, and use them well. Once finished, it simply had to become the title story.[6]

: : :

As the decade came to a close, more and more of Bradbury's time was devoted to "SF-come-alive" as he called it, the emotion-charged essays that he now used as his window into Humanity's future. But the three major essays he had written for *Life* magazine had exacted a heavy toll. By nature he was not disposed to plan, research, and produce analytical prose on the Space Age or on any other topic. He was intoxicated by the additional fame this kind of writing brought to his reputation, yet he was also terrified by the process. Masked as an essayist, he couldn't afford to wait for the Muse to bring up the subjects his subconscious *really* wanted to write about; he had to make the self-conscious effort to meet an editorial deadline, never knowing if his imagination could bring his metaphor-rich poetic style into play effectively. Early in 1969, Bradbury used an unexpected decision-point to call the question in his mind.

Susan had spent the previous summer studying at Oxford, and he and Maggie knew that it was only a matter of time before all four of their daughters would begin lives of their own. In early March 1969 he alerted Dave Maness at *Life* that he would be taking his wife and children to London for perhaps the last summer they would be able to travel as a family. Bradbury made it clear that the dates (from late June to early September) were inflexible, given his need to travel by land and sea, and the ocean liner tickets were already purchased. The Apollo 11 moon landing dates were not yet set, as they depended on the results of the upcoming Apollo 9 and 10 missions, but it was already clear that Bradbury would probably be in London when *Life* needed him most.

There was a lot going on between the lines in his letter; he referred to his role as peripheral anyway, "helping out," as he put it, and noted that the trip might actually be a positive move in terms of creativity ("distance really does wonders for me and my ideas"). He spent most of the letter suggesting that he try out "familiar" essays for *Life*, short pieces placed up front "where Loudon Wainwright often tries out his familiar essays." Bradbury wanted to be a part of the event he had been waiting for all his life, but he clearly wanted some distance from the kind of in-depth essay he had been assigned in the past. In the end, he was not assigned an Apollo 11 feature for *Life*. The magazine's major coverage would fall to Norman Mailer, whose *Of a Fire on the Moon* serialization would open with a cover photo of Mailer on the August 29, 1969, issue.

The family would not go to Ireland during this summer idyll; Bradbury would never return there, for he remembered only Ireland of the winter of 1953–54, so inspiringly beautiful yet so heartbreakingly sad. But a ghost from that long fall and winter emerged unexpectedly in March 1969, just as the Bradburys were planning the trip; Ricki, John Huston's former wife and mother of both Anjelica and Tony, died in a tragic automobile crash. The Bradburys had felt a great sympathy for Ricki during the preproduction work on *Moby Dick*; she often seemed to them like a vulnerable young princess trapped in a Greek tragedy. In New York, Len and Beth Probst, who had provided the Bradburys with relief throughout the long Dublin winter so many years earlier, found the news of Ricki's death in the back pages of the *New York Times*. Len Probst expressed the emotions they all felt in a note to Bradbury: "Suddenly, we were all back in Ballsbridge, she radiant, lovely and alive without John and without that doomed look. . . . It was sad and seemed somehow foreordained. I wonder how John took it, if he expected it?"

Bradbury had recently renewed his friendship with the Probsts; he had not forgotten his friend's unfavorable review during the short 1965 New York run of *The World of Ray Bradbury*, but his own work as an occasional reviewer for the *Los Angeles Times* had tempered his feelings; he was not really suited for this kind of writing, but the experience provided a more forgiving perspective of the reviewer's craft. Bradbury enlisted the Probsts in the campaign to convince Maggie that the necessary stopover in New York would be more enjoyable than she imagined.

To this point, Maggie had been the sole dissenter concerning the London trip. She was becoming more and more insular, even within the world of four rapidly maturing young women that she oversaw and guided on a daily basis. Maggie knew that she was sometimes too selective in her friendships, and even more selective in the wider range of people with whom she could, as Mrs. Ray Bradbury, easily associate. She read most of the time, and the public would never know just how much her husband valued her close reading of his typescripts. She valued privacy, but she also knew that this third overseas trip would be different; there was no writing component for her husband, and it would be their first extended vacation as a family. Perhaps the weeks in London would be a good thing; Maggie quietly acquiesced, and plans soon began in earnest.

A personal invitation to the launch from NASA administrator Dr. Thomas O. Paine soon confirmed that the moon landing would fall in the midst of the London vacation, and Bradbury began planning alternate media options for London. In late June 1969, the family made the Atlantic crossing aboard the SS *United States*, reprising their first 1953 storm-tossed crossing in far more enchanting weather. "[T]he sea, most nights, so still and calm," he reported back to Congdon on June 30, "it was like sailing on pure black oil, a vast breathing sheet of liquid on which the moon rode . . . and the ship without the slightest roll to or fro . . . so that you felt you were on a slow train instead of a boat . . . incredible . . ." (ellipses Bradbury's). They traveled in a cabin next to the former King Edward VIII of England and his wife, the Duke and Duchess of Windsor—an improbable pairing that Bradbury, from his perspective, considered "a nice dividend."

There were many enjoyable activities that summer; these included a return visit to the John Soane museum and its many mysterious antiquities, which had been the grand discovery of the 1957 trip.[7] But he became anxious as the July 20th Apollo 11 launch date approached. Bradbury was, in a manner of speaking, just as remote from the American media as Armstrong, Aldrin, and Collins, but without the communication links that they enjoyed. This was incredibly and unexpectedly frustrating, for he wanted to celebrate with the public back home. In fact, the celebration was more important to him, in many ways, than his more self-conscious standing as America's leading visionary writer on America's Space-Age endeavors.

There was suspense right up to the last moment, as the unmanned Soviet Luna mission raced Apollo for the prize of a first lunar landing; when Luna failed, the rivalry was tempered by a brief but promising moment of cooperation as the Soviets shared their data feeds with NASA. That evening, London time, Bradbury arrived at the BBC to appear on the David Frost show to offer comments after the successful landing by Armstrong and Aldrin. But he was upstaged by other guests, including Sammy Davis Jr. and Englebert Humperdinck, who were brought out to Frost ahead of him. Bradbury was like a man possessed, thinking only of the historical moment, and no explanation of the guest sequence could calm him. He walked out of the studio without ever making an appearance on the show.[8]

Bradbury went over to the NBC London studios, where he publicly chastised a panel that included political activists Lord Peter Ritchie-Calder and Bernadette Devlin for dwelling on politics when Mankind had just taken its first step toward the stars. By great good fortune, he was able to salvage an NBC-TV interview with Roy Neal and what turned out to be a widely broadcast television interview with Mike Wallace at the London newsroom of CBS. The next afternoon, July 21, 1969, Walter Cronkite broadcast a tape delay of the Wallace interview from his live news anchor desk at NASA Houston, and Bradbury was finally able to share his transatlantic moment of celebration.

The interview started slowly, prompted by brief questions from Mike Wallace. First came the philosophical insights he had taken from Nikos Kazantzakis ("We are God himself coming awake in the universe"), then the awful future facing Earthbound Mankind that he had presented to Oriana Fallaci and other audiences

("Someday the sun will either explode or go out"). Toward the end of the interview, Wallace asked about the military implications of the Apollo 11 achievement. Bradbury's voice, which had been slowly rising with enthusiasm, now reached a dramatic peak, for this was the symbol of the choice that the rocket had represented to him for more than two decades: nuclear war, or salvation in the stars. Bradbury presented space exploration as the great moral substitute for war: "War is a great toy to play with. Men and boys love war . . . let us eliminate war because the proper enemy is before us. All of the universe doesn't care whether we exist or not, but *we* care whether we exist . . . this is the proper war to fight."

There was no scientific introspection here; Bradbury was not capable of it, and never pretended to be. But Walter Cronkite's live studio audience at NASA-Houston burst into applause for the final words of the writer who still listened to the whispers of the boy within. Here were the dreams of that young boy, headed for the stars, in "King of the Gray Spaces," written in 1942, his earliest quality science fiction tale: "We were just a lot of kids. With cut fingers, lumpy heads and whining tenor voices. We liked our game of mibs as well as the next rumple-hair; but we liked the rockets more."[9]

: : :

He had missed *Life* magazine's ride to the Moon; he would never write another Space feature for his *Life* editors during the few remaining years before its demise. Bradbury would still interact intermittently with NASA, most notably with Apollo 12's Alan Bean and the Apollo 15 crew, which named Dandelion Crater in his honor, and Apollo 17's Harrison Schmitt. At the same time, he was already beginning to hitch a ride to Mars, and on out to the outer solar system, with Caltech's planetary scientists and the Jet Propulsion Laboratory. Embedded in Bradbury's wide-ranging May 1970 address for the Caltech Alumni Association was a lengthy articulation of his Space-Age vision, and this presentation would become the core of many future lectures.

But the most significant moment in his early association with Caltech was his participation in an amicable debate on "Mars and the Mind of Man" on November 12, 1971, just as Mariner 9 was about to begin its unprecedented orbital mapping missions above the Red Planet. In this discussion, Bradbury joined his good friends Arthur C. Clarke, astronomer Carl Sagan, and one of the architects of the Mariner Mars missions, Caltech's Dr. Bruce Murray.[10] It was Bradbury's first chance to visit with Clarke since writing a favorable 1968 review for the uncut version of the Clarke-Kubrick groundbreaking film, *2001: A Space Odyssey*. Clarke deeply appreciated Bradbury's support, and no doubt knew that *2001* represented what Bradbury himself had tried so hard to do with his *Martian Chronicles* screenplays (he also appreciated Bradbury's candor in say-ing—in print—that 2001 would have been even better if Stanley Kubrick had not interfered with the Clarke screenplay).

The following day, Bradbury received his full baptism into the Space Age when he joined the JPL scientific teams to witness the Mars Orbit Insertion (MOI) of Mariner 9. It was a long day, culminating in transmission of the first survey pho-tographs, and Bradbury finally had the opportunity to meet Wernher von Braun. Like many Americans of his generation, Bradbury approached the meeting with ambivalence. In the end, he found common ground based on their shared vision for Mankind's future in space. For his part, von Braun had no such misgivings and commemorated their meeting with this note: "To Ray Bradbury, who had it all figured out long ago."[11]

Bradbury and the other Mariner 9 panelists were able to present their final reflections a year later, as Bruce Murray began to gather the debate transcrip-tions, interspersed with sensational mission photographs of Mars, for Harper & Row's *Mars and the Mind of Man*. Bradbury penned both the foreword and the afterword, expressed partially in poetry. He had now attained his full public stature as a dreamer of futures, combining fiction, essay, and poetry as he defined the impulse to reach for Mars in terms of the Westering spirit of earlier pioneers:

> And yet I would not see our candle blown out in the wind. It is a small thing, this dear gift of life handed us mysteriously out of immensity. I would not have that gift expire. Crossing the wilderness, centuries ago, men carried in covered cows' horns the coals of the previous nights' fires to start new fires on the nights ahead. Thus we carry ourselves in the universal wilderness and blow upon the coals and kindle new lives and move on yet once more.

By the early 1970s, Bradbury's ability to create dreams of the Cosmos was no longer limited to the short story form; very few subsequent stories, other than those nested in typescripts from his early career, were set on other worlds. He preferred to present his far-traveling dreams of the Cosmos in essay form, or in dramatic, spoken form. The process was not unlike apotheosis; narrative passages from his early fantasies of space travel and colonization, words from his more recent lectures, articles, and poems, even his presence in a room—a room full of astronauts, students, or librarians, it didn't matter—all served as reminders of why Mankind explores.

41 | "Take Me Home"

Bradbury had witnessed the Apollo 11 moon landing through various media miracles and had spoken to a national American audience by satellite feed from London. But he returned to North America by water, just as an earlier age of pioneers had done, and then set out on his customary train journey across the North American continent. Rail travel was not just a way around his fear of air travel; it was also a way to shed skin, a psychological metaphor he had used in his Pasadena City College lecture: "The jet doesn't give you time esthetically to prepare yourself for a new experience or to leave old experience behind properly. . . . [B]y the time I got home I had a whole new skin on, because I had time to weigh in the balance myself and my life, my past, my present, and my future on that train coming home."

Along the way, he had discovered a new identifier for the kinds of stories he was writing, a category that, like Gilbert Highet's earlier recognition of Bradbury as a fabulist, did not have the limiting associations of a genre label. In February 1967, he would tell the freshman class at Caltech that he was a moralist who wrote cautionary fables. In approving the six-volume boxed set of Bradbury paperbacks that Bantam released in 1969, he reflected on what linked five of them: "The five books . . . all have something in common in the fantasy–science fiction fields with here or there a touch of what might be called, for lack of a label, magic-realism."[1] One could also apply this new designation to *Something Wicked This Way Comes*, the sixth title in the boxed set, the 1962 novel that capped the two decades of outstanding fiction for which he is best remembered.

But his early stories had also revealed Bradbury as one of the most significant neoromantic writers of midcentury America; he rarely used this designation, but he was sometimes amazed when editors and critics tried to punish him for it. In 1969, when *Playboy* rejected a freelance interview because his responses were "too often couched in romance," his reaction was swift and sure: "All of my work has been touched with romance, particularly my Space Fiction concerning our future on other worlds. I have always considered romance as absolutely necessary in the life of boys, young men, and, for that matter, men, which means a kind of special wild love, a fanatic thing, that pulls or drives them to make a reality of the particular dream romanticised."[2]

By the late 1960s, he was also pleased that these young men's dreams were also the dreams of young women, and he was heartened to find a growing proportion of women attending his frequent student lectures at Caltech. As for those literary folks who didn't value the romantic core of his work, he regarded them as "the sort that would build only tenements in cities, and no fountains to refresh the soul. What in hell is the use of a dwelling, as mere roofing, without something to make your insides sing?"

His plays had become great consumers of time and creativity during the 1960s, and these adaptations revealed perhaps more than any of his early fiction his instinctive need to write for his own enjoyment and create worlds that he could share with audiences that shared his sensibilities no matter what the larger literary world might think. He knew that plays like *Any Friend of Nicholas Nickleby's Is a Friend of Mine*, which brought both Charles Dickens and Emily Dickinson into his Green Town memories of 1920s Illinois, would not advance his stature in American letters, but he simply didn't care: "Super-realists are dumbfounded by the play," he explained to Congdon. "They won't buy Charlie Dickens or Emily on any level. But the people I really love and trust, in turn really love and trust the play."[3]

The consequences of shifting his time and attention to stage adaptations (and even more extensively to cinema and television adaptations) included a marked and ultimately irreversible decline in his production of masterful short fiction, but this had little impact on his overall creativity or his basically optimistic state of mind. The surviving opening fragment for "A List of My Failures," an unpublished article written in 1962, maintained his own cautionary view that an established name is no guarantee of future sales. He viewed "failures" in the more positive context of "setbacks," and always felt that setbacks had the value of teaching the writer new lessons of the writing craft.

Such setbacks and distractions from storytelling were never part of the public perception. The injection of older unpublished stories into his later story collections sustained public enthusiasm for his storytelling, but successive generations of readers almost always entered his world through the now-classic titles of the 1950s and early 1960s, preserved in perennial paperback and library editions or through the pages of both commercial and textbook anthologies. By the beginning of the 1970s, Bradbury stories had appeared in more than 230 trade anthologies and nearly 170 textbooks.[4] Wise publishing decisions by Don Congdon and affiliated overseas agencies had also made Bradbury one of the most widely published contemporary American fiction writers in foreign-language editions.

: : :

In many ways, the visionary Bradbury who emerged as an inspirational cultural force after 1954 was a very different creative figure from the phenomenal storyteller of earlier times. In terms of character and intellect, he emerged with greater powers from his 1953–54 European sojourn. By successfully negotiating the challenges of writing the *Moby Dick* screenplay for John Huston in Ireland and London, Bradbury found many doors open when he returned home to Hollywood. By fully embracing the great art and architecture of the Italian Renaissance under Bernard Berenson's subtle tutelage, he refined his ability to distinguish the enduring from the ephemeral.

But it could also be argued that the world Berenson showed him, and Huston's passport to endless Hollywood temptations, greatly diminished his focus as a storyteller. Much of his subsequent fiction would not, as a body of work, have established an enduring reputation if he had not already *been* Ray Bradbury. And to some degree, fortune had propelled him into the mainstream in the first place. Would he have broken into literary prominence without the blessing of Martha Foley, who placed his work in four of the *Best American Short Stories* annual anthologies, or Herschel Brickell, who fought his own judges to foreground Bradbury in two O. Henry Prize anthologies of the 1940s?

Bradbury always acknowledged the debts he owed to those editors and publishers who believed in him early on, and without a doubt the great fictions he created between 1943 and 1953 justified all the chances that Bradbury took to place them in front of a wide range of major writers and critics. But most of his subsequent work of quality was deeply grounded in that first amazing decade; "The Day It Rained Forever," the last of his *Best American Short Stories* selections in 1958, was written within months of his 1954 return to America. Other significant stories published in later times, including "I Sing the Body Electric!" evolved from manuscripts of the late 1940s and early 1950s. Nearly all the significant creative arcs that followed his return—*Something Wicked This Way Comes, The Halloween Tree, Death Is a Lonely Business,* and *From the Dust Returned*—were harbored within the islands of creativity where he felt safest: the light horror stories, edgy terror tales, and fantasies where he had found his first success as a writer of short fiction.

Style was his great constant companion, woven so deeply into his subconscious identity that the growing complexities of his career could not attenuate it. There was still that occasionally unnerving encounter with Otherness as only Bradbury could imagine it. The metaphors still came, the emotional hit was always palpable, but the structures of his short stories were often diminished, the emotional impact somehow off-line or too sentimental. Not surprisingly, new generations were catechized by the same great story collections and novelized story cycles as those readers who came before.

But this more mature Ray Bradbury was still a creator, even as he chose to weave the best of his newer tapestries from older fabrics. He was still a presence to be reckoned with, more valued as an independently minded visionary than ever before. Heinar Kipphardt's In the Matter of J. Robert Oppenheimer, which Bradbury saw during its short New York stage run in 1969, proved more troubling than sanative for him, bringing back too many memories from the McCarthy era's climate of fear. Yet conservative thinkers like Russell Kirk found Bradbury inspiring for the way he came to stand against consumer-driven materialism, "mindless power," and "the perversion of right reason into the mentality of the television-viewer."[5]

The outspokenness Bradbury had exhibited through the repressions of the McCarthy era and the activism of the 1960s followed an independent path that eventually took him beyond the few activist groups he had joined during those decades. As early as 1963, he privately voiced his sense of being one of the principled outsiders: "Many of them don't join groups because they have found what many of us have found, that by working alone, speaking alone, we have known greatest strength, the strength of the individual, that person we are always speaking of with great pride in America, but who doesn't get the attention he deserves. . . . If some do not join groups it is not because they are afraid, but because they want no one speaking for them. They would rather speak for themselves." These words lay out the underlying motivation of the man who had cried "Cowards!" to the entire Writers Guild of America West after a forced blacklist vote in 1954.

He was still uncomfortable with literary labels as well, even the ones, like "a teller of tales," that he had worn in earlier times with little sense of a burden. By the fall of 1970, his draft introduction for Doubleday's edition of Avram Davidson's collected stories indicates his growing sense that an unconventional prose genius like Davidson's (and, by extension, his own) was eclipsed by the continuing dominance of genre conventions in magazine fiction: "A teller of tales. The designation is almost an insult in our time. We have been so put upon by your New Yorker slice-of-life writer and all of the other non-talents of our age appearing in magazine after magazine, that when we come upon such as Avram Davidson we go into a mild shock of surprise. For this is what story writing once was, and can be again, if we leave it in such capable hands."[6]

Fame was, potentially, his worst enemy. The urge to gain critical recognition had an impact on his behavior that he would never admit, even to himself. His willingness to walk away from certain film and television deals was sometimes based more on pride than on the good business sense of Don Congdon. Disdain for the newcomer, rising at times to jealousy, magnified the creative trespasses of Rod Serling in Bradbury's mind, resulting in a parting of ways that both men mishandled. His desire to dominate the early film negotiations for *Something Wicked This Way Comes* damaged his relationship with some of his best allies, including director Blake Edwards and Twentieth Century–Fox executive Elmo Williams. To be sure, there were many Hollywood agents and producers who were on the make, and Bradbury usually had the discernment to let Congdon or his Hollywood agents deal with them. But what really saved Bradbury from a full descent into the hellbound consequences of fame was his unquestioning love of the authors who inspired him. He reflected on his very special form of salvation in a private 2002 interview:

> [O]ne of the reasons for my success is, I've never wanted to be famous. I've just wanted to be loved—there's a difference, a difference. . . . You find that a book like *Fahrenheit* is in every library in the country and most of the schools. . . . But I didn't intend that; that wasn't the reason. I wrote it because it was a great idea and I loved the idea. . . .
>
> The great American novel for me is *Tender Is the Night*, by F. Scott Fitzgerald. Not because it's a "great American novel," but because I *love* it. The *texture* is there . . . the asides, the observations, the richness. It's a long way around to the point that the reason I have a sustained reputation is because people I know, know that I loved everything that I did, and I was not straining to be popular.[7]

As he matured into the middle years of his career Bradbury was able to make a deal with his ego about the great American novel, in much the same way he had made a deal with his subconscious to write his first drafts spontaneously, as the Muse and his characters moved him, with no regard for logic or revision. Here was the will to believe in the underlying wonderment of creative fiction, a respect for authorship that subordinated the drive for gain and fame to the drive to stay true to the author's craft. Most of the time, though not always, this world view kept him from delivering the hurtful blow in his written or spoken words.

The second and third decades of Bradbury's professional career—the 1950s and 1960s—were successful by almost any standard of measurement. The largely private record of Hollywood disappointments after the mid-1950s make the literary and media achievements of his midcareer years even more remarkable. He fought his way beyond the boundaries of genre labels and saw adaptations of his fiction for stage, cinema, and television (often by his own hand) liberate his stories and novels from the pages of bound books.

At times, his outspoken views on society, technology, and politics operated beyond the boundaries set by liberals and conservatives alike, and such moments inevitably extended into the politics of literature. During UCLA's 1963 Conference on Culture, he countered a rapidly aging Aldous Huxley's despair over the gulf between science and the arts by asserting that "the poetry of science is coming to birth in science fiction. . . . Science and aesthetics must join hands on the rim of Space right now." He went on to proclaim science fiction as the future of the literary mainstream, paving the way for Isaac Asimov, Eric Rabkin, and other writers and scholars to extend the field through even more public statements over time.[8]

Here, during these unbound years, is where Bradbury began to consciously articulate in his mind the love of craft and love of literature that would inform his mid- and late-career motivation and his discipline as a writer. With Huston, Berenson, and, in later years, Federico Fellini, Bradbury discovered a wider world of aesthetic inspiration. He needed a way to explain his origins and his development, and eventually he would come to see it this way: *it was a function of making one's own luck by being honest and true to the loves that inspire creativity*. This lesson, in various combinations and contexts, would become a recurring motif in the public lectures that dominated the last four decades of his life.

As with his interviews and essays on writing, his lecture career began with years of regional speaking engagements. Throughout the 1960s he became ever more popular as a public speaker at the national level, but his availability was limited by his unwillingness to fly and his abiding tendency to run his own engagement schedule. This all changed in 1970, when he was approached by Ruth Alben Davis, who had recently launched a speaker's bureau that emphasized loyalty and service to clients. She had experience in the world of publicity and quickly realized that Bradbury had a broad-based popularity that transcended nearly all cultural boundaries.

The timing was perfect, for Bradbury had become, largely by his own efforts, a lay spokesman for the Space Age. His editors at Life magazine had opened the doors at NASA and elsewhere for a decade, but Bradbury's own very public celebrations of the moon landing in the summer of 1969 led television viewers to realize what magazine readers had known for a decade—that Ray Bradbury was representative of all Americans who found meaning and excitement in the nation's Space-Age achievements.

A generation earlier, he had written a modern fable of Mars that highlighted, in frightful symmetry, the options for success or failure facing those who might someday establish humanity's first beachhead on another planet. Over time, The Martian Chronicles became a Space-Age classic that helped propel science fiction into the future mainstream; by the early 1970s, he could also speak publicly and compellingly of our coming journey to Mars, and read his own poetry about reaching it, to a generation of space enthusiasts who had been inspired by his tales. He did this unashamedly by invoking the first literary dream of his youth, come full circle from his juvenile reading of the Edgar Rice Burroughs hero John Carter, whose ten-volume saga was based on the premise that Carter could pass, first by accident and eventually by sheer force of will, between his American homeland and the great technowarrior civilizations of a highly romanticized Mars.

From this point on through the four remaining decades of his life, Bradbury would often repeat this dream, for he was now beginning to live it out; his 2003 introduction to the Modern Library's *A Princess of Mars* is perhaps as eloquent as any version he would ever tell: "At the age of nine, ten, and eleven, I stood on the lawns of summer, raised my hands, and cried for Mars, like John Carter, to take me home."[9] He had long since left Burroughs behind, without ever forgetting him: "You must close part of your mature mind to appreciate his wonders." And indeed, the wonders never vanished from Ray Bradbury's imagination; "Take Me Home," a final retelling of this lifelong wish, was his last publication, appearing in *The New Yorker* on June 4, 2012—the day before he slipped gently and painlessly away from this world.

Notes

Unless otherwise indicated in individual note citations, Ray Bradbury's unpublished papers cited in this volume are located in the following repositories: The Albright Collection contains the manuscripts of published and unpublished works through all periods of his career and letters to Bradbury through 1970; the Center for Ray Bradbury Studies (Indiana University School of Liberal Arts, IUPUI) holds letters to Bradbury since 1970; the Rare Book and Manuscript Library of Columbia University's Butler Library is the depository for Bradbury's letters to his agent, Don Congdon; Syracuse University's Bird Library holds Bradbury's letters to Frederik Pohl and to the editors of the *Magazine of Fantasy & Science Fiction* (F&SF); the Lilly Library at Indiana University (Bloomington) contains Bradbury's F&SF letters addressed specifically to Anthony Boucher and some of the many Bradbury letters written to Doubleday editor Walter Bradbury (no relation); the Library of Congress holds a number of other Bradbury letters to his Doubleday editors; and the University of Tulsa preserves Bradbury letters to his British publisher, Sir Rupert Hart-Davis, in its Hart-Davis Collection. Portions of chapters 1 through 5 were condensed and rewritten from my essay on Bradbury's *Moby Dick* experience in the *New Ray Bradbury Review*, volume 1 (The Kent State University Press, 2008); portions of chapters 6 and 8 were excerpted and rewritten from that essay and from my introduction to the Bradbury-Berenson correspondence in volume 2 of the *New Ray Bradbury Review* (2010). A number of chapter titles derive from literary allusions relevant to Bradbury's reading life, including chapters 3 (T. S. Eliot), 15 (Eugene O'Neill), 20 (Langston Hughes), 26 (Stanley Weinbaum), 30 (John Wyndham), 32 (Edith Wharton), 33 (William Dean Howells), 37 (Hugh Kenner), and 39 (Eugene O'Neill). Unless otherwise noted, all interviews with Bradbury were conducted in Los Angeles.

Chapter 1. Loomings

1 Bradbury, interview with the author, Oct. 2, 2004. In *The Hustons* (New York: Scribner's, 1989), biographer Lawrence Grobel places the premiere on Feb. 2, 1951, but other sources indicate that subsequent Los Angeles openings line up better with Bradbury's recollection of the date.

2 Huston to Bradbury, undated (early Mar. 1951). The letter can be dated with some certainty by reference in a letter from Bradbury to William F. Nolan dated Mar. 2, 1951. Details of the dinner are available from many sources, but are taken directly from Bradbury, interview (UCLA Oral History), ch 8, 302, and Bradbury, interview (Eller), Oct. 2005.

3 Huston to Bradbury, Dec. 27, 1951. Huston refers to Korda only by his surname, but context indicates that he meant Alexander Korda rather than his brother, the director Zoltan Korda.

4 Huston to Bradbury, Feb. 1, 1953.

5 Bradbury, interviews with the author, Oct. 25, 2002, Oct. 8, 2005, and Oct. 8, 2006.

6 Grobel, *The Hustons*, 416.

7 Bradbury, interview with the author, Pasadena, Oct. 7, 2006. The factors surrounding Bradbury's decision to accept Huston's offer are found in Bradbury, interview (UCLA Oral History), ch 8, 303–308. His purchase of a second copy of the novel comes from Weller, *The Bradbury Chronicles* (New York: Morrow, 2005), 211.

8 Bradbury, Fairfax High School lecture, Los Angeles, 1958 (tape recording).

Chapter 2. Strangers in a Strange Land

1 Bradbury, Congdon interviews, II, 107–108.

2 Bradbury's annotation on the first two pages of that draft establishes the date he began to compose the screenplay. His business itinerary during the brief New York stopover is found in Congdon to Bradbury, Sept. 8, 1953, and Bradbury to Nolan, Sept. 29, 1953.

3 A more detailed description of the voyage, including the recollections of Regina Ferguson, may be found in Weller, *The Bradbury Chronicles*, 214–216. Bradbury's annotated copy of *Moby Dick* confirms that he finished his first reading after arriving in Paris.

4 Bradbury, "Questions and Answers on 'Moby Dick'" (1955), unpublished 7-page typescript with 2-page revision of the opening questions.

5 Bradbury to the author, Apr. 14, 2005 (email). In the fictionalized *Green Shadows, White Whale* (New York: Knopf, 1991), Bradbury moved the conversation about Fedallah to the evening of Bradbury's first dinner with the Huston family in Ireland.

6 A fragment page of the Capa story, dated Dublin, Oct. 1953, and 1961 fragment titled "A Wake for Bob Capa," are the only pages known to survive from Bradbury's Paris encounters (Albright Collection).

7 Bradbury attended the screening. A detailed discussion of the activities surrounding Huston's London itinerary is found in Weller, *The Bradbury Chronicles*, 218.

8 Bradbury, interview with the author, Oct. 12, 2005.

9 Bradbury, interview with the author, Oct. 25, 2007.

10 Bradbury, interviews with the author, Oct. 12, 1998, and Oct. 8, 2006; Bradbury, interview (Congdon), 1970, 106.

11 Grobel, *The Hustons*, 400, 408–9, 417, and Peter Viertel, *Dangerous Friends* (New York: Doubleday, 1992), 204.

12 Godley, *Living Like a Lord* (New York: Houghton Mifflin, 1956), 218–219.

13 Grobel, *The Hustons*, 430, and Viertel, *Dangerous Friends*, 205.

14 Viertel, *Dangerous Friends*, 205. In this memoir, Viertel also maintains that the Bradbury family took rooms at Courtown, but concedes in a subsequent letter to Bradbury that he had misremembered these details (Viertel to Bradbury, Sept. 10, 1992).

Chapter 3. Indecisions, Visions, and Revisions

1 Excerpt from Bradbury's American Film Institute seminar appearances (1969, 1981, 1982), published in *Conversations with the Great Moviemakers of Hollywood's Golden Age*, ed.

George Stevens Jr. (New York: Alfred A. Knopf, 2006), 384. The date is not specified, but it is most likely from the 1981 or 1982 seminars.

2   Bradbury to Hart-Davis, Oct. 12 and Nov. 26, 1953. The cover page of Bradbury's surviving first draft is annotated in the author's hand with dates of the stages of composition.

3   The summary of the Beaumont exchange is drawn from Bradbury to Forry Ackerman, Oct. 15, 1953; Bradbury to Beaumont, Oct. 21 and Dec. 4, 1953; and Beaumont to Bradbury, Oct. 30, 1953.

4   Bradbury, interview with the author, Mar. 12, 2011.

5   Grobel, The Hustons, 417.

6   Bradbury to Writer's Guild of America, West, Nov. 16, 1955, offers a full breakdown of the evolution of the screenplay both before and after completion of the first draft in January 1954. See also Bradbury (UCLA Oral History), ch 6.

7   The doubloon sequence was established between Bradbury's first revision and cutting of his complete screenplay (Jan. 20, 1954) and Lorrie Sherwood's preparation of the full script with shot sequences (Feb. 22, 1954). The discards from Bradbury's typewriter suggest that he had this sequence fairly well developed in early February. For the dramatic effect of his 1991 novelization, Bradbury moved his development of the doubloon sequence into the final days of his months with Huston.

8   Bradbury to his parents, Jan. 7, 1954.

9   The interim count of 140 is noted in Bradbury to his parents, Jan. 7, 1954. The final first draft length of 159 pages is found in Bradbury to August Derleth, Jan. 14, 1954 (Wisconsin) and Bradbury to Hart-Davis, Jan. 17, 1954 (Tulsa). The title page of Bradbury's surviving "A" draft also records the date of completion and the final number of pages.

10 Bradbury, interview (UCLA Oral History), 237–238.

11 Both of these typescripts survive in the Albright Collection, along with a number of discarded leaves from earlier and later stages of work.

12 Bradbury to Hart-Davis, Jan. 17, 1954.

13 Bradbury, interview with the author, Oct. 9 and 13, 2005.

Chapter 4. Fatal Attraction

1   Bradbury, interview (UCLA Oral History), ch 6, 248–259 (background), 249 (quotation).

2   Bradbury's novelization of this insight, fictionally moved in time to the end of his Dublin stay, appears in Green Shadows, White Whale, ch 32.

3   Joseph Conrad, The Mirror of the Sea, 5th edition (London: Methuen, 1915), chapter XXII, "The Character of the Foe."

4   Bradbury, interview with Herrmann biographer Steven C. Smith, Dec. 14, 1984 (Bradbury photocopy).

5   Bradbury to Forry Ackerman, Feb. 24, 1954.

6   Bradbury, interview (UCLA Oral History), ch 8, 309, 338.

7   Grobel, The Hustons, 417.

8   Bradbury's annotated transcription of the hoax telegram still survives in his papers.

9   The most significant pranks are summarized in Weller, The Bradbury Chronicles, 221–225.

The best primary source remains Bradbury's UCLA Oral History interview (Cunningham), ch 8, and his novelization of these events in *Green Shadows, White Whale* (1992), chapters 24, 27, and 31.

10 Bradbury, interview with the author, Oct. 7, 2006.

11 Weller, *The Bradbury Chronicles*, 226, from an interview with Viertel.

Chapter 5. A Whale of a Tale

1 The only full account of this downward spiral is found in Bradbury, interview (UCLA Oral History), ch 8, 317–335. Weller describes the dispute over Ray's mode of travel to London (226–227), but no secondary sources connect the disintegration of the relationship with the direct cause.

2 Bradbury, interview (UCLA Oral History), ch 8, 320–321.

3 Grobel, *The Hustons*, 390.

4 Information on this dinner is both plentiful and problematic. Richard Brooks, quoted in Grobel's *The Hustons*, remembers a large group gathering at the White Elephant restaurant that included the key cast and crew from *Beat the Devil* (419). He may be conflating the March 1954 dinner with one given the previous summer as production of the Bogart film ended. Viertel does not indicate that the March group was this large, and his description of the final exchange between Huston and Bradbury differs from that of Brooks in its details (*Dangerous Friends*, 216–217). Lorrie Sherwood (quoted by Grobel, *The Hustons*, 419) maintained that Bradbury reached into the cab and punched Huston, but no other sources make this claim. In general, Weller seems to follow the Cunningham interview and unspecified interviews of his own (227–228). In this study I have followed Bradbury's own account in the UCLA Oral History interview, ch 8, 335–340, within the larger context provided by my October 2005 and 2006 interviews with Bradbury. Viertel, who shows some weakness of recall at other points in *Dangerous Friends*, remembers that the disparagement of Ray's friends involved Anita Loos and her husband rather than the Probsts.

5 Bradbury, interview (UCLA Oral History), ch 8, 340.

6 Bradbury, interview (Atkins), 1974, quoted in Grobel, *The Hustons*, 418. Bradbury had originally placed the harpooner Tashtigo in the absent Fedallah's place, lashed to the great whale; but in his April 2nd sequence of rewritten pages, 'Tashtigo' is deleted and 'Ahab' is penned in the margin, in Bradbury's hand.

7 Bradbury, interview with the author, Oct. 8, 2005.

8 Arthur C. Clarke, *2001: A Space Odyssey* (New York: New American Library, 1968), 141.

9 Bradbury, interview with the author, Oct. 8, 2005.

10 Bradbury, interview with the author, Oct. 8, 2005.

11 Russell to Ruth Simon (Hart-Davis), Mar. 13, 1954.

Chapter 6. "Floreat!"

1 William F. Nolan, "The Ray Bradbury Index," in *The Ray Bradbury Review*, first supplement (San Diego, privately printed, Mar. 1954).

2 Bernard Berenson, *Sunset and Twilight* (New York: Harcourt, Brace, and World, 1963), 343.

3 Bradbury's half-page of idea notes from the luncheon is dated May 10, 1954.

4 Bradbury, interview with the author, Oct. 2, 2004.

5 Bradbury's half-page typed note (Bradbury Center) verifies that Berenson suggested this idea during the May 10, 1954, luncheon at Villa I Tatti. Horace Gold's earlier idea along these lines is found in Gold to Bradbury, Oct. 3 and Nov. 4, 1950 (Jonathan R. Eller), *Becoming Ray Bradbury* (Urbana: University of Illinois Press, 2011), 215–216.

6 Bernard, *Sunset and Twilight*, 345.

Chapter 7. A Place in the Sun

1 Bradbury to Hart-Davis, June 29, 1954 (Tulsa).

2 Eller, *Becoming Ray Bradbury*, 241, n 4. Bradbury's reading of Jimenéz in translation can now be pinpointed to July 1953, when he took time from his final *Fahrenheit 451* revisions to start a never-finished story inspired by Jimenéz's work.

3 Congdon to Bradbury, Aug. 18, 1953.

4 Nelson Algren to Stanley Kauffmann (Ballantine), Sept. 30, 1953 (Bradbury's cc).

Chapter 8. Post-Scripts

1 Bradbury to Hart-Davis, June 29, 1954 (Tulsa).

2 Bradbury's endpaper inscriptions show that he purchased Jay Leyda's edition of *The Complete Stories of Herman Melville* and *Redburn* in October 1953, and *White-Jacket* in November; all three were English editions purchased in Dublin. After returning to America in June 1954, he acquired secondary volumes that included Newton Arvin's *Herman Melville* (1950), Jay Leyda's *The Melville Log* (1951), Lewis Mumford's *Herman Melville* (1929), and Lawrence Thomson's *Melville's Quarrel with God* (1952).

3 Bradbury to Clifton Fadiman, undated (cc, Albright Collection). Fadiman's response, dated Aug. 25, 1954, reveals his conviction that Bradbury had struck an effective balance between action and character: "[A] great deal of the cavernous heart of the book is retained; Ahab has stature and some of the symbolism comes through."

4 Moulin Productions (Walter E. Mirisch) to Bradbury, May 6, 1955.

5 Mary Dorfman (WGAW Credit Arbitration Secretary) to Bradbury, June 1, 1955.

6 It was a rationale that Huston had asserted in claiming coauthorship credit with more than one of his screenwriters. Albert Bant, given coauthored screen credit on *The Red Badge of Courage*, later visited Bradbury at his home and told him that his experience had been similar. Bradbury had similar discussions with his good friend Ben Maddow, a member of his writing group and the principal screenwriter for Huston's production of *The Asphalt Jungle*.

7 Bradbury, interview (UCLA Oral History), ch 8, 343–344.

8 Bradbury to Bernard Berenson, Mar. 23, 1956.

9 Bradbury, interview with the author, Oct. 2, 2004.

10 Bradbury, interview with the author, Oct. 14, 2005.

Chapter 9. Invitations to the Dance
1 Bradbury, Introduction, in *Forbidden Planets* (New York: DAW Books, 2006), 1. "I turned down the project and later regretted it because when I saw the film with the Id on the screen, I realized this was the most important idea in the picture."
2 Congdon to Bradbury, Mar. 29, Apr. 12, 1955.
3 Bradbury to Congdon, Mar. 31, 1955.
4 Bradbury to Berenson, Aug. 4, 1955.

Chapter 10. Pictures within Pictures: *The October Country*
1 Bradbury to Derleth, Feb. 19, 1956 (Madison).
2 Carlos Baker, "A Chamber of Horrors," *New York Times Book Review* (Dec. 11, 1955): 30.
3 Boucher to Bradbury (cc editorial attached), Dec. 14, 1955.
4 "Djinn and Bitters," *Time* 66 (Nov. 21, 1955): 121.

Chapter 11. Laughton and Hitchcock
1 Ray Bradbury to Walt Bradbury, Aug. 28, 1955 (Lilly).
2 Sir Michael Redgrave, *In My Mind's Eye: An Autobiography* (London: Weidenfield and Nicholson, 1983), 173–174. "For the dummy itself I enlisted the help of ventriloquist Peter Brough, who was, strange to say, an almost national figure on radio. Cavalcanti's first idea was that the dummy should be modeled to look like me. I wanted a figure which would look as different as possible, a caricature of a cheeky, overgrown schoolboy, like Brough's Archie Andrews."
3 Bradbury's notecard submission files show that he sent Lewton "Homecoming," "Skeleton," "The Smiling People," and "The Man Upstairs."
4 Other correspondence on this issue includes Congdon to Bradbury, June 28, July 7 and 14, 1955.

Chapter 12. "The First to Catch a Circus in a Lie Is a Boy"
1 The correspondence documenting the strained publishing history of Bradbury's *Dr. Lao* anthology includes Saul David (Bantam) to Bradbury, Oct. 6, 1952; Feb. 26, Mar. 27, and June 8, 1953; June 29, Sep. 1, and Sep. 28, 1954; Jan. 17, Feb. 9, and Mar. 5, 1956.
2 Bradbury to Bob Gottlieb (Simon & Schuster), Oct. 31, 1962.
3 Congdon to Bradbury, Dec. 13, 1955. Congdon relayed this news along with Bantam's sense of urgency: "Saul says he doesn't know why it's taking you so long to write the introduction for them, but couldn't something be done about it by the first of the year."
4 William Tenn, "The Fiction in Science Fiction," *Science Fiction Adventures* (Mar. 1954), 67. Sturgeon's following response to Bradbury is quoted in Tenn, who seems to reflect a tougher criticism than Sturgeon actually expressed in surviving letters. The Sturgeon introduction is discussed in detail in Eller, *Becoming Ray Bradbury*, 188–190.
5 Saul David's rejoinder (from his Jan. 17 letter) refers to "SHE and the Abe Merritt

things," suggesting that Bradbury's submitted draft introduction may have read "H. Rider Haggard and A. Merritt." If so, Bradbury's substitution of Burroughs for Haggard would represent an intent to strengthen his argument by drawing a sharper divide between general fantasy and more juvenile-focused pulp fiction.

6 Congdon to Bradbury, Jan. 12, 1956.
7 Bradbury to Boucher, Feb. 11, 1956 (Syracuse).

Chapter 13. Various Wines

1 Bradbury to Rhymer, Dec. 1, 1949, 2 pp. photocopy, Albright Collection. NBC director Warren Lewis had offered Bradbury access to recordings of the programs, prompting Bradbury to write Rhymer and request a list of the creator's favorite episodes.
2 Bradbury to Mr. Koenig, May 3, 1961, 1p. photocopy, Albright Collection. Both the Rhymer and Koenig letters cited in this discussion appear to be Bradbury's file copies.
3 Bradbury, interview with the author, Oct. 23, 2007.
4 Bradbury, "Since We Heard That Magic Word: Turnabout!" foreword to Forman Brown's *Small Wonder: The Story of the Yale Puppeteers and the Turnabout Theatre* (Metuchen, N.J.: Scarecrow, 1980), v-vi.
5 Bradbury, interview with the author, Oct. 13, 2005, and Oct. 23, 2007. Laughton's *Don Juan in Hell* had the greatest impact of all: "I came out riven, wanting to work for Charles Laughton, because he directed it" (2005).
6 Bradbury, "A Life in the Arts," Mar. 1995 (dramaticpublishing.com).
7 James Curtis, *James Whale: A New World of Gods and Monsters* (Boston: Faber and Faber, 1998), 381. Curtis misdates the set designs to spring 1957, but the Laughtons were in New York from October 1956 through May 1957. Correspondence places the design phase in the spring of 1956.

Chapter 14. The End of the Beginning

1 Bradbury may never have known that Hermann Bondi and Thomas Gold, who developed Steady State with Fred Hoyle, were initially inspired by Ealing Studio's 1945 British film *Dead of Night*, which Bradbury considered a masterpiece of psychological terror. Like Bradbury, Bondi and Gold were drawn to the recursive nightmare at the center of the film, but where Bradbury was attracted to the circular plot as a narrative strategy, this circularity led the two physicists to conceive a dynamic universe (expanding as Hubble had proven) that constantly creates matter, with no beginning and no end.
2 Ken Crossen's review of *The Golden Apples of the Sun*, in *Future Science Fiction* 4 (Nov. 1953): 40–41, 63.
3 Brian Aldiss, "The Autumn People," *Oxford Mail* (Aug. 9, 1956); "SF," *Oxford Magazine* (June 5, 1958); "Brian W. Aldiss," in Charles Platt, *Dream Makers* (New York: Ungar, 1980, 1987), 80: "One of the things I first like[d] about science fiction was that it did give me strange backgrounds; for instance, in the early work of Ray Bradbury."
4 Michael Edwards, "Time Machine," *The Isis* (Jan. 23, 1957): 19; J. G. Ballard, introduction

to *The Complete Short Stories*, vol.1 (London: Flamingo, 2001; New York: HarperCollins, 2006) C. S. Lewis to Mr. Rutyearts, Apr. 28, 1951 (Wheaton).

5   Congdon to Bradbury, Apr. 25, 1955. His further comments are from Congdon to Bradbury, July 13, 1956.

Chapter 15. Strange Interlude: *Dandelion Wine*

1   Bradbury to Anthony Boucher, Feb. 11, 1956 (Syracuse).
2   Bradbury to Congdon, Mar. 6, 1956 (two drafts, unsent). Congdon's subsequent negotiations with Susskind are documented in Congdon to Bradbury, July 8, Sept. 14, Oct. 3, 16, Nov. 8, 20, 26, and Dec. 12, 1956.
3   Bradbury, interview with the author, Oct. 13, 2005; William Thomier and Robert F. Fink, "James Whale," *Films in Review* 13:5 (May 1962): 289; Curtis, *James Whale*, 381.
4   Prospects for the long-format television options are found in Congdon to Bradbury, July 11 and Aug. 8, 1956.
5   "A Portrait of Genius: Ray Bradbury," a self-administered interview in *Show* (Dec. 1964): 55.

Chapter 16. Return to Hollywood

1   Bradbury, interview with the author, Oct. 2002.
2   Bradbury to Boucher, June 28, 1957.

Chapter 17. "And the Rock Cried Out"

1   *Tell It on the Drums* (now simply titled *Kimberly*) was deferred for the time being; Reed was scheduled to direct, but it remained an unproduced property when H-H-L closed down in 1959.
2   This recollection and the following comment on Huston are from Bradbury to Nolan, July 3, 1957.
3   Congdon to Bradbury, May 14, 1953.
4   Bradbury, interview with the author, Oct. 9, 2006, and Bradbury to Nolan, July 3, 1957.
5   Bradbury, interview with the author, Oct. 12, 2005.
6   Marie D. Moore (Matson Associates) to Bradbury, July 10, 1957.
7   Fritz Blocki, "Floodlights and Footlights," Los Angeles *Evening Outlook*, Aug. 17, 1957. Forry Ackerman, subject of this article, appears to be Blocki's source.
8   Bradbury to Boucher, June 28, 1957.

Chapter 18. Berenson at Sunset

1   Bradbury to Berenson, July 13, 1956, and Feb. 28, 1958.
2   Ray Bradbury to Walt Bradbury, Oct. 30, 1957 (Lilly).
3   UCLA Oral History Interview (1962), 428.
4   Bradbury to Arielle Dombasle and her former husband, Dr. Paul Albou, Aug. 8, 1999 (draft).

5　The French reception of Bradbury is surveyed in William F. Touponce, *Ray Bradbury and the Poetics of Reverie*, 2nd edition (San Bernardino: Borgo Press, 1998), ch VII .

6　Bradbury, interview with the author, Oct. 13, 2005.

Chapter 19. The Unforeseen

1　Carnell to Bradbury, Aug. 13, 1957.

2　Bradbury, interview with the author, Oct. 12, 2005. Bradbury recalled that the evening with the Highets occurred on the way over to Europe in June 1957, but the separate travel arrangements for Maggie on that leg of the trip made such a date impossible. Only the dates of the return trip support the visit.

3　Haberstroh to Fulton, Sept. 26, 1957 (forwarded to Bradbury).

4　Bradbury, interview with the author, Oct. 24, 2002.

5　Bradbury to August Derleth, Oct. 16, 1957, notes Aurthur's minor borrowings from Huxley and Orwell. The steps toward legal action are documented in Bradbury to Congdon, Oct. 14 and (c. 15), 1957; Congdon to Bradbury, Nov. 6, 1957.

Chapter 20. Dreams Deferred

1　UCLA Oral History Interview (1962), 453, 465–466.

2　Hill to Bradbury, Dec. 2, 1957.

3　Congdon to Bradbury, June 18, 25 and July 24, 1958; Bradbury to Congdon, June 22, 1958. Bradbury turned down Preminger's *The Man With the Golden Arm* and *Anatomy of a Murder*.

4　The final stages of the Bryna negotiations with Bradbury are discussed in Oscar Godbout, "Bradbury Writes Television Series," *New York Times*, July 18, 1958, 45; *Daily Variety* (Oct. 31, 1958): 1, 4; "Bryna Hurls 'Rock' in H'Wood's Own H-Bomb Film Race," *Hollywood Reporter* (Nov. 11, 1958): 1; Bradbury to Congdon, Aug. 1, 3, 10 and Oct. 24, 1958; Congdon to Bradbury, Aug. 7, 1958; Benjamin to Congdon, Nov. 11, 1958.

5　Ray Bradbury, interview with Donn Albright for the author, April 2006.

6　Marie Moore (Matson Agency) to Bradbury, July 10, 1957; Congdon to Bradbury, Nov. 27 and Dec. 9, 1957.

7　Bradbury, interview with the author, Oct. 8, 2006, Oct. 23, 2010; Bradbury, UCLA Oral History Interview (1962), 353.

8　Congdon to Bradbury, Mar. 8, 1957.

Chapter 21. The Great Wide World

1　The sublime also attracted; Bradbury once recommended "the vast and horrible bulk and shadow" of Piranesi's torture chambers as subject for his friend, popular magazine cartoonist Charles Addams (undated note, the Albright Collection).

2　Bradbury, interview with the author, Oct. 7, 2006.

3　Bradbury, signed editorial letter under "Not Child Enough," the *Nation*, 186:26 (June 28, 1958).

4　Bradbury, interview with the author, Oct. 11, 2005.

Chapter 22. *The Dreamers*

1 UCLA Oral History Interview (1962), 446.
2 "Set 2 'Dreamers' Plotters," Hollywood Reporter (Oct. 22, 1958): 3.
3 Bradbury to Congdon, Jan. 1, 1959.

Chapter 23. Dark Carnivals

1 Congdon to Bradbury, May 2 and 15, 1958.
2 Harry Lang, "Looking Around," Los Angeles Examiner, Nov. 15, 1952, sec. 1-5; "Florabel Muir Reporting," the Los Angeles Mirror, Nov. 12, 1952, 8; UCLA Oral History Interview (1962), 378–379.
3 Bradbury, interview with the author, Apr. 6, 2009; Variety 95:3 (Mar. 8, 1957): 1, 4.
4 Bradbury, interview with the author, Oct. 2010; UCLA Oral History Interview (1962), 382–383. Bradbury indicated in the UCLA Oral History that the unnamed writer wanted Bradbury's name to drive up the asking price. In the 2010 interview, Bradbury indicated that the writer was actually on the edge of the Hollywood Ten, and not one of them.
5 Discussions of these early Russian publishing efforts appear in Congdon to Bradbury, Mar. 14, 1956; Boucher to Bradbury, Mar. 11, 1957; and Bradbury to Boucher, Nov. 6, 1957.
6 Mike Connolly, "Rambling Reporter," Hollywood Reporter (Aug. 27, 1954): 2.
7 Photostat copy of Plaintiff's exhibit 16 (Bradbury Center); Gene Beley's Ray Bradbury Uncensored! (New York: źUniverse, 2007), Chapter 17.
8 Bradbury's letter is undated, but was date-stamped by the Matson Agency on June 19, 1959.

Chapter 24. Medicines for Melancholy

1 Bradbury to Congdon, Dec. 24, 1958.
2 Bradbury to Congdon, Jan. 20 and Mar. 1, 1959.
3 All of these emerging Hollywood friendships of the 1950s are described in Bradbury, interviews with the author, Oct. 9, 2005, and Oct. 8, 2006.
4 Norman Lloyd, Stages: A Director's Guild of America Oral History (Metuchen, N.J.: The Scarecrow Press, 1990), 177. Interviewed by Francine Parker.
5 Mike Connolly, "Hollywood" column, Chicago Sun-Times, Apr. 14, 1959, 51.
6 Bradbury, interview with the author, Oct. 13, 2005, and Oct. 19, 2008.

Chapter 25. Escape Velocity

1 Bradbury to Congdon, Apr. 2, 1961.
2 Bradbury to Congdon, Feb. 18, 1960.
3 Knopf's follow-up letters to Bradbury suggest that this incident led to Kauffmann's departure from the firm shortly afterward.
4 For a full discussion of the evolving drafts of Something Wicked This Way Comes, see Jonathan R. Eller and William F. Touponce, Ray Bradbury: The Life of Fiction (Kent: Kent State University Press, 2004), 268–282.

5 Bradbury to Condon, July 11 and 24, 1960.
6 Bradbury to Congdon, July 17, 1960.
7 Bradbury to Congdon, Sept. 27, 1960. Bradbury also raised the cautionary example of *The Rock Cried Out* screenplay, and how Stanley Kramer's production of *On the Beach* had provided the major studios "a reason for not doing my screenplay, which seemed too far off trail and dangerous for them."
8 Congdon didn't think that Bradbury owed Beaumont a script option for *Something Wicked*, even if *Dr. Lao* fell through for him (Congdon to Bradbury, Sept. 30, 1962).
9 Bradbury to Congdon, June 26, 1960.

Chapter 26. Martian Odyssey

1 Bradbury to Ben Benjamin, Mar. 14, 1963; Bradbury to Don Congdon, Mar. 23, 1963. Evidence of Bradbury's long-term friendship with Julian Blaustein prior to 1960 is found in Bradbury to Blaustein, Aug. 9, 1960.
2 Bradbury's contract had been hurried through just before the walkout so that he could pick up with work immediately after the strike settlement.
3 Bradbury to Congdon, July 29, 1960.
4 Bradbury to Hart-Davis, Oct. 30, 1960.
5 Bradbury to Congdon, Apr. 14, 1961.
6 UCLA Oral History Interview (1962), 244–245.
7 The decline of the *Martian Chronicles* work at MGM is described in Bradbury to Congdon, Mar. 18 and Apr. 14, 1961; Ben Benjamin to Congdon, Feb. 17 and Apr. 6, 1961; and Congdon to Benjamin, Apr. 23, 1961.
8 Bradbury to Bob and Nan [Kirsch], Nov. 27, 1960.
9 Bradbury, interview with the author, Oct. 6, 2004.
10 Bradbury to Siegel, Dec. 21, 1960.
11 Bradbury, interview with the author, Oct. 10, 2005.

Chapter 27. "Cry the Cosmos"

1 Bradbury to Tim Seldes (Doubleday), Sept. 26, 1962 (cc).
2 Bradbury, interview with the author, Oct. 2, 2004.

Chapter 28. In the Twilight Zone

1 Quoted at length in Roger Anker, "Be Careful What You Ask For: Serling, Beaumont, and Bradbury," part 2, in *Dark Discoveries* 15 (fall 2009): 26–27. In his letter, Serling misattributed "The Long Years" as "Marionettes, Inc." It's possible that the error originated in Beaumont's letter to Serling.
2 Late-life reflections by William F. Nolan and George Clayton Johnson on Serling's learning curve in fantasy and science fiction are quoted in Anker's "Be Careful What You Ask For" (part 2), 25.
3 Bradbury to Congdon, Sept. 27, 1960.
4 Bradbury to Congdon, Mar. 28, 1962.

5 Bradbury, interview with the author, Apr. 6, 2009.
6 Bradbury to Oscar Dystel (Bantam), May 7, 1962 (cc).

Chapter 29. *Something Wicked This Way Comes*
1 Bradbury to Congdon, Jan. 20, 1961.
2 Patrick McGilligan, *Alfred Hitchcock: A Life in Darkness and Light* (New York: Regan Books, 2003), 611.
3 Joyce Emerson, "What Became of Science Fiction?" Sunday Times (London), May 8, 1960.
4 Kingsley Amis, "The Words Are Wild," *London Observer*, Feb. 24, 1963.
5 Bradbury, interview with the author, Mar. 2012. I'm also grateful to Professor Robert Woods of Faulkner University for conversations on the character parallels between the Williams and Bradbury novels.
6 Nate Monaster (WGA) to Bradbury, Nov. 16, 1962.
7 Bradbury, interview with the author, Oct. 4, 2004.
8 Bradbury, interview with the author, Oct. 23, 2007.
9 Bradbury to Congdon, Jan. 3, 1964 (misdated 1963).

Chapter 30. Out of the Deeps
1 Bradbury to Congdon, June 9, 1960.
2 Congdon to Bradbury, May 1, 1961.
3 Bradbury, interview with the author, Oct. 8, 2006.
4 Bradbury initially tried to secure distribution through MGM, but that possibility ended when the studio dropped the option on his *Martian Chronicles* screenplay (Bradbury to Julian Blaustein [cc], June 27, 1960).
5 Bradbury to Schlesinger, Apr. 30, 1962 (cc). Vice President Johnson represented the President at the Seattle conference.

Chapter 31. Machineries of Joy
1 Bradbury, interviews with the author, Oct. 8 and 12, 2005. Nortman Corwin had suggested the Desilu option.
2 Bradbury, interview with the author, Oct. 2, 2004. The substance of the Brook and Bradbury negotiations are found in Ramsay (Peters Agency) to Bradbury, March 6, 22 (with encl.), and 31 (telegram), 1963; Ramsay to Congdon, Jan. 17, 1964; and Bradbury to Ramsay, Jan. 20, 1964 (cc); Jeanie Sims to Bradbury, Feb. 4, 1964.
3 Bradbury to Gottlieb (Simon & Schuster), June 3, 1962.
4 Bradbury, interviews with the author, Oct. 5, 2004, and Oct. 8, 2005.
5 Bradbury to Robert Terry (General Service Studio), Nov. 12, 1962.
6 Bradbury, interview with the author, Oct. 2, 2004. The final break came when Bradbury discovered what he perceived as another conflict of interest: Famous Artists attempted to close a deal for *The Martian Chronicles* with Paramount's Henry Hathaway, a director

that the agency also represented. This transition is also documented in Bradbury to Congdon, Mar. 23 and Apr. 16, 1963.

7 The initial phases of the Pakula-Mulligan work (along with the Gene Kelly sidebar) are documented in Bradbury to Congdon, May 8 and 9, June 5, and Aug. 3 and 9, 1963; Congdon to Bradbury, July 15, Aug. 2 and 15, 1963.

8 Pakula to Bradbury, Dec. 23, 1963.

9 *Daily Variety* (July 17, 1964): 1; and *Hollywood Reporter* (Nov. 6, 1964): 7.

10 Bradbury to Congdon, May 17 (re Williams) and Oct. 1, 1966 (re Truffaut).

11 Bradbury to Congdon, Mar. 4 ("[T]he story out of *Chronicles*, the screenplay, is not, to me anyway, an exceptional story. Good, yes, but not great.") and Mar. 9, 1966 ("[B]y the time I finished two years of work on the screenplay I was so exhausted I couldn't tell good work from mediocre-less-than-good.").

Chapter 32. A Backward Glance

1 The tale of the *Vintage Bradbury* introduction is chronicled in Congdon to Bradbury, Apr. 28, May 26, and Nov. 5, 1964, and Bradbury to Congdon, Nov. 23, 1964.

2 Congdon to Bradbury, Mar. 25, 1965.

3 Wogan (NBC) to Bradbury, Oct. 17, 1963, Apr. 7 and Aug. 17, 1965; Bradbury to Wogan, Mar. 17, 1965; Bradbury to Congdon, Aug. 3 and 19, 1966. Bradbury offered to take a payment cut to secure a higher fee for Corwin, but that proved unnecessary.

4 Bradbury, interview with the author, Oct. 12, 2005.

5 Anthony Jones (Peters Agency, London) to Congdon, May 27, 1969 (Bradbury cc); Bradbury to Anthony Jones, June 5, 1969 (Congdon's cc).

6 Ballantine to Bradbury, June 6 and 17, 1966 (the latter confirming Don Congdon's approval of the Bal-Hi issue); Bradbury to Ballantine, June 10, 1966.

Chapter 33. Stops of Various Quills

1 Bradbury to Congdon, June 29, 1963.

2 His work on the Fair narration is described in Bradbury to Congdon, June 29, July 8, and Aug. 1, 1963.

3 Bradbury to Sam Kingsley (New York Worlds Fair), Mar. 1, 1965 (cc).

4 Bradbury's rough draft of his Pasadena College Convocation speech (Apr. 22, 1966), 8–10.

5 The negotiations for *Nemo* are documented in Congdon to Bradbury, Aug. 2, 1963, May 26, July 22, Aug. 17, and Sept. 4, 1964.

Chapter 34. *The World of Ray Bradbury*

1 Bradbury, interview with the author, Los Angeles, Oct. 2002.

2 Bradbury to Congdon, Feb. 19, 1964.

3 Bradbury to Congdon, Feb. 15, 1965.

4 Bradbury, interviews with the author, Oct. 7, 2004, and Oct. 12, 2005.

5 Bradbury, interview with author, Oct. 7, 2005.

Chapter 35. If the Sun Dies

1 The comparison to Uriah Heep may have had deeper roots in American culture; Robert Caro would make the same association in one of his biographical volumes of Johnson's life; Richard Nixon was apparently tagged with this label as well.

2 This passage and those subsequent passages quoted here are from "Ray Bradbury Speaks on 'Film in the Space Age,'" in *American Cinematographer* (Jan. 1967): 34–35, 64–67.

3 The final report of the FBI Los Angeles office, and the covering memo to the FBI director, are both dated Aug. 15, 1968; these documents and related materials were declassified (with redactions) on May 9, 2003, after a Freedom of Information release request by Sam Weller.

Chapter 36. Truffaut's Phoenix

1 Bradbury, interview with the author, Apr. 6, 2009.

2 Lewis Allen (Allen-Hodgdon Productions) to Bradbury, Jan. 25, 1965.

3 Bradbury's carbon copies of his letters to Allen are dated Mar. 27 and May 3, 1964.

4 Bradbury, "*Fahrenheit 451* Revisited," *UCLA Magazine* (Summer 2002).

5 Bradbury to Congdon, undated (receipt stamp Sept. 6, 1966).

Chapter 37. A Colder Eye

1 Lorraine Williams to Bradbury, Nov. 30, 1965.

2 Bradbury to Congdon, Feb. 13, 1965.

3 Bradbury to Congdon, Nov. 24, 1965: "[Edwards] is better at straight drama, or at least my recollection tends to see him that way."

4 Bradbury to Congdon, May 28, June 6, and Nov. 9, 1966.

5 Bradbury to Congdon, Mar. 16, 1966, and Dec. 27, 1968.

6 Bradbury to Congdon, Mar. 18, 1966.

7 Bradbury to Congdon, Apr. 4, 1967; also Mar. 6, 1967.

8 Bradbury to A. C. Spectorsky (*Playboy*), May 17, 1965.

9 Bradbury to Congdon, July 18, 1967.

10 Bradbury to Congdon, Mar. 1, 1968; Bradbury, interview with the author, Oct. 7, 2004.

11 Bradbury to Congdon, Mar. 22, 1968.

12 Kaye to Bradbury, Nov. 27, Dec. 9, 1968.

13 Bradbury, interview with the author, Oct. 4, 2004; Congdon to Bradbury, Sept. 24, 1967.

14 Bradbury, interview with the author, Oct. 5, 2004; Bradbury to Congdon, June 6, 1967, and Dec. 27, 1968; Congdon to Belafonte, June 3, 1966, and Nov. 8, 1968 (Bradbury cc); Chiz Schultz (for Belafonte) to Congdon, Dec. 26, 1968.

15 Peggy Robertson (Hitchcock Productions) to William Tennant (Ziegler-Ross), May 31, 1968 (fwd Bradbury).

Chapter 38. The Isolated Man

1 Bradbury to Pohl, undated, c. Oct. 1968 (cc).

2 Detailed accounts of Bradbury's involvement can be found in Wes Herschensohn, *Resur-*

rection in Cannes: The Making of The Picasso Summer (Cranbury, N.J.: A. S. Barnes, 1979); other sources are Bradbury, interview with the author, Oct. 2, 4, 2004, Oct. 18, 2008, Oct. 28, 2010, and Mar. 12, 2011, and Congdon to Bradbury, Oct. 16 and Dec. 28, 1967.

3 "Bradbury, Format and Wald Talking 'Illustrated' Deal," Daily Variety (Sept. 2, 1960): 3; "1st Format Feature: 'Illustrated Man,'" Daily Variety (July 24, 1962): 6. Bradbury's further reflections are recorded in his interview with Arnold Kunert, "Ray Bradbury on Hitchcock, Huston and Other Magic of the Screen," Take One (Canada, Sept. 26, 1973): 21–22, and in Bradbury, interview with the author, Oct. 23, 2010, and Mar. 12, 2011.

4 Bradbury, interview with the author, Oct. 5, 2004.

5 Bradbury to Congdon, Oct. 18, 1968.

6 Bradbury, interview with the author, Oct. 12, 2005.

7 Bradbury, interview with the author, Oct. 12, 1998.

8 Congdon to Bradbury, Aug. 29, 1966: "Just as you did in the Disney piece for Holiday, you got up on your soap box and lectured through most of the piece."

Chapter 39. A Touch of the Poet

1 Eller, Becoming Ray Bradbury, 57–58.

2 Henry FitzGerald Heard to Bradbury, Jan. 18, 1951.

3 Bradbury to Congdon, Sept. 6, 1970.

4 Bradbury to Congdon (re Loyola), Mar. 9, 1966; John Ciardi to Congdon, Aug. 3, 1967.

5 The composition of the musical adaptation is discussed in Bradbury to Congdon, Apr. 12, May 1, and May 14 (with encl), 1966.

6 Bradbury to Congdon, Apr. 4, 1967; elaborated in Bradbury, interview with the author, Oct. 10, 2006.

7 Congdon to Bradbury, Oct. 1, 1968.

8 Bradbury, interview with the author, Oct. 7, 2004.

Chapter 40. "Christus Apollo"

1 Bradbury to Congdon, Sept. 5, 1968.

2 For a full analysis of this important poem, see Eller and Touponce, Ray Bradbury, 18–21.

3 Congdon to Bradbury, Oct. 1 and 31, 1968. The transition to Knopf is summarized in Bradbury to Congdon, Oct. 14, 1968.

4 William B. McIntyre to Rod Steiger, Sept. 21, 1968 (Bradbury cc).

5 These seven collections do not include the three retrospective "best of" collections: The Vintage Bradbury (1965), The Stories of Ray Bradbury (1980), and Bradbury Stories (2003). For a detailed analysis of the collections through 2001, see Eller and Touponce, Ray Bradbury, ch 7 and Table 13.

6 Bradbury, interview with the author, Oct. 21, 2002; Bradbury to Congdon, Feb. 15, 1969.

7 Bradbury, interview with the author, Oct. 7, 2006.

8 Anon., "Londoner's Apollo Diary," Evening Standard, July 21, 1969, 10. Bradbury recounted his David Frost and NBC panel experiences in his May 1970 Caltech Alumni

Day address, published as "Reflections from the Man Who Landed on the Moon in 1929," *Engineering and Science* 34:1 (Oct. 1970): 18–19.

9 These opening lines are from the original December 1943 serial publication in *Famous Fantastic Mysteries*, before Bradbury revised the story as "R Is for Rocket" (1962).

10 A detailed discussion of Caltech's "Mars and the Mind of Man" conference and the retrospective commentaries of Bradbury and the other participants can be found in Robert Crossley's "Mars as Cultural Mirror," in *Visions of Mars* (Jefferson, N.C.: McFarland, 2011), 165–174.

11 Bradbury, interview with the author, Oct. 9, 2006. Photocopies of von Braun's inscription, signed "with admiration," are preserved in the Center for Ray Bradbury Studies.

Chapter 41. "Take Me Home"

1 Bradbury to Congdon, Oct. 17, 1967.
2 Bradbury to Congdon, July 2, 1969.
3 Bradbury to Congdon, Aug. 13, 1968.
4 These totals, which include the United States, Canada, Great Britain, and Australia, are from the unpublished *October's Friend*, a catalog of the Albright Collection by Jim Welsh and Donn Albright.
5 Russell Kirk, *Enemies of Permanent Things* (New York: Arlington House, 1969), 117.
6 The final introduction appeared as "Night Travel on the Orient Express, Destination: Avram," in Avram Davidson, *Strange Seas and Shores* (Garden City, N.Y.: Doubleday, 1971).
7 Bradbury, interview with the author, Oct. 2002.
8 Art Seidenbaum, "Literature Neglects Science, Huxley Says," *Los Angeles Times*, Apr. 8, 1963, part II, 1, 8; Bradbury, interview with the author, Mar. 2012.
9 Bradbury invoked the spirit, if not the exact words, of this great romantic moment from his early reading; the closest that Burroughs comes to these lines occurs in the opening pages of *The Gods of Mars*, the second novel in the series, and indeed Bradbury's favorite: "With scarcely a parting glance I turned my eyes again toward Mars, lifted my hands toward his lurid rays, and waited."

Index

Balcony, The (film), 196

Ball, Lucille, 208

Ballantine, Ian, 222; Fahrenheit 451, 7, 24, 41–43, 223; correspondence with, 42, 224

Ballantine Books, 90, 161; The Autumn People, 222; censorship, threatened with, 63; Fahrenheit 451, 7, 20, 42–43, 103, 223–24; The October Country, 55, 61–63, 103; Stanley Kauffmann, editor at, 7, 41, 162; Tomorrow Midnight, 222

Ballard, J. G., 94

Bantam Books, 12, 76, 162, 189; censorship, threatened with, 63; The Circus of Dr. Lao and Other Improbable Stories (anthology), 74, 79; Dandelion Wine, 149; God on Tomorrow Morning proposal, 161; The Martian Chronicles, 124, 220; The October Country, 63; Oscar Dystel, editor at, 161; Saul David, editor at, 74; six-volume boxed set of Bradbury paperbacks, 277; Timeless Stories for Today and Tomorrow, 74; 20,000 Leagues under the Sea, 121, 202–3, 230

Barker, Clive, 63

Barker, Lex, 13

Barrault, Jean-Louis, 254–55

Barrymore, John, 176

Barzun, Jacques, 40

Basilica di Santa Maria del Fiore (Duomo), 35

Beach, Grant, 118

Bean, Alan, 275

Beat the Devil (film), 10, 13

Beaumont, Charles (Charles Nutt): Bradbury correspondence with, 17; decline and death of, 256; "Mother's Day," 184; screenwriting conflict, 164–65; Twilight Zone, writer for, 182–86, 188

Beckett, Samuel, 232

Beerbohm, Max, "The Duke and the Dairymaid," 101

Beethoven, Ludwig van, 94

Belafonte, Harry, 255, 260

Bel Geddes, Barbara, 155

Bellini, Giovanni, 36

Benedek, Laslo, 100, 156, 211; Death of a Salesman, 211

Benet, Steven Vincent, John Brown's Body, 67

Benjamin, Ben, 149–50, 154, 212; "And the Moon Be Still as Bright," 130; Dark Carnival original screenplay, 100; and Don Congdon, 55, 59, 108, 168, 170; Fahrenheit 451 film, 60; Fahrenheit 451 plagiarism lawsuit, 125–26, 149, 211; The Friendly Persuasion (West) film adaptation, 57; "The Illustrated Man" film adaptation, 140; The Martian Chronicles, 168, 170–71; negotiates 1952 film deals, 55; Report from Space, 108

Berenson, Bernard: Bradbury's 1954 visit to, 33–34, 39, 89; Bradbury's 1957 visit to, 114–17, 119–20; correspondence with, 48–54, 86–87, 116, 123; death of, 176, 256; decline of, 117, 138; shared aesthetics with Bradbury, 134–36; tutelage of Bradbury, 35–38, 117, 124, 279, 282

Bergson, Henri, 35, 179, 239

Berlioz, Hector, Evenings with the Orchestra and The Trojans, 137

Bespoke Overcoat, The (film), 114

Best American Short Stories, 158, 279; of 1947, 7, 226

Best Plays of 1964–1965, The, 234

Betjeman, John, 42

Bewick, Thomas, 135

Bible, 23, 48

Billy Budd (film), 244

Blaustein, Julian, 167, 168, 169, 171, 212

Bloch, Robert, 74

Block, Irving, 55

Bloom, Claire, 259–60; as Clarisse, 245

Bluestone, George, 248

Bogart, Humphrey, 215

Bondarchuk, Sergei, 195

Bonestell, Chesley, 136, 159

Bonner, Anthony, 202

Book-of-the-Month Club, 43; *Book-of-the-Month Club News*, 133

Booth, Margaret, 172

Borges, Jorge Luis, Bradbury compared to, 94

Borman, John, 108

Borowsky, Marvin, 142

Botticelli, Sandro, 136, 238

Boucher, Anthony, 62, 75; on censorship, 145; correspondence with, 80, 108–9, 112, 114, 145–46; "The Eerie Ebb of Science Fiction," 192–94; *Fahrenheit 451*, 20; as H. H. Holmes, 20, 192–94; *Something Wicked This Way Comes*, 193–94

Bourguignon, Serge, 259

Bowen, Robert, 133

Bracelli, Giovanni Battista, *Bizarie*, 135

Brackett, Leigh, 75, 127, 140

Bradbury, Alexandra (fourth daughter), 140

Bradbury, Bettina (third daughter), 110

Bradbury, Elizabeth (sister), 250

Bradbury, Esther Moberg (mother), 122, 250–51

Bradbury, Leo(nard Sr) (father), 122–23, 250

Bradbury, Leonard Jr "Skip" (brother), 250

Bradbury, Marguerite "Maggie" (McClure) (wife), 11, 12, 51, 145; art studies with Bradbury, 54; with Bradbury and Truffaut, 243; in England (1957), 110–11, 114; in England (1969), 272–73; in Ireland with Bradbury (1953–54), 15; in Italy (1954), 21, 34, 38; raising a family, 166, 168, 240; worries about fame and Hollywood, 121–24, 141

Bradbury, Ramona (second daughter), 12, 123

Bradbury, Ray, and aesthetics, 134–36, 282;

Christianity 48, 178–81, 239–40; Climate of Fear, 42, 44, 280; controversy, nonconformism, and antiauthoritarian views, 41–42, 72–73, 121, 144–47, 237, 241, 260–62, 280; cosmology, 90–91, 178–81, 239, 269–70; fame, 124, 136, 238; horror and terror film genres, 71–72, 164, 248–49, 262; Impressionism, 95, 135; intellectual magazines, 237, 270; modernism (literature), 41, 232, 238, (art) 136; mythopoeia and mythmaking, 94, 269–70; postmodernism, 37; realism, 232–33, 278; reluctance of working with others, 127, 175, 236; Renaissance, discovery of, 34–36, 39, 51, 54, 135–36, 238, 279; romanticism, 135–36, 277; screenwriting, 49–50, 108, 140, 142, 168–71, 173–74; the Space Program, 89–90, 161, 205–7, 219, 228–29, 238–39, 270–71, 273–76, 282–83; Surrealism, 118–19, 135; television and playwriting, 69, 86, 155, 156–57, 234, 266; Theatre of the Absurd, 232–33; writers, advocacy for, 261; writing, art of, 81, 117, 225–27, 278, 280; writing science fiction, 33, 272, 277; writing verse, 264–65, 269–70

—Books

The Autumn People, 222

Bradbury Stories, 222

Dandelion Wine, 37, 82, 96, 106, 129, 144, 149, 212, 221, 224; adaptation concepts, 158, 212; evolution of the story cycle, 103, 104, 105; and reviews, 133–34, 193

Dark Carnival (story collection), 9, 55, 56, 72, 100; stage adaptation, 253, 265–68; stories refashioned for *The October Country*, 55, 56, 61–62, 210, 249

Death Is a Lonely Business, 279

Fahrenheit 451: Bal-Hi edition, 224; film and television negotiations, 55, 59–60, 102, 106, 108, 126; final revisions of,

157; *The October Country*, 62–63; Something Wicked This Way Comes, 192–93; *The World of Ray Bradbury* (plays), 233–36

Ealing Studios, 67, 71, 249; *Dead of Night*, 139

EC Comics, 63–65; adaptations reprints, 222

Edwards, Blake, 251, 255–56, 281

Edwards, Michael, 94

Einstein, Albert, 239

Eiseley, Loren, 177; "Buzby's Petrified Woman," 76

El Greco (Doménikos Theotokópoulos), 141

Ellin, Stanley, "Faith of Aaron Menefee, The," 191, 194

Ellis, Antony, 99

Ellison, Harlan: *Again, Dangerous Visions*, 265; *Dangerous Visions*, 257

Elmer Gantry (film), 171

Evans, Peter, 110–11

Examiner, 145

Fadiman, Clifton, 48; introduction to *The Martian Chronicles*, 132

Fallaci, Oriana: 1964 interview, 239, 240, 274

Famous Artists, 55, 200; "And the Rock Cried Out" option, 109; Bradbury's departure from, 211–12; Bradbury's dissatisfaction with, 149–50; the *Dark Carnival* screenplay, 100; the *Fahrenheit 451* plagiarism suit, 125–26, 149; film offers declined by Bradbury, 106, 116; "The Fox and the Forest" adaptation, 102; the *Martian Chronicles* MGM option, 167, 171

Famous Fantastic Mysteries, 91

Fantastic Voyage (film), 231

"Fatal Planet" (Block and Adler), 55

Fate of a Man (film), 195

Faulkner, William, 119, 172; Bradbury compared to, 94

Federal Bureau of Investigation (FBI), 144; file on Bradbury, 241; report by informant, 147

Fellini, Federico, 212, 282

Ferguson, Regina, 12, 14, 21

Fiction (French edition of *The Magazine of Fantasy & Science Fiction*), 146

Finney, Albert, 257; Terrence Stamp compared to, 244

Finney, Charles G., 74, 164; *The Circus of Dr. Lao*, 77–78

Finney, Jack: "Body Snatchers," 156; "Missing Persons," 76

Fitzgerald, Barry, 154

Fitzgerald, F. Scott, 172; *Tender Is the Night*, 281

Flon, Suzanne, 13

Florida Quarterly, 264

Flynn, Errol, 215

Foley, Martha, 158, 279

Fonda, Jane, 244–45

Forbidden Planet (film), 55, 168

Format Films, 188, 205–7, 259

Fosdick, Raymond, 91

Foster, Hal, 136

Four Horsemen of the Apocalypse, The (film), 140, 167

"Four of Us Are Dying, The" (*The Twilight Zone*), 188

Fowler, Gene, 176

Foxwell, Ivan, 72

Fra Angelico, 36, 39, 238

Frank, Mary, 155

Frankenheimer, John, 125, 157

Franklin, Michael, 195

Franz, Arthur, 154

Freeman, Fred, 159

French surrealists, Bradbury compared to, 94

Friar, Kimon, 179

Friendly Persuasion (film), 55–56, 106, 145

Frost, David, BBC talk show, 274

Frost, Robert, 191
Fry, Christopher, 263
Fulton, John, 108, 121, 130–31
Fuseli, Henry (Johann Heinrich Füssli), 135

Gaines, William M., 222
Galaxy, 257, 264
Galileo (Galileo Galilei), 239
Gandy, Joseph Michael, 135
Garreau-Dombasle, Man'Ha (Germaine Massenet), 118–19; *Sati*, 118
Garreau-Dombasle, Maurice, 118
Gassman, Vittorio, 251
Gaver, Jack, 235
Gay, John, 106–7, 148
General Artists, 212
General Motors, World's Fair exhibit, 204
Genn, Leo, 113
Giroux, Claude, 233–35
Givray, Claude de, *Fahrenheit 451* screenplay, 243
Godley, John (Lord Kilbracken), 15, 49
Goldenberg, William, 253, 266
Goldsmith, Jerry, 269
Goldwyn, Sam[uel] Sr, 215
Goldwyn, Samuel Jr, 56, 251–52, 255
Gomberg, Sy, 154–56, 208
Good Morning Miss Dove (film), 55, 106
Gottlieb, Bob, 162, 207, 265; *Fahrenheit 451*, 224; *I Sing the Body Electric!* 271; *Leviathan '99*, 201; *The Machineries of Joy*, 210; *Something Wicked This Way Comes*, 164
Gould, Harold, 233–35
Goya, Francisco, 135
Grandville, J. J. (Jean Ignace Isidore Gérard), 135
Graves, Ralph, 177
Greatest Story Ever Told, The (film), 211
Great Gabbo, The (film), 71
Great Race, The (film), 251
Great War, The (film), 195

Greene, Graham, 109, 114; *The Quiet American*, 109; *The Third Man*, 114
Green Town stories, 266, 278; *Dandelion Wine*, extracted for, 101–3; the Green Town novel, 144; influences, 81–83
Gregory, Paul, 67, 208; break with Laughton, 70, 84, 87, 100–101; *Fahrenheit 451* adaptation with Charles Laughton, 68–70; interest in Bradbury's Irish plays, 154
Grobel, Lawrence, 26, 29
Grubb, Davis, *The Night of the Hunter*, 67–68, 85
Guide for Living (Pope Pius XII), 160–61
Guzman, Don, 20

Haberstroh, Alex, 121
Haggard, H[enry] Rider: *She: A History of Adventure*, 79
Haggott, John, 60
Halevy, Julian, 137
Hall, Peter, 209
Hamilton, Ed[mond], 127
Hammer Films, 223
Hamner, Earl: and *The Martian Chronicles* musical, 100
Harper & Row, publisher, 276
Harper's, 76; Bradbury critique of, 237, 270; *The Circus of Dr. Lao and Other Improbable Stories*, review of, 75; *Dandelion Wine*, review of, 133; *Fahrenheit 451*, review of, 20, 43
Harris, Richard, 258
Harrison, Joan, 113, 194
Harryhausen, Ray, 14, 202
Hart-Davis, Rupert, 47, 193, 210; Bradbury meeting with, 14, 32, 114; correspondence with, 21, 32, 39, 126, 178; *The Golden Apples of the Sun*, 14
Hawthorne, Nathaniel, 262; Bradbury compared to, 94; "Earth's Holocaust," 76
Hayden, Hiram, 161

JONATHAN R. ELLER is a Chancellor's Professor of English at Indiana University-Purdue University in Indianapolis, the senior textual editor of the Institute for American Thought, and director of the Center for Ray Bradbury Studies at IUPUI. *Becoming Ray Bradbury* was a runner-up for the 2011 Locus Award for best nonfiction book in the science fiction and fantasy field.

The University of Illinois Press
is a founding member of the
Association of American University Presses.

Composed in 10.2/14 Quadraat
with DIN 30640 Std display
by Celia Shapland
at the University of Illinois Press
Manufactured by Sheridan Books, Inc.

University of Illinois Press
1325 South Oak Street
Champaign, IL 61820-6903
www.press.uillinois.edu

10/14

Lewes Public Library
111 Adams Ave.
Lewes, DE 19958
302-645-4633